Speaking in Court

Andrew Watson

Speaking in Court

Developments in Court Advocacy from the Seventeenth to the Twenty-First Century

palgrave
macmillan

Andrew Watson
Sheffield Hallam University
Sheffield, UK

ISBN 978-3-030-10394-1   ISBN 978-3-030-10395-8   (eBook)
https://doi.org/10.1007/978-3-030-10395-8

Library of Congress Control Number: 2018968324

This Palgrave Macmillan imprint is published by the registered company Springer Nature Switzerland AG.
The registered company address is: Gewerbestrasse 11, 6330 Cham, Switzerland

I would like to thank those who have helped in the research, writing and production of this book. Their knowledge, patience and encouragement was vital at every stage and is greatly appreciated. Special thanks are due to Leslie Blake, Richard de Friend, Peter Murray and Suzanne Carthy.

To Jacqui Watson Z"L, Reggie Watson Z"L and Nicola Edwards Z"L: Wonderful and splendid people – may their memory be for a blessing and may peace be upon them (Zikhronam livrakha v' alav ha-shalom).

Table of Cases

Cases cited by name.

Table of Statutes

Statutory Instruments

Court of Appeal (Recording and Broadcasting) Order 2013.
Higher Courts Qualification Regulations 2000.
Higher Courts Qualification Regulations 1998.
Higher Courts Qualification Regulations 1992.

Contents

1

Introduction and Structure

There are few comprehensive histories about how courtroom advocacy has evolved in this country and about the important factors that have shaped it. This may be partly because advocacy in court is usually regarded by its practitioners as an intensely practical activity, firmly anchored in immediate concerns. Nonetheless, an attempt can be made to trace how advocacy has changed, to examine some of the influences on its development and to consider what may well affect it in the future.

Chapter 2 starts with the roughness and uncouthness of much Tudor and Stuart advocacy, and continues with the timid reserve which to some extent replaced it in the late seventeenth century. These aspects began to be displaced by greater eloquence of distinguished eighteenth century judges and barristers – very likely themselves responding to greater refinements in the English language and awareness amongst the educated of its possibilities to persuade. Growing knowledge amongst the higher echelons of society about the classical literature and of Greek and Roman rhetorical style affected advocacy, especially before the House of Lords, when it acted as a court, for example in the long running impeachment trial of Warren Hastings, and also before special juries. Because of the influence of the classics and ancient rhetoric on advocates, which was still present, though weakening, well into the twentieth century, there is an Excursus (Classical Rhetoric), **available**

© The Author(s) 2019
A. Watson, *Speaking in Court*, https://doi.org/10.1007/978-3-030-10395-8_1

on the internet (Historyadvocacy.wordpress.com) about classical rhetoric, concentrating on Cicero and Quintilian who were much studied in Britain and North America. The ancient world also shows that styles of advocacy were not fixed and evolved due to a variety of influences.

The effect of contemporary poetry, used to awaken generous sympathies in jurors, and of literature, including that of Sir William Blackstone which may be regarded as such, in enriching vocabulary and providing advocates in the later eighteenth century with more allusions on which to draw is considered, as is the florid and emotional style, taken to new heights by barristers from Ireland. Contributions by prominent barristers to advocacy, conspicuously Thomas Erskine, who also did much to establish the moral basis for its practise, are described. Mention is made of previous cases becoming binding authority before courts in the eighteenth century, the doctrine of *stare decisis*, and the effects of this on advocates, who had to adapt their submissions to take account of this key change.

In the eighteenth century (Chap. 3) lawyers started to appear for prosecutors in felony cases. To redress the balance judges began to allow prisoners to instruct counsel to conduct examination in chief, cross-examination and argue points of law. The effects of this on advocacy, particularly the development of cross-examination and a more determined and aggressive approach by barristers on behalf of their clients, are examined. Advocacy in criminal trials which essentially became adversarial in nature, but remained short in length, became increasingly affected by rules of evidence. The lengthy campaign, and opposition to it, ending in the Prisoners' Counsel Act 1836, to remove the felony prisoners' handicap of not being allowed counsel on their behalf to address the jury is recounted. The Act gave prisoners the right to a full defence by counsel in felony cases, importantly including addressing the jury. Also described in this chapter is the limited scope for advocacy in civil trials in the eighteenth and early nineteenth centuries.

Next considered (Chap. 4) is the forceful advocacy for prisoners, often matched by counsel for the Crown that was a frequent result of the Prisoners' Counsel Act 1836. It was usually delivered, as was advocacy in civil cases, with much melodrama and floridity of language before common jurors who, because of their often limited education, were especially susceptible to theatricality, intense appeals to emotion and allusions to religion, then very strong. How public opinion, developing rules of professional etiquette, and the judiciary came to limit the bounds of the forensic licence granted by the Act of 1836 is examined.

Scenes of discourtesy, and worse, between counsel and towards judges in court in the 1830s, 40s and 50s are described, as is what was the press and public reaction to them. Some reasons for this behaviour, and the poor quality of advocacy often associated with it, are offered, including the inability of some judges to control proceedings in court, drink and tiredness. Although not without some setbacks, the second Tichborne case in 1871–72 being a vivid example, conduct generally improved later in the nineteenth century, due much to evolving etiquette at the bar and a greater determination by its members to enforce standards,

Key changes in 1851 to rules concerning criminal indictments, which limited arguments in court about their validity, are outlined. Tentative conclusions are then drawn about the effect on advocacy of the reduction, in the first half of the nineteenth century, of the number of offences punishable by death.

The dominant style of advocacy before juries in the second half of the nineteenth century, up until roughly the 1880s, was declamatory, melodramatic and lachrymose. It was frequently marked by aggressive, intimidating and wide ranging – "blunderbuss" – cross-examination and also by long and repetitious closing speeches in the course of which strong appeals to emotion were made, often invoking the Deity and the Bible or the spirit of justice. (Special jurors, because they were usually more educated, would often be treated to more allusions to the classics references to history, and quotations from literature and poetry than common jurors.) A number of examples of this style are presented in Chap. 5.

Even though histrionics continued to thrive during this period, some leaders of the bar, including Hardinge Giffard (later Lord Halsbury), John Holker, (a future Attorney General), Charles Russell (who became Lord Chief Justice) and Edward Clarke, began to significantly change the style of advocacy. Their approach was quieter, more learned and less inclined to violent appeals to emotion, florid speech and to widely quoting from literature and verse. In the bar's tradition of copying what appeared to succeed, they began to be emulated by junior members.

Chapter 6 shows how opportunities for passionate appeals to emotion, flowery passages and histrionic gestures fell as trial by jury in civil actions declined with the establishment of County Courts, where the overwhelming majority of cases were heard by judges alone, and the Common Law Procedure Act 1854 which, provided both parties consented, permitted issues of fact in the higher courts to be tried by judges without juries. Judges had little taste for sensational appeals, floridity, and theatricality but did have a high regard for fact, law and logically structured argument. Accordingly advocacy before them adjusted and shortened in length. Some barristers lamented what they saw as the decay of forensic oratory, due to the reduction of trials by jury; others accepted the altered style that was required as a necessary adaptation to changed circumstances. Chances to address juries in criminal matters also reduced with the growth of summary trial before magistrates in the second half of the nineteenth century. Specialist statutory tribunals, formed to implement new regulatory legislation and to resolve disputes between the state and the subject, or between subjects, did not employ juries. Indeed the majority of them had little or no need for advocates.

The Judicature Acts 1873–75 much lessened prospects for winning civil cases by advocates taking points at the beginning of trials, based on principles of law developed over centuries, about inadequacies and defects in opponents' pleadings, but gave them more flexibility to bring new evidence and advance freshly thought legal argument.

Chapter 7 returns to criminal matters. After a long campaign, prisoners were given the right to give evidence on oath by the Criminal Evidence Act 1898. Advocates were placed in the position of having to advise clients whether they should step into the witness box. If they did, counsel's closing speech had to take into account the evidence they had given. No longer was an advocate free to suggest to the jury any story his ingenuity could devise as a possible explanation of the proved facts: In short it revolutionized the style of defence advocacy in many criminal cases. Skills in re-examination, necessary to minimise damage inflicted in cross-examination, became vital.

In both civil and criminal cases, advocacy at the turn of the twentieth century was affected by rules concerning the content of opening speeches. It was also influenced by having to accommodate increasing numbers of expert witnesses. Examination of witnesses, especially cross-examination, had become a much more precise and subtle art, far removed from indiscriminate and instinctual performances frequently seen earlier.

At the end of the nineteenth century and during the first quarter of the twentieth century the advocacy of Rufus Isaacs, Edward Carson, F. E. Smith and Edward Marshall Hall, who regularly opposed each other in court in greatly publicized cases, was an important influence on other barristers of the period and beyond (Chap. 8). The first three were the heirs of Giffard, Holker, Russell and Clarke, but who further advanced their form of advocacy employing a deceptively conversational or low-key approach and carefully planned often deadly cross-examinations. They avoided long and emotive closing speeches. Blunderbuss advocacy, unpredictable in its effect and often dangerous to its user, was replaced by the lethal precision of the sniper's rifle. Marshall Hall's advocacy, on the other hand, with its blatant appeal to emotion, sometimes sprinkled in tears, fell squarely within the tradition of nineteenth century histrionic advocacy.

In severely bomb damaged Second World War London, George Keeton (Chap. 9) wrote, in 1943, about *"a silent revolution in methods of advocacy as practiced by the English Bar over the last fifty years"*.[1] Changed standards of etiquette, professional rules and greater control exerted by judges over these years had led to a vast increase in courtesy in interactions with judges and between counsel. The conduct of prosecutions had also improved. They were generally no longer carried out in a sneering hectoring manner with witnesses mercilessly browbeaten or bullied. Dramatic types of nineteenth century advocacy, in which counsel was prepared to use mannerisms, tricks of speech and gestures to heighten the effects of their pleas to juries, was replaced by a conversational and matter of fact tone. The idea that to cross-examine meant to examine crossly had almost vanished. Appeals to juries were now to reason combined with a controlled, subtle and focused appeal to emotion. Jury trials in civil cases had continued to decline. Advocacy before judges was concerned with facts and the law, not oratorical flourishes. Fewer criminal trials before juries took place as the jurisdiction of the magistrates widened further. The

---

[1] G. W. Keeton, *Harris's Hints on Advocacy*, Stevens and Sons, 1943, page 10.

more restrained and conversational style of advocacy before criminal juries may have been to some extent influenced by that of the civil courts, where the leaders of the bar appeared more often and increasingly without juries. Two of the most distinguished advocates in the first half of the twentieth century were Patrick Hastings and Norman Birkett. Their triumphs ensured that their style of advocacy would influence other barristers. Hastings was a master of unembellished and unornamented speech of brevity. Unlike Hastings, Norman Birkett believed that the advocate ought to use a greater range of speech, informed by celebrated literature.

Other factors lay behind the mainly conversational and matter of fact advocacy that had become established, including a widely held suspicion of rhetoric and, very importantly, more informed and better educated juries. Jurors were less susceptible than their predecessors to theatrical gestures and melodrama, which had largely been replaced in literature and on the stage by introspection and realism, references to God and the Bible, elegant and flowery, but empty, speech and appeals to strong emotion and prejudice. In a more scientific age jurors expected more of an appeal to reason. The success of barristers such as Giffard, Holker, Russell and Clarke may have been because they early on appreciated fundamental changes happening to juries and also a shift in the prevailing emotional style in Britain, driven by many different reasons, from sentimentalism towards stoicism, discipline and restraint – a development identified to the run from the 1870s up to the First World War, now studied in detail by historians of emotion.[2]

Attempting to catch the eye of the press to help create a reputation, useful to generate work, was an important factor behind the emotive, vividly worded and aggressive advocacy of the early Victorian period and afterwards. The decline of court reporting in the newspapers, removing

---

[2] The history of emotions is a developing field of historical research at the intersection of anthropology, sociology, psychology and the life sciences. Concerned with the experience and expression of human emotion, especially variations in different times and cultures it rests on the assumption that emotions – feelings and their expressions – are shaped by culture and learnt and acquired in social contexts. What is felt and shown towards certain people or things depends on social norms or rules. Emotion, according to many historians, is as fundamental a category of history, as class, race and gender. See Jan Plamper, *The History of Emotions: An Introduction*, Oxford University Press, 2015.

much of the gallery from the stage, may well have contributed to the more subdued form of speech.

The book continues by considering alterations in advocacy before juries in the second half of the twentieth century and what has accounted for them (Chap. 10). Changes scrutinized include: the falling away in the use of Aristotle's ancient order of closing speeches, which usually ended with an emotive peroration; the enormous expansion of eligibility to serve on juries, a *democratisation*, brought about by the Juries Act 1974, leading to great changes in the way jurors were addressed and to different allusions and references made by advocates; the reduction, and eventual abolition, by the Criminal Justice Act, 1988, of peremptory challenge of jurors; the removal of certain offences from Crown Court jury trial; prosecutions conducted in more measured tones and more methodical and less aggressive defences, although the latter was not always being seen in sexual offences cases; decline in weight attached by juries to police evidence; less heavy drinking by some barristers and the positive effects this brought to performance in court; the rise of plea bargaining and the need to mitigate effectively after guilty pleas; the introduction of Social Enquiry Reports and their effect on pleas in mitigation; the need to make, and respond to, submissions arising out of key changes in evidence and procedure concerning the exclusion of confessions, when adverse inferences can be drawn from silence to questions put to the accused and from admission of a defendant's bad character and increased employment of expert witnesses in trials.

However, it is in civil cases, that the greatest changes to advocacy have occurred in the last sixty or so years. A number of developments and their consequences are examined (Chap. 11). These include; the Legal Aid and Advice Act 1949, which made advocacy available to more people; relaxation of the rules against hearsay; a better rapport between judges and advocates; changes in civil and court procedure from the 1990s; the growth of informed judicial intervention in trials at first instance; the Woolf reforms leading to substantial modifications of the stages in civil trials, the introduction of advocacy on paper, precipitating a debate about whether the oral tradition of English advocacy was threatened; joint witness reports; the decline of allusions to the classics, literature, poetry and history and use of Latin in advocacy; changes in advocacy in the County

Court; clients' perceptions of the "new" advocacy; conditional fees and behaviour in court and the presence in court of litigants in person; *McKenzie* friends; Mediation and Collaborative Law; and greater use of the Welsh language in court advocacy.

A most important influence on advocacy, particularly that of junior practitioners, has been the introduction of systematic instruction on the subject. Not many decades ago the prevalent view had been that attempts to teach advocacy would be of little value – facility in the art being mainly regarded then as innate. The origin of advocacy teaching in England and Wales is traced and the content of the current courses outlined (Chap. 12).

In England and Wales since 2013 the broadcasting of some Court of Appeal proceedings has been permitted. The debate which preceded this change is described in Chap. 13 and the effects of televising courts on advocacy and advocates considered, with reference to limited available overseas research. This is followed by the question of dress in court. It has been said by some that the traditional attire of judges and barristers, often seen as emblematic of British courts, has contributed to pomposity of speech and needlessly theatrical behaviour, – an opinion vehemently opposed by others. Views on the long running question of dress are presented. Comparatively recent rules, which have probably settled the matter, at least for some time, are explained. The effects on advocacy of wearing the Moslem niqab and burqa by advocates, judges and witnesses in court are then pondered.

In Chap. 14 a number of developments already bearing on the practice of advocacy, and likely to be more weighty in future, are dealt with including: the extension of rights of audience in the higher courts to solicitors, representing an important departure from the past when they were confined to barristers; large firms of solicitors conducting "in-house" advocacy; increased employment by the Crown Prosecution Service ("CPS"), in the Crown Court of its own lawyers with higher rights of audience rather than instructing independent advocates; CPS use of employees, *Associate Prosecutors*, who are not qualified lawyers to conduct more prosecutions in the Magistrates' Courts; granting rights of audience before the lower courts to Fellows of the Institute of Legal Executives; and, in a period when more persons can act as advocates, the creation of new formal quality control bodies. Lastly, new technology in the courtroom, and the very significant ways advocacy may be influenced by it, is examined.

Considerable alterations in advocacy have occurred not just in Britain but throughout the common law world. For purposes of comparison some attention is paid to the United States in Additional Chapter 1 (Major Alterations in Advocacy in America Also) and Additional Chapter 2 (Jury Advocacy and the Decline of Trials in America), available on the internet (Historyadvocacy.wordpress.com). In the first of these the place of the Greek and Roman classics and rhetoric in advocacy in late eighteenth century America and in the first half of the nineteenth century is explored. Use by many attorneys of an apologetic, dispassionate and formulaic type of criminal advocacy bearing much of the influence of Cicero, provides a strong contrast to the extravagant, melodramatic and flowery styles of address in the English courts at the time. However, changes in procedure, laws of evidence and the prevailing general style of public oratory led, in the third quarter of the nineteenth century to attorneys assuming the mix of flamboyance, appeal to emotion and aggression which has been their hallmark before juries ever since. Interestingly this came about at a time when by contrast in England and Wales advocacy was becoming more fundamentally subdued in style.

As in England and Wales, there was discussion about whether advocates should be allowed to express belief in the causes of their clients and later the adoption of professional rules forbidding the practice. Further, like in England, attorneys in the United States found it both necessary to adjust to laws granting accused persons the right to give evidence on oath and also to the presence of expert witnesses in court. Attorneys in criminal cases, had to be able to conduct plea bargaining, a procedure which arose independently in a number of jurisdictions in the early mid nineteenth century, and deliver pleas in mitigation.

The late nineteenth century saw the beginnings of bench trials. These became more frequent in the century which followed. Taking the jury out of the court had a huge impact on advocacy. Unlike jurors, judges had no time for stirring speeches, sensationalism and histrionics. Strict attention to evidence and law by attorneys was required.

Influences on advocacy in the United States over the last half century or so are examined in the **second Additional Chapter on the internet.** Methods of witness preparation and trial consultancy, neither of which have direct

English equivalents, are investigated. Reasons for the reduction in trials and the profound consequences for advocates and advocacy are discussed.

The conclusion reached is that advocacy in England and Wales, and the United States, has been far from fixed and immutable over the last three centuries but was, and remains, very fluid. It certainly did not develop according to an over-riding logical plan, but has grown piecemeal and at an uneven pace, the result of a complex interplay of many influences. Research for this book has attempted to identify as many of these as possible. A nonexhaustive list of principal factors, the relative importance of each has varied over time, includes: the effect on juniors of successful styles and approaches used by senior advocates; judicial tastes for the advocacy of lawyers, especially in the absence of jurors, when it is usually for the practical and the unadorned; changes in court procedure made by judges; reforms in the law of evidence concerning who and what may be put before courts and informing the content of submissions made; alterations in civil and criminal procedure and in the substantive law; the amount of media reporting of cases in court; public and press opinion about the acceptable limits of advocates' tactics and oratory; the forming, by advocates, of professional rules of conduct and how much they are followed; levels of respect and civility between the bench and the bar; the standing of the judiciary and its power to control proceedings in court; the extent to which juries are used in trials and the social origins of those serving on them; greater education of jurors and less susceptibility to melodramatic appeals to emotion; awareness by advocates that in addressing juries they have to take into account contemporary use of language and, when making allusions, draw on popular culture, itself far from still, formed by newspapers, novels, radio, films, television and increasingly the computer internet; the school educational curriculum, which has substantially evolved, usually received by lawyers and judges; general styles of public speaking and discourse in society; the formal teaching of advocacy, only introduced comparatively recently; and a relationship, although not a simplistic one, between quality of advocacy and the amount parties and the state are prepared to pay for it. Probably new technology is chief amongst elements that will exert an influence on future forensic oratory. Another important factor may be the effects of widening the pool of advocates.

It is hoped this book is able to convey that advocacy is not static as might be thought by those who regard courts and the law as very conservative. On the contrary it is very changeable, being subject to a complex interplay of factors, the importance of each has varied over time.

By use of diverse sources, the author of this book also hopes it might make a small contribution to the growing body of *external legal history*[3] which examines law and legal phenomenon within wider historical, social, economic and political contexts and may also be of interest to readers other than lawyers.

Echoing Counsellor Pleydel in Sir Walter Scott's Guy Mannering, "*A lawyer without history or literature is a mechanic – a mere working mason; if he possesses some knowledge of these he may venture to call himself an architect*", the author would be delighted if this book helped to provide some background and context for those teaching and learning professional advocacy skills.

Although cross cultural relationships are not simple, study of how and why advocacy has changed in Britain and the United States over the years may also assist comprehension of future developments in other countries, where court oral advocacy has recently been given greater importance.[4]

---

[3] *External legal history* may be compared with *internal legal history*, a phrase used to describe the activity of tracing the history of legal rules and legal principles which largely confines itself to internal sources such as statutes and case law and secondary sources concerned with articulating the meaning of the law within traditional doctrinal or theoretical legal analysis. See D. Ibbetson, *What is legal history a history of?*, in Andrew Lewis and Michael Lobban (eds) *Law and History* (2003) 6 Current Legal Issues pp. 863–879.

[4] One such country is Japan where in May, 2009, a new mixed court system (*Saiban-in Seido*), in which six randomly chosen citizens sit as lay judges with three professional judges to try serious criminal cases, previously tried by judges alone, was introduced after five years of planning. Hitherto, language used by judges and advocates in court was highly technical. Little examination of witnesses occurred and there was much reference to written evidence and submissions. Documents would be read to judges, usually in a dry way and with hardly any eye contact, in the knowledge they would be reviewed by them later. All this took place in a context of a shared unspoken understanding between judges prosecutors and defence lawyers and in which subtle signals to each other, including rhythmic breathing, were employed. Considerable preparation was undertaken to ensure that the style and content of lawyers' addresses to the lay members of the court would be comprehensible to them. This included holding mock trials and training prosecutors, defence lawyers and judges, often drawing on foreign expertise about oral advocacy to lay persons.

At a time when there is much interest in the effect of one influence – new technology – history reminds us that advocacy is shaped by many factors.

The methodology of this book consists of a literature survey and a series of semi-structured interviews with advocates, judges, trainers and academics to ascertain their views on the past and changes in advocacy over recent decades and their predictions for the future. Deep gratitude is expressed to them for their valuable time, patience and helpful suggestions.

See Colin Jones, *An American Lawyer's View of the Law Judge System*, Heibonshinsho, Tokyo, 2009 and A Watson, Popular Participation in Japanese Criminal Justice. From Jurors to Lay Judges, Palgrave Macmillan, 2016. Jury trial was restored in Spain. Reforms to civil procedure in 1993 and 2003 in Finland, partly to reduce delay caused by repeated adjournments and to establish a more concentrated form of hearing, have resulted in greater orality during court proceedings and have lessened reliance on written evidence and legal submissions. See Laura Ervo, *Scandinavian Trends in Civil Pre-trial Proceedings*, Civil Justice Quarterly., Volume 26, October, 2007, pp. 466–483.

2

Distinguished Advocates, Judges, Classical Learning and Other Influences on Advocacy in the Eighteenth and Early Nineteenth Centuries

Ferocity and Bitterness

There are few records of the advocacy of early lawyers; their words having long since evaporated. Those that do exist, chronicled in the lives of jurists such as Edward Coke and Francis Bacon and in the State Trial Reports,[1] show that lawyers in Tudor and Stuart times were not accustomed to principles of restraint and moderation. Advocacy in these periods was marked, as a rule, by what Bernard Kelly, author of *Famous Advocates and their Speeches*[2] described, in the introduction to his work written almost a century ago, as a *fierce bitterness, or rather savagery, hardly to be realized at the present day*. For instance, in the treason trial of Sir

---

[1] These reports, made between 1163 and 1858, chiefly cover cases of high treason but also include bigamy, sedition, seditious libel, murder involving high ranking officials or peers, riot, piracy, witch craft, bribery and corruption. The quality of reporting, especially in early cases, is variable, but increased in the late seventeenth century, when good shorthand writers were employed. It is difficult to say how representative the cases reported in the State Trials are of criminal trials more generally, of which there are few records. See Sir James FitzJames Stephen, *A History of the Criminal Law of England*, London, Macmillan and Co., 1883, Vol. I, Chapter XI, page 345.

[2] Sweet and Maxwell, London, 1921.

© The Author(s) 2019
A. Watson, *Speaking in Court*, https://doi.org/10.1007/978-3-030-10395-8_2

Walter Raleigh, in 1603, the Attorney General, Sir Edward Coke, addressed the defendant, who was about to speak in his own defence:

> *Thou art a scurvy fellow; thy name is hateful to all the realm of England for thy pride. I will now make it appear to the world that there never existed on the face of the earth a viler viper than thou art.*[3]

In the midst of other opprobrious epithets aimed at Raleigh, Coke said:

> *Thou art a monster, thou hast an English face, and a Spanish heart. Thou viper! For I thou thee, thou viper.*[4]

> "*It becometh not a man of virtue and quality to call me so*" was Raleigh's dignified rebuke adding, "*but I take comfort in it, it is all you can do*".

Coke then asked Raleigh "*Have I angered you?*" Raleigh replied, "*I am in no case to be angry*". In other instances, during the trial, similar language was used by Coke towards the prisoner, until he was told by the bench not to be impatient and to allow Raleigh to speak. Admonished, Coke sat down in anger and was only with much difficulty persuaded to proceed. When at length he did, it was with a fresh torrent of invective in which Raleigh was accused of the darkest treasons and called a "*damnable atheist*". As well as displaying intemperate language, Coke adduced evidence against the prisoner which, even by the then lax practice of trials for treason, was obviously illegal. It was principally upon this proof that Sir Walter Raleigh was convicted.[5]

---

[3] The Trial of Sir Walter Raleigh, 1 State Trials (1730) page 205.

[4] In the opinion of Sidney W. Clarke, writing in 1896, (William Andrews ed. *The Lawyer in History, Literature and Humour*, William Andrews and Co, London, 1896 page 56) the phrase "if thou thou'st him some thrice", said by Sir Toby Belch in the course of directing Sir Andrew Ague-Cheek, in Act iii, Scene 2 of Twelfth Night, probably first performed in Middle Temple Hall on 2nd February 1602, to convey a challenge to the disguised Viola was an obvious allusion by Shakespeare to the violent invective thrown by Coke at Sir Walter Raleigh in court. Conversely, appreciation of Shakespeare in succeeding centuries was to ensure that his words were much alluded to in trials by generations of advocates in numerous lands.

[5] F R Wrottesley, *The Examination of Witnesses in Court*, Sweet and Maxwell, London 1910. Chapter 3. Pages 89–90.

Coke, as Attorney General, is also remembered for splenetic performances in other trials, including that of the Earl of Essex (1600).[6] Many historians have been so appalled by his offending speeches that they have felt unable to give Coke anything like his fair share of credit in defending the common law against the royal prerogative and for his influential written works on the law.[7] Nevertheless, though not readily defensible according to modern ethical notions, Coke's conduct seems to have complied broadly with the rhetorical standards expected of crown counsel in treason trials at the period.[8]

Edward Coke was a skillful rhetorician – rhetorical technique, largely derived from the Latin classics, formed an important component of Elizabethan education in Grammar schools[9] – with a forceful ability to persuade.

---

[6] State Trials 43 ELIZ 1600, 1333–59. At his trial, the Earl of Essex told the jury that Coke was *"playing the orator* and displaying *the trade and talent of those who value themselves upon their skill in pleading innocent men out of their lives"*. David Jardine, *Criminal Trials*, Charles Knight, London, 1832, Volume 1, Page 321.

[7] See John Hostettler, *Champions of the Rule of Law*, Waterstone Press, 2011, Chapter 2, especially page 46.

[8] Bernard Kelly, *Famous Advocates and their Speeches: British Forensic Eloquence from Lord Erskine to Lord Russell of Killowen*, London, Sweet and Maxwell, 1921, page 2. Sir James FitzJames Stephens, however, concluded, after surveying the State Trial Reports that, in the rancorous ferocity of his advocacy, Coke was unrivalled in any English court of justice, except perhaps those in which Judge Jeffries presided, following the Restoration. Sir James FitzJames Stephens, *A History of The Criminal Law of England*. Vol. I, Chapter XI, page 333.

[9] Coke had attended Norwich Grammar School. (For further details of his background and career, see Cuthbert W. Johnson. *The Life of Sir Edward Coke*, 2 Volumes, Henry Colborn, London, 1837.) Many lawyers, members of the gentry and of commercial families, who served as jurors, were educated at grammar schools (On the Elizabethan grammar school curriculum and the prime place within it of Latin and reading Cicero, Ovid, Virgil and Horace, see Alison Plowden, *Elizabethan England*, RDA Limited, 1982, Chapter 3.). Boys at Grammar school were also taught adoxography, the art of eruditely praising worthless things. It has been said Coke mastered a reverse skill and with his words sent scores of men to their deaths. Sadakat Kadri, *The Trial. A History from Socrates to O.J. Simpson*, Harper, London, 2006, page 82. Probably the first English treatise on adoxography, *The Defence of Contraries*, written by Anthony Munday, was published in 1593. The work contains essays celebrating deformity, ugliness, poverty, blindness, sterility and stupidity. In its preface is a claim that it would be particularly useful to lawyers. Francis Bacon, typical of those from particularly wealthy backgrounds, did not attend grammar school but was educated privately by tutors.

Late sixteenth and early seventeenth century judges, members of what Dr. Ian Williams (Interviewed on the 5th May, 2010) described as *"the classically educated humanist elite"*, occasionally referred to the classics in their judgements (no records of their use by advocates before them

Away from State Trials, Coke's great rival and foe Francis Bacon, recalled both as Lord Chancellor and a founder of modern science, had a reputation for eloquence both in the courts and parliament.[10] Regarding Bacon's oratory Ben Jonson wrote[11]:

There happened in my time one noble speaker, who was full of gravity in his speaking. His language, where he could spare or pass by a jest, was nobly censorious. No man ever spoke more neatly, more pressly, more weightily, or suffered less emptiness, less idleness, in what he uttered. No member of his speech but consisted of his own graces. His hearers could not cough or look aside from him without loss. He commanded where he spoke and had his judges angry and pleased at his devotion. No man had their affections more in his power. The fear of every man that heard him was lest he should make an end.

However it has been said that Bacon did not always exert himself fully if he saw little chance of success or personal advantage:

---

appear to exist, although, in Dr. William's view, it is highly likely that they were employed to persuade Privy Counsellors, not usually legally trained but educated in the classics, who sat in Star Chamber Cases, with common-law judges, and in treason cases.). Examples kindly supplied by Dr. Williams, from his research, included: Berkeley J's reference to Aesop's *Fables*, Plato and Diogenes in *Hastings v Douglas* (1634) CUL. Gg.ii.19,f.506; Aristotle's *Politics* and Demosthenes in *Zangis V Whiskard* (1595) BL. MS. Add. 25,211, f. 126, per Harris sjt; Reference to *the Philosopher* (presumably Aristotle) in *Lord Cromwell's Case* (1601) 2 Co.Rep., ff.72 73: Reference to Virgil by Francis Bacon in *The Case of Impeachment of Waste* (undated) in *Arguments of Law of Sir Francis Bacon, Knight, In Certain Great and Difficult Cases*. In *The Works of Francis Bacon*. Ed. Spedding J., Ellis R. L. and Heath D.D., vol. 7, p. 532 and Bacon's reference to Julius Caesar's works and his departure from England in *Lowe's Case* (undated) in *Arguments of Law of Sir Francis Bacon, Knight, in Certain Great and Difficult Cases*. In *The Works of Francis Bacon*. Ed. Spedding J., Ellis R. L. and Heath D.D. vol. 7, p. 548. Dr. Williams was in no doubt that, although no explicit reference was made to it, the judges and jurors in the Trial of Walter Raleigh would have implicitly understood Coke's portrayal of Raleigh to be Cicero's Cataline, the arch traitor.

[10] See Thomas H. Macauley's biographical essay, *Lord Bacon* in *Critical and Historic Essays*, London: Longman, Green and Longman, 1877, pp. 356–414. Also see F.E. Smith, First Lord Birkenhead, *Famous Trials*, Hutchinson and Co, Ltd., *Francis Bacon* pp. 395–399, who describes Bacon's career and his trial, conviction and ruin in 1621 for taking bribes from parties in a case which he sat as a judge. Although seldom discussed, it is broadly accepted that in England, right until the impeachment of Lord Macclesfield, in 1725, there was a steady tradition of judicial corruption, a hidden and silent influence on the success of advocacy at trials. Bribes were resisted by some judges but, it would seem, taken by many. Andrew Dewar Gibb, *Judicial Corruption in the United Kingdom*, W. Green and Son, Edinburgh, 1957.

[11] *On Lord Francis Bacon*, published in 1625, Harvard Classics, 1910, Vol 27, page 60.

When engaged in some cause celebre – the Queen and the Court coming to hear the arguments or taking a lively interest in the result – Bacon no doubt exerted himself to the utmost and excited applause by the display of learning and eloquence; but on ordinary occasions, when he found himself in an empty court, and before an irritable judge, he must have been unable to conceal his disgust – and eager to get home that he might finish an essay or expose some fallacy by which past ages had been misled – if he stood up for his client as long as he felt there was a fair chance of success, we may believe that he showed little energy in a hopeless defence, and that he was careless about softening defeat by any display of zeal or sympathy.[12]

Coke, then Attorney General, and Bacon, the first Queen's Counsel, bitterly clashed in the Court of Exchequer when Bacon made an application in a case in which he had neither a brief nor a fee:

Coke: *"Mr Bacon if you have any tooth against me, pluck it out, for it will do you more hurt than all the teeth in your head will do you any good".*

Bacon: *"Mr Attorney, I respect you; I fear you not, and the less you speak of your own greatness, the more I will think of it".*

Coke: *"I think scorn to stand upon terms of greatness towards you, who are less than little, – less than the least".* [Here he added some similar expressions with an insolence which cannot be expressed].

Bacon: *"Mr Attorney, do not depress me so far; for I have been your better, and may again when it please the Queen".*[13]

The Arrival of Eloquence

William Forsyth (1812–1899), in his highly influential book, *Hortensius: or the Advocate*, first published in 1849, on the conduct and duties of an advocate, then highly topical, but which also presented a history of advocacy from ancient Greece onwards, saw eloquence only becoming important at the English Bar in the late eighteenth century:

---

[12] John, Lord Campbell, *Lives of the Chancellors*, London: John Murray, 1856, Volume III, page 12.

[13] John Lord Campbell, *ibid*, page 28.

Forensic eloquence in this country seems to have been almost unknown until the latter part of the eighteenth century….. and we search in vain that voluminous and interesting repository of cases, the State Trials, where the higher efforts of judicial oratory ought, if anywhere, to be found, for 'thoughts that breathe, and words that burn' in the efforts made by our advocates in former days for their clients. We find, indeed, immense learning and research; a wonderful familiarity with precedents, the pole-star of the English lawyer; and sound and logical argument, interrupted however too often by puerilities and laboured truisms, and conveyed in the stiff and formal periods in which our ancestors used to enunciate their thoughts.[14]

Bernard Kelly traced the beginnings of what he terms *British Forensic Eloquence* to the early, rather than late, eighteenth century. In his account,[15] the roughness and uncouthness of early advocacy, and the timid reserve and uninspired dullness which had to some extent replaced it in the late seventeenth century,[16] was supplanted through the efforts of a number of influential men. One such was Lord Cowper (1664–1723) who was appointed the first Lord Chancellor of Great Britain in 1707. Praised by Kelly for his *melodious voice* and *perfect elocution*, he was gifted with eloquence, which assisted his rise in the Whig Party, and appeared in many important cases, including that of *Ashley V White*[17] in 1703, establishing the constitutional principle that a qualified voter in an elec-

---

[14] William Forsyth, *Hortensius or the Advocate*, London: J. Murray, 1849, page 20.

[15] Bernard Kelly, *Famous Advocates and their Speeches*, Sweet and Maxwell, London, 1921, page 2.

[16] Heneage Finch (1621–1682), 1st Lord Nottingham, called to the Bar (Inner Temple) in 1645, appointed as Solicitor General in 1660, Attorney General in 1670 and five years later Lord Chancellor, spoken of as the *father of equity* and known as the *English Cicero*, the *English Roscius* and *silver tongued*, appears as a seventeenth century eloquent exception to this. However, according to Forsyth (Hortensius, 1879 Edition, page 312.) none of his speeches remain that would justify these descriptions. There is evidence that judges who sat in the reign of Charles II disapproved of long or elaborate speeches by counsel. Lord Guilford, for example, had little toleration for speeches at all. According to contemporary reports, he would strongly discourage counsel from making them after the conclusion of evidence. Mr. Commissioner Kerr at the Old Bailey had the ledges in front of counsel's seats cut away, so that they had nowhere to rest their papers, thus reducing the length of their speeches. Another Stuart judge much annoyed by the length of some written pleadings, which would subsequently have to be read aloud in court, ordered the draftsman to parade through the courts with his head through them. (Richard Du Cann, *The Art of the Advocate*, 1993, Penguin Books, page 21.)

[17] 1703 92 ER 126.

tion has a right akin to a property interest and in the absence of a valid statute denying that right he would have an action for damages against those preventing its exercise. As Lord Chancellor he made important contributions to the development of the law of equity. Also remembered for helping to shape equity, especially as Lord Chancellor from 1733 to 1737, and eloquence in court is Charles Talbot, 1685–1737, made 1st Baron Talbot in 1733 when he was appointed to the Woolsack. Called to the bar in 1711, he rapidly acquired a reputation for persuasiveness appealing to both the hearts and heads of juries. Indeed on his death the following anonymous memorial verse was published[18]:

> *How the heart listened while he pleadings spoke.*
> *While on the enlightened mind with willing art*
> *his gentle reason so persuasive stole that the charmed*
> *hearer thought it was his own.*

Another contribution was made by PhillipYorke, Lord Hardwick (1690–1764), who became Lord Chancellor in 1738. Generally seen as the creator of the modern systematised English law of equity, in the words of William Forsyth, he was "the oracle of equity".[19] Whilst at the bar, Lord Chesterfield praised his restrained manner in crown prosecutions. Contrasting Yorke to the former "bloodhounds" of the Crown, Chesterfield described him as naturally humane moderate and decent.[20] Early in his career Phillip Yorke conducted the prosecution of Christopher Layer for treason as a Jacobite in 1720. This case further elevated his reputation as a forensic orator which was already considerable in cases involving equity. In 1723 he rose to Attorney General. In that post Bernard Kelly,[21] described how he brought a variety of learning and richness of illustration to his speeches making them *"among the finest speci-*

---

[18] Quoted by Brian Gibbens QC, Former Recorder of Oxford, *Elements of Modern Advocacy*, New Law Cassettes, Butterworths, London, 1979.

[19] William Forsyth, *Hortensius or the Advocate*, London, John Murray, 1849, page 13.

[20] *Characteristics of Lord Hardwicke, by Lord Chesterfield*, European magazine and London review, Volume 41, 1802, page 250.

[21] Bernard Kelly, *Famous Advocates and their Speeches*, London: Sweet and Maxwell, 1921, page 3.

mens of their kind". Lord Campbell in *Lives of the Lord Chancellors*[22] considered that Lord Hardwicke's judgements combined a luminous method of arrangement with elegance and lucidity of language.

William Murray, Lord Mansfield, (1704–1793)[23] also had an effect on advocacy. As a judge he is recognized as the founder of English mercantile law which, having found it in chaos, left in a form almost equivalent to a code. Highly educated, an outstanding Classics scholar[24] when at Oxford, he mixed with the best of literary society and was an intimate friend of Alexander Pope. Indeed it was said that the *"graceful and fluent"*[25] periods in his much admired court oratory and judgments were strongly influenced by Pope, whose witty and eloquent work was much concerned with uniting elegant form and matter.[26]

Murray's early work at the bar centred on important Scottish appeal cases.[27] His English practice was small until 1738 when a single speech in a much reported cause célèbre[28] before a jury placed him at the head of the bar. From that time he had all the work he could attend to. Separating him from the greater number of his contemporaries at the bar William Murray was noted for his self-control and "being prudent to the point of timidity".[29] He received criticism for being moderate and dispassionate

[22] Lord Campbell, *Lives of the Chancellors*, London, John Murray, Volume V.

[23] *Lord Mansfield*, C. H. S. Fifoot, Oxford, Clarendon Press, 1936.

[24] Later in life, in 1775, William Murray, then Lord Mansfield, commissioned a portrait, *Lord Mansfield Chief Justice of England*, attributed to David Martin, depicting him seated, in front of a bust of Solomon, reading Cicero. The picture was purchased for display in his very substantial London home, Kenwood House, beside Hampstead Heath. This property was acquired, and much altered, mainly with the proceeds of his highly successful career in law.

[25] Bernard Kelly, *Famous Advocates and their Speeches*, London, Sweet and Maxwell, 1921, page 3.

[26] There is an anecdote that Pope undertook to teach Murray oratorical delivery shortly after his call to the Bar, and that one day a neighbour entering his Chambers, 5 King's Bench Walk, found him gesturing before a mirror with Pope giving instructions. See Lord Campbell, *The Lives of the Chief Justices*, Volume II, London: John Murray. 1858, page 33.

[27] Prominent amongst these was, in 1737, as counsel in the Houses of Parliament for Edinburgh to oppose the imposition of penalties on that city following the Porteous Riots. His considerable eloquence in this cause was greatly noted. See Edmund Heward, Lord Mansfield: *A Biography of William Murray 1st Earl of Mansfield 1705–1793*. Chichester: Barry Rose, 1979, pp. 18–21. The story of the Porteous Riots is graphically told by Sir Walter Scott in *The Heart of Midlothian*.

[28] The case of William Sloper, a wealthy young man, who had the misfortune to be found in bed with an actress Maria Cibber. Proceedings, with the object of obtaining as much money as possible from him, were begun by her husband. William Murray acted as junior counsel for William Sloper. See Edmund Heward, *ibid*, pp. 21–23.

[29] *Lord Mansfield*, C.H. S Fifoot, *ibid*, Oxford, Clarendon Press, 1936, page 37.

and was unfavourably compared with Edward Coke. When asked about this, he replied, "*I would not have made Sir Edward Coke'd speech to gain all Sir Edward Coke's estates and all his reputation*".[30] As solicitor general (1742–54) Murray prosecuted the Scottish Jacobite lords, Balmerino, Kilmarnock and Lovat. In 1756 Murray was raised to the peerage, as Lord Mansfield, and made Lord Chief Justice, a post he held until 1788. During this time he instituted a number of procedural reforms in the Court of King's Bench which bore on advocacy. One of these was to allow barristers to submit only a single motion each day and, if necessary, to continue with it the following day. Hitherto the number of motions they were permitted to make was unrestricted and barristers were heard in order of seniority. That had meant almost all work went to senior barristers, who were often so overworked they frequently had insufficient time to read their briefs, to the detriment of those who instructed them.[31]

English, spoken by the educated in the eighteenth century became more refined, in no small measure due to the influence of Jonathan Swift, Richard Steele, Joseph Addison, Samuel Johnson, Lord Chesterfield and other writers and arbiters of taste. Verse flourished as well.[32] Public speakers had more words to decorate their speeches as many Latinisms were substituted for common words of Anglo-Saxon derivation which were seen as low, slangy or imprecise. The Century also saw a greater awareness of the possibilities of language to persuade, thus Lord Chesterfield advised his son to master oratory, "*the art of speaking well*", not because of what

---

[30] C.H.S. Fifoot, *ibid*, page 37. The speech to which Murray referred was that made by Coke in the prosecution of Sir Walter Raleigh.

[31] Edmund Heward, *Lord Mansfield: A Biography of William Murray Ist Earl of Mansfield 1705–1793*. Chichester: Barry Rose, 1979, pp. 46–47. Other changes brought about by Lord Mansfield included reducing the number of reserved judgements after hearings had finished and restricting rehearing of cases to when only real doubt existed about the first.

[32] The period also experienced works written in verse on a vast range of subjects including law. An example is *Coke's Reports in Verse* published by the legal bookseller John Worrall in 1742 and reissued in the early 1800's. Each case is summarized in a rhyming couplet appearing in the same order as the full cases in Coke's Reports, with the case name at the head of the couplet. According to research undertaken by John Kleefeld, author of *From Brehons to Brouhahas: Poetic Impulse in the Law*, a paper delivered at the Institute of Advanced Legal Studies on the 17th June, 2009, this slim volume sold widely but particularly amongst law students. Mr. Kleefeld was interviewed on the 26th June, 2009.

people would think of him if he did not, but because it was foolish to neglect an accomplishment which would serve him well in later public life, whether it be in parliament, the pulpit, or at the bar. According to Chesterfield: "*It is not enough to speak*" the hearers' language in "*its utmost purity, and according to the rules of grammar, but he must speak it elegantly, that is he must use the best and most expressive words and put them in the best order. He should likewise adorn what he says by proper metaphors, similes, and other figures of rhetoric; and he should enliven it, if he can, by quick and sprightly turns of wit*".[33] On the forensic skill of Lord Mansfield, Lord Campbell wrote his observations "*seemed to suggest trains of thinking rather than to draw to conclusions; and so skillfully did he conceal his art that the hearers thought they formed their opinion in consequence of the working of their own minds, when in truth it was the effect of the most refined dialectic*".[34] In taking this approach he appeared to follow Pope's advice in his versified *Essay on Criticism*:

> *Men must be taught as if you taught them not*
> *And things unknown proposed as things forgot.*[35]

An indication of Mansfield's eloquence may be seen in extracts from his famous verdict in 1772 in the famous case of James Somerset[36] which, although Mansfield carefully avoided a general pronouncement of principle,[37] effectively ended slavery in Britain in 1772:

> *On the part of Somerset, the case which we gave notice should be decided this day, the Court now proceeds to give its opinion. The state of slavery is of such a*

---

[33] Lord Chesterfield's letter to his son November 1st 1739. *Chesterfield's Letters*. J M Dent and Sons, last reprinted 1975, pp. 3–4. Alexander Pope saw poetry as a means of aiding public speaking. In *The First Epistle of the Second Book of Horace*, in John Butt (ed), *The Poems of Alexander Pope*, vol. IV 1737, reprinted by Methuen, London 1939, page 189, Pope wrote: *What will a Child learn sooner than a song?/ What better teach a Foreigner the tongue?/ What's long or short, each accent where to place?/ And speak in public with some sort of grace?*

[34] Quoted by A. W. Cockburn QC, *In Limine An Address on Advocacy to the Christ Church Law Club*, May 15th, 1952, published and gestetnered by the Faculty of Law, University of Southampton.

[35] *Works of Alexander Pope*, Book XX, Wordsworth, 1995.

[36] *R v Knowles, ex parte Somerset*, 1772, 20 State Trials 1; 98 Eng Rep 499; 1 *Lofft* 1 (KB 1772).

[37] See Wilfred Prest, *William Blackstone and the Historians*, History Today, July 2006, page 49.

nature, that it is incapable of being introduced on any reasons, moral or political; but only positive law, which preserves its force long after the reasons, occasions, and time itself from hence it was created, is erased from memory: it's so odious, that nothing can be suffered to support it but positive law. Whatever inconveniences, therefore, may follow from a decision, I cannot say this case is allowed or approved by the law of England; and therefore the black must be discharged.

It is believed, although not recorded in his judgment, that Lord Mansfield said further:

The air of England is too pure for a slave to breathe, and so everyone who breathes it becomes free. Everyone who comes to this island is entitled to the protection of English law, whatever oppression he may have suffered and whatever be the colour of his skin.[38]

Classics and Rhetoric

In the eighteenth century, forensic oratory was shaped by the fact it was sometimes, particularly in important cases, addressed to special jurors[39] and peers in the House of Lords, when that body was acting as a court.

---

[38] See Lord John Campbell, *Lives of the Chief Justices*, Volume II, page 418. Also Lord Denning, then Sir Alfred Denning, attributed similar words to Lord Mansfield in *Freedom Under the Law, The Hamlyn Lectures*, London; Stevens and Sons, 1949, page 7.

[39] Most trials, both criminal and civil were before common juries, selected from the general pool of those eligible to serve as jurors. However four non-standard common law types of juries existed in England. These were:

The Gentleman Jury – men of high social and economic status;

The Struck Jury – principal landowners selected from a list of forty-eight names;

The Professional Jury – members of special knowledge or expertise, and

The Party Jury (known by the Latin phrase "jury de medietate linguae") – a jury for defendants at special risk of suffering prejudice. It was composed either wholly or in half of persons of the same race, sex, religion or origin.

The first three types were first recognized by a statute in 1730 (3 Geo.II.c.25) under the general term "special jury". The background of special jurors meant that they could usually be relied upon to find for the Crown in political cases and tried many in the late eighteenth century. This feature continued well into the first third of the nineteenth century when out of the small number of criminal cases tried each year by a special jury, a significant number were political prosecutions (some 183 between 1816 and 1834 – Woodward, L. *The Age of Reform* 2nd edition, Oxford, 1962,

Members of these groups usually shared a background of education in the classics, as did judges and many lawyers. At public schools and grammar schools the school curriculum was dominated by Greek and Latin. Teaching methods tended to be very traditional.[40] Nonconformists were excluded from most public schools. They formed what became known as Dissenting Academies such as those at Daventry, Warrington and Hackney, the centre of dissenting education in London. The education received at these schools was more closely linked to the world of business and additionally comprised science and accountancy.[41] The grip of Latin

---

p. 31) The special jury was employed extensively in civil cases from 1770 to 1790, roughly corresponding to Lord Mansfield's period as Lord Chief Justice of the Court of Kings Bench, when he used juries of merchants (The Professional Jury) in the shaping of a coherent body of commercial law. After Lord Mansfield, special juries of merchants continued to be influential, especially during the first half of the nineteenth century under Lords Ellenborough and Campbell. The Parliamentary Select Committee on Special and Common Juries of 1867 found a burgeoning use of special juries in the Court of Common Pleas, Chancery, in the Divorce Court and in a great many Sheriff Courts dealing with compensation cases. They attracted some criticism as an adjunct to the class system (Oldham, James, *The Seventh Amendment and the Anglo-American Special Juries*, NYU Press, 2006, Chapter 8). The Juries Act 1870 defined the class of persons entitled and liable to serve on special juries. As before, they were every man whose name was on the jurors' book for any county and who was legally entitled to be called an esquire, or was a person of higher degree, or a banker or merchant. An additional qualification of occupying a house of a certain high rateable value was added. A special juryman received a fee of one guinea for each cause, unlike common jurors who were unpaid. Either party to a case could obtain an order for a special jury but had to pay the additional expenses incurred unless the judge certified that it was a proper case to be tried by a special jury. Under the 1870 Act a special jury could not be ordered in cases of treason or felony and could only be ordered in misdemeanours when the trial was before the King's Bench Division of the High Court, or the civil side at assizes. The Party Jury was abolished in the Naturalisation Act of 1870, which also gave foreigners the right to serve on juries. Special Juries remained on the statute book until 1949 (1971 for London) and the last case using a special jury was in London in 1950. (Neil Vidmar, *World Jury Systems* Oxford University Press, 2000). Perhaps the most famous post war action heard by a special jury was the much publicized libel case of *Laski v The Newark Advertiser Co. Ltd and Parlby*, tried by Lord Goddard, then Lord Chief Justice of England, in 1947, and in which Sir Patrick Hastings, *see later* Chap. 9, appeared for both the defendants.

[40] Shelley, it has been calculated, got through some 75,000 lines of Greek and Latin poetry and prose during his time at Eton, 1804–10, many of them being constantly repeated. Eton gave priority to three authors: Homer, Virgil and Horace. Pote and Williams, Eton publishers, produced other books of classical authors which were used at Eton, Harrow and other schools. The 1806 edition of *Potae Graei* included extracts, inter alia from Homer, Hesiod, Theocritus, Euripides and Sappho. Other books published at this time included Aeschyles, Aesop's Fables and selections from Ovid and Tibullus. Ian Gilmour, *The Making of the Poets. Byron and Shelley in Their Time*, Pimlico, London, 2003. Page 100.

[41] On the variety of schools and education in the eighteenth century see Nicholas Hans, *New Trends In Education In The Eighteenth Century*, Routledge and Kegan Paul, 1951.

and Greek at public schools remained strong and it was only during the following century that attempts were made to extend what was taught with, for example, Samuel Butler's introduction of mathematics and history at Shrewsbury School and Thomas Arnold's provision of lessons in geography, modern history and foreign languages at Rugby. University education at Oxford and Cambridge, available only to professing Anglicans, still concentrated on Aristotle's logic and upon classical languages.[42]

Amongst the eighteenth century educated classes, of which lawyers were a part, there was considerable interest in classical rhetoric (as indeed there was in the grand tour of Italy and the art and architecture of ancient Rome and Greece, which was imitated in neo-classicism,[43] with the British, at the heart of an expanding territorial and trade empire, forming an image of themselves as the new Rome). This was heightened by the publication of the texts on rhetoric by George Campbell in 1776,[44] and Hugh Blair in 1783,[45] both figures of the Scottish Enlightenment. Earlier, during the 1760s, Adam Smith had written and lectured about rhetoric theory.[46]

Because rhetoric from classical times was an important influence on advocates and advocacy in Britain during the eighteenth, nineteenth and even parts of the twentieth century, this book contains an excursus on classical rhetoric which is intended to provide readers with a helpful background.

---

[42] Instead of going to university, Dissenters attended senior classes at the Dissenting Academies where a much wider curriculum was taught, including English, contemporary literature, history geography and politics. See Irene Parker, *Dissenting Academies in England*. Cambridge University Press, 1914. Some nonconformists attended universities in Scotland, where there was also an emphasis on classical languages.

[43] For an account of the range of classical influence on eighteenth century English society see Jeremy Black, *Culture in Eighteenth Century England. A Subject for Taste*, Hambledon and London, 2005, Chapter 8. See also, Mark Bradley, *Classics and Imperialism in the British Empire*, Oxford University Press, 2010, which explores interactions between classics and imperialism during the heyday of the British Empire from the late 18th to its collapse in the twentieth century.

[44] *Philosophy of Rhetoric*, 1911, Funk and Wagnalls, London and New York.

[45] *Lectures on Rhetoric and Belles Lettres* (with an introduction by Linda Ferreira-Buckley and S. Michael Halloran), 2005, South Illinois University.

[46] *Lectures on Rhetoric and Belles Lettres*, 1985, Indianapolis, Liberty Classics. Also see, J.C. Bryce (Ed) *Rhetoric and Belle Lettres*, 1983, Oxford: Clarendon Press, 1983.

Forensic speeches, of the classical variety, were distinguished by the length and complexity of their sentences, many allusions to Greek and Latin literature and by strict subordination of style to sense, at least in the best advocacy. In the worst, concern to create an impression of balance and articulation over-rode presenting arguments clearly and accurately.[47] The subtlety and complexity of this style, rich in alliteration, antithesis, parallelism and other rhetorical devices and language, can sometimes obscure the meaning of particular passages from modern readers not highly trained in Latin and Greek syntax, and who are obviously unable to hear the deliverer's tone and inflection of voice and to observe his facial expressions and bodily gestures.[48]

The great exponents of the 'classical' style of forensic advocacy, in the later eighteenth century were the trial managers, officers appointed by the High Court of Parliament to prosecute in impeachment proceedings, Edmund Burke (1729–1797), Charles James Fox (1749–1806) and Richard Brinsley Sheridan (1751–1816), who were politicians as well as lawyers (Sheridan, of course, was also an accomplished, though by far from affluent, playwright and friend of the Prince of Wales), in the

---

[47] Robert Graves, a classical scholar as well as a novelist, presents Modestus, in *Count Belisarius*, Cassells, 1938, Chapter 2, as a person *in classical times* who was given to strained rhetorical oratory, overly concentrating on style and numerous allusions, considered by him to assist clarity, an opinion not shared by certainly most listeners.

[48] Being absent when oratory of whatever style is delivered was considered by Sir Norman Birkett, more than half a century ago, in a Presidential Address to the Holdsworth Club of the Faculty of Law in the University of Birmingham, 7th May, 1954:

> For the great utterances when recalled are without the fire and glow of the advocate's presence; the dramatic setting has vanished; and the magical moments have irrevocably gone. It is clear that the thing said can hardly be separated from the moment of its saying and great advocacy reaches its heights only at the very moments of its performance. It is designed and intended for one particular occasion. Then and then only are to be seen the many elements which in combination make advocacy what it is. The advocate himself with his own distinctive personality, his quick mind and understanding heart, his readiness, his resources, his courage; the particular occasion with all its dramatic possibilities; the particular theme, whether noble and lofty or tragic and pitiful: the form and beauty of the words the advocate employs; the fire and glow and vehemence; the gestures, the voice, the expression – all these things are for the moment, and once gone, are gone beyond recall. That is why the modern reader of past forensic oratory falls to wondering how those triumphs were ever achieved. It is not merely that the oratory suited to one age is quite unsuited to another; it is that the one vital element of true advocacy is missing.

impeachment trial before the House of Lords of Warren Hastings for alleged misdeeds in India.[49] Hastings faced seven charges. After a trial which extended from 1788 to 1795 he was finally acquitted of them all. The speeches made by Edmund Burke and Richard Brinsley Sheridan contained strong appeals to the emotions of their listeners. In a period which was certainly not embarrassed by sentiment, advocates, understood the truth of Lord Chesterfield's letter to his son written in 1746.[50]

Wherever you would persuade or prevail, address yourself to the passions; it is by them that mankind is to be taken. I bid you strike at the passions......If you can once engage people's pride, love, pity, ambition (or whichever is their prevailing passion) on your side, you need not fear what their reason can do against you.

This is part of Sheridan's opening which he, in finely wrought and studied sentences, sought to excite strong feelings of hostility against Warren Hastings:

The coolness and reflection with which this act was managed.......proves the prisoner to be that monster in nature, a deliberate and reasoning tyrant; other tyrants of whom we read..........were urged on to their crimes by the impetuosity of passion. High rank disqualified them from advice, and perhaps, equally prevented reflection. But in the prisoner we have a man born in a state of mediocrity; bred to a mercantile life; used to system, and accustomed to regularity; who was accountable to his masters and therefore compelled to think and deliberate on every part of his conduct. It is this cool deliberation I say, which renders his crimes the horrible and his character the more atrocious.

---

[49] See Marshall, P J. *The Impeachment of Warren Hastings*, Oxford University Press, 1965. Also see F. E. Smith, The First Earl Birkenhead, *Famous Trials*, Hutchinson and Co, Ltd., 1930, *The Trial of Warren Hastings*, pp. 151–166, for a concise and lively account and for criticism of the trial managers: *But it is one thing to deliver a philippic, another to manage a prosecution* (Page 161). For a brief history of impeachment trials in Britain and the United States, see Andrew Watson, *Impeachments – Past, Present and Future?* Justice of the Peace 1999, Vol. 163, pp. 468–472 and pp. 491–494.

[50] From Dublin Castle on the 8th February, 1747. Unable to locate in *Lord Chesterfield's Letters*, J. M. Dent and Sons, reprinted in 1975, but quoted by Richard DuCann, *The Art of the Advocate*, Revised Edition, Penguin Books, 1993, page 193.

Edmund Burke's 15 speeches in the prosecution of Hastings show much of the influence of Demosthenes.[51] The peroration of his final speech, much admired as a piece of discourse, contains many tropes, figures of thought and of diction as taught in the handbooks of classical rhetoric including Cicero and Quintilian.[52]

The trial managers were also quite willing to use theatricality to achieve their objective. According to an account given by the historian Edward Gibbon, Sheridan affected to be so overcome by the horrors described in his opening speech that he concluded it by collapsing into Burke's arms.[53] Nor was drama restricted to the floor of the House of Lords. It was reported on another occasion that Sheridan's famous and glamorous wife, the singer Elizabeth Linley, fainted in the middle of one of Burke's speeches detailing the torture of Indian women.[54] (Histrionics from advocates and members of the audience was, of course, not entirely unknown in classical times, see Excursus (Classical Rhetoric) **available on the internet**

---

[51] George Kennedy, *Classical rhetoric and its Christian and secular tradition from ancient to modern times*, Croom-Helm, 1980, pp. 231–232. For a more detailed description of methods employed by Demosthenes, see Hans Julius Wolff, *Demosthenes as Advocate: The Functions and Methods of Legal Consultants in Classical Athens*, in Edwin Carawan, *Oxford readings in the Attic orators*, Oxford University Press, 2007, Chapter 5. Michael Grant, *Cicero Selected Works*, Penguin, 1960, page 30, considered that Burke's attack on Warren Hastings owed much of its *balance, symmetry and resonance to Ciceronian oratory* and noted that Burke explicitly referred to Verres, the corrupt governor of Sicily, who was successfully prosecuted by Cicero.

[52] Just to present one example, Burke, at the conclusion of a speech which lasted four days, set out a number of separate and quite distinct reasons to convict Warren Hastings:

I impeach Warren Hastings, Esquire of high crimes and misdemeanours.

I impeach him in the name of Commons of Great Britain in Parliament assembled, whose Parliamentary trust he has betrayed.

I impeach him in the name of all the Commons of Great Britain, whose national character he has dishonoured.

I impeach him in the name of the people of India whose laws, rights and liberties he has subverted, whose properties he has destroyed, whose country he has laid waste and desolate.

I impeach him in the name and by virtue of those eternal laws of justice which he has violated.

I impeach him in the name of human nature itself, which he has cruelly outraged, injured and oppressed, in both sexes, in every age, rank, situation, and condition of life.

Classical rhetorical devices used here include anaphora, where a phrase, *I impeach him*, is repeated at the beginning of successive lines and tricolon, a sentence of three clearly defined parts of equal length usually independent clauses and of increasing power, in the fourth sentence.

[53] See Fintan O'Tool, *A traitor's kiss: The life of Richard Brinsley Sheridan 1751–1816*. Granta Books, 1998.

[54] Bernard Kelly, *Famous Advocates and their Speeches*, London, Sweet and Maxwell, 1921, page 12.

Historyadvocacy.wordpress.com). Displays by Sheridan, Burke and Linley were in keeping with the emotional climate of the time – a period of sentimentality in which feeling and expression, encouraged by novels, was celebrated. Widely read works of the time included those by Henry Mackenzie (*The Man of Feeling*), Samuel Richardson (*Pamela, or Virtue Rewarded*) Oliver Goldsmith, (*Vicar of Wakefield*), Lawrence Sterne, (*Tristan Shandy*) and Henry Brooke (*The Fool of Quality*) – all of which relied on emotional responses by readers to their characters.

Henry Brougham (1778–1868), who become Lord Chancellor of England from 1830 to 1834, practiced as a barrister from 1806, after his call to the English Bar.

Brougham's greatest forensic triumph is generally held to have been the cross-examination of unsavoury witnesses and his magnificently eloquent closing speech in the "trial", before the House of Lords in 1820, of Queen Caroline, accused by her husband George IV of infidelities as a ground for annulment of the royal marriage.[55] The peroration of his final speech was said to have been written and rewritten by him seventeen times. His speeches were heard, and later read, with enthusiasm. The peroration from his opening speech has often been quoted:

Such my lords is the Case now before you! Such is the evidence in support of this measure- evidence inadequate to prove a debt – important to deprive of a civil right – ridiculous to convict of the lowest offence – scandalous if brought forward to support a charge of the highest nature which the law knows – monstrous to ruin the honour, to blast the name of an English Queen.[56]

Following Caroline's acquittal, Brougham became one of the most popular figures in Britain. His forensic style, which was to affect other advocates of the time, was influenced by the oratory of classical antiquity, particularly that of Demosthenes and Cicero, about whom he wrote arti-

---

[55] See Arthur Aspinall, *Lord Brougham and the Whig Party* (originally published in 1927), Nonsuch Publishing, 2005, Chapter 6. Sir George Hayter's very large and detailed oil on canvas, *The Trial of Queen Caroline*, painted between 1820 and 1823, may be seen in the National Portrait Gallery, London.

[56] *Speeches of Henry Lord Brougham*, Adam and Black, Edinburgh, 1838, vol 1, page 227. It was quoted in Hornal V Neuberger Products Ltd. [1957] 1 Q. B. 247 a case concerning the burden and standard of proof in civil actions, by Lord Justice Hodson, page 263.

cles in the *Edinburgh Review*. He also published translations of Demosthenes's "*Chersonese oration*" and "*On the Crown*".[57]

Amongst his admirers, Brougham was considered to be the "*Solon, Lycurgus, Demosthenes of the British Senate and Courts*".[58]

Thomas Erskine, His Triumphs and the Morality of Advocacy

Brougham was a great devotee of the late eighteenth century barrister, and fellow Scot, Thomas Erskine (1750–1823) and published commentaries on his speeches.[59] As a leader of the English Bar, Erskine[60] was

---

[57] In his masterpiece "*On the Crown*", Demosthenes (384–322 BC), who is generally considered to have been the greatest of all Greek orators and an inspiration to Cicero in Roman times, defended Ctesiphon, who had been charged by Aeschines on a legal technicality with offering a golden crown to Demosthenes to honour him for his services to their city of Athens. Ctesiphon was acquitted, thus also vindicating Demosthenes, and Aeschines, a rival orator and supporter of Philip II of Macedonia, was forced into exile. This was achieved not by the sort of measured and reasoned argument that Socrates might have employed but by brilliant rhetoric and the ability to condense long and complex episodes in a few masterly dramatic phrases. In the Attic plain tradition, Demosthenes's style was relatively straight forward, though he made use of his body to accentuate his words. George Keeton (*Harris on Advocacy* Eighteenth Edition, Stevens and Sons, 1943, Chapter 1), commenting on Demosthenes's denunciation, saw it as an acknowledged model of the prosecutor's art, although it contained much that would not be permitted under modern advocacy; "*he used every trick in the orator's art — suggestion, abrupt transition from second to third person and back again, prejudice (against one of low alien birth), and the implied comparison between the mediocre talents of Aeschines and his own brilliance to bring his accuser to confusion*". From the eighteenth century generations of those attending public schools and grammar schools in Britain studied, read and translated the speeches of Demosthenes, Socrates, especially *The Apology* with its appeal to reason rather than emotion, and those of Cicero, particularly his speeches against the anti-republican conspirator Cataline, in which he used similar forensic methods to those of Demosthenes.

[58] Bernard Kelly, *Famous Advocates and their Speeches*, Sweet and Maxwell, London, 1921, Page 82. Henry Brougham's oratory, in and out of court, and ability in law was not universally lauded. William Hazlitt, the essayist, wrote, in his *Spirit of the Age*, published in 1825, "*Mr Brougham speaks in a loud and unmitigated tone of voice, sometimes almost approaching a scream. He is fluent, rapid, vehement, full of his subject, with evidently a great deal to say, and regardless of the manner of saying it.......As a lawyer, he has not hitherto been remarkably successful. He is not profound in cases and reports, nor does he take much interest in the particular cause or show much adroitness in the management of it*". William Hazlitt, *Spirit of the Age*, now published by Kessinger Publishing Co, 2004, *Mr Brougham*, pp. 136–137.

[59] See, for example, *The Speeches of the Right Honourable Lord Erskine When at the Bar, with a Preparatory Memoir by the Right Honourable Lord Brougham*. Edited and published by James Ridgway. 4 Volumes. London, 1810.

[60] On the career of Thomas Erskine, see John Hostettler, *Thomas Erskine and trial by jury*, Chichester, Barry Rose Law Publishers, 1996.

profoundly influential on courtroom oratory. It was the judgment of Lord Campbell, in his *Lives of the Lord Chancellors* that as an advocate Erskine was *"without an equal in ancient or modern times"*.[61] His memory and reputation endured throughout the nineteenth century[62] and in the early twentieth century. Bernard Kelly[63] variously described him as *"that heaven born advocate"*, the *"Demosthenes of the English Bar"* and *"a genius"*. Erskine's greatest achievements were as a jury – lawyer. His speeches are characterized by vigour, cogency and lucidity, and often by real literary merit. As a young man, he had contributed to his self-education by extensive reading, particularly of English literature. Whilst posted to Minorca, as a commissioned officer in the army, Erskine closely read Shakespeare, Dryden and Pope.[64] Perhaps this, and a lack of formal education beyond a preliminary stage (it was said that, as a result of a patchy school education, due to the limited financial resources of his family which, though aristocratic, had fallen hard times, his Latin was never more than moderate and that he had no Greek whatsoever[65]), may explain why he made few allusions to Greek and Latin classics and little use of ancient styles of oratory but concentrated on English literary worth in his speeches.

An aspect of Erskine's advocacy, held in much esteem by Brougham, was his courageous and passionate close identification in court with the causes he represented. Erskine's successful defence against nine counts of treason, before an Old Bailey jury in 1794, of Thomas Hardy, a principal member of the "Friends of The People", which was allegedly planning an armed revolt similar to the French Revolution-in Britain, and who had helped form a group called the London Corresponding Society. Hardy, a shoemaker by trade, consistently maintained his objective was parliamentary reform. Sir John Scott, appointed Attorney General during the previous year and who subsequently rose to Lord Chancellor, known as Lord

---

[61] Volume VI (1845).

[62] In late Victorian times, Sir James FitzJames wrote, *Erskine was the most popular and effective advocate who ever appeared before the English Bar.* Sir James FitzJames Stephen, *A History of The Criminal Law of England.* Macmillan and Co., 1883, Chapter XXII, page 454.

[63] *Famous Advocates and their Speeches*, London: Sweet and Maxwell, 1921, Chapter One, Historical Introduction.

[64] Richard Hamilton, *All Jangle and Riot – A barrister's history of the Bar*, Professional Books, 1986, page 144.

[65] Sean Gabb, *Thomas Erskine: Saviour of English Liberty*, Freeman, July 1989, Vol 39, No 7.

Eldon, directed the prosecution which lasted five days. He opened with a speech that was nine hours long and included a minute examination of Hardy's deeds and the reading of seized papers. Next came the prosecution witnesses, government spies and others arrested, but who had been intimidated into turning King's evidence. Erskine's opening speech was seven hours in length. He destroyed the Crown's case reminding the jurors that treason was strictly to plot against the sovereign's life and could not consist of merely offending the government. The prosecution had made much of Hardy's "further intentions" beyond parliamentary reform. Erskine told the jury that they had to concentrate on facts, not on probabilities. "I am not vindicating anything that can promote disorder in the country" he said, "but I am maintaining that the worst possible disorder that can fall upon a country is when subjects are deprived of the sanction of clear and positive laws". The seized papers according to Erskine indicated a desire to reform parliament, not to overthrow it. The credibility and consistency of the Crown's witnesses were strongly attacked. After concluding his opening speech with a voice dying away to a near whisper, he called witnesses for the defence. Following closing speeches, the jury, after deliberating for three hours, returned an acquittal. At the time Erskine's opening speech was widely seen as a forensic masterpiece, combining, in beautiful language, appeals to emotion with the reason of hard logic. In our own age, one writer[66] considered it *"perhaps the greatest ever delivered in an English court and certainly the greatest that anyone has found in the voluminous series of the State Trials"*.

The government continued with its prosecutions for treason. Next was that of John Horne Tooke, an elderly clergyman and philologist who had corresponded with Dr. Johnson and was a friend and colleague of Whig leaders. Showing astute tactics, Erskine let Horne Took largely conduct his own defence. At one crucial point, however, Erskine took firm command by asking the Prime Minister, compelled to attend by a writ, if he and Horne Took had once collaborated in introducing a Reform Bill. Pitt uncomfortably equivocated and the public gallery erupted with laughter. The jury found Horne Took not guilty in eight minutes. In the wake of the acquittals of Hardy and Horne Took, a jury trying John Thelwall, a

---

[66] Sean Gabb, *Thomas Erskine: Saviour of English Liberty*, Freeman, July 1989, Vol 39, No 7, page 4.

young agitator who genuinely did admire the Jacobins in France, nearly automatically found him innocent. In this, and the two earlier trials, Erskine gave his services free of charge. His forensic efforts undoubtedly helped curb the repressive measures taken of the Pitt Ministry taken in response to the insecurity and hysteria in Britain in the aftermath of the revolution in France. Shortly after Thelwall's trial other prisoners were released. Certain of obtaining convictions the government had drawn up 800 arrest warrants, of which 300 were signed. They were now abandoned. After studying Erskine's speeches in cases of the highest political importance, Sir James FitzJames Stephen found that, although he was "*fearless*" and "*independent*", he hardly ever collided with the judges by misrepresenting the law or attempting to induce juries to break it.[67]

Reflecting on Erskine's career, which notably included successfully defending Lord George Gordon in 1781 on a charge of High Treason, after the enormously destructive anti-Catholic Gordon Riots in London, and representing Thomas Paine, in a case he did not win, indicted for seditious libel in 1792, some[68] have seen his genius not so much in his sentences, which could strike as insipid, but in taking what was confused or obscure and making it absolutely plain, and in the arrangement of a great mass of points into one smooth and persuasive flow of argument. This combined with a clear and melodious voice (interestingly he carefully trained himself out of any traces of a Scottish accent, possibly because English jurors might otherwise have considered him uncouth and less persuasive, remembering adverse remarks made about Scottish Enlightenment figures David Hume and Adam Smith when south of the border[69]), facial expressions and gestures, calculated to reinforce the effect

---

[67] Sir James FitzJames Stephen, *A History of The Criminal Law of England*, Macmillan and Co., London 1883, Chapter XXII page 454. In his view, in nearly thirty years as a barrister and a judge, counsel generally took the law as they found it and did not invite jurors to ignore it. He also, however, presents illustrations when they did. They are drawn, before his time as a barrister, from the famous trials for libel which led to Fox's Libel Act 1792, the trials of the Chartists in 1841, 1842 and 1843, the later trials for trade conspiracies and from a long series of Irish trials starting after the 1798 rebellion.

[68] See, for examples: *Carrol C. Arnold, Lord Thomas Erskine Modern Advocate* in Thomas Benson Edited *Landmark Essays on Rhetoric*, Hergamoras Press, California, 1993, pp. 89–105, especially pp. 97–98; and Sean Gibb, *Thomas Erskine: Saviour of English Liberty*, Freeman, July, 1989, Volume 39, No 7.

[69] John Andrew Hamilton, *Thomas Erskine, First Baron Erskine (1750–1823)*, Dictionary of National Biography, 1885–1900, Volume 19, pp. 437–438. Whilst a gentleman commoner at

of his speech, made him almost irresistible in argument. In addressing juries Erskine frequently began by displaying modesty, even self-deprecation, and ended in a similar manner, emphasising that it was the evidence, not his endeavours, which demanded the verdict he sought.[70]

In defending those charged with grave crimes, Erskine, Brougham and other counsel were prone to flights of rhetoric and dramatic description, to histrionic tricks and even tears. Sarcasm and aggression towards witnesses was also quite frequently employed. Characteristic of Erskine's advocacy was his repeated invocations of the deity. It has been said of him that *"there was a special vigour firing all of Erskine's eloquence that bespoke a self-righteousness rooted in intense religious zeal rather than the law book learning of the lawyer"*.[71]

Trinity College, Cambridge, in 1776, Thomas Erskine won a prize in English declamation. Also see Sean Gibb, *ibid.* Of note, it is said that within the British advertising industry the most appealing and trustworthy accents nowadays are Scottish.

[70] The following, at the end of his closing speech for Lord George Gordon, is an example of the use of this oratorical device, not unknown in ancient Rome:

> *Gentlemen, I feel entitled to expect both from you and the court the greatest indulgence and attention. I am indeed a greater object of your compassion than even my noble friend whom I am defending. He rests in conscious innocence and in well-placed confidence that it can suffer no strain in your hands. Not so with me. I stand before you a troubled, and, I am afraid, a guilty man, in having presumed to accept the awful task which I am now called upon to perform- a task which my learned friend who spoke before me, though he has justly risen by extraordinary capacity and experience to the highest in his profession, has spoken of with distrust and diffidence which becomes every Christian in a cause of blood. Mr Kenyon has such feelings, what must be mine! Alas gentlemen who am I? A young man of little experience, unused to the bar of criminal courts, and sinking under the dreadful consciousness of my defects. I have, however, this consolation, that no ignorance nor inattention on my part can possibly prevent you from seeing, under the direction of the judges, that the Crown has established no case of treason.* (Extract printed in S. C. Sarkar, *Hints on Modern Advocacy and Cross-Examination*, S. C. Sarkar and Sons (Private) Ltd., Calcutta, 1924, 4th Edition, pp. 172–173)

[71] David Mellinkoff, *The Conscience of a Lawyer*, 1973, St Paul, West Publishing Co, page 247. The author draws attention to what Erskine said in his prosecution of the publisher of Tom Paine's *Age of Reason* (Erskine lived by the Cab-rank Rule, see below) *The people of England are a religious people, and with the blessing of God, so far as is in my power, I will lend my aid to keep them so.* Rv Williams (1797), 26 How. St.Tr.653, 668 (1816–1826).

According to Lord Campbell, in his *Lives of the Lord Chancellors*,[72] Erskine would take pains to dress himself when out of London on circuit in a way to attract the favourable attention of the juries he was to address.

Erskine's defence of Thomas Paine in 1792 had a significant effect on the practice of advocacy which endures to this day as a distinctive feature of the Bar, known as the "Cab-rank" rule. In that year Paine, a radical writer whose writings had done much to support the American Revolution at critical times, was charged with seditious libel arising from publication of Part II of his work *The Rights of Man*. This book, a bestseller which sold the then huge number of one and a half million copies, was critical of the monarchy and the aristocracy, proclaimed the need for universal public education, for children's allowances and old age pensions, for public provision of work and wages for the unemployed and for the financing of these measures by a progressive income tax.[73] His trial was listed *in absentia* before the Lord Chief Justice, Lord Kenyon, and a Special Jury, selected by Crown lawyers and commenced on 18th December 1792.

Paine, wisely as it transpired, on the advice of the poet and artist William Blake and the moral philosopher Jeremy Bentham, had already left the country for what he thought was the safety of Revolutionary France, although later he was to be proved cruelly, and nearly fatally, wrong.

Thomas Erskine, who was not strongly in sympathy with his views, received a brief to act for Paine. Erskine's friends, who believed he might soon be appointed Lord Chancellor, urged him not to accept. In reply to one friend, he was reported as having said, "*But I have been retained, and I will take it by God*".[74] Erskine's decision to act for Tom Paine certainly cost him a valuable retainer as an adviser to the Prince of Wales.[75] In the

---

[72] Volume IV, referred to by Richard Du Cann, *The Art of the Advocate*, Penguin Books, 1993, page 53.

[73] See Geoffrey Robertson, *The Justice Game*, London, Chatto and Windus, 1998, 478–480 and also Andrew Watson, *Advocacy for the unpopular*, Part 1, Justice of the Peace, Vol. 162, 1998, 476–480 at 477–478.

[74] John Hostettler, *Thomas Erskine and trial by jury*, Barry Rose, Chichester, 1996, Chapter 8, page 91.

[75] See Andrew Watson, *Advocacy for the Unpopular*, Justice of the Peace. Volume 163, 1998, pp. 478–480.

course of his speech to the special jury at the Old Bailey, criticized by some as largely a hymn of self-praise and for hardly offering jurors any arguments against convicting Paine,[76] Erskine said:

> *I will for ever, at all hazards, assert the dignity, independence and integrity of the English Bar, without which impartial justice, the most valuable part of the English Constitution, can have no existence. From the moment that any advocate can be permitted to say he will, or will not stand between the Crown and the subject arraigned in the court where he daily sits to practice, from that moment the liberties of England are at an end. If the advocate refuses to defend, from what he may think of the charge or of the defence he assumes the character of the Judge; nay, he assumes it before the hour of judgment: and, in proportion to his rank and reputation puts the heavy influence of perhaps, a mistaken opinion in to the scale against the accused, in those favour the benevolent principle of English law makes all presumptions......[77]*

The Special Jury found Tom Paine guilty of seditious libel even before the Lord Chief Justice had an opportunity to sum up the case. He was sentenced to outlawry, a punishment medieval in origin, under which he was to be put to death if he returned to England and his property was seized. The cab-rank rule expounded by Erskine, building on pre-existing rules of professional etiquette, fared considerably better. Like hackney carriage drivers who are obliged to convey all those who can pay their fares, the essence of the rule is that barristers (it has never applied to solicitors) are obliged to act for all who have the wherewithal to instruct them, in areas of law in which they are competent, no matter what they personally think about the client or his or her case. The cab-rank rule was rapidly adopted as a moral basis for advocacy and in its early years was much championed by Lord Brougham.[78] A frequent toast at barristers'

---

[76] For example Geoffrey Robertson, *The Justice Game*, Chatto and Windus, London, 1998, page 378. This view is not shared by Hostettler, *Thomas Erskine and trial by jury*, Barry Rose, Chichester and Sean Gabb, *Thomas Erskine: Saviour of English Liberty* Freeman, July 1989, Vol. 39, No. 7, who summarise Erskine's arguments to the jury. See page 96 and pp. 3–4 respectively.

[77] *Speeches of the Right Honourable Lord Erskine*, James Ridgway, 1810, Volume 1, pp. 90–91.

[78] See, for instance, Brougham's speech to the House of Lords in 1840, 55 *Parliamentary Debates*, House of Lords (5th Series) August 10, 1840, cols. 1401–2. Cited by David Pannick, *Advocates*, Oxford University Press, 1992. page 141.

dinners was *"To Erskine and Independence"*. The rule, deriving from 1792, operates in England and Wales, Scotland, Northern Ireland, the Republic of Ireland, Australia, New Zealand and South Africa and a small number of other countries.[79] It was not without its detractors who, far from seeing it as a noble ethic to ensure that even the grossly unpopular should not go unrepresented, perceived the rule to be pure convenient self-interest by the Bar enabling its members to take any case they pleased for remuneration. Some reference[80] was made to Jonathan Swift (1667–1745), himself a disappointed litigant, in *Gulliver's Travels* in which he said of lawyers:

> *they were a society of men bred up from their youth in the art of proving by words multiplied for the purpose that what is white is black and black is white according as they are paid.*[81]

As in earlier times, lawyers in the eighteenth century were the object of popular suspicion.[82] William Hogarth, Isaac Cruickshank, James Gillray, Thomas Rowlandson and others, satirized the legal profession (either asleep or, worse, distracted by matters most uncourtly) as they did aristocrats, the French and politicians.

It has been said the cab-rank rule contributed much to advocacy strengthening it by the experience of acting both for the Crown and defendants and for plaintiffs and defendants in civil matters.[83]

The British nobility during the eighteenth century were forced to recognize the great lawyers as their equals because Parliament was The High

---

[79] Andrew Watson, *Advocacy for the Unpopular*, Justice of Peace, Volume 162, 1998. page 476.

[80] See Richard DuCann, *The Art of The Advocate*, Penguin, 1993, page 14.

[81] Jonathan Swift, *Gulliver's Travels*, 1726. Reprint, Harmondsworth Press, Middlesex, 1985, page 291. Detractors who were educated in the classics doubtlessly also referred to Homer's Iliad:

> [1] *Yea, when men speak, that man I most detest*
> *Who lacks the verity within his breast.*

[82] See Kirsten Olsen, *Daily Life in 18th Century England*, The Greenwood Press, Westport, Connecticut, 1999, pp. 204–220. A number of caricatures and cartoons of lawyers from the period are shown in this book.

[83] Interview with Anthony Arlidge QC. Held on 30th October, 2007.

Court of Parliament and politics were conducted in legal terms. The development of advocacy affected the House of Commons, where a great speech could be decisive in winning a vote, as much as the courts: one closely affected the other. In both, however, eloquence too easily still sank to mere abuse. Use of impressive forensic skills in parliamentary debates helped propel Spencer Perceval (1762–1812) up through the legal offices of Solicitor General and Attorney General to become Prime Minister in 1809 until 1812,[84] when he was assassinated in the lobby of the House of Commons, the only British Prime Minister to have been murdered. In the nineteenth century barristers were to account for one fifth of the members of the House of Commons, were well represented in every government and provided a steady flow of recruits to the House of Lords.[85]

Romilly and Copley

Another barrister, praised in his time, whose style of advocacy is credited with having influenced others in the late eighteenth century was Sir Samuel Romilly (1757–1818). Well educated and a good classical scholar he was called to the bar in 1783 and soon developed an extensive, and highly lucrative,[86] practice, mainly in chancery matters. His great abilities were recognized by the Whig party. He was made solicitor general in 1806 in the cabinet of Lord Grenville and remained until it fell. Thereafter, he devoted his great eloquence to exposing the barbarity of the criminal law, under which, in the "Bloody Code", a vast number of offences (nearly two hundred) were punishable by death, and campaigning for its humane reform. In this, and as a barrister in court, he was said to have *"marshalled his premises and deduced his conclusions with mathematical precision, and his diction was as chaste as his logic was cogent. The unerring instinct with which he exposed a fallacy united to no small power of sarcasm*

---

[84] Alan Harding, *A Social History of English Law*, Penguin, 1966, page 291.

[85] Daniel Duman, *The English and Colonial Bars in the Nineteenth Century*, Croom Helm, London, 1983, Chapter 6.

[86] Daniel Duman, *The English and Colonial Bars in the Nineteenth Century*, Croom-Helm, London, 1983, page 145.

and invective, made him formidable in reply while the effect of his easy and impressive elocution was enhanced by a tall and graceful figure, a melodious voice and features of classical regularity".[87]

John Singleton Copley, Lord Lyndhurst (1772–1863), who, in 1827, 1834 and 1840, became the only North American born Lord Chancellor to date, was recognized as a great advocate in patent cases. Unusually for one who specialized in civil matters, he also excelled in criminal trials. A Luddite machine breaking case, *Rv Ingham*[88] heard at Nottingham Assizes in 1812, in which his client was charged with hostile activities towards 'proprietors of a silk and lace cotton factory', saw him take the point that one of the two factories involved made cotton lace, and the other silk lace; neither of them made 'silk *and* cotton lace'.[89] On this technical point the indictment facing the prisoner was bad and consequently he was acquitted. At that time the rules of criminal pleading remained very strict.[90] Copley was carried shoulder high in triumph by his friends, work flooded in and the next year he was appointed a serjeant. In 1816 Copley's civil practice was boosted by his advocacy in *Boville and Moore and Others*, before Chief Justice Gibbs and a special jury in the Court of Common Pleas at the Guildhall in London.[91] He successfully defended an action brought against his clients for infringement of a patent. Copley gained distinction for the clear way he explained the intricacies of the machine concerned, having intensively studied it for two days' previously in Nottingham.[92]

---

[87] Dictionary of National Biography (Ed Sidney Lee, 1897), Vol. 49, page 190. See also R.A. Melikan, *Romilly, Sir Samuel (1757–1818)*, published 2004, Oxford Dictionary of National Biography. For more on the life and achievements of Sir Samuel Romilly, see John Hostettler, *Champions of the Rule of Law*, Waterside Press, 2011, Chapter 11.

[88] Unreported in the law reports.

[89] *Dictionary of National Biography*, Volume IV pp. 1108, T.M.

[90] Richard Hamilton, *All Jangle and Riot*, Professional Books, 1986, pp. 261–262. However, after the Criminal Procedure Act 1851 trivial indictment flaws and variances no longer won an accused his or her freedom – see Bentley, David, *English criminal justice in the nineteenth century*, Hambledon Press, London, 1998, Chapter 13.

[91] Unreported in the law reports, but a short hand note was taken by W. B. Gurney and printed by G. Woodfall for the use of the Plaintiff in 1816.

[92] Copley was able to convince the court that the Plaintiff's machine was only an improvement on the Spinning Jenny invented by Mr. Heathcote, some years ago, who was then enabled to obtain

Copley's defence of Arthur Thistlewood and James Watson at the Old Bailey in 1817 attracted much publicity. In December 1816, a mass meeting took place at Spa Fields.[93] A revolutionary organization, the Society of Spencean Philanthropists, planned to encourage rioting at this meeting and then take control of the government by seizing the Tower of London and the Bank of England. The meeting was dispersed by the authorities and the leaders, including Thistlewood and Watson, arrested and later charged with high treason. Against much evidence, Copley secured their acquittal. His performance was greatly acclaimed. Lord Campbell, who was present at the Court of Kings Bench Westminster, described his address to the jury, of which unfortunately no written record survives, "*as one of the ablest and most effective ever delivered in a Court of Justice*" and "*the whole as a close chain of reasoning on the evidence as applicable to the charge*".[94] Compliments were paid to him including comparisons to Cicero, again reflecting admiration and influence of the classics in that that age.[95] Throughout his career at the bar, Copley enjoyed a reputation for *tempered advocacy*; he was said to be scrupulous and dignified, an excellent speaker with a talent for cross-examination, who never overstepped the bounds of courtesy.[96]

Advocacy from Ireland

In 1793 711 barristers practised in Ireland, compared with only 604 for the whole of England and Wales.[97] The busy centre of Irish law, the Four Courts in Dublin, had acquired something of a reputation as a theatre

---

substantial reward for his invention. *National Dictionary of Biography*, Volume IX, page 1109. T.M.

[93] See Malcolm Chase, *Arthur Thistlewood, radical and revolutionary*, Oxford Dictionary of National Biography.

[94] Lord Campbell, *Lord Chancellors and Keepers of the Great Seal of England*. John Murray, London, 1869, Volume VIII, Chapter 2, page 17.

[95] *Dictionary of National Biography* Volume IV, page 1109.

[96] Gareth Jones, *Copley, John Singleton, Baron Lyndhurst (1772–1863)*, published 2004, Oxford Dictionary of National Biography and see Sir Theodore Martin, *A life of Lord Lyndhurst from letters and papers in possession of his family*. John Murray, London, 1883.

[97] *A Brief history of the Irish Bar from the 18th Century to the Present*. The Bar Council of Ireland, 2012. By 1835 in England and Wales the number in practice had increased to 1300 and in 1846

where parties, witnesses and barristers frequently had groups of cheering supporters and where cases often involved a noisy battle of wits and free trading of insults. A good barrister was considered a major prize and many women attended the Four Courts with the hope of seeing their heroes in action. The Act of Union with Great Britain in 1800, and the disappearance of the Parliament of Ireland[98] had been resolutely opposed by most of the Irish Bar. This led to many eloquent and persuasive speeches on the subject and to Dublin becoming a *"great school of oratory, in which all the graces and treasures of language, intellect and learning were united to sway or to convince"*.[99] These developments in oratory were transferred to forensic address in the courts.

The type of forensic address to juries was typically, emotive, flamboyant, delivered with gusto and contained a profligacy of words. A simple statement of facts was seldom enough. An illustration of this form of advocacy may be seen in an excerpt from a speech by John Philpot Curran (1750–1817) in 1804 (Curran, the "Irish Erskine" was a leading member of the Irish Bar and had defended with brilliance, though without success, the United Irishmen, following their failed uprising in 1798). A master of rich word painting, fiery denunciation, use of ridicule, pathetic description and gifted with a prodigious memory, enabling him to deliver vast speeches without any note, Curran acted in 1805 for a young and poor clergymen, the Reverend Massey, whose twenty four year old wife had been allegedly enticed from him, although she appeared to go quite voluntarily, by the rich and elderly Cornish aristocrat, the Marquess of Headfort. The Marquess and the clergyman's wife made off together whilst her husband was preaching in church on Sunday:

---

had grown to 3080, including 28 serjeants at law and 74 Queens Counsel.

[98] See Maire and Connor Cruise O'Brien, *A Concise History of Ireland*, Thames and Hudson, 1985, Chapter 5.

[99] Bernard Kelly, *Famous advocates and their speeches*, London: Sweet and Maxwell, 1921, page 19. The essayist, William Hazlitt, writing in 1825, saw Irish oratory rather differently: *It is a sort of aeronaut; it is always going up in a balloon, and breaking its neck, or coming down in a parachute. It is filled full with gaseous matter, with whim and fancy, with alliteration and antithesis, with heated passion and bloated metaphors, that burst the slender, silken covering of sense; and the airy pageant, that glittered in empty space and rose in all the bliss of ignorance, flutters and sinks down to its native bogs.* A little further Hazlitt writes of *Irish orators playing with words, ranging them into all sorts of fantastic combinations.* William Hazlitt, *Spirit of the age*, Republished by Kessinger Publishing Co, USA, 2004, page 133. It is not possible to discover the extent to which Hazlitt's opinions were shared.

The Cornish plunderer intent on spoil, callous to every touch of humanity, shrouded in darkness, holds out false lights to the tempest-tossed vessel [the wife], and lures her, and her pilot [the husband], to that shore on which she must be lost for ever; the rock unseen, the ruffian invisible, and nothing apparent but the treacherous signal of security and repose; so this prop of the throne, this pillar of the State, this stay of religion, this ornament of the Peerage, this common protector of the people's privileges and of the Crown's prerogative, descends from these high grounds of character to muffle himself in the gloom of his base and dark designs, to play before the eyes of the deluded wife and the deceived husband, the fairest lights of love to the one and the hospitable regards to the other, until she is at length dashed on that hard bosom where her honour and her happiness are wrecked and lost forever.............[100]

As can be seen, allusion is piled on analogy, metaphor and simile and syllogism is strongly present. These were elements of contemporary English advocacy, but they were taken further in Ireland.[101]

Like the Scots, the Anglo-Irish were an important source of barristers for the English Bar, either by Irish barristers transferring to practice in England or by young men qualifying directly to become barristers in London.[102] They frequently took the style of advocacy in Ireland with them, which had an effect on that in England. An example was Charles Phillips (1787–1859), called to the Irish Bar in 1812 and later admitted

---

[100] See F. Roderick O'Flanagan, *The Munster Circuit*, Sampson, Low, Marston and Searle, London, 1880, Chapter XIV *Immorality Rebuked*.

[101] The Reverend Massey was awarded £10,000 by the jury. In both Ireland and England actions for criminal conversion *crim con*, by which a cuckolded husband was allowed to sue his wife's seducer for damages, usually attracted many spectators in court and were widely reported in the newspapers (See Ben Wilson, *The Making of Victorian Values: Decency and Dissent in Britain: 1789–1837*, Penguin, 2007, Chapter 5.) Cases were often brought as a prelude to an action for a divorce *mensa et thoro*, effectively a claim for judicial separation. In England they were heard by a *special jury of gentlemen of fortune*, (Lord Mansfield encouraged their use.) consisting of twenty four jurors selected from freeholders of substance, knights and urban gentry. Damages set by them could be as great as £15,000, indicating the high value placed on a gentleman's honour. Once awarded the defendant either paid up, came to an arrangement with the husband or was arrested, his goods seized and put into a debtors prison. The Divorce Reform Act 1857 abolished the action of criminal conversion in England and Wales.

For another example of Curran's richly worded and emotive advocacy to a special jury, see an extract of his speech, contained in *Great Orators, Statesmen and Divines*, Edinburgh, W. P. Nimmo, Hay and Mitchell, 1914, pp. 75–79, on behalf of Michael Hamilton Rowan, indicted for seditious libel, delivered 29th January, 1794. Curran also makes generous allusions to Leonidas and Sparta.

[102] Bernard Kelly, *Famous Advocates and their Speeches*, Sweet and Maxwell, London, 1921, page 19.

to the Bar of England and Wales in 1821 at Middle Temple. He was Curran's biographer[103] and friend. Phillips, with his florid advocacy, became the leading criminal barrister at the English Bar.

Catholics had been prevented from being lawyers since 1688. The Catholic Relief Act of 1791 allowed them to be called to the Bar of England and Wales (similar Acts permitted them, in 1792, to join the Bar of Ireland and, in 1793, the Bar of Scotland). Following the Catholic Relief Acts appreciable numbers of Catholic Irishmen started to practice at the Irish Bar. Perhaps the most renowned of these was Daniel O'Connell (1775–1847). In 1794 he was admitted to Lincoln's Inn. Two years later O'Connell transferred to the King's Inn, Dublin and was called to the Irish Bar in 1798. For the next decade he practiced mainly in the south of Ireland and established a great reputation for eloquent advocacy in court which, on occasion, was also combined with considerable daring and some theatricality.[104] Like Curran, he was not embarrassed to use emotion on jurors. A great many anecdotes circulated about him. When defending in case of murder, O'Connell was repeatedly interrupted by a hostile but inexperienced judge. Rather than tolerate what he saw as badgering O'Connell told the judge *"since you refuse me permission to defend my client, my Lord, I leave his fate to your hands, his blood be upon your head if he is condemned"*, and left the courtroom. The judge was apparently so terrified that he acquitted the defendant.[105] In another murder case, the key piece of evidence was a hat identified by a prosecution witness. On cross-examination, O'Connell held up the hat and "read" the defendant's name from the inside. He asked the witness to confirm that the name was on the hat when it was discovered, and the witness had not merely written the name on the hat. Then, he held up the hat, which had no name in it, and demanded that the case be closed.[106] In the political sphere, O'Connell later used his lawyer's forensic and organizational skills in campaigning for the removal of barriers to Catholics holding public office

---

[103] Charles Phillips, *Curran and his contemporaries*. William Blackwood, 1850.

[104] National Dictionary of Biography, Volume XIV, pp. 816–817.

[105] Patrick M. Geoghegan, *King Dan, The Rise of Daniel O'Connell 1775–1829*, Gill and Macmillan, 2008, Page 78.

[106] Patrick M. Geoghegan, *King Dan, The Rise of Daniel O'Connell 1775–1829*, Gill and Macmillan, 2008, Page 78.

in both England and Ireland (achieved in the Catholic Emancipation Act 1829) and for the repeal of the 1800 Act of Union between Great Britain and Ireland. His work for these causes outside and inside Westminster, where he was the wild card in politics, made him the first key figure of Irish national awareness since the failed uprising against British rule in 1798.

Of his oratorical ability it was said:

> *He had the power to make other men hate or love, laugh or weep, at his good pleasure…Daniel O'Connell, by virtue of being more intensely Irish, carrying to a more extravagant pitch all Irish strength and passion and weakness, than other Irishmen, led and swayed his people by a kind of divine, or else diabolic right.*[107]

O'Connell was aware of the danger of being carried away by his own oratory and was seen, on occasions, to have a piece of paper before him on which was written: "*A speech is a good thing, but never forget the verdict is the thing*".[108]

Catholic Irish barristers joined the English Bar and young talented Catholic Irishmen began to qualify as English barristers without first becoming barristers in Ireland.[109] Whilst their forensic oratory had at times direct, forceful, tumultuous and passionate aspects, its practitioners drew on a spoken and literary tradition, as deep and abundant as that of the Anglo-Irish, and which valued graces, treasures and lyricisms of language allied to intellect and learning.[110] Their presence at the English Bar

---

[107] John Mitchell, *Jail Journal*, 1854, New York, The Citizen, page 15.

[108] Richard Du Cann, *The Art of the Advocate*, 1993, Penguin Books, page 196.

[109] Bernard Kelly, *Famous Advocates and their speeches*, London, Sweet and Maxwell, page 12 and page 18.

[110] Some had an awareness of Brehon law, Ireland's indigenous system of law dating from Celtic times, which survived until the seventeenth century, when it was finally supplanted by English Common Law. It was administered by Brehons, the successors to Celtic druids. Their role was to preserve and interpret the law rather than expand it. Great attention was paid the use of elegant language in judgements, which were sometimes delivered in verse. See Laurence Ginnell, *The Brehon Laws: A Legal Handbook*, T. Fisher Unwin, London, 1894. Also see John Kleefeld, *From Brehons to Brouhahas: Poetic Impulses in the Law*, a paper delivered at the Institute of Advanced Legal Studies on 17th June, 2009.

stimulated and influenced the style of effective advocacy.[111] In the late nineteenth century this was particularly true of Charles Russell, called to the bar at Lincolns Inn in 1859, and who, after a distinguished career, became Lord Chief Justice of England in 1894, the first Catholic to hold that position for many centuries.[112]

Jewish Members of the Legal Profession

Francis Henry Goldsmid (1808–1878) was admitted to Lincoln's Inn in 1833. He was the first Jewish barrister and became a QC in 1858.[113] In a century which saw the removal of legal disabilities against Jews, more entered the legal profession as barristers and solicitors, expanding the pool of talented advocates, and some became eminent judges. Amongst them were Judah Phillip Benjamin, Sir George Jessel, Arthur Cohen and Rufus Isaacs.[114] Particularly because integration, and through it success, was emphasized, especially amongst established Jewish families, patterns of speech in court, as in other places of public life, did not depart from the mainstream.[115]

William Blackstone, Literature and Poetry

Publication by William Blackstone (greatly influenced by Lord Mansfield's wide learning and forceful thinking), of his *Commentaries on the Laws of England*, in four volumes originally between 1765 and 1769, was of

---

[111] In 1835 the number of barristers originating in Ireland and practicing at the English Bar was 21 (8.7 of the total). By 1885 the figure had risen to 50 (7.9 of the total). The corresponding statistics for barristers of Scottish origin are 10 (4.1) in 1835 and 37 (5.9 of the total) in 1885, Daniel Duman, *The English and Colonial Bars in the 19th Century*, Croom Helm, 1983, page 12. The influence of both greatly exceeded their numbers.

[112] See Chapter 5.

[113] Louise S Goldsmid (his Wife), *Memoirs of Sir Francis Goldsmid Bart*, 1882, C Kegan Paul and Co.

[114] Arthur Goodhart, *Five Jewish Lawyers of the Common Law*, Oxford University Press, 1949.

[115] Interview with Gerald Rabie, barrister and scholar of British Jewish history, London, 30th July, 2009.

much significance in the development of advocacy in the late eighteenth and early nineteenth century.

At the age of 15, William Blackstone (1723–80), having been an outstanding pupil at Charterhouse School and noted as a promising poet, entered Pembroke College, Oxford, where he wrote poetry and a treatise on architecture. He became a fellow of All Souls in 1743. After graduating in civil (Roman) law at Oxford University Blackstone was called to the Bar at Middle Temple and practiced common law. Difficulty in obtaining clients and a preference for academic life prompted him to abandon the bar and return to Oxford. Prominent in college business and university politics, he also began a popular course of lectures on English law and government, subjects not previously taught at Oxford or Cambridge, then the only universities in England. The success of these lectures led to his appointment in 1758 to a newly endowed professorship of English Law.[116]

Blackstone's course of lectures formed the basis of his Commentaries which comprised the first methodical treatise since the Middle Ages on common law, suitable not only for lawyers, but also for a lay readership. As an exposition of English law it was a phenomenal success read widely not only in Britain but also the colonies. An edition published in Philadelphia in 1771 sold at least fourteen hundred copies.[117] Written in a clear, dignified, graceful and attractive style, which put them within the category of literature, though loosing no opportunity for embellishment, Blackstone's Commentaries performed for educated society much the same service as was rendered to the people of ancient Rome by the publication of previously unknown laws; they were provided with a good general knowledge.[118] They also became an important, though not uncontroversial, element in the education of lawyers.[119] In the opinion of

---

[116] Wilfred Prest, *Blackstone and his Commentaries*, Hart Publishing 2009, *Introduction*.

[117] On the reception of Blackstone in the United States, see *Shick v. United States*, 195 US 65, 66 (1904) and Lawrence M. Friedman, *A History of American Law*, Simon and Schuster, 1973, pp. 88–89.

[118] Somewhat later they were to be caricatured by Jeremy Bentham as reactionary, glorifying the status quo and opposed to all reform: see Wilfred Prest, *William Blackstone and the Historians*, History Today, July 2006.

[119] John Scott, Lord Eldon, who served as Lord Chancellor (1801–1806 and 1807–1827), was particularly critical and said that lawyers had been made cheap by learning the law from Blackstone's.

Bernard Kelly the elegance of style of the Commentaries *"enriched the vocabulary of the Bar, and so may be said to have influenced in a very high degree the oratory of the Courts, which from this time forward became increasingly ornate"*.[120]

An increasing tendency to quote from poetry added further to more decorous advocacy.[121] By the late eighteenth and early nineteenth centuries, the store of verse on which it was possible to draw had grown considerably with the works of the Romantic poets, including Wordsworth, Coleridge, Blake and later Shelley, Keats, Byron and Heine. Allusions to the still evolving novel could also sharpen an appeal to emotion.[122] Pieces from Byron and Sir Walter Scott came to be considered by barristers as especially helpful in awakening generous sympathies of jurors. It can be surmised that Sir Walter Scott, who was not only a great imaginative writer but also a devoted practical lawyer and Clerk of Session of the Scottish Supreme Court, would have thoroughly approved of the purposes to which his work was put. Indeed in *Guy Mannering* he put the following words in the mouth of Counsellor Pleydel[123]:

> *A lawyer without history or literature is a mechanic – a mere working mason; if he possesses some knowledge of these he may venture to call himself an architect.*

The Romantic movement and the Gothic novel, pioneered by Horace Walpole in *The Castle of Otranto* (1794) and Ann Radcliffe, *The Mysteries of Udolpho* (1794), represented a move by sections of educated society

---

He asserted the superiority of *Coke on Littleton* written by Sir Edward Coke and first published in 1629. As a student, John Scot had abridged this work for his own use. Bernard Kelly, *Famous Advocates and their Speeches*, London, Sweet and Maxwell, 1921, page 18.

[120] Bernard Kelly, *Famous Advocates and their Speeches*, London: Sweet and Maxwell, 1921, page 18.

[121] Bernard Kelly, *Famous Advocates and their Speeches*, London, Sweet and Maxwell, 1921. The author wrote, pp. 20–21, *"The Courts of law could not but imitate the general spirit which shone forth in speeches and addresses of the highest excellence"*. On the use of poetry and other literature before jurors in the nineteenth century see also J.A. Foote, *Pie powder from the Law Courts*, John Murray, London, 1911, pp. 85–90.

[122] On nineteenth century sentimental novels drawn upon in speeches to jurors see Michael Millender, *The Transformation of the American Criminal Trial 1790–1875*, Doctoral Dissertation, Department of History, Princeton University, Chapter 7.

[123] Walter Scott, *Guy Mannering*, 1815, P. D. Garside edition, 1999, Page 259.

away from cold classical formalism, so dominant in education and intellectual thought and endeavour, towards wider interests and deeper sympathies, thus widening the scope in forensic oratory for appeals to emotion.[124]

More Firmer Shape of Stare Decisis

The eighteenth century was not only when more refined language and literary allusions became available for use by advocates, but also when important changes in legal argument employed by advocates took place.

Although by the seventeenth century courts were paying more attention to precedents, valuing them more significantly than ever before, judges did not consider themselves bound by individual previous court decisions. Emphasising their obligation to abide by statutes, they declined to follow precedents referring to the Roman Law maxim *judicandum est legibus non exemplis* (adjudication is to be according to declared law, not precedent) and their consciences if they thought a judgement of another court was erroneous.[125] Not until the eighteenth century did the modern doctrine of *stare decisis*, i.e. earlier decisions must be followed when the same points arise in litigation, begin to take shape, a process that that was not completed until the first decades of the next century.[126]

---

[124] In his *Rhetoric*, Aristotle identified three modes of persuasion: *Logos*, the art of deductive logical proof; *Pathos*, playing on the audience's emotions to put them in a certain frame of mind and *Ethos* which relies on the good character of the speaker to influence others. Clearly appeals to emotion by advocates alluding to literature corresponds with *Pathos*. Citing literature also relates to *Ethos* in that it invokes the authority of the author, or subject, of the work, who may be greatly respected, and enlists him or her in the advocate's cause.(Aristotle, himself, categorized literary figures *as ancient witnesses*.) Also, in the eyes of jurors, it may have enhanced the advocate as a literate and erudite person, even if some members of the jury were unfamiliar with the literary references made. In eighteenth and nineteenth centuries, times of great social deference, this apparent learning may have contributed to persuading jurors who were often less educated than the advocate. For those of similar education, citations they recognized from literature may have confirmed, psychologically, that the advocate was one of them and, therefore, safe to trust.

[125] See Neil Duxbury, *The nature and authority of precedent*, Cambridge University Press, 2008, Chapter II, pp. 31–37.

[126] J. H. Baker, *An Introduction to English Legal History*, Butterworths, 2002, Chapter 12, pp. 195–201. See also Gerald J. Postema, *Philosophy of the Common Law*, in *The Oxford Handbook of Jurisprudence and Philosophy of Law*, ed. J. Coleman and S. Shapiro, Oxford University Press, 2002, pp. 588–622 at 589. For the somewhat later crystallization of *stare decisis* in the United

The consequences for advocates of precedent moving from the periphery to the nub of the common law system were substantial.[127] Submissions before courts had to be constructed more with cases as the building bricks of legal argument, reducing reliance upon broad principles of law. This necessitated greater research beforehand of law reports to identify those that appeared relevant because of their factual similarity. If previous cases did not entirely resemble the facts of the present case, compelling reasons had to be put why they should, nonetheless, be followed. Conversely, arguments had also to be fashioned to persuade judges not to follow cases that were unfavourable to clients' cases, including because they were not sufficiently similar, were really confined to their specific facts, or had been decided in error.

States, see Frederick G. Kemplin, *Precedent and Stare Decisis: The Critical Years*, 1800 to 1850 (1959) 3 American Journal of Legal History, pp. 28–54.

[127] See Laurence Goldstein edited *Precedent in law*, Oxford, Clarendon Press, 1987: *The Rule of Precedent*, Theodore M. Benditt, pp. 89–106; *Theories of Adjudication and the Status of Stare Decisis*, Peter Wesley-Smith, pp. 73–87 and *Changes in the Doctrine of Precedent during the 19th Century*, Jim Evans, pp. 35–72.

3

Prohibition Against Counsel in Felony Trials and the Consequences of its Erosion

Many believe that English justice has always possessed certain fundamentally fair qualities, including a right to legal representation in court. It, therefore, often comes as a quite a revelation, if not a shock, to learn just how little opportunity existed well into the nineteenth century for professional advocacy on behalf of defendants, known as "prisoners" until the last century, in serious criminal trials. Until the reign of King Henry I (1100–1135), persons tried both for felonies, serious offences rendering those guilty liable to lose everything, including their lives, and for misdemeanours, lesser matters, were allowed to make their defence in court by counsel. The *Leges Henrici Primi*, written in the early twelfth century, referred to circumstances in which an accused was or was not entitled to counsel. It shows that persons indicted for felony were not.[1] Somewhat

---

[1] See *Leges Henrici Primi: Edited With Translations and Commentary by L J Downer*, Oxford University Press 1972. See also Frederick Pollock and William Maitland, *The History of English Law Before the Time of Edward 1st*, 1898, Cambridge University Press, pp. 99–101. The rule was justified in a leading thirteenth century case about rape when a prisoner was told *because the King is a party in this case* (all felony cases were brought in his name) *and sues ex officio, for which reason it is not proper that you should have counsel against the king.* Year Books 30 and 31 Edw. 1. (Rolls Series) pp. 529–30. A narrow exception to the rule against representation for felons and traitors existed where a case gave rise to a debatable point of law. The reports for 1309–10 record that a lawyer appeared on behalf of a defendant when a point of law was concerned. Herman Cohen, *A History*

© The Author(s) 2019
A. Watson, *Speaking in Court*, https://doi.org/10.1007/978-3-030-10395-8_3

strangely, the prohibition did not extend to trials of misdemeanours: the accused was entitled to a full legal defence, although the right was seldom exercised if he or she had allegedly committed only a petty crime. One reason for the apparent anomaly of retaining entitlement to representation in misdemeanours may have been that they included civil or regulatory offences such as failure by landowners to maintain roads; lawyers had long been involved in matters where the legal issue centred on property rights.[2]

Justifying the rule in the early seventeenth century, Lord Coke[3] said that:

> *No counsel is allowed in cases of felony, because the evidence ought to be so clear that it cannot be contradicted.*

In adopting this passage in the murder trial before the House of Lords in 1678 of Lord Cornwallis,[4] Lord Nottingham, the Lord High Steward, stated:

> *No other good reason can be given why the law refuseth to allow the prisoner at the Bar counsel on matters of fact, in the result of which his life may be concerned, but only this, because the evidence by which he is condemned ought to be so very evident, and so plain, that all the counsel in the world should not be able to answer it.*[5]

---

of the English Bar and Attornatus to 1450, Sweet and Maxwell, London, 1929, page 210. For more on how this exception was interpreted, see S.C.F. Milsom, *Historical Foundations of the Common Law*, 1981, Butterworths, London, p. 413.

[2] Barristers, whose advocacy work was therefore confined to civil disputes and misdemeanours, were not generally recognized as forming a distinct order of legal practitioners in the same way as attorneys and sergeants until roughly the eve of the Civil War (1642–1649). The main force which opened up the courts to barristers, thus expanding the opportunity for advocacy in civil cases, was a huge growth in the volume of litigation during the second half of the seventeenth century, as the economy developed further. The quantity of business handled by the two major central courts of Common Pleas and Kings Bench more than trebled in this period. Wilfred Prest, *The Rise of the Barrister: A Social History of the English Bar 1590–1640* Oxford: Clarendon Press, 1986, page 5.

[3] *The Third Part of the Institutes of the Laws of England*, W. Rawlins, London 1644, page 137.

[4] See Colin Rhys Lovell, *Trial of Peers of Great Britain*, The American Historical Review, Vol 55, No 1 (Oct 1949) pp. 69–81.

[5] Quoted by Lord Lyndhurst in his speech to the House of Lords on the second reading of the Prisoners Counsel Bill and reported in the *Morning Chronicle* on Friday 24th June 1836. For a

In the late seventeenth century dissatisfaction intensified after a succession of celebrated state trials which involved miscarriages of justice.[6] By the Treason Trials Act of 1695[7] counsel was allowed to make a full defence, including addressing the jury, for the accused, who was also permitted to have a copy of the indictment against him five (later extended to ten) days before trial. In 1708 a prisoner was permitted to have a list of witnesses against him and a list of the jurors in the case.[8] These rights, however, only applied to persons accused of treason and other state crimes.[9] In the 18th and early nineteenth century Thomas Erskine, Henry Brougham (see preceding Chapter) and other barristers appeared in such cases.

Prisoners in ordinary trials continued to be denied the right to counsel. In the early part of the eighteenth century the nature of trial on indictment showed marked inquisitorial features, very different from today. Judges were highly interventionist and could exercise considerable influence over the jury's verdict. Although prosecutions were in the name of the King, there was no system of public prosecution and most prosecutions were conducted by victims of crimes or by private individuals acting for them.[10] Most cases were simple confrontations between alleged victims and those they accused, orchestrated by the judge and without the help of lawyers on either side. The Judge examined and cross-examined

---

similar justification to that given by Lord Nottingham, some decades later, see William Hawkins, *Treatise of the Pleas of the Crown*, London, 1721, book 2, page 400.

[6] For an account of these, during the reigns of Charles II and James II, see Sir James Fitzjames Stephens, *A History of The Criminal Law*, Vol. I, Chapter XI, pp. 369–416.

[7] 7 William III.c.3.

[8] Anne, c. 27, s. 14. In 1702, it was also enacted, by 1 Anne, st. 2, c 9, that in cases of treason and felony the prisoner's witnesses should be sworn, as well as witnesses for the Crown. See, Allyson N. May, *The Old Bailey Bar 1783–1834*: Copy of 1997 thesis held at Lincoln's Inn Library, page 4.

[9] The fact they were not extended to all felonies demonstrated to Sir James Fitzjames Stephens *the slightness to which public attention was then, or indeed till a far later time, directed to the defects of the criminal law*. Sir James Fitzjames Stephens, *A History of The Criminal Law of England*, Macmillan and Co., 1883, Chapter XI, page 417.

[10] When counsel was instructed to prosecute their role, from at least Tudor times until changes in procedure and the law of evidence in the eighteenth century, appears to have been to draw pointedly to the attention of the prisoner every part of the case against him. Cross –examination of witnesses was predominantly undertaken by judges. Sir James FitzJames Stephens, *A History of the Criminal Law of England*, Macmillan and Co., 1883, Vol. I, Chapter XI.

the prosecutor, the accused and the witnesses and frequently gave a running commentary as the case unfolded to the jurors, who quite often interrupted to ask questions. Prisoners were afforded the opportunity of questioning the prosecutor's witnesses and to answer evidence given against them. From 1702 they were also permitted to call witnesses as to fact and those who could testify as to their general character and reputation.[11] Unlike prosecutors, however, they could not compel their witnesses to attend, and since trials were not scheduled, defendants did not know when witnesses needed to be in court. The immediate and unrehearsed responses by the accused to the evidence as it was presented were widely held to the best indication of innocence or guilt.[12] It was felt that the accused himself would give a more open and honest account of the truth than could he supplied by a lawyer speaking for him or her.

As the eighteenth century unfolded there was an increase in the use of prosecution counsel, partly as a result of increasing wealth of those who brought prosecutions. Prosecutors had always been allowed to have lawyers but very few did so until the 1720s and 1730s. Their use was encouraged by the growing government practice, which began in the late 1690s, of funding prosecutions for the most serious offences, such as seditious words and libel, treason, coining and violent offences including murder, rape and robbery. Once present in court, the use of lawyers seems to have been adopted by the prosecutors in other types of cases.[13] Engagement of lawyers was further encouraged by a statute of 1752 which allowed the courts to reimburse prosecutors' expenses if the prosecutor was poor and a conviction was obtained. A 1778 statute extended payment of expenses to all prosecutors of successful cases. Amongst Judges, this led to a sense

---

[11] Neither category of witness was permitted to give sworn evidence. This placed them at a lower level than prosecution witnesses, whose testimony was on oath. See G. Fisher (1997), *The Jury's Rise as Lie Detector*, 107 Yale Law Journal, p. 603.

[12] J M Beattie, *Scales of Justice: Defence Counsel and the English Criminal Trial in the Eighteenth and Nineteenth Centuries*, Law and History Review, Vol 9, No 2, pp. 221–267; pp. 230–32.

[13] Numbers of counsel instructed to prosecute property crime increased with the formation in large numbers throughout the country of Associations for the Prosecution of Felons. These were established to spread the cost of investigating crime and paying legal fees. See John Hostettler and Richard Braby, *Sir William Garrow, His Life, Times and Fight for Justice*. Waterside Press, 2009, p. 31.

that imbalance and unfairness existed against prisoners.[14] To redress the scales they began, without legislation, to allow accused felons to employ counsel as early as the 1730s at the Old Bailey in London and the Middlesex Sessions. Counsel appeared on sufferance of the bench and were limited to examining and cross-examining witnesses, a task previously performed by the Judge, and to arguing points of law. In the trial of Elizabeth Woodcock, for instance, tried in 1754 for stealing a few shillings from a drunken man in an alehouse, Lord Chief Justice Ryder stopped the case after the alleged victim's evidence had been undermined by counsel on her behalf.[15] The number of trials, however, at the Old Bailey in which counsel was actually employed by prisoners was very small during the middle decades of the eighteenth century and never rose above one or two in every session. Undoubtedly many would have been prevented or deterred from employing a barrister by the fees but also by what a lawyer might do, particularly as many did not appear to have gone out of their way to make much out of their limited opportunities to defend their clients.[16] Things altered radically in the 1780s. In 1786 nearly two hundred men and women on trial for felonies at the Old Bailey had the help of lawyers. Whilst still only amounting to one fifth of those tried that year, it represented a sudden and very striking increase in

---

[14] See John H. Langbein, *The Origins of the Criminal Trial*, Oxford, 2003, pp. 171–172. Also John Beattie, *Garrow for the Defence*, History Today, Feb. 1991, Vol. 41, Issue 2, page 50 and Allyson N. May, *The Bar and the Old Bailey, 1750–1850*, University of North Carolina Press, 2003, page 25.

[15] Lincoln's Inn Library, Harrowby MSS, doc. 14, pp. 4–6.

[16] John Beattie, *Garrow for the defence*, History Today, Feb 1991, Vol. 41, Issue 2, page 49. According to Professor Robert Shoemaker, of Sheffield University and co-founder of the Old Bailey on Line Project, there is some evidence that in the eighteenth century prisoners in Newgate Prison, which was full of prisoners awaiting trial, some of whom had been tried before in Old Bailey, the Middlesex Sessions Court in Clerkenwell or elsewhere, and with convicted prisoners awaiting punishment, shared information about law, procedure and tactics and even conducted mock cross-examinations and closing speeches. The very effective cross-examination of witnesses against her, bringing out numerous inconsistencies in their evidence, and polished closing speech of Sarah Malcolm, an Irish laundress tried for three murders in 1733, was attributed by Professor Shoemaker to this informal form of advocacy training. Largely because of her efforts her trial lasted nearly five hours; the average length in the eighteenth century being half an hour. After a much longer period of deliberation than usual, the jury, nonetheless, found her guilty and she was subsequently executed. *Voices from the Old Bailey*, Series Two, Episode Four, *Whose Law was it anyway?*, BBC, Radio 4, August, 17th, 2011.

cases defended by counsel and in the number of lawyers practicing at the Old Bailey. The fraction of prisoners represented grew to a quarter by 1800.[17] Importantly, the increased employment of lawyers by prisoners was accompanied by a clear shift in their behaviour and attitudes, particularly in their determination to act as advocates. Still not allowed to address the jury on their clients' behalf or comment on the evidence, they became much more anxious to take advantage of the opportunities afforded by cross-examination of prosecution witnesses in felony trials. Cross-examination became the prime focus for those with a strong sense of duty to defend their clients and was marked by growing assertiveness, increased sharpness, more use of sarcasm, and a preparedness to continue in the face of judicial hostility: a more committed advocacy.[18] Because of the prohibition on defence speeches, the significance of a question had to be apparent from the question itself and it has been suggested that this is one reason why it became permissible to ask leading questions in cross-examination.[19] There is little doubt that cross-examination provided lawyers the opportunity to develop their taste for advocacy, or that this stage of the trial changed remarkably in the eighteenth century. Barristers also involved themselves more in legal argument to challenge the validity of indictments, which had at the time to be very carefully drawn[20] and often

---

[17] David Bentley, *English Criminal Justice in the 19th Century*, Hambledon Press, 1998, page 108. A similar growth in representation by counsel had occurred in provincial practice. See P. King, Crime, Justice and Discretion in England, 1740–1820. Oxford University Press, 2000, p. 228.

[18] David Cairns, *Advocacy and the Making of the Adversarial Criminal Trial, 1800–1865*, Oxford, Clarendon Press 1998, page 31. This form of advocacy entered new territory, going far beyond counsel asking prosecution witnesses polite questions, the hallmark of most advocacy before the 1780s. See Geoffrey Robinson in Forward to John Hostettler and Richard Braby, *Sir William Garrow, His Life, Times and Fight for Justice*. Waterside Press, 2009.

[19] David Cairns, *Advocacy and the Making of the Adversarial Criminal Trial*, 1800–1865, Oxford, Clarendon Press, page 49. See also John Hostettler and Richard Brady, *Sir William Garrow. His Life, Times and Fight for Justice*. Waterside Press, page xiv. Some judges nonetheless continued to doubt the propriety of defence counsel putting leading questions in cross-examination (Rv Hardy (1794) 24 St Tr 199) and objection was still being taken to it as late as 1836 (Parkin v Moon (1836) 7 C& P 408).

[20] The slightest flaw in an indictment then could result in an acquittal. The complexity of drafting indictments is illustrated by the four volumes, each numbering over 700 pages, of indictment precedents compiled by John Silvester, a contemporary of William Garrow, *infra*, at the Old Bailey. Sometimes persons attending court in the public gallery, more and more seen in the eighteenth century as part of gentleman's education, and keen to contribute to increasingly legalistic debates

after their cross-examinations made submissions on the admissibility of suspect evidence such as: hearsay; confessions; that given by witnesses prosecuting for reward, for example thief-takers, those income directly depended on successful prosecutions[21] and the testimony of accomplices who had been promised they would not be prosecuted (Indeed it was mainly because of concerns about perjured testimony and deliberate perversions of the truth, which plagued criminal justice in the eighteenth century, that judges first permitted prisoners to be represented by counsel in the 1730s.[22]). Submissions to the Judge by barristers on law were sometimes, in reality, points made to sway jurors who heard counsel's arguments.[23] Of assistance to advocates acting for prisoners was, certainly by the 1780's, judges were directing jurors that defendants had a presumption of innocence and the onus lay on the prosecution to prove its case. Hitherto this had been seen as an aspiration, rather than a legal axiom.[24]

Prominent amongst those undertaking this more ardent advocacy was William Garrow (1760–1840). Called to the bar in 1783, at 23 years of

---

would interrupt to identify defects in indictments and put forward points in favour of prisoners. Douglas Hay, *Property Authority and the Criminal Law*, in Douglas Hay et al., *Albion's Fatal Tree*, Penguin, 1988, page 33.

[21] From 1692, Parliament passed a series of statutes rewarding the apprehension and conviction of people guilty of serious crimes. Special proclamations added further rewards. The government might pay as much as £140 for catching and convicting a highwayman and £420 for three. These sums contributed to perjury by thief-takers. Exposure of false convictions procured by them led to scandals. See John H Langbein, *The Origins of Adversary Criminal Trial*, Oxford, 2003, pp. 148–150.

[22] Also to limit this mischief, judges introduced a rule which required corroboration of accomplice evidence in the 1740s. The rule existed for about 40 years. See Albert Alschuler, *Comments on the Origins of the Adversary Criminal Trial*, The Journal of Legal History, Volume 26, No1, April, 2005 pp. 79–85. In 1786 three proscriptions against lying on oath, taken from the Old Testament, were painted on the walls of the Old Bailey, *The Times*, 28th April, 1786.

[23] David Bentley, *English Criminal Justice in the Nineteenth Century*, Hambledon Press, 1999, page 108.

[24] Court records show similar directions on the standard and burden of proof were being given by judges in Massachusetts a decade earlier. John H. Langbein, *Privilege and Common Law*, in Richard H. Helmholz et al., *The Privilege Against Self-Incrimination: its origins and developments*. University of Chicago Press, 1997, page 234 By contrast, depicting a common view in the seventeenth century, it is perhaps worth noting that in the trial of Sir Walter Raleigh in 1603 one of Sir Edward Coke's colleagues for the prosecution told jurors that the defendant had to prove his innocence. The effect this had on them cannot be measured, but they returned a verdict of guilty in barely fifteen minutes.

age, he immediately began to practise at the Old Bailey and on the Home Circuit. In his first year, he appeared in nearly a hundred cases at the Old Bailey. More than 80 percent of these were for the defence. Well over half his clients were acquitted. During Garrow's first ten years at the bar he was instructed in more than a thousand criminal cases.[25] Becoming a shooting star, Garrow came to dominate the criminal bar in his day becoming a King's Counsel in 1793. Although possessed of a commanding presence in court and a keen mind, his pre-eminence was built on devastating cross-examination. William Garrow set a pattern in examining unreliable witnesses to expose weaknesses in cases against his clients. He frequently battered prosecution witnesses with relentless questioning. Sarcasm was often cruelly employed. Sometimes he indulged in playful repartee with witnesses, or was amusing at their expense; the object of both being to diminish their credit and lessen the weight of their evidence. He treated all witnesses in the same manner. In particular he was indifferent to elevated social position and with it any notion that this gave witnesses greater honour and credibility and therefore should not be vigorously probed[26] Garrow could indeed be rude to witnesses: in one case a witness employed in the kitchen of the prosecutor was addressed by him variously as *cook, Mrs. Cook* and *cookey*, rather than by her name.[27] The most abusive of his cross-examinations, however, were of those who came into court determined to lie for reward.[28] Garrow's behaviour occa-

---

[25] The Old Bailey Papers record many of William Garrow's cases from 1784 to the early 1790s. Hundreds of these are now readily available from the website *The Proceedings of the Old Bailey, London 1674 to 1834*. OBP Online. (www.oldbaileyonline.org) Records of his cases on assize circuits are also occasionally available.

[26] An example of Garrow's indifference to high social status in the conduct of cases is given by John Hostettler and John Braby, *Sir William Garrow, His Life, Times and Fight for Justice*, Waterside Press, 2009, pp. 63–65: Baron Hompeschv. The farmer and his dog. Greatly angered, the Baron challenged Garrow to a duel, which he declined. The landed gentry and gentlemen were especially threatened by his courtroom tactics which they saw as a threat to their honour.

[27] *Rv Twite*, Old Bailey Session Papers 1788, no. 480, pp. 597–601.

[28] Allyson May, *Advocates and Truth –Seeking in the Old Bailey Courtroom*, The Journal of Legal History. Volume 26, No 1, April, 2005, page 73. See also John Hostettler and John Braby, *ibid*, pp. 54–59, who present a series of cases in which Garrow cross-examines both professional and first-time thief-takers.

sionally led to rebukes from opposing counsel or judges[29] but what is striking is the extent to which his conduct was tolerated by the judiciary. In addition to his powers of cross-examination, Garrow was a master of court procedure. Further he was learned in criminal law and, on the basis of a strong knowledge of past cases, able to argue legal points, especially those concerning evidence, often displaying great rhetorical skill.[30]

The quality of William Garrow's court advocacy was enhanced by a willingness to meet his clients, often in disease ridden prisons, to discover more about their cases and to take instructions from them. This was rare amongst his contemporaries, who usually left such work to attorneys.[31] After becoming a King's Counsel in 1793, Garrow's criminal work diminished, although he continued his highly profitable career in the civil courts. He later entered Parliament and was subsequently appointed Solicitor General and afterwards Attorney General. Garrow also served as a judge. In his time at the criminal bar William Garrow's style of advocacy was both admired and emulated by many of his contemporaries. As a figure in history and law Garrow was essentially forgotten in the 1840s. Rediscovery of him began in the 1990s. Since then the first ten years of his career in the development of the criminal trial has become much discussed.[32] More than any other, motivated by practical concern to win cases by the best means available, rather than a grand reforming plan, Garrow is now recognized to have largely established the art of cross-examination, the essential feature of adversary trial. His, and others', insistent questioning of witnesses raised matters of immediate concern to judges. These were resolved by them in post-circuit meetings at Serjeant's

---

[29] For instance in the Trial of William Bartlett OBP Online (www.oldbaileyonline.org) 11th January, 1786. Ref:t1786111-30.

[30] John Beattie, *Garrow for the defence*, History Today, February 1991, Vol. 41, Issue 2.

[31] John Hostettler and Richard Braby, *Sir William Garrow, His Life, Times and Fight for Justice*, Waterside Press, 2009, page xiv.

[32] For an account of Garrow's rediscovery see John Hostettler and Richard Braby, *Sir William Garrow, His Life, Times and Fight for Justice*, Waterside Press, 2009, pp. ix–xii. *Garrow's Law*, a four part, much acclaimed, prime time BBC TV *drama*, shown during November, 2009, starring Andrew Buchan as William Garrow, substantially based on cases in which Garrow appeared, has firmly placed him in popular history. For an article on Garrow, *From the Bar to the small screen*, by Mark Pallis, the Legal and Historical Consultant to *Garrow's Law*, see Counsel, January 2010, pp. 27–29.

Inn.[33] Here rules of evidence, essential in an adversarial system, were laid down, including those dealing with hearsay, accomplices and best evidence. These rules, born in response to advocates, were further developed in the nineteenth century and, in themselves, became an increasing influence on the practise of advocacy.

In Garrow's own time, some were incensed by what they considered to be his belligerence, bad manners, coarseness of language and willingness to make sport of those he cross-examined. The aggressive advocacy adopted by many criminal barristers from the 1780's may have contributed to a widespread sense that there was something almost ungentlemanly about the trade. Certainly, they were parodied in the press. Contempt for the skills of criminal practitioners is apparent in the Dictionary of National Biography entry for George Bond (1750–1796) famous in his day as a barrister at the Surrey Sessions: "*He belonged to a class of lawyers now happily approaching extinction, whose chief strength consists in playing upon the susceptibilities of ignorant juries. Enthralled by his course and vulgar humour, the jurors of his native county, Surrey, were almost at his mercy, and tradition says that a not uncommon form of verdict at the Surrey Sessions was "We find for Serjeant Bond and costs".*"[34]

Unlike Garrow, most barristers who worked at the Old Bailey were not set to be leaders of the legal profession. Criminal work occupied a relatively lowly place within the broader legal profession. Many practitioners sought to move on to civil work or had to practise in other metropolitan courts to earn a living.[35] Some of the successful barristers became judges and, from the criminal bench, perpetuated the culture and ways they had helped to create.

---

[33] J. M. Beattie, *Scales of Justice: Defence Counsel and the English Criminal Trial in the Eighteenth and Nineteenth Centuries*, Law and History Review, 1991, vol. 9 (2) p. 224.

[34] Quoted by Allyson May, *The Bar and the Old Bailey 1750–1850*, University of North Carolina Press, page 140. After surveying the careers of members of London's nascent criminal bar, Allyson May (*Advocates and Truth – Seeking in the Old Bailey Courtroom*, The Journal of Legal History, Volume 26, No1, April, 2005, pp. 72–73.) considered them in a more kindly light. *Regardless of their not unnatural interest in earning a living ....on the whole they were principled men rather than the thugs and bullies portrayed in the press. They believed that the lawyer's duty is to his client, and that it was not counsel's duty to prejudge a client.*

[35] See Allyson N. May, *The Bar and the Old Bailey 1750–1850*, University of North Carolina Press, 2003, Chapter 3.

The shift from a type of trial with clear inquisitorial aspects towards an essentially adversarial, one, the "Adversarial Revolution", had a number of consequences: criminal trials became more structured with distinct prosecution and defence cases, rather than *a rambling altercation* between the accused and witnesses[36]; evidential objections by counsel became more frequent[37]; with a greater recognition of the burden of proof defendants did not need to take any part in their defence until the completion of prosecution case, by which time the full prosecution case would be known, and not speak at all if counsel could establish grounds for acquittal at that stage; and a significant movement in power took place towards lawyers from judges, whose role began to increasingly resemble that of an umpire, or trial manager.

The continuing prohibition on counsel making speeches to the jury, i.e. a *full defence*, was to some extent mitigated by barristers circuit etiquette which required that prosecuting counsel be restrained in jury addresses, or sometimes completely abstain from making one.[38] Also

---

[36] David Cairns, *Advocacy and the Making of the Adversarial Criminal Trial, 1800–1865*, Clarendon Press, Oxford, page 30. See also David Lemmings, *Criminal trial procedure in 18th Century England: The Impact of Lawyers*, Journal of Legal History, Vol 26, No1, April 2005, pp. 73–82. Sir James Fitzjames Stephen estimated that allowing a witness to tell his own story had been replaced, in trials involving counsel, by rules of examination in chief preventing the asking of leading questions (those which suggest the desired answer) by the beginning of George III's reign (1760). According to him, this practise, which still exists, was introduced to keep witnesses to the point and was a recognition that all evidence must be confined to the issue, a rule he saw as coming from the civil to the criminal courts in the early eighteenth century. Sir James Fitzjames Stephen, *A History of The Criminal Law of England*, Macmillan and Co., London, 1883, Chapter XII, pp. 430–431.

[37] By 1790 courts enforced a rule excluding proof of a defendant's prior criminal acts and other proof of bad character. They also followed a rule against admitting involuntary confessions, including those obtained by threat or promise of favour. (Warickshall's case, 1 Leach, 263 decided in 1783, is one of the earliest cases on this subject.) Although the rule requiring corroboration of accomplice evidence, introduced in the 1740s, was abolished in the 1780s, judges cautioned jurors against giving too much weight to uncorroborated accomplice testimony. The hearsay rule now operated, subject to several exceptions, and was justified on the basis of the right to cross-examine witnesses. Further, judges told juries to convict only on proof of guilt beyond reasonable doubt. See Albert Alschuler, *Comments on The Origins of the Adversary Trial*, The Journal of Legal History, Volume 26, No1, April, 2005, pp. 79–85. The existence of these rules helped shape the practice of advocacy. Hitherto, it had been strikingly little constrained by rules of evidence. See Sir James FitzJames, *A History of The Criminal Law of England*, Macmillan and Co., 1883, Chapter XI.

[38] David Cairns, *Advocacy and the Making of the Adversarial Criminal Trial*, 1800–1865. Clarendon Press, Oxford, pp. 39–46.

defence counsel were given considerable latitude in their styles of cross-examining prosecution witnesses such as their questioning might incorporate a far from impartial summary of evidence. Further, it became allowed for a prisoner's statement, which opened the defence case, to be drafted by counsel giving it more of a defence, and less of a testimonial, quality. A number of legal historians[39] believe that the absence of counsel able to conduct a full defence, *full defence counsel*, made jurors more inclined to acquit out of sympathy for prisoners unable to defend themselves adequately and because of a knowledge of the penalties that were possible on conviction.

It is of note that, despite the use of counsel to cross-examine prosecution witnesses and argue points of law on behalf of prisoners, the length of trials remained very short. A good example of this brevity is the Old Bailey trial, in January 1790, of William Hayward, a coachman, who was charged with stealing a harness worth ten pounds from his master, William Champion Crespigny, Esquire, of Cavendish Square.[40] Mr. Hayward was represented by William Garrow, who had received a full and well researched brief drawn up by a solicitor. Nearly all the trial was taken up by evidence given by Mr. Crespigny, his servants, and a coachmaker who had sold the harness at Mr. Hayward's request. All were closely cross-examined by Garrow, especially Mr. Crespigny who was subject to a barrage of questions. Mr. Hayward said nothing on his own behalf and called no witnesses. Little was said by the judge about the evidence. The jury reached their verdict without leaving the room. Mr. Hayward was acquitted. The trial lasted less than half an hour. According to a study conducted on trial proceedings at the Old Bailey, albeit some years later, this short amount of time may in fact have been longer than most trials.[41]

---

[39] J. M. Beattie, Scales of Justice: *Defence Counsel and the English Criminal Trial in the Eighteenth and Nineteenth Centuries*, Law and History Review, Vol. No2, pp. 254–257. David Cairns also considers the severely restricted role of counsel inclined juries to show a "*favourable disposition*" towards prisoners and to leniency. *Advocacy and the making of the Adversarial Criminal Trial, 1800–1865*, Clarendon Press, Oxford, page 53 and page 55.

[40] David Beattie, *Garrow for the* defence, History Today, Volume 41, Issue 2. Feb 1991.

[41] See *Trial Procedures*, Introduction to Old Bailey Session Papers On Line, www.oldbaileyonline. org. Astonishingly in 1833, it was calculated that the average trial at the Old Bailey took eight and

Judges' permission for prisoners in felony cases to have counsel examine and cross-examine witnesses allowed more scope in forensic advocacy and increased the overall amount of it.

Fox's Libel Act 1792, Defamation and Civil Juries in Scotland: Expanding the Scope for Advocacy

In 1792 Fox's Libel Act was passed which enabled juries to determine what was criminal libel, as well as the fact of its publication. Previously what constituted a libel was a matter for the Judge alone to rule upon. The statute resulted in a further opportunity for advocacy with counsel making eloquent, vehement and rhetorical addresses in defence of the subject's liberties. An example of this was Henry Brougham in his successful defence of the radical brothers John and Leigh Hunt against a charge of libel for publishing criticism of the government for severe corporal punishment, in the armed forces, where it was prevalent.

During the nineteenth century the civil law of defamation, with its division, after 1812 between libel and slander,[42] developed very considerably and with this came an increase in actions before juries in courts.[43]

By a number of Acts between 1815 and 1830, juries in civil cases were introduced into Scotland, widening the role of forensic advocacy there too. In the main this was welcomed by members of the Faculty of Advocates, whose number had doubled over two decades before 1815.[44]

---

a half minutes, although it is unknown whether this calculation was made only on cases where prisoners had no help from counsel.

[42] Embedded in the law by the Court of Common Pleas case of *Thorley V Lord Kerry* 1812 4 Taunt 355.

[43] Interview on 12th March, 2008 with Paul Mitchell, of the School of Law, Kings College, London and author of *The Making of the Modern Law of Defamation*, Hart Publishing, Oxford, 2005.

[44] For reasons underlying the introduction of jury trials in Scottish civil cases, see Nicholas Phillipson, *The Scottish Whigs and the Reform of the Court of Session*, 1990, Edinburgh, The Stair Society.

The Prisoners' Counsel Act

A number of prosecutors began to depart from the restraint expected in felony cases by using their opening statements in cases not merely to outline the facts, but to slant the case against the defendant. Also in the 1800s, and very likely as a response, certain barristers, notably including William Garrow, asserted that they would make observations to juries on behalf of prisoners.[45] The co-ordinated and well resourced court prosecutions by the Bank of England and other banks of forgers and coiners, during and in the years immediately after the Napoleonic Wars, further convinced many judges of the fairness of allowing prisoners to be fully represented by counsel.[46]

Between 1821 and 1836 repeated parliamentary attempts, beginning with a Bill introduced by William Martin, perhaps now best remembered for pioneering legislation against cruelty to animals, were made to remove the felony prisoners' handicap of not being allowed to have counsel address the jury on their behalf. The rule was even enforced against children and the infirm. England and Ireland were the only European countries denying prisoners the right of a full defence and were also out of step with the practice in the United States and the colonies. The arguments for reform left many in Parliament and the Bar unmoved.[47] What is striking about the campaign to allow counsel to address juries fully was that it was largely driven by a small number of Whig politicians, chief amongst them being Henry Brougham. There is little evidence that it was sustained by popular support, contrasting heavily with other reforms con-

---

[45] In the Trial of John Taylor, William Garrow declared, "what the law of England will not permit me to do *directly* [By which he meant address the jury.], I will do *indirectly*, where I can." Quoted in P. King, *Crime, Justice and Discretion in England, 1740–1820*, Oxford, 2000, page 229.

[46] Allyson May, *Reluctant Advocates: The Old Bailey Bar and the Prisoners' Counsel Act, 1836*. Paper delivered to the Institute of Advanced Legal Studies, London, 26th March, 2006. Also Allyson May, The Bar and the Old Bailey, 1750–1850, University of North Carolina Press, 2003, page 27. On the prosecution of coining and forgery see Randall McGowan, *From Pillory to Gallows. The Punishment of forgery in the age of the financial revolution, Past and Present*. 199, 165 (1) pp. 107–140.

[47] For a full analysis of arguments for and against allowing felony prisoners a full defence, and a description of the campaign to change the law, see Allyson May, *The Bar and the Old Bailey 1750–1850*, The University of North Carolina Press, Chapel Hill and London, 2003, Chapter Seven. See also David Bentley, *ibid*, page 105 for a useful summary.

tributing to the dismantling the old regime, such as widening the electoral franchise, the abolition of slavery, Catholic emancipation, and restrictions on the width of the death penalty.[48] Nonetheless, a Bill, introduced by William Ewart to remove the restriction received Royal Assent in 1836. In the House of Commons Daniel O'Connell, who, like Ewart, was much influenced by Jeremy Bentham, spoke strongly on its behalf, alleging several instances where a speech from counsel would have saved the accused from unmerited conviction. Sir Frederick Pollock, later to become Lord Chief Baron, described the existing state of affairs as a disgrace to the country. After securing a great majority, the Bill went up to the House of Lords where it received considerable support, particularly from the Lord Chancellor, Lord Lynhurst and the Lord Denman, the Lord Chief Justice.

Earlier in 1836, the campaign to permit prisoners to have a full defence by counsel had received strong backing in the Second Report of Her Majesty's Commission on Criminal Law, published earlier that year. The Commissioners, Thomas Starkie, Henry Bellenden Kerr, Andrew Amos and John Austin, much swayed by Brougham, discarded the old notion that the judge was in anyway counsel for the prisoner and emphasized the power of competent advocacy to uncover the truth:

> *The advocate possesses more certain means than the Judge, of distinguishing between true and false testimony, between that which is substantial and that which is merely colourable. When the charge is false, he possesses through his intimate knowledge of the real facts, an almost infallible key to the truth; he can show that all the evidence truly given is consistent with the innocence of the accused, and is prepared to examine into and comment upon those discrepancies upon which innocence must frequently depend for its manifestation.*[49]

The Commissioners had also heard much hostile evidence from members of the judiciary and counsel. Indeed most barristers and judges were

---

[48] Allyson May, *Reluctant Advocates: The Old Bailey Bar and the Prisoners' Counsel Act, 1836*. Paper delivered to the Institute of Advanced Legal Studies, London, 26th March, 2006.

[49] In Parliamentary Papers: Reports from Commissioners: Church, Education, Law etc., 36 (London, 1836), page 193.

against granting a full defence in felony trials. The gist of much of the opposition appears in submissions to the House of Lords Committee on the Prisoners' Counsel Bill made by Charles Phillips, who had dominated the Old Bailey Bar since the 1820s,[50] and in letters he wrote to Henry Brougham. Phillips and his colleagues believed that the adversarial process in civil cases and trials of misdemeanours often resulted in verdicts against the evidence, rather than increasing the number of true ones. He predicted that the same would happen in criminal cases with juries being misled in much lengthened trials. Charles Phillips was concerned that cases would be coloured by the prosecution to the disadvantage of prisoners and that professional rivalries between barristers would be fought out in court. Also, as prosecutors generally had more resources, prisoners would suffer by having the best talent deployed against them. Because future employment depended on success, barristers briefed by the prosecution might behave with less moderation. Permitting counsel to speak for their clients in felony trials, Phillips wrote to Brougham, would:

> *Make life and liberty subjects of a trial of skill. Verdicts will often depend, not on innocence, but on eloquence. Those who are employed as advocates must act as advocates and the most awful of considerations may become the victim of sophistry. Look at your Courts of Common Law – one fourth of their time consumed in motions for new trials, on the ground that the verdicts were given against the evidence. How obtained? The speech of Wilde did it!!.*[51]

According to him, "four fifths of the practical men" (barristers with a criminal practice) were against the changes sought. His view may not, however, have been shared by the majority of junior barristers at the Old Bailey.[52] Some other established members of the criminal bar may have resisted reform mainly out of self-interest: Allowing defence counsel to

---

[50] Charles Phillips, the 'Garrow' of the 1830s, was employed in over 2300 cases at the Old Bailey between 1825 and 1834 and had an active criminal practice on the Oxford circuit as well.

[51] University College London: Brougham papers, volume 24, page 444.

[52] It is possible they believed the reform might lead to more briefs from prisoners and, therefore, it was in their advantage to support it. Divisions of opinion in the bar were discussed by Allyson May in *Reluctant Advocates: The Old Bailey Bar and the Prisoners' Counsel Act 1836.* a paper delivered to the Institute of Legal Studies, London, 26th March, 2006.

address the jury could be expected to greatly increase their workload with little prospect of remuneration for it, given the limited means of most of their clients.

The Prisoners' Counsel Act, when a Bill, suffered amendments in Parliament. The most important dissension was about whether defence counsel should have the last word. In civil cases and misdemeanours, where speeches for the defendant were permitted, the barrister for the plaintiff, or prosecutor was allowed to reply at the end of the trial if the defendant had called any evidence. To avoid the possible destructive consequences of a reply, the defence frequently adduced no evidence. The speech in civil cases was *"counsel's most potent opportunity to influence the jury. Here counsel in a civil trial would attack, doubt, interpret, defend and reason upon the evidence; praise, justify, excuse, pity or sympathise with the client; and challenge, cajole, persuade and lead the jury by their noses to a verdict in his client's favour. The speech was so highly valued in civil trails that defence counsel were often prepared to call no evidence, so as to deprive the plaintiff's counsel of a reply and ensure the defence had the last word"*.[53] Clause 2 of the prisoners' Counsel Bill would have given counsel for the prisoner the right to the final word in a closing speech whether or not he had called any evidence in his defence, but it was struck out by the House of Lords; thus putting the rule in felonies on the same footings as misdemeanours. (It was not to be until the Right of Reply Act in 1964 that defendants were unconditionally given the last word in criminal jury trials.) The Prisoners' Counsel Bill was changed because Judges felt that giving the defendant the closing word might place them in the awkward position of having to correct the view of defence lawyers when summing up a case and might give the jury the impression they were biased against the prisoner.

By letting the defence counsel address the jury in felony case, the Prisoners' Counsel Act took criminal trials away from the traditional notion of a sober investigation of truth and made them more akin to a civil trial: a contest between professional advocates with both sides striv-

---

[53] David Cairns, *Advocacy and the Making of the Adversarial Criminal Trial*, 1800–1865. Clarendon Press, Oxford, 1998, page 55.

ing for a verdict in their favour. In this fight, the Act strengthened the hand of the defence advocate in that it gave the accused the right to inspect and copy depositions of evidence taken by magistrates at committal proceedings. Counsel now had a better picture of the prosecution's case against their clients and could plan accordingly, with less chance of being ambushed by fresh evidence. The statute made possible the rise of the form of criminal trial with which we are familiar today, with its underlying assumption that the truth is the product of adversarialism. This significant change in procedure was to profoundly affect advocacy.

The first case in London after the implementation of the Prisoners' Counsel Act was heard on 14th October, 1836. In *R v M'Pherson*, John Adolphus, counsel for the prisoner, was reported as saying that it was a most important alteration in the practice of the criminal law and he hoped it would prove as great a blessing to the community as the benevolent persons who framed and supported it could expect.[54] For the great majority of prisoners, who could not afford to instruct counsel, it proved no blessing and was cruelly irrelevant. In murder cases, judges increasingly assigned counsel, unpaid, to prisoners who could not afford them, a practice they had begun in the 1820s. Judges, however, varied in their willingness to do so and counsel was rarely assigned in trials for offences other than murder. The assistance they could render was often limited by being brought in at the eleventh hour.[55]

Because of the prosecution's right of reply to defence evidence under the Prisoners' Counsel Act 1836, defence counsel often voluntarily excluded evidence to ensure they had the last word before the Judge summed up the case to the jury. In most cases the defence consisted of cross-examination of prosecution witnesses and a closing speech. This *"encouraged aggressive advocacy which was likely to be anticipated and matched by prosecuting counsel"*[56] who dispensed with their traditional restraint in conducting cases. As mentioned earlier, some prosecutors

---

[54] *Morning Chronicle*, 14th October, 1836.

[55] David Bentley, *English Criminal Justice in the Nineteenth Century*, Hambledon Press, London, 1998, page 108.

[56] David Cairns, *Advocacy and the Making of the Adversarial Criminal Trial*, 1800–1865. Clarendon Press, Oxford, page 125.

even before the reform of 1836 were abandoning restraint and this had been one reason put in support of the change in procedure. More aggressive cross-examination by defence counsel, particularly those in the Old Bailey, often employing speculation, sarcasm, abusiveness and nastiness, had begun in late eighteenth century. This greatly intensified after the Act.

Although the police, quietly, working with the Home Office did to some extent fulfil this role, but only in selected cases, there was no public prosecutor to take criminal cases to court before the Prosecution of Offences Act 1879 created the office of Director of Public Prosecutions.[57] People had to find their own lawyers, an expense many were reluctant to make, especially in more minor cases, or present prosecutions themselves. This considerable omission in the legal system, combined with the inability of most prisoners to afford representation, served to restrict the amount of advocacy heard in the criminal courts long after defendants were granted the right to a full defence.

Features of Civil Trials

There are few records of advocacy heard before juries in civil trials during the 18th and beginning of the nineteenth century, however sufficient is known to say they were very different from modern trials and the scope for counsel more limited. Witness rules prevented parties to cases giving evidence (nothing similar to the rule in felony cases by which a defendant could give unsworn testimony existed) and also any witness deemed to have an interest in the outcome of the case.[58] Little or no cross-examination of those who did testify took place and only loose, if any, limits on the

---

[57] *A Modern Legal History of England and Wales*, Butterworths, London, pp. 227–228. See also A. H. Manchester Philip Kurland and D. W. M. Waters, *Public Prosecution in England 1855–1879: An Essay in English Legal History. Duke Law Journal.* Volume 1959. Fall. Number 4.

[58] On the witness disqualification rules in England and the United States, see Kenneth S. Abraham and G. Edward White, *The Transformation of the Civil Trial and the Emergence of American Tort Law.* University of Virginia School of Law, Public Law and Legal Theory Research Paper Series, 2016–17, pp. 20–72.

admission of hearsay testimony (either oral or written evidence if the third party is not present in court) were imposed. In addition to seeking to ensure jurors were not misled by the tactics or legal arguments of counsel judges felt at liberty to explain the meaning of witness evidence to them. Judges could, as did Lord Mansfield, disregard a jury finding if it did not match their sense of a just outcome.[59] In all civil actions the parties involved had the right to be assisted by counsel. Trials began with an address by the plaintiff's counsel in which legal argument was put and comment made upon evidence likely to be produced during trial. After evidence and arguments for the plaintiff had been presented counsel for the defendant opened with legal arguments and comments and called evidence. At the end of the defendant's case, the plaintiff's counsel was permitted a reply. Although individual judges occasionally departed from this three step procedure, it was generally followed.[60]

The period spanning roughly 1780–1850, especially the decades between 1820 and 1850, saw major developments in civil trials with Lord Denham's Act of 1841 which abolished the witness disqualification rule concerning non-party witnesses and an Act of 1851 removing the prohibition on parties giving evidence. Restrictions on hearsay evidence were tightened considerably and cross-examination of witnesses became routine.[61] These changes meant a greater role for counsel and skills in examining and re-examining witnesses, likely including their client, and cross-examining witnesses for the opposing side. They also resulted in more legal argument about admissibility of evidence.

---

[59] See James Oldham, *The Mansfield Manuscripts*, Volume II, pp. 1541–1623.

[60] Thomas Starkie, *A Practical Treatise of the Law of Evidence, and Digest of Proofs in Civil and Criminal Proceedings*, J. and W. T. Clarke 1824 pp. 381–82.

[61] See T.P. Gallanis, The Rise of Modern Evidence Law, 84 IOWA L REV (1999) pp. 511–535.

4

Victorian Advocacy: Emotion, Melodrama, Floridity and Juries

Early Victorian advocacy to persuade juries, in both criminal and civil cases had much of the theatrical about it. Barristers knew they could acquire fame through their performance in court and the public at large regarded the courts as legitimate places of entertainment, a situation that was to continue for many decades. In *The Victorian Bar*, J. R. Lewis[1] wrote about a *"long affinity between stage and bar"*; how there was a well-established tradition of barristers on the circuits presenting amateur theatrical performances, especially of Shakespeare, and how several leading counsel claimed earlier professional experience of the boards.[2] As in the Four Courts in Ireland, the public in England booed and hissed,

---

[1] *The Victorian Bar*, London, Robert Hale, 1982, page 13.

[2] The link between advocacy and acting was acknowledged by Basil Montagu in *Essays and Selections*, London, William Pickering, 1837. In expounding the duty of an advocate owed in civil cases to his client, he wrote, at pages 266 to 267, "except when a man's life was at stake, it was expedient that a judge and a jury should hear the opposite statements of men better able than individual suitors to do justice to their respective causes. The advocate might in the course of his duties be required to profess that which he did not feel and to support causes in which he did not believe or which he knew to be wrong. This, however, was nothing *but a species of acting without an avowal that it is acting*. The advocate did not mix himself either with his client or his cause; he lent his exertions but not himself. He exercised no discretion as to whom to plead for; to do so would prejudice the suitor".

© The Author(s) 2019
A. Watson, *Speaking in Court*, https://doi.org/10.1007/978-3-030-10395-8_4

applauded their favourites, cheered and catcalled. Doorkeepers to the principal courts sometimes charged for entry to the show. Trials of public interest at the Old Bailey, which with enlargement by statute of its geographical jurisdiction in 1834 became the Central Criminal Court, were an event in the social world, attended by large, and occasionally aristocratic audiences.[3] Sometimes, as part of their training, prospective barristers underwent a declamatory course at a drama school along with young hopefuls for the stage. This contributed to a style of court advocacy that was "*melodramatic, declamatory and lachrymose*".[4] Emotion was heightened by frequent appeals to God and for the heavens to show, by some sign, the client's purity of heart and deed. Barristers sometimes deployed humour, often involving that Victorian form of wit the pun, popularized by the poet Thomas Hood, amongst others, and for which there was great appetite, and richly present in burlesque theatre.[5] A number used gestures, that would have been at home in that exaggerated art form, such as elevation of the eyebrows or knowing glances to jurors to credit them with an intelligence not to be taken in by a witness in the box. Some had the ability by a wink or gesture to make the whole court erupt with laughter thereby leading jurors away from damaging points in

---

Some barristers wrote plays. One, for instance, was Thomas Noon Telfourd (1795–1854), perhaps best remembered for his defence of Edward Moxon, charged with blasphemy for publishing a popular complete works of Percy Bysshe Shelley, in 1840. A classical scholar, Telfourd produced *Ion*, a tragedy based on a drama from Euripides, performed in Covent Garden in 1836, and *The Athenian Captive*. Both were rich in sentiment, which was so popular in the 1830s. His *Glencoe* was a tragedy based on Scottish history. Noon Telfourd had been the pupil of Joseph Chitty (below at note 5), renowned for tearful melodrama in court. Thomas Noon Telfourd became a Judge of Common Pleas. A portrait of him hangs in Middle Temple.

[3] Bernard Kelly, *Famous Advocates and their Speeches*, Sweet and Maxwell 1921, page 21. Steven Cowan, a historian of education and of the labour movement at the Institute of Education, London (Interviewed on the 6th June, 2010.), explained that many people would use watching court proceedings *as a sort of base for their self-education*. The presentational style of barristers *had been copied in the late eighteenth century by radicals like John Thelwall* (who was successfully defended at court by Thomas Erskine, see Chap. 2.) *and in the following century went on to influence the rather loquacious delivery of the early socialists and trade unionists who were so keen to impress their hearers with the depth of their education*.

[4] J.R. Lewis, *The Victorian Bar*, Robert Hale, London, 1982, page 120.

[5] Henry James Byron, 1835–1884, who, after abandoning his studies at Middle Temple for the Bar, found great playwriting success in burlesques and other punny plays. The pun appeared much in the humorous magazines he edited.

issue.[6] Certain barristers could shed tears to compound their emotional defences of lay clients.[7] Crying in court was not restricted to them. Tears were sometimes shed by defendants, not always spontaneously, but advised beforehand, by witnesses under pressure of cross-examination, by jurors, hearing upsetting evidence and by and those in the public gallery. Between 1750s and the 1850s weeping judges, distressed by evidence and by passing severe sentences, especially that of death, were a regular feature of public justice, although by the 1870s Victorian "men of feeling" had disappeared from the bench.[8]

So great was the association between acting and performance by barristers in front of juries that the *Spectator* in 1849 suggested it might be sensible to transfer the courts to the theatres *"which would be more convenient in more ways than one, the Judge, counsel and other performers would welcome the better ventilation, and the orchestra would be on hand to accompany Mr. Charles Wilkins and the other eloquent gentlemen in the chanting parts of the oratory"*.[9] Similarly *Punch*, some years earlier, had informed the

---

[6] Showing that by the second half of the twentieth century this technique had largely disappeared, Geoffrey Robertson QC,: *Sir John Mortimer, creator of Rumpole of the Bailey*, 16th January, 2009, The Times Obituary, recalled how, *almost alone at the bar*, the late John Mortimer QC, perhaps best known for the *Rumpole* books, *could laugh a case out of court*, especially in his closing speeches. Geoffrey Robertson frequently appeared in court as John Mortimer's Junior.

[7] One such was Sir Fitzroy Kelly who later became Solicitor General, Attorney General and eventually join the Bench as Chief Baron of the Exchequer. He cried very conspicuously in the course of his highly sentimental defence of the notorious murderer John Tawell in 1845 (Tawell was the first suspect to be arrested after his description was telegraphed from one part of the country to another). In this he was far from alone. *The Examiner* of 24th May, 1856 reported that *since the trial of Thurtell, there has hardly been a remarkable case in which counsel for the prisoner has not wept for his client, or protested his solemn belief in his innocence......* The case of Thurtell, in which Joseph Chitty, who had a huge junior practice and was a prolific writer of legal textbooks, shed copious tears for his client, took place in 1823/24, some years before the Prisoners' Counsel Act. It was almost the last famous trial under, what Eric Watson, *The trial of Thurtell and Hunt*, in the *Famous English Trial Series*, William Hodge and Co, Edinburgh and London, 1920, described as the *old Tudor procedure* and the presiding judge as *inquisitorial*. It was the first trial *by newspaper* and the first in which there was any serious collision between judges and the press about the latter's investigations and reporting of proceedings.

[8] Thomas Dixon, *Weeping Britannia*, Oxford University Press, 2015, pp. 174–179. Sir James Shaw Willes, a judge between 1855 and 1872, known for great intellect, literary sensibility and mercy in criminal cases, was one of the last "weeping judges".

[9] Quoted by J. R Lewis, *The Victorian Bar*, Robert Hale, 1982, page 14. Sergeant Wilkins, earlier in 1849, represented Mr. Mannings who had been charged jointly with his wife for the murder of her lover. Wilkins sought to place the entire responsibility on Mrs. Mannings, *see later*.

public that an application was about to be made for a regular licence for the "*Criminal Drama*" at the "*Great National Theatre Royal, Old Bailey*". A cartoon following this announcement showed the Central Criminal Court disguised as a kind of showman's booth, with a large painted canvas displaying a sensational murder trial in progress, the judges all ranged, the galleries packed and the defending counsel in tears.[10]

Melodrama, as a form of theatre, had become popular from the late eighteenth century and lasted until the early twentieth century. The first drama in Britain to be labelled "melodrama" was Thomas Holcroft's *A tale of Mystery* in 1802. Melodrama consisted of short scenes interspersed with musical accompaniment and was characterized by simple morality, good and evil characters and exaggerated acting style.[11] Characters were stereotypical and usually a villain, a wronged maiden and a hero appeared. The emotions of the actors were played out in the music and accompanied by dramatic tableaux. Because of musical interludes, melodrama was not considered a "play" and thus evaded the Licensing Act 1737, which, until its repeal in 1843, restricted plays to two London theatres only – in Drury Lane and Covent Garden, where chiefly Shakespeare was performed, although modern dramas were sometimes staged. Early melodrama aimed to appeal to working class audiences. Heroes and heroines were almost invariably working class and the villains aristocrats, or members of the squirarchy. Reflecting the fascination of Wordsworth, Coleridge, Byron, and others of the Romantic movement, in nature and exotic travel, settings of early melodramas were often ruined castles and wild mountains. In the choice of these locations there was also clearly a connection with the Gothic novel, a strong theme of which being jeopardy of the innocent. The 1820s and 1830s saw a craze for domestic melodrama and for real life horror stories. "Maria Martin or Murder in the Red Barn", was based on the true story of the murder of a young girl in Suffolk in 1827. Later in the century, popular novels were also turned into melodramas.[12] Synonymous with stage spectacle, exaggeration, and

---

[10] Bernard Kelly, *Famous Advocates*, London: Sweet and Maxwell, 1921, page 23.

[11] See M. W. Disher, *Melodrama: Plots that thrilled.* New York Macmillan, 1954.

[12] Dion Boucicault's hugely successful adaptation in 1852 of Alexander Dumas's *The Corsican Brothers* is an example.

dripping in sentimentality, melodrama's popularity cut across social class.[13]

From the eighteenth century and well into the nineteenth century, stage performances of Shakespeare for mass audiences bore many similarities with melodrama complete with soliloquies as declamatory turns, music, scenery, thunder, lightning and wave machines.[14] Burlesque also helped to satisfy a huge growth in demand for theatrical entertainment in the early nineteenth century and beyond. A burlesque took a well-known play, story, opera or pantomime and satirized it in an exaggerated style with music.[15] Political and social events were also "burlesqued". Leading Victorian pantomime writers started writing burlesques and filling them with puns and word play loved by audiences of the time. Many men who sat as jurors, were drawn to, and influenced by, what they saw in popular theatre (hundreds of theatres were built in Victorian Britain) and by what they read in popular novels, where melodrama and rich sentimentality were often important ingredients; a fact not lost on those who addressed them as counsel.[16]

Juries

Eighteenth century courtroom oratory in state trials, where defendants had the right to full defence counsel, and that heard in civil trials, where special juries were empanelled, often involved jurors, with some classical learning, because of their social and educational background.[17] This was not shared by the vast majority of Victorian common jurors – jurors

---

[13] Queen Victoria watched seven performances of Boucicault's *The Corsican Brothers or The Fatal Duel*: Richard Fawkes, author of *Dion Boucicault – A Biography*, speaking at *Victorian Fancies*, National Theatre, London, 2010.

[14] Terence Hawkes, *Meaning by Shakespeare*. London: Routledge, 1992.

[15] See V. C. Clinton-Baddeley, *The Burlesque Tradition in English Theatre*, Methuen, 1952; also see Robert Tanitch, *The London Stage in the Nineteenth Century*. Haus Publications, 2010.

[16] Wilkie Collins (1824–1889), the author of melodramatic, "sensationalist" and widely read novels, including *Basil*, *The Woman in White* and *The Moonstone*, and plays, had studied at Lincolns Inn to become a barrister.

[17] See Chap. 2, *Classics and rhetoric*.

selected from the general pool of those eligible for service defined by a property qualification – who tried most of those indicted for felonies and civil matters. A small number of prisoners, on either their own application or that of the prosecutor, were tried by special juries, composed of persons of the rank of esquire or above, bankers or merchants. It could reasonably be supposed that they would have been exposed to public school, if not university, classical education, as would those of the growing middle classes who had attended grammar schools. The popular poetic work of Thomas Macauley *Lays of Ancient Rome* (1842), and later the Victorian – Hellenistic verse of Alfred Tennyson and others, did much to expand awareness of classical themes amongst a wider population.[18] Also, for those lacking a Latin education, a knowledge of Roman historical events was available in Edward Gibbon's *Decline of the Roman Empire*, much read in the nineteenth century, despite its controversial view of religion, and John Dryden's translation of Plutarch's Lives.[19] English translations of the Greek and Roman myths were also readily obtainable, including Alexander Pope's *Iliad* and the *Odyssey* in rhyming couplets, George Chapman's Homer[20] and John Dryden's *Virgil*. The importance of Greek, Latin and the classics for early Victorian gentlemen, or those aspiring to that status, is brought out in the novels of Charles Dickens including *David Copperfield* and *Great Expectations*.[21]

---

[18] A significant result of Macauley's *Minute on India*, which dealt with what should be taught in educational institutions in India, was that knowledge of Shakespeare achieved great prominence in the sub-continent and found its way into general and court oratory there.

[19] Roman History was central to a number of popularly read novels including Edward Bulwer-Lytton's *The Last Days of Pompey*, published in 1834, and *Antonina or the Fall of Rome*, by Wilkie Collins (1850). Myths and history of ancient Greece and Rome were an important theme in Nineteenth Century Art. Prominent amongst artists steeped in tradition of admiration for classical antiquity were Frederic Leighton, J.W. Waterhouse Lawrence Alma – Tadema who produced many admired and much exhibited works. Classical myths, Greek and Roman history, and its reception and influence in nineteenth century Britain, were sometimes burlesqued, notably in stage productions by Robert Brough.

[20] The *Odyssey* was translated in the seventeenth century by Chapman in iambic pentameter and the *Iliad* in iambic heptameter. Editions of Chapman's *Homer's Hymns*, the *Georgics of Virgil*, *Hesiod's Words and Days*, *Hero and Leander*, and *Juvenal's Satires* were published in the nineteenth century.

[21] See also Christopher Stray, *Classics Transformed, Schools, Universities, and Society in England*, 1830–1916, Clarendon Press, 1998, Chapter 3, who explained how possession of knowledge of Latin, Greek and the Classics meant membership of an elite and was a barrier for those without it.

Complaints were made about the low intellectual quality of common jurors.[22] It was said that educated men were rarely found on them. Indeed an article in the *Law Times* of 1849 asserted:

> *The composition of the jury list seems to be conducted on the principle of selecting the most uneducated and incompetent persons in the county with the requisite property qualification.*[23]

Shortly afterwards, a further piece in the same journal claimed that every lawyer could recall at least fifty instances which revealed the jury's lack of understanding.[24]

Common law juries largely consisted of shopkeepers and small farmers.[25] A practice of not including special jurors on common jury panels existed. School education did not become available to all children, even in an elementary form, until 1870. It is, therefore, safe to assume that many of those who qualified as common jurymen would barely have been literate and may well have found it difficult to assess the evidence in more complex cases.[26]

This was re-iterated in an interview with Mr. Stray, held on the 2nd July, 2010. Samuel Smiles in *Self Help*, published in 1859, Chapter XI, gives examples of persons, including the young Samuel Romilly (Chap. 2 of this book), who had risen far above their humble origins by acquiring Greek, Latin and the Classics.

[22] To Serjeant Wilkins was attributed the famous remark that his excuse for drinking a pot of stout at midday was that he wanted to fuddle his brain down to the intellectual standard of a British jury. J. R. Lewis, *The Victorian Bar*, Robert Hale, London, 1982, page 69.

[23] Anonymous (1847–48), 10 *Law Times* 319.

[24] Anonymous (1848–49). 11 *Law Times* 425. In similar vein the Jurist, 11th August, 1849, regretted that *juries were usually composed of persons with a scarcely sufficient education to understand the ordinary conversational language of educated men and quite incapable of any close or acute reasoning.*

[25] David Bentley, *English Criminal Justice in the Nineteenth Century*, Hambledon Press, London, 1998, page 92. For a description of how juries in other jurisdictions of the British Empire were composed see Richard Vogler, *The International Development of the Jury: The Role of the British Empire*, International Review of Penal Law Vol. 72, 2002. The article outlines the transplantation of English common law juries overseas with colonisation and Empire, beginning with North America.

[26] A. H. Manchester, *A Modern Legal History of England and Wales 1750–1950*, London: Butterworths, 1980, pp. 90–99.

The great majority of persons exempted from jury service came from the educated and prosperous.[27] Those who were not exempt could buy their way out of it comparatively easily. The law's insistence on land as the basis of qualifying for jury service[28] excluded men whose wealth consisted of personal property. An awareness by advocates of a lack of education amongst common jurors, it is submitted, was a great influence on the style and content of advocacy in the nineteenth century.[29]

A common denominator between most jurors was knowledge of Christianity hence allusions to, and quotations from, the Bible were made by barristers to common juries,[30] rather than drawing on the classics. The style of oratory generally in England had been affected by the rise of Methodism and by the Evangelical revival in the previous century; the deliberate appeal of great eighteenth century religious preachers such as John Wesley and George Whitfield, and their early nineteenth century successors, to wide audiences, sometimes in the open air and numbering tens of thousands, gave political and forensic oratory, as well as preaching, a new forcefulness as well as emotional appeal. It was said of George Whitfield (1714–1770), who exerted a major influence on pulpit oratory in the eighteenth and nineteenth centuries on both sides of the Atlantic, that his preaching, in an overwhelmingly commanding voice, was singularly

---

[27] Section 2 of the 1825 Juries Act (6 George IV.), "*An Act for consolidating and amending the Laws relative to Jurors and Juries*", set out persons who were exempt. The list included: Peers, Judges, Ministers of Religion, Serjeants and Barristers, Members of the Society of Doctors of Law, Advocates of Civil Law, Attornies, Solicitors and Proctors, Officers of the Courts, Coroners, Gaolers, Surgeons, Doctors, Apothecaries, Members of the Army and Navy, Ship Pilots, Royal Household Staff, Officers of Customs and Excise, Sheriff's Officers, High Constables and Parish Clerks.

[28] The Juries Act 1825 Sections 1, 8 and 50 and afterwards by the Juries Act, 1870, Section 7.

[29] For disquiet about the standards of jurors, see the Second Report of the Common Law Commissioners, 1836. Concern about the poor quality of common law jurors persisted for decades. The Juries Act 1870 declared that special jurors were not to be exempt from common juries, but the practice continued. Proposals by the Attorney General, made between 1873 and 1874, to bolster the common jury by making it necessary to include four special jurors and to give powers to trial judges in felony cases to direct trial by special jury foundered. David Bentley, *English Criminal Justice in the Nineteenth Century*, Hambledon Press, 1998, page 93.

[30] Vivid examples of references to the Bible and the Almighty mentioned in this book include Charles Phillips defence of Francois Courvoisier in 1840, this Chapter; Edward Kenealey's defence of Thomas Castro/Arthur Orton (1873–74), also in this Chapter; further in this Chapter, the speeches of Thorne-Cole to jurors at the London Sessions in the 1870s and 1880s; and Digby-Seymour for defendants in the 1867 Fenian Trial in Manchester, Chap. 5.

lucid and simple and that he seldom troubled listeners with complex argument and intricate reasoning. Simple Bible statements, apt illustrations and personal anecdotes, were commonly used as was strong pathos and frequent resort to weeping.[31] It was reported he could raise tears in his audience by the merely pronouncing the word *Mesopotamia*.[32] That many jurors were used to this form of religious address was appreciated by barristers who consciously, or subconsciously, adapted it to their use.[33]

Restrictions on the Extent of Forensic Licence

In the "trial" of Queen Caroline, in 1820, an investigation before the House of Lords to determine the truth of allegations of adultery against her, Henry Brougham, set out the principle that it was the duty of the advocate:

> *To save his client by all expedient means, to protect that client at all hazards and costs to others and among others to himself* …[34]

---

[31] Thomas Dixon, *Weeping Britannia*, 2015, Oxford University Press, pp. 72–81.

[32] For more on George Whitefield see, J.C. Ryle, *Christian Leaders of the 18th Century*, Banner of Truth, 1869, *Estimation of Whitefield's Ministry*. According to Simon Schama, evangelical passion, which *remains a brilliant strand in the weave of American discourse* and rhetoric, goes back to the Great Awakening in the 1740s *when flocks thrilled to Methodist preachers such as George Whitefield*. Mile High Stadium, *The Times*, August, 2008. Further, on the Great Awakening and its affect on American Discourse, see Christopher Grasso, *A Speaking Aristocracy*, University of North Carolina Press, 1999, Chapter 2.

[33] Serjeant Charles Wilkins, *d* 1857, was renowned for his ability to rouse emotions through colourful speech, florid over-emphasis, flamboyant gestures, use of the *bon mot* and for playing on the passions and the prejudices of the jury. J. R. Lewis described him as epitomizing the early Victorian years of the Bar (*The Victorian Bar*, Robert Hale, London, 1982. page 68.). His advocacy drew on his earlier public performances as a Wesleyan preacher in Methodist Chapels, ale house comedian and actor.

Words, phrases and rhymes from the King James Bible, first published in 1611, had long become part of English speech in and out of court (See Melvyn Bragg, *The Book of Books: A Biography of the King James Bible*, BBC Books, 2011.). It is worthy of note that Gilbert Gray QC (1929–2011), one of the Bar's greatest jury advocates in the last decades of the twentieth century, was said to have based his rousing courtroom style on the rolling cadences and richness of language he had heard as a boy in his local Salvation Army Hall and Methodist chapel (Daily Telegraph, Obituary, April, 26th, 2011).

[34] Henry Brougham, *Speeches of Henry Lord Brougham*, Edinburgh, Adam and Black, Volume 1, page 105.

Brougham derived this precept of individual heroism in advocacy from earlier state trials where special efforts and unflinching loyalty by barristers (for example that shown by Thomas Erskine) to their clients were required. After barristers were given the right, under the Prisoners' Counsel Act, 1836, to directly and uninhibitedly address juries in felony cases some counsel interpreted Brougham's broad "all *expedient* means" description of the advocate's duty to his client as a licence to try to win by any *effective*, means. Other barristers formed a more restrained view about what was permissible, adopting that part of Lord Langdale's speech in Hutchinson v Stephens in 1837[35] in which he emphasized that an advocate's zeal should be qualified by "*considerations affecting the general considerations of justice*". The question of how far counsel could go was discussed much in the mid-nineteenth century.[36] An early contribution was made by Charles Dickens in his novel Pickwick Papers, published in 1837. Although a civil case for breach of promise to marry,[37] Dickens's character Serjeant Buzfuz[38] in *Bardell v Pickwick* abuses his right of free

---

[35] (1837) 1 Keen 659.

[36] For accounts of this, see Jan-Melissa Schramm *Testimony and Advocacy in Victorian Law, Literature and Theology* Cambridge University Press, 2000, Chapter 3 and Allyson May, The Bar and the Old Bailey, University of North Carolina Press. Chapel Hill and London. 2003, Chapter 8, which also includes discussion on acceptable limits of advocacy before the Prisoners' Counsel Act, 1837

[37] See Sir William Holdsworth, *Charles Dickens as a Legal Historian*, Chapter *Bardell and Pickwick*, New Haven: Yale University Press, 1928.

[38] From the thirteenth century Serjeants-at-law were the highest order of counsel, and as a class formed a professional collegiate society centred at Serjeants Inn. They became identifiable by a coif, or black patch on the crown of the wig. Until 1845, when it was abolished by Act of Parliament, Serjeants held a valuable monopoly of practice as leading counsel in the Court of Common Pleas. Elevation from barrister to Serjeant was a mark of professional success and allowed greater fees to be charged. A serjeant was allowed to sit in the House of Lords, though not allowed to speak. Judges in the three superior courts of Common Law were chosen from the serjeants. Following custom, if a barrister below the rank was selected he would formally be appointed as a serjeant before being sworn as a judge. In the nineteenth century there were seldom more than forty serjeants in existence at one time. The Judicature Act 1873 removed the requirement for a barrister to become a serjeant before attaining a place on the Bench. This, combined with the earlier loss of their monopoly in the Court of Common Pleas, and the rise of the rank of Queens Counsel, especially since the early 1830s, when numbers appointed multiplied (see Daniel Duman, The *English and Colonial Bars in the Nineteenth Century*, Croom Helm, 1983, page 35.), as the sign of professional distinction, led to the order of serjeants being widely viewed as anomalous. It was dissolved in 1877. Serjeant's Inn in Chancery Lane was sold and the proceeds divided between the thirty six

speech before the jury by rhetorical excess, theatricality and gratuitous insults.[39]

The Old Bailey trial, in June 1840, of Francois Courvoisier, a Swiss valet, indicted for the murder of his master Lord William Russell at his house in Park Lane, was attended by persons of high society and much reported in all the major newspapers. This case focused public and professional attention on what was acceptable in full defence advocacy and sparked a debate on the subject which lasted over ten years. Courvoisier was defended by the Anglo-Irish barrister Charles Phillips (1787–1859). As a barrister in Ireland, on the Connaught Circuit, Phillips had established a genius for florid oratory, fiery denunciation and pathetic description principally in seduction and breach of promise cases, where strong appeals to emotions could be made. He transferred to the English Bar in 1821. At first, seen as too rich in description and imagery, he was not an immediate success before English juries and was given the title of Councillor O'Garnish by some of his colleagues.[40] An opponent in one case, none other than Henry Brougham (who later became his friend), spoke to the jury of *the horticultural address of my learned friend*.[41] During the eighteenth, nineteenth and early twentieth centuries amongst the inhabitants of the British Isles there was a keen sense of difference of emotional styles between the home nations and even regions within them.[42] Stereotypically the Irish and Welsh had a reputation for emotional excitability in speech. Phillips's fortunes turned and he soon acquired a very large practice at Middle Temple, perhaps partly as a result of a growing appreciation by juries of a more passionate style of address. He came to be regarded as one of the greatest forensic orators of the age.

---

former members. The QC's became the inheritors of the prestige of the serjeants. (Baker, J.H. *The Order of Serjeants at Law: A Chronicle of Creations, with Related Texts and a Historical Introduction.* London, Seldon Society, 1984). For an account of Serjeants in Ireland, see Hart, A. R. *A History of The King's Serjeants at Law in Ireland.* Dublin: Four Courts Press, 2000.

[39] Madeline House and Graham Storey suggest that Dickens modelled Serjeant Buzfuz on Charles Phillips. *Dickens's Letters, Volume 11*, Oxford, Clarendon Press, 1965, pp. 86–87.

[40] David James O'Donoghue, *Charles Phillips*, Dictionary of National Biography, 1885–1900, Volume 45.

[41] *The Georgian Era Memoirs*, London: Vizetelly, Branston and Co, 1833, page 522.

[42] Thomas Dixon, *Weeping Britannia*, Oxford University Press, 2015, pp. 206–207.

In passion, declamatory eloquence[43] and liberal embellishment of speeches by floral language, rather than a great knowledge of the law, Charles Phillips was certainly not alone, but he was the leading light.[44] His intonation, physical presence and ability to cross-examine led to many briefs at the Old Bailey and London Sessions. Despite opposing full representation by counsel to prisoners in 1836, *see earlier*, Chap. 3, he nonetheless took full advantage of it.

In defending Courvoisier, Phillips not only represented the defendant as not guilty to the jury, after Courvoisier had privately admitted to Phillips that he had committed the crime on the third day of the trial, but also sought to blame another servant, who was completely innocent, and accused the police of planting evidence of guilt in the defendant's rooms. In his closing three hour speech,[45] Phillips told the jury that the author of the crime was known to God alone. "*The almighty God above knows who did this deed of violence*". Very soon after his conviction, Courvoisier's confession to Phillips became public and was reported in *The Times*.[46] A virulent reaction to Phillips's speech, made in the full knowledge of his client's guilt, followed in the daily press and the periodicals. Some barristers were also uncomfortable with the idea that counsel made aware of his client's guilt must continue to defend him on the basis he was innocent.

In large editorial articles, which appeared regularly for several weeks after the trial, the influential weekly periodical the *Examiner* called Phillips's line of defence the *lie* of defence and roundly condemned him for exceeding the limits of forensic licence on his clients behalf:

---

[43] Charles Phillips was noted for his use of alliteration, as his opening of a libel case in 1830 shows:

Who shall estimate the cost of a priceless reputation – that impress which gives this dross its currency, without which we stand despised, debased, depreciated............

Quoted by Richard DuCann, *The Art of the Advocate*, Penguin, 1993, page 217.

[44] Bernard Kelly, *Famous Advocates and their Speeches*, Sweet and Maxwell, 1921, London, page 19.

[45] Partly reproduced in David Cairns, *Advocacy and the Making of the Adversarial Criminal Trial 1800–1860*, Oxford: Clarendon Press 1998, Appendix 3. The controversy over Phillip's behaviour is discussed in pages 129–136.

[46] *Courvoisier's Confession of Guilt*, The Times, 22nd June, 1840.

Whether all this accords or not with professional morality, it is not for us to decide; but if it does, the public will probably be disposed to think that the profession should change its name from the profession of law to the profession of the Lie.

We should like to know the breadth of the distinction between an accomplice after the fact and an advocate who makes the most unscrupulous endeavours to procure the acquittal of a man whom he knows to be an assassin.[47]

Charles Dickens wrote two letters on the subject of the Courvoisier case to the *Morning Chronicle*. In the first (dated 21st June, 1840.) he accused Charles Phillips of damaging the very morality of advocacy. A rapid response came in a letter to the paper from a *Lawyer of Middle Temple*, likely to have been Phillips, stressing counsel's obligation to obtain, by every means, his client's acquittal. If this could not be achieved, then counsel should at least ensure his client was "*legally convicted*". Dicken's promptly reacted with a second letter, dated the 26th June, in which he accepted the importance of an independent bar and the right of counsel to take a brief from any client and, within bounds, to do his best to save him,[48] but strongly denied "*the right to defeat the ends of truth and justice by wantonly scattering aspersions upon innocent people*".

In 1845 what was described as the War between the Bar and the Press occurred. Arising from a small dispute between Serjeant Telfourd and *The Times*, it rapidly escalated into a major skirmish. *The Examiner* again portrayed the lawyer as a liar.[49] Punch produced numerous jokes at the expense of the bar. Seemingly striking at the very idea of paid advocacy, or at least its contemporary practice, the recently founded satirical journal presented barristers thus:

And yet these men are but creatures of the Attorneys: they go where the latter bid them........If an honest man is to be bullied in a witness-box, the barrister is

---

[47] The *Examiner*, 28th June, 1840.

[48] Dickens never appeared to waver in this belief. In *Great Expectations*, written nearly twenty years later, the importance of cross-examination, as a means of avoiding injustice, is shown by the stranger's cross-examination of Mr. Wopsle. *A Dicken's Anthology*, Selected by Sidney Macer-Wright, Heron Books, 1957, *Brow Beating as a Fine Art*, pp. 55–59.

[49] For example see, The Bar and the Press, *The Examiner*, 16th August, 1845.

instructed to bully him. If a murderer is to be rescued from the gallows the barrister blubbers over him, as in Tawell's case; or accuses the wrong person, as in Courvoisier's case. If a naughty woman is to be screened, a barrister will bring Heaven itself into court, and call Providence to witness that she is pure and spotless, as a certain great advocate and school-master abroad did for a certain Queen Caroline. They are sold to the highest bidder these folks of the long robe.[50]

Not purely confined to criminal matters, the issue of putting forward a case counsel knew to be false arose again during the 1840s.[51] In 1847, Digby Seymour (*later,* see Chap. 5) in the Mirfield Murders Case, attempted to entirely fix the blame on his client's co-defendant, who was separately represented, for a murder with which they were charged. It was widely rumoured that he had confessed to Seymour before the trial began that he alone was responsible for the crime. Digby Seymour denied that the confession took place. He admitted that he had strong reason to believe his client was guilty, but justified his conduct on the grounds that he had no evidence irreconcilable with the guilt of the other defendant.[52] His explanation drew much hostility from the press. Another, and colourful, example of counsel putting forward something he knew to be untrue, which was condemned by the Judge, jury, press and legal journals alike, occurred in 1853 when a barrister called William Sleigh defended a burglar by saying he had an arrangement to meet the lady of the house in bed. This was entirely Sleigh's invention and he publicly defended his conduct in doing so.[53]

---

[50] Mr. Punch to the Gentlemen of the Press, *Punch,* 1845, pp. 64–65. (Mr. Punch may have been W. M. Thackeray.) Sir Fitzroy Kelly's tearful and sentimental defence of the notorious murderer John Tawell in the same year had attracted much criticism. See, for example, The Times (From the Examiner) March 31st 1845. Mr. Punch's reference to "*a certain great advocate and school master abroad*" can only be to Lord Henry Brougham.

[51] The nature of the duty owed by counsel to a guilty client did not form part of the politicians' discussion at the time of the passage of the Prisoners' Counsel Act 1836: Allyson N. May, *The Bar and the Old Bailey,* 1750–1850 Chapel Hill 2003 pp. 202–3.

[52] (R v Reid and McCabe 1847). See Allyson May, *The Bar and the Old Bailey 1750–1850,* pp. 224–225.

[53] Andrew Watson, *Changing Advocacy,* Justice of the Peace, Volume 165, 22nd September, 2001, page 748. Before reaching thirty, William Campbell Sleigh (1818–1887, called to the bar at Middle

The case of Mr. and Mrs. Mannings in 1849 again focused attention on the duty of counsel to his lay client. The Mannings were charged with murdering their lodger, Patrick O'Connor. The trial was much reported and commented upon.[54] Both were found guilty and hanged. Mr. Manning was represented by Serjeant Wilkins and his wife by William Ballantine, then the leading practitioner at the Old Bailey, where the trial took place. Wilkins defended Mr. Mannings by seeking to blame his wife (who like Courvoisier happened to be Swiss) and mounted a violent attack on her. Ballantine declared he would not follow these tactics.

I will do that which it is my duty as an advocate; but if my duty as an advocate requires that I should cast upon the male prisoner the sort of observations and accusations which have been made against the woman, I would feel that my profession was a disgrace, and the sooner I abandoned it for one more creditable, the sooner I would be a respected, an honourable, and an upright man, and placed in a better position to respect myself.[55]

Ballantine's behaviour was praised widely while that of Wilkins much criticized. Debate about the licence of counsel was re-kindled, in the course of which Phillips' conduct of Courvoisier's defence was again scrutinized.[56]

Harsh and widespread criticism of saving clients by all *expedient* means, or rather its distortion to mean winning by any available means, led to the notion becoming discredited within the profession. There was an acceptance of views expounded by William Forsyth in *Hortensius or the advocate, An historical essay on the Office and Duties of an Advocate* (1849).[57] In essence, Forsyth approved the line taken by Lord Langdale,

---

Temple in 1846), had been married three times, divorced twice and bankrupt two times. These details were brought to public attention in 1853, but did not prevent him being created a serjeant at law in 1868, the same year he patented an invention for *an improved appliance for protecting trousers from mud.*

[54] See for example the *Examiner*, 27th October, 24th November and 8th December, 1849.

[55] The Times, 27th October, 1849.

[56] Jan-Melissa Schramm, *Testimony and Advocacy in Victorian Law, Literature, and Theology*, Cambridge University Press, 2000, page 118.

[57] London: John Murray, 1849, page 436.

in 1837, that the advocate *"cannot acquire rights greater than are possessed by his principal. He may not assert that which he knows to be a lie. He may not connive, much less substantiate a fraud"*. Sometime later, the Bar expressed a similar, but binding, opinion on the correctness of counsel defending on a plea of "not guilty" a person charged with an offence, when he had confessed to counsel he was guilty of the offence charged.[58] Applied retrospectively in *Courvoisier* it would have meant that Phillips was right in testing the strength of the prosecution evidence against his client, but wrong in suggesting his innocence. Roughly by 1850, the bar had come to accept the full defence in felony trials introduced by the Prisoners' Counsel Act 1836, to which it had been largely opposed, and also that justice was promoted by ensuring that a morally guilty client received a fair trial in which evidence against him should be properly proved.[59] This was supported in the legal periodicals,[60] but not the popular press.[61] The question of the morality of forensic licence, especially advocates acting for defendants whom they knew, or suspected to be guilty, appears in Victorian novels.[62]

For many members of the Bar cases such as Courvoisier and the Mirfield murders illustrated that interviews between counsel and criminal clients were to be discouraged as tending to destroy the impersonal nature of advocacy and, moreover, to avoid being put in situations of

---

[58] Sir Gervais Rentoul, *The Art and Ethics of Advocacy*, Haldane Memorial Lecture 1943, pp. 18–19.

[59] See Allyson May, *The Bar and the Old Bailey, 1750–1850*, University of North Carolina Press, Chapel Hill and London, 2003, Concluding Chapter.

[60] See Allyson May, *The Bar and the Old Bailey, 1750–1850*, University of North Carolina Press, 2003, pp. 228–233.

[61] Jan-Melissa Schramm, *Testimony and Advocacy in Victorian Law*, Literature and Theology, Cambridge University Press, 2000, pp. 117–144.

[62] In Anthony Trollope's Orley Farm (published in monthly shilling parts between 1861 and 1862), for example, the central theme is the looming and actual trial of Lady Mason for perjury, committed many years earlier in a bitterly fought court battle about the validity of a codicil, which she had forged, to her late husband's will. After his closing speech on her behalf, in the later criminal trial before the jury, Mr. Furnival, her leading barrister, sits down:

> *And yet as he sat down he knew that she had been guilty! To his ear her guilt had never been confessed; but yet he knew that it was so, and knowing that, he had been able to speak as though her innocence were a thing of course.* (Anthony Trollope, *Orley Farm*, London: Folio, 1993, page 617)

great embarrassment. Such a view was still to be found well into the twentieth century.[63]

Objections raised by the press and public to needless attacks by barristers on the character of witnesses or parties also played a significant part in restraining the bar's forensic licence. Standards of etiquette were formulated, which were later entrenched as rules of professional conduct, requiring counsel, so far as possible, to be satisfied that allegations were true before putting them to witnesses.

Judicial Limitations on the Licence of Advocates

Judicial pronouncement further limited counsel's licence in felony cases. In the trial of the strychnine poisoner William Palmer in 1856[64] the Chief Justice, Lord Campbell, politely rebuked Sergeant Shee (later to become Mr. Justice Shee[65]), who the prisoner's leading counsel, for expressing his personal opinion of Palmer's innocence. Shee said, in a closing speech which had included an appeal to the heavens and was widely seen as brilliant specimen of legal oratory:

> *"I commence his defence. I say in all sincerity, with an entire conviction of his innocence I believe that never was a truer word pronounced than the words "Not Guilty to the Charge."*"[66]

---

[63] Patrick Hastings, *later*, Chap. 9, for instance, steadfastly refused to see his clients in the cells at court. In this he was not alone. (Explained in an interview, on the 30th October, 2007, with Anthony Arlidge QC, who was called to the bar in 1962, Treasurer of Middle Temple in 2003, and widely held to be the leading barrister in England and Wales in criminal defence work.)

[64] Palmer, a young surgeon, was tried at the Old Bailey for the murder by strychnine poison of a betting man at Rugeley. The case excited enormous interest and was much reported, not only in Britain but also throughout Europe and beyond, because of the use of what was then an obscure drug and the general air of mystery surrounding the affair. So great was feeling against him in Staffordshire that Parliament passed a special Act (18& 20 Vict. C.16) permitting cases to be transferred to London where there was a clear risk of prejudice against a prisoner locally.

[65] William Shee (1804–1868), the son of Irish parents, was the first Catholic barrister to be appointed a judge of the superior courts since James II. The high point of his career as a barrister was his defence of Palmer.

[66] Rv Palmer: Verbatim Report. Transcribed by Mr. Angelo Bennett of Rolls Chambers, Chancery Lane, (London: J. Allen, 1856), page 175.

The Lord Chief Justice told the jury:

> *I most strongly recommend to you that you should attend to everything that Serjeant Shee said to you with the exception of his own private opinion. It is my duty to tell you that opinion should not be any ingredient of your verdict.......* *it is the duty of the advocate to press his argument on the jury, but not his opinion.*[67]

In telling the jury that Sergeant Shee's opinion ought not enter into their verdict, the Lord Chief Justice was reiterating a principle that had been established in the state trial of, Thomas Paine in 1792 when Thomas Erskine had said to the jury:

> *I will now lay aside the role of the advocate and address you as a man.*

This was met with the judge by:

> *You will do nothing of the sort. The only right and licence you have to appear in this court is as an advocate.*[68]

In an earlier case, when he defended the Dean of St Asaph, charged with seditious libel, in 1784, Erskine openly placed himself in even closer personal alliance with a client and his cause.[69] Indeed in the case which first brought him to public notice, the trial of Captain Baillie (a criminal libel prosecution arising from allegations of corruption and mismanagement

---

[67] Verbatim Report, pp. 307–308.

[68] R v Paine (1792) 22 How.St. Tr.358, 412 (1816–1826).

[69] Rv Shipley (1783–1784), 21 How.St.Tr 847 (1816–1826). Erskine's client was indicted for seditious libel. Prosecuting counsel said to the jurors: "*I declare upon my honour...... that I not only think it is a most enormous, and most mischievous libel*" (page 889). In reply Erskine said ......"*following the example of my learned friend, who has pledged his personal veracity in support of his sentiments, I assert, upon my honour to be unaltered, and I believe I may say, unalterable opinion, formed upon the most mature deliberation; and I choose to place that opinion in the very front of my address to you, that you may not, in the course of it, mistake the energies of truth and freedom for the zeal of professional duty. This declaration of my sentiments, even if my friend had not set me the example by giving you his, I should have considered to be my duty in this cause.......*" (page 899.) He ended his closing speech by "*As a friend of my client, and a friend of my country, I shall feel much sorrow, and yourselves will probably hereafter regret it, when the season of reparation is fled*". (page 929) Excerpts from David Mellinkoff, *The Conscience of a Lawyer*, pp. 245–246.

made by the Captain at the Greenwich Hospital for Seamen), in 1778, Erskine had said "*I speak not as an advocate alone. – I speak to you as a man……….*" Erskine drew a distinction between ordinary cases, when a lawyer ought not to argue his personal opinion, and cases affecting the public right where it would be wrong not to do so. Injection of a lawyer's own personal opinion has been identified with an older tradition of advocacy which did not find the practice objectionable, but quite proper, doing what the layman often thinks the lawyer does anyway – personally vouch for the client and his case.[70]

The rule forbidding advocates to express personal opinions in their clients' cases, expounded by Lord Kenyon in 1792 in the Thomas Paine trial, was frequently broken in the nineteenth century. Lord Brougham and Thomas Denham voiced personal support for Queen Caroline when defending her in 1820. In 1837 the *Legal Observer*[71] bemoaned that young barristers, in particular, were inclined to the very grave error of avowing personal belief in the causes of their clients and the credibility of witnesses and other evidence. Such behaviour, which in the periodical's view often carried great weight with juries, involved the advocate in a lie, blunted his sense of right and wrong and brought the profession into public disrepute.

Lord Campbell's re-assertion in Palmer's case of the prohibition of personal belief in cases was accepted by the bar, as a point of professional etiquette, in felony cases. Any doubt that it did not apply to civil cases was dispelled ten years later in the case of the self-styled "Princess Olive", who sought, unsuccessfully, to establish her membership of the Royal Family. Much of her claim depended on some documents. Her counsel, Walter Smith started to assert his belief on his *word and honour as a gentleman* that they were genuine when Lord Chief Justice Cockburn interrupted him with:

> *I insist on your not finishing that sentence. It is a violation of a fundamental rule, which every advocate ought to observe, to give the jury your personal opinion.*[72]

---

[70] David Mellinkoff, *The conscience of a lawyer*, 1973, West Publishing Co, St Paul, pp. 237–247.

[71] *Legal Observer* 15 (1837): 216–217.

[72] Ryves and Ryves v The Attorney General (1866) in The Annual Register, vol. 108, pt. II, page 255.

The main practical consequences of this fundamental rule of advocacy were that advocates ceased to overtly vouch for their clients and prefaced their comment and opinion to jurors with the words *"you may think that......"*.

Scenes in Court and Discourtesy

Not only was bullying cross-examination of witnesses an aspect of advocacy in the early decades of Queen Victoria's reign, and those closely preceding them, but so was rudeness to Judges and fellow barristers. Numerous slanging matches occurred amongst counsel themselves and between barristers and Judges, who were not always able to control them. On occasions the conduct of counsel was so bad that jurors sometimes actually stood up in protest.[73] Bad behaviour was not confined to the Old Bailey Bar, which for many years had enjoyed a foul reputation, or even the criminal bar. Mr. Sergeant Adams, sitting as a judge at the Middlesex Sessions in the 1840s and 1850s "appeared only to occupy the bench as a mark for the impertinence of barristers". Frequent scenes between Judge Chilton and the Bar at Greenwich were reported in the *Kentish Mercury* in 1847. In 1848 the Recorder of Hull Sessions was reduced to tears by the disrespect of a barrister called Dearsley. A vendetta, involving barristers and Judge Ramshay, occurred in the Liverpool County Court in 1850 and 1851.[74] Quarrels between Counsel in court were not uncommon and were satirised in cartoon form in one edition of *Punch* with the caption *Unseemly Squabbles*.[75] The Bar was scandalized in 1847 when two Chancery Queen's Counsel exchanged blows in open court.[76] Richard Bethell (who, in time, as Lord Westbury, became Lord Chancellor of England), renowned for his sharp tongue, once had his noise bloodied by opposing counsel as they walked from the courtroom. On another

---

[73] David Bentley, *English Criminal Justice in the 19th Century*, Hambledon Press 1998, Chapter 11.

[74] For these and other examples of similar behaviour see J. R. Lewis, *The Victorian Bar*, Robert Hale, London, 1982, pp. 22–27.

[75] Reproduced as a photographic plate, *Illustration 8*, in J.R. Lewis, *The Victorian Bar*, Robert Hale, London, 1982.

[76] *The Times*, 27th July, 1847.

occasion he was challenged to a duel by another opponent over an argument which had occurred in a case. He did not accept.[77] It was, however, the Old Bailey that consistently retained the worst reputation for unpleasant disputes between counsel and between bench and Bar. It is not entirely facetious to suggest that a florid style of oratory, and some scenes in court, was to some extent connected to the lunches supplied daily, at the expense of the sheriffs, in the Old Bailey and other courts. At the Old Bailey two dinners attended by judges and counsel, were served. The first was at three 'o' clock, for judges and aldermen sitting in the evening and counsel (evening sessions were abolished in 1844 and with them the 3 pm lunch which was transferred to earlier in the afternoon) and the second at five 'o' clock, for those coming off duty. These meals usually comprised beefsteaks and marrow-puddings and were accompanied by plentiful supplies of port and sherry. They were expensive for their providers. Mainly on account of this, by 1877, at the Old Bailey, they had become *mere epicurean memories.*[78] The Honourable Charles Ewan Law, the Recorder at the Old Bailey (1835–1850), was described as *dignified in manner before dinner always.*[79] Earlier, some of the utterances of

---

[77] See J. R. Lewis, *The Victorian Bar*, Robert Hale, London, 1982, page 24. There was a precedent for duelling. In 1816, John Adolphus, who acted for the defendant in the first case after the Prisoners' Counsel Act was implemented in 1836, quarrelled with another counsel, Peter Alley, in a late sitting Old Bailey trial. Unable to settle their differences, the pair fought a duel with pistols in Calais. Both survived, though Alley's arm was injured. See James P. Gilchrist, *A Chronological Register of Principal Duels*. Bulmer and Nicol, 1821, page 252.

[78] Bernard Kelly, *Famous Advocates and their Speeches*, Sweet and Maxwell, 1921, pp. 21–22.

[79] William Ballantine, *A Barrister's Life*, Richard Bentley, London, 1880, page 66. A contemporary of Ballantine wrote the following about the Old Bailey meals and their effect on standards: *The Dinners were good, the wines abundant, and the results visible at the evening sittings. A barrister who had been cross-examining, and speaking for eight hours, was not unlikely to take a little wine for his stomach's sake, and was sometimes called down to defend a prisoner without any clear notion that he was not to prosecute. The juries who came to sit at five, of course had dined, and living men have seen a judge (not one of the fifteen) descend the stairs, holding fast by the banister, not in wantonness of care, afterwards trying prisoners, when unable to read the dispositions accurately, or to understand the witnesses answers yet getting through the work from memory and habit. The witnesses, who had been waiting all day in the Old Bailey public houses, were often very drunk. One Alderman must always be in the court; no one knows why, but such is the law, and his worship was frequently in a state of modified sobriety. Quarrels of the most discreditable order might be expected from a court so composed. It is better not to attempt a description of the rows. Those who have been present at them will remember; those who have not would disbelieve. Mr Adolphus and his Contemporaries at the Old Bailey*, Law Magazine, 34 (1846) pp. 62–63.

Serjeant Arabin, who sat as a judge at the Old Bailey from 1830 to 1839, had either the distinct whiff of alcohol about them, or signs of a more deep seated confusion. Examples include:

> *No man is fit to be a cheesemonger who cannot guess the length of a street* and *If ever there was a case of clearer evidence than this of persons acting together, this was that case*[80]

The quality of advocacy may not have been added to by tiredness. While the legal terms lasted, the courts sat for very long hours.[81] On the very last day of term, they might sit until midnight to clear their lists of cases.

Standards were not helped either in criminal and civil matters by the practice of many barristers wandering from court to court and taking contemporaneous instructions, to the detriment of those whose briefs they had accepted earlier.[82] Often leading barristers had numerous cases on the daily cause list, a feature which endured for the rest of the century and beyond. To cover them required juniors, who often did most of the work. Juniors and clients would sometimes complain of leaders rushing into court and taking control of their cases with little idea of what had happened in their absence.

Largely as a result of public disapproval, which impacted on the Bar's evolving etiquette, the conduct of barristers at the Old Bailey and elsewhere gradually improved over the second part of the nineteenth century.[83] The process was not without a number of setbacks. In 1876,

---

[80] Richard Hamilton. *All Jangle and Riot*, Professional Books, 1986, page 271. For other pronouncements made by Serjeant Arabin, and anecdotes told about him, sitting as a judge, see Sir Robert Megarry, *Arabinesque at law*, 1969, Wildy, Simmonds and Hill. In *R v Harris* (Cited by Megarry as Arab.AP., ex rel W. B.1834), Charles Phillips, counsel for the prosecution and Serjeant Arabin, sitting as a judge, conducted a conference after which the prisoner pleaded guilty. Arabin said to Phillips, *you must distinctly understand that I know nothing of the arrangement.* In an example of rudeness from counsel to the bench, not unknown at the time, Phillips replied, *Yes my lord it is thoroughly understood that your Lordship knows nothing.* (Megarry page 6)

[81] Allyson May, *The Bar and the Old Bailey*, University of North Carolina Press, 2003, pp. 171–172 and John H. Langbein, *The Origins of the Adversary Trial*, Oxford, 2003, page 25.

[82] Richard DuCann, *The Art of the Advocate*, Penguin Books, 1993, pp. 40–42.

[83] Edward Purcell, recollecting the criminal bar, in the late 1870s and early 1880s, when he began his career, wrote: "*The coarseness, vulgarity and violence that made "Old Bailey barrister" an opprobrious*

for instance, at the Middlesex Sessions Court, Ribton Cooper was reported to have shouted at opposing counsel, William Sleigh, *It's no use you putting on those monkey faces with me!* In the commotion that followed, the judge ran out of the building and did not return until the uproar had subsided.[84] However vastly far more serious had been Dr. Kenealy QC's[85] conduct in defending Arthur Orton, the *Tichborne claimant,*[86] on counts of perjury at the Old Bailey in 1873–1874. The

---

description were fast dying out, but were not extinct. The older generation persisted in their bad old ways, not by any means mollified by finding their business passing to younger men of a "different type". Forty *years at the Criminal Bar; Experiences and Impressions,* Fisher Unwin, London, 1916, page 48.

[84] J. R. Lewis, *The Victorian Bar,* Robert Hale, London, 1982, page 120.

[85] Edward Vaughan Kenealy was born in Cork in 1819, educated at Trinity College, Dublin, called to the Irish Bar in 1840 and then to the Bar of England and Wales, at Middle Temple in 1846, where he rapidly rose and became a silk in 1868, working in London and also on the Oxford Circuit. He was eloquent (perhaps rather waspishly, J.B. Atlay, the distinguished barrister and author of *Famous Trials of the Century,* 1899, Grant Richards, London, page 354, wrote he *was the master of a tremendous flow of words, and of the gift which in Irishmen is sometimes eloquence, in Englishmen invariably bathos.*) energetic, tenacious and courageous and possessed a stock of quotations and knowledge of poetry for the benefit of jurors. Despite these skills he had a reputation for lacking discretion, inclination to completely disregard the feelings of opponents, making reckless and unsupported statements and failing to appreciate that quarreling with judges was only effective if the jury was on his side. (J. R. Lewis, *The Victorian Bar,* Robert Hale, London, 1982, page 116. See also B. W. Kelly, *Famous Advocates and their Speeches,* Sweet and Maxwell, 1921 pp. 113–118).

[86] After the death, in 1866, of the eleventh baronet, Sir Alfred Tichborne, whose family was of ancient lineage, originating before the Norman Conquest, Arthur Orton, alias Thomas Castro, who had been a butcher in Australia, came forward and claimed to be Sir Alfred's elder brother, Roger Charles. He had been educated at Stoneyhurst College, served in the Army and was thought to have been lost at sea, off the coast of South America, in 1854. Lady Tichborne recognized him as her son, despite his coarseness of speech, ignorance of French (Roger Charles had as a child been brought up in France) and the Classics, lack of knowledge of family history and military matters and difference in appearance to Roger Charles. Other members of the family were unconvinced. When Lady Tichborne died, Orton sought to claim his inheritance. To fight his case in court and gain support he sold shares in his hoped for fortune and toured music halls where he denounced the British establishment before working class audiences. The case of Tichborne *v* Lushington, in the Court of Common Pleas, began in 1871 and lasted 102 days (See J. Atlay, *Famous Trials of the Century,* London, 1899, Grant Richards, pp. 263–283). The Claimant was represented by Serjeant Ballantine, whose opening speech lasted a day and a half and Hardinge Giffard. The Defendants retained Sir John Coleridge, who cross-examined for twenty two days, and Henry Hawkins. The jury considered the Claimant was not Roger Tichborne and, with his consent, counsel elected to be non-suited. The trial cost the Tichborne family nearly £92,000, making it the most expensive in Victorian Britain. (The National Portrait Gallery, London, possesses a lithograph of the court scene, entitled *Scraps in Court, -Tichborne v. Lushington,* made by Andrew Maclure in 1871. Amongst others, Arthur Orton, William Ballantine, William Bovill, Henry Hawkins, and John Coleridge are depicted.) At the end of the civil trial, Arthur Orton was committed, by Sir William

trial lasted 188 days, of which 66 days were occupied with speeches by counsel. Instead of seeking to rely on the standard and burden of proof to show that the prosecution's case was too uncertain to justify a conviction, Kenealy, inexplicably, took on the onus of trying to prove that the defendant was Roger Tichborne. His theory, without any evidence behind it, was that the Tichborne family and their Crown advisers, were guilty of bribery and conspiracy. Henry Hawkins opened for the Crown with a short dramatic speech and then called his witnesses. In cross-examination, many of them were subjected by Kenealy to wild and offensive accusations, often completely unconnected with issues in the case, and fierce vituperation when they objected. Henry Hawkins constantly protested; the judges (Lord Chief Justice Cockburn and Justices Mellor and Lush, sitting in banc.) intervened; there were also clashes with the special jury. The trial descended into a continual scene of outburst, protest and quarrel. There was no improvement when Kenealy opened his case and presented his witnesses. His closing speech lasted for twenty one days. Very little of it was concerned with a summary of the evidence and with putting a consecutive and coherent case before the jury.[87] He started by calling on God:

> *I commence my observations in defence of the accused by reverently invoking the Supreme Judge of the Universe that, in this mighty trial, He may give us that light which is His own essential attribute; that He may guide us by us by wisdom, by impartiality, by the spirit of justice justice, the most celestial of all human qualities – unto a true verdict on the issue between us; that we may not be misled by any temporal consideration, by fear, by favour, by affection, to deviate in the least degree from the glorious path of sun-bright rectitude, but that we*

Bovill, Chief Justice of the Common Pleas, to stand trial for perjury at the Old Bailey where Dr. Kenealy led his defence. The claimant was convicted and sentenced to 14 years penal servitude. Before imposing this long, and it has been said, in view of Kenealy's behaviour, possibly vengeful sentence, Lord Justice Cockburn said that *the Claimant set a wind blowing through England that will take a generation to quiet.* Because of widespread fascination with the aristocracy, and that the story was replete with ingredients of a great Victorian novel, including money, class, drink, family squabbles, long lost heirs and intricate legal doings, both cases received intense press publicity and were much discussed at all levels of society. Interest has persisted with a comparatively recent film, *The Tichborne Claimant,* loosely based on the facts of the cases, being produced in 1998.

[87] J. B. Atlay, *Famous Trials of the Century,* Grant Richards, London, 1899, page 379.

may, all of us bear in mind, according to the justice we mete out here, so shall be the justice administered to ourselves in the dread hereafter. There is not one of us that will not have to stand before that awful throne, which shimmers far away in the future, to answer for life on earth; there is not one of us who will not have to give a reason for the motives by which he was influenced in all the essential acts of his existence....[88]

Dr. Kenealy later alleged: Lord Chief Justice Cockburn had prejudiced the case; that the prosecution was the most corrupt and wasteful since the Stuart period; and that forgery, perjury and bribery were the tools of *verminous* witnesses for the Crown.[89] In his closing speech for the prosecution, Henry Hawkins spoke of *"Justice being insulted in her seat"*. Lord Chief Justice Cockburn, in summing up, described Kenealy's advocacy as *"one unceasing torrent of invective, of dirty, foul slime"*.[90] The jury convicted the prisoner on all counts and formally complained, in writing about Kenealey's conduct after the case had finished:

We find..............; that the charges of bribery, conspiracy and undue influence made against the prosecution in this case are entirely devoid of foundation, and we regret extremely the violent language and demeanour of leading counsel for the defendant, and his attacks on the counsel for the prosecution, and on several of the witnesses produced in the cause.[91]

The way Kenealy ran the defendant's case led to many questions and comments in the legal and general press about the role of advocacy and forensic excess – themes that had been much heard earlier, especially in the 1840s, following the granting of full defence by counsel in felony cases in 1836. Questions were also asked about how determined the bar

---

[88] Address to the jury on behalf of Thomas Castro/Arthur Orton, Old Bailey, 1874. Reproduced by Bernard Kelly, *Famous Advocates and their speeches*, London: Sweet and Maxwell, 1921, pp. 116–117.

[89] In J. B. Atley's opinion, *never was a prisoner's chance of acquittal more recklessly sacrificed to the almost insane vanity and headstrong willfulness of counsel, ibid,* page 379. In what might be seen as some mitigation on his behalf, Francis Cowper (*Holker and Kenealy*, Graya, No 67, Easter 1968, page 17) suggested that ill-health (Kenealy suffered from diabetes) partly accounted for his impossible conduct.

[90] J.B. Atlay, *Famous Trials of the Century*, Grant Richards, London 1899, page 380.

[91] J. B. Atlay, *Famous Trials of the Century*, Grant Richards, London, 1899, page 385.

was to root out conduct like that which had been exhibited recently and, more fundamentally, should the regulation of advocacy be left in its hands. In Kenealy's case the bar acted swiftly and decisively. His fellow barristers on the Oxford Circuit called upon him to answer allegations before the Bar Mess that he had spoken to witnesses in a way that exceeded the licence granted to the bar and had "*exhibited improper demeanour to the bench*". Dr. Kenealy declined to appear and was expelled.[92] In practical terms this meant no junior barrister on that Circuit could work with him[93] Next, the Benchers of Gray's Inn held an inquiry into his conduct, the outcome being that he was removed from being a bencher and disbarred from further practice, then an extreme step, especially when a Queen's Counsel was concerned.[94] It may be that excesses of counsel and the inability of some judges to deal with them, especially in the 1840s, memories of which were revived by Kenealy's conduct in R v Castro, explained *The Barrister's Dream* in *The Hunting of the Snark*, by Lewis Carroll, in 1876. In the fifth part of this nonsense poem the barrister:

> *dreamed that he stood in a shadowy Court,*
> *Where the Snark, with a glass in its eye,*
> *Dressed in gown, bands and wig, was defending a pig*
> *On a charge of deserting its sty.*

In a later verse the snark tells the jury "*My poor client's fate now depends on your votes*" The verse continues:

> *Here the speaker sat down in his place,*
> *And directed the Judge to refer to his notes*
> *And briefly to sum up the case.*

The next verse reads:

---

[92] Reported in the Law Journal, April 11th, 1874.

[93] On the role of Circuit bar messes, where barristers frequently dined, in fostering a professional spirit amongst them and in maintaining standards, see A. H. Manchester, *A Modern Legal History of England and Wales 1750–1950*, London, Butterworths, 1980, page 68.

[94] For an account of the proceedings in Gray's Inn, see, Sir Malcolm Hilbery, *The Kenealy Scandal*, Graya, No 62, Michaelmas Term, 1965 pp. 125–137.

But the Judge said he never had summed up before;
So the Snark undertook it instead,
And summed it so well that it came to far more
Than the Witness ever had said!.

Remembering the late 1870s and 1880s, when he was beginning his forty year long career as a barrister before the criminal courts, Edmund Purcell wrote of the:

bludgeon being too often the weapon of the advocate. The judge was denounced and insulted; the witnesses, especially the police, were accused of willful perjury; the address to the jury was clamour and vituperation. It was only gradually that subtlety and plausibility took the place they now occupy in the armoury of the advocate.[95]

Judges, particularly at the London Sessions, often encountered great rudeness from the Bar. Purcell recounted:

Bench and Bar, "Scenes in Court" were frequent headings in the newspapers; observations were made to the judge, which today would scarcely be credited. I have heard Thorne Cole, a loud-voiced advocate, who was a terror to Sir P. Edlin, in addressing the jury, compare him somehow to Nebuchadnezzar and denounce him as the coiled-up boa-constrictor, who was about to spring on the unhappy prisoner[96]

Describing Thorne-Cole, Purcell wrote, "*His strength was not so much in winning acquittals as in giving his clients as it used to be described a 'glorious funeral'. He was full of noise and declamation; shouted and beat the desk with a vigour that made poor Edlin start and tremble with the dread of what was coming next. His powers of vituperation, often quite original, relieved his speeches from the monotony of mere abuse*".[97]

---

[95] *Forty Years at the Criminal Bar; Experiences and Impressions*, Fisher Unwin, London, 1916, page 48.

[96] Purcell, *ibid*, page 49.

[97] Edmund Purcell, *Forty Years at the Criminal Bar*, page 28.

Certain judges, in an age before the Court of Criminal Appeal[98] and hence almost absolute masters of their courts, were not always known for impartiality. Some frequently intervened during proceedings and tinged their summings up to assist the prisoner. Rather more, however, including Sir Peter Edlin, did so to thwart his or her case. In such circumstances attacks on judges can be explained as counsel attempting to act in the best interests of prisoners.

The movement in the later nineteenth century towards courtesy in courts may to some extent have resulted from the steadily growing dignity of the bench, especially since the Judicature Acts of 1873–5 which transformed the civil court structure. A rise in their standing has been seen as responsible for increased judicial control over legal proceedings and for a greater acceptance of that control by the Bar than earlier in the century.[99]

Important Changes in Procedure and Evidence Affecting Advocacy in Criminal Trials

An aspect of advocacy in the criminal courts that persisted until the middle of the nineteenth century was the requirement that written indictments had to be very tightly drawn. The law required indictments to be certain. Both the offender and the offence had to be accurately described and in minute particularity. Even in simple cases indictments would be long documents. Complex rules of criminal pleading governed this area.[100] Amendments were not permitted so the effect of counsel being able to point to a defect was that a prosecution would fail. It would also collapse if there was a variance between the indictment and the evidence called to support it. In order to minimise the risk of this happening the pleader would usually include in the indictment a number of alternative

---

[98] The Court of Criminal Appeal was established by the Court of Criminal Appeal Act 1907; rights to appeal to it, either against conviction or sentence, were given to those convicted on indictment.

[99] G.W. Keeton, *Harris on Advocacy*, Stevens and Sons, 1943, page 10.

[100] See Chitty, *Practical Treatise on Criminal Law*, 1st Edition 1816, pp. 168–304.

counts founded on the same events scarcely different from each other except in small particulars but designed to cover all possible combination of facts the evidence might prove. This approach, however, tended to lengthen the size of indictments and increased the chances of formal errors within them.

Where a defect or flaw existed in an indictment, or the indictment varied between the evidence, counsel for the prisoner would normally take the point by a motion in arrest of judgement after the verdict had been delivered. Many displayed great ingenuity in their arguments. Unmeritorious acquittals did occur.[101] The issue caught the public eye in 1841 when Lord Cardigan was tried at the Old Bailey for the murder of 'Harvey Garnett Phipps'. It was proved that he had killed 'Harvey Garnett Phipps Tuckett'. The judge had no option but to direct the jury to acquit him[102] (leaving Lord Cardigan free, fifteen years later in the Crimean War, to lead the calamitous charge of Light Brigade into the Russian guns, remembered by the poetry of Tennyson.). Calls for root and branch reform were made in the press[103] and the Criminal Law Commissioners in their Eighth Report (1845) considered there was a clear need for change. Reform eventually came in 1851 with Lord Campbell's Criminal Procedure Act. This statute: set out a list of defects that should not invalidate an indictment[104]; specified that all formal objections had to be made before the jury was sworn and not afterwards and gave the court power upon such objections to order the indictment to be amended.[105] Also, where variance occurred between the indictment and the evidence called to prove it, the judge was given power to amend the indictment if any variance was not material to the merits of the case and did not prejudice the prisoner in his defence.[106] Further, the Criminal Procedure Act simplified forms of indictment for certain offences including murder,

---

[101] For some examples see David Bentley, *English Criminal Justice in the Nineteenth Century*, Hambledon Press, 1998, page 135.

[102] Richard DuCann, *The Art of the Advocate*, Penguin Books, Revised Edition, 1993, page 93.

[103] See *The Times* leader, 31st December, 1841.

[104] Section 24.

[105] Section 25.

[106] Section 1.

manslaughter and theft and forgery of documents.[107] After the Act trivial indictment flaws and variances no longer resulted in acquittal and barristers had to adjust to this in their practice of advocacy.[108]

Slightly later there were other changes in procedure to which advocates also had to adapt. During the first half of the nineteenth century many judges, reacting to the prosecution's refusal to call a witness whose name appeared on the back of an indictment, would call the witness themselves or insist that the Crown tender them for cross-examination. After 1860 this practice ceased.(Nonetheless, the Crown was obliged to have at court witnesses it decided in its discretion not to call in case the defence wished to do so.) This change put counsel for the prosecution in a stronger position to run his case as he saw fit. At a time when calling evidence by the defence gave the Crown the last word with the jury, counsel for the prisoner had to weigh the tactical advantage of having the final speech against what might be gained by calling any of these witnesses.

A Crown witness who proved hostile by going back on what he or she had said at committal would be confronted with his deposition and warned by the judge against perjury. In 1865 the Crown's hand was strengthened by being given the right to cross-examine witnesses found to be hostile on their depositions.[109]

Affecting the task of advocacy by counsel acting for the Crown and for prisoners was greater acceptance by judges at trials of circumstantial evidence – relevant indirect evidence which allows a court to infer the existence, or non-existence, of a fact in issue. The sensational trial and conviction in 1864 of Franz Muller[110] for murder in a railway carriage was a landmark case in this direction.[111] Counsel now had to submit

---

[107] Sections 4 and 5.

[108] It was not, however, until the Indictments Act 1915, that prolixity of indictments was addressed.

[109] Criminal Procedure Act, 1865, Section 3.

[110] See Leslie Blake, *Famous cases: R v Muller – The nature of circumstantial evidence*, Estates Gazette, October 14th, 1995.

[111] Two years later, in *R v Exall* (1866) 4 F&F 922, Lord Chief Baron Pollock, most probably remembering the intricacies of Muller's case, famously likened circumstantial evidence to "a rope of several cords": "*One strand of the cord might be insufficient to sustain the weight, but three stranded together may be of sufficient strength. Thus it may be in circumstantial evidence – there may be a combination of circumstances, no one of which would raise a reasonable conviction or more than a mere suspicion; but the three taken together may create a conclusion of guilt with as much certainty as human affairs can admit of*.

before judges that pieces of evidence were, or were not, sufficiently relevant to be admitted as circumstantial. If allowed into trial it became necessary for them to the make the most of, or to minimise, its significance before jurors.

The Removal of the 'Bloody Code' and Consequences for Advocacy

When the nineteenth century began well over two hundred offences were punishable by death under English law.[112] Frequently judges and jurors, who considered capital punishment too severe in cases before them, undervalued stolen goods to below the amount for which it could be imposed. To avoid the death penalty being passed some jurors found prisoners not guilty. The majority of those who were convicted of capital crimes were spared execution by royal discretionary pardon and sentenced to transportation or imprisonment. Some received no punishment at all. In making decisions about pardoning the King-in-cabinet considered the prisoner's character, the nature of the offence, the strength of the evidence against him or her and the prevalence of the particular crime. The recommendation from the judge was decisive in most instances.[113] The death penalty was removed for pick-pocketing in 1808. In the 1820s, during the period Robert Peel was Home Secretary, major dismantling of the 'Bloody Code' took place. Within five years in excess of one hundred felonies were declared non-capital. The pace of reform was continued in the 1830s and by 1840 the number of capital offences was confined to seven. It was reduced to four in 1861: murder, treason, arson in royal dockyards and piracy with violence.

Penalties substituted for offences which previously carried the death penalty were transportation, until its abolition in 1867, and imprisonment. Judges were given much discretion, which they tightly guarded, on

---

[112] In the years after 1660, the number of capital offences increased from about 50 to around 160 in 1750 and rose further. See W R Cornish and G de N. Clark, The Era of the Bloody Code, *Law and Society in England 1750–1950*, Sweet and Maxwell, London, 1989, pp. 544–568.

[113] W R Cornish and G de Clark, *ibid*, page 564.

the severity of sentence. Given this, it became increasingly important for counsel to put before them, as compellingly as possible, mitigating factors, about both the offence and the prisoner, that might reduce punishment. It might reasonably be surmised that judges' greatly widened sentencing powers following the removal of the 'Bloody Code' promoted development of the speech in mitigation. Rather surprisingly, what evidence there is points to the rarity of pleas in mitigation throughout the nineteenth century.[114] The author of a relatively recent paper,[115] which drew on the results of a study of trials for felonious assault, formerly a capital offence, reported that most counsel tried to put as many features that could be seen as mitigating before the jury in the course of the trial. This appeared to be in the hope that, if they were not inclined to acquit entirely the prisoner, jurors might find him or her guilty of a lesser offence, especially if at least some evidence had been given of provocation or intoxication. If the accused was convicted of an offence there seemed little need to cover, in a separate plea in mitigation before the judge, ground that had already been covered.[116]

---

[114] David Bentley, *English Criminal Justice in the Nineteenth Century*, Hambledon Press, 1998, page 279.

[115] Dr. Phil Handler, *Penal Reform and Trial Practice in England, 1808–1861*. Paper delivered on 6th February, 2008 at the Institute of Advanced Legal Studies, London.

[116] Interview with Dr. Handler held on 6th February, 2008.

5

Signs of Changes in Styles Before Juries

In the second half of the nineteenth century, thereabouts until the beginning years of the 1880s, the dominant style of advocacy before juries in criminal and civil cases remained melodramatic, declamatory and lachrymose.[1] Aggressive and intimidating cross-examination of witnesses took place, sometimes, unless restrained by judges, descending into bullying.[2] Questions asked often had more to do with a blunderbuss than

---

[1] J. R. Lewis, *The Victorian Bar*, Robert Hale, London, 1982, pp. 119–120, describes how prospective barristers would sometimes attend a course on declamation with John Cooper, who had given up the stage himself to teach young hopefuls. His classes on declamation were attended by a mixture of aspiring barristers and actors. Recollecting the criminal bar in the 1870s and early 1880s, Edward Purcell, *Forty Years at the Criminal Bar*, page 27, wrote of "*many advocates who deliberately took a dramatic approach to advocacy and were prepared to adopt mannerisms, tricks of speech and gestures to heighten the effect of their pleas* and of *the prevailing fondness for noise*".

[2] Lord Chief Justice Cockburn's comments in 1874 on the treatment of witnesses indicate this was particularly bad in England:

> *I have watched closely the administration of justice in France, Germany, Holland, Belgium, Italy, and a little in Spain, as well as the United States, in Canada, and in Ireland, and in no place have I seen witnesses so badgered, brow beaten, and in every way so brutally maltreated as in England. The way in which we treat our witnesses is a national disgrace, and a serious obstacle, instead of aiding the ends of justice. In England the most honourable and conscientious men loathe the witness-box. Men and women of all ranks shrink with terror from subjecting themselves to the*

© The Author(s) 2019
A. Watson, *Speaking in Court*, https://doi.org/10.1007/978-3-030-10395-8_5

with a precise forensic weapon. Closing speeches were frequently long and repetitious. Appeals to emotion, and prejudice, usually reaching their peak in the peroration, were often greater than those to reason. The Diety and the Bible were regularly invoked. Vivid and floral language was employed and poetry liberally put to use to awaken generous sympathies. Special juries, in particular, would be treated to quotations from, and allusions, to English literature, history and the classics. This style of advocacy was parodied in Gilbert and Sullivan's

---

wanton insult and bullying misnamed cross-examination in our English courts. Watch the tremor that passes the frames of many persons as they enter the witness box. I remember to have seen so distinguished a man as Sir Benjamin Brodie shiver as he entered the witness box. I dare say his apprehension amounted to exquisite torture.

Calling for judges to exercise more control over the way cross-examination was conducted, the Lord Chief Justice continued:

Witnesses are just as necessary for the administration of justice as judges or jurymen, and are entitled to be treated with the same consideration, and their affairs and private lives ought to be held as sacred from the gaze of the public as those of the judges or the jurymen. I venture to think that it is the duty of the judge to allow no questions to be put to a witness, unless such are clearly pertinent to the issue before the court, unless such as are clearly pertinent to the issue before the court, except where the credibility of the witness is deliberately challenged by counsel and that the credibility of a witness should not be wantonly challenged on slight grounds. (Irish Law Times, 1874, quoted in Francis L. Wellman, *Wellman's Art of Cross – Examination*, 4th Edition, 1936, pp. 188–189)

Nearly a decade after Lord Justice Cockburn's comments, and demonstrating continuing concern about cross-examination, Sir James Fitzjames Stephen, who at the time had nearly thirty years' experience in the courts firstly as a barrister and then as a judge, wrote, in similar terms, that "*it was the highest importance that judges and counsel bear in mind the abuse to which cross-examination is liable and should do their best not to ask questions conveying reproach on character, except in cases in which there is a reasonable ground to believe that they are necessary*".

Like Cockburn, Stephen was not only exercised about the subject of questions put to witnesses but also the way in which they were asked. "*Cross-examination is not infrequently converted into an occasion for the display of wit, and for obliquely insulting witnesses. It is not uncommon to put a question in a form which is in itself an insult, or to preface a question or receive an answer with an insulting observation. This naturally provokes retorts, and so cross-examination so conducted ceases to fulfil its legitimate purpose and becomes a trial of wit and presence of mind which may amuse the audience, but is inconsistent with the dignity of justice, and unfavourable to the object of ascertaining the truth*". Stephen principally blamed judges for this state of affairs by not stopping examinations unnecessary for any proper purpose and for failing to prevent questions in improper forms. Sir James Fitzjames Stephen, *A History of The Criminal Law of England*, Macmillan and Co., 1883, Chapter XII, pp. 435–436.

Trial by jury – a short comic operetta, first staged in 1875, about a trial of an action in the Court of Exchequer for breach of promise to marry.[3]

Advocates of Their Time

Mentioned is now made of some prominent advocates of the period, whose cases were greatly reported and whose style, because of their successes, influenced those of other barristers. In a small profession which lacked formal training in advocacy, watching and emulating the style and techniques of leading advocates was central to the education of younger lawyers.

A writer of several books on Welsh literary history, and originally employed in the Printed Book Department of the British Museum, John Humphreys Parry (1816–1880) decided to qualify for the Bar. He was called at Middle Temple in 1843. With a pleasing heavy set appearance, a deep Welsh voice and clear talent, especially for cross-examination, he achieved rapid success and soon built up a large practice at the Old Bailey, the Middlesex Sessions and on the Home Circuit, of which he soon became an acknowledged leader.[4] In 1856, he was made a serjeant. Amongst the great cases in which he figured, were for the prosecution in the trial of the Mannings in 1849, charged with the brutal murder of their lodger, the excise man O'Connor (Chap. 4), and for the defence of Franz Muller in 1864, indicted with the murder of Mr. Briggs on the underground railway.[5] In 1873–74 he appeared for the prosecution in

---

[3] George Gilbert, when a practising barrister on the Northern Circuit, later as a magistrate for Middlesex and who also involved himself in much litigation about his work, would have been familiar with courtroom advocacy of his time. It is said he compiled his notes for *Trial by jury* in 1868. Still performed today, it is often produced in the Royal Courts of Justice, and until recently at the former Bow Street Magistrates Court, as part of the annual Covent Garden Festival.

[4] B. Kelly, *Famous Advocates and their Speeches*, London: Sweet and Maxwell, 1921, page 109.

[5] His closing speech for Franz Muller was widely praised as a memorable piece of advocacy (Kelly, *ibid*, Page 109.), especially those parts which dealt with: the influence of the press on public (the jury's) opinion; that counsel's personal opinion was to be ignored; and for circumstantial evidence to be complete.

Regina V Castro, the Tichborne claimant perjury trial. Parry was considered to have a great deal of Charles Dickens's Buzfuz about him,[6] but his theatrical performances won him considerable support and work from attorneys and were copied by others at the bar. His opponent in many cases, William Ballantine, described Parry's noise and thunder as *"passion passing for eloquence"*.[7] Despite this, J Alderson Foote, in his book of reminiscences of decades of practice as a barrister in Victorian England wrote[8]:

> *Parry was an oldish man when I remember him, but to my mind he was the most persuasive advocate that ever addresses a jury. He had not the overwhelming force of Russell, nor the incisive persistence in cross-examination of Hawkins, nor the silver tongue of Coleridge; who were all in their own peculiar style unapproachable. But he had persuasion, which after all, is the end to which other qualities are the means; and I doubt if any other advocate of his day could have shown a higher average of successes.*

William Ballantine (1812–1887) became a barrister of Inner Temple in 1834. Long before he was appointed a serjeant in 1856, he established himself as one of the leading criminal advocates of his day at the Old Bailey, where he remained for his working life, surpassing others in cross-examination and retention of essential facts.[9] For many years he dabbled in the theatre and journalism. Ballantine's clients were numerous and ranged from Prince Louis Napoleon (Napoleon III of France) to the Gaekwar (Prince) of Baroda, in Western India, tried in 1875 with attempting to poison the British Resident. For this case he received £10,000, then an enormous sum. He appeared for the claimant in Tichborne v. Lushington which straddled 1871 and 1872. Attracting crowds and huge press interest, the case hinged on whether the claimant,

---

[6] J. R. Lewis, *The Victorian Bar*, Robert Hale, London, 1982, page 62.

[7] *See*. J. R. Lewis, *ibid*, page 63.

[8] John Alderson Foote *Pie powder from the Law Courts: being dust from the law courts, collected, and recollected on the Western Circuit by a circuit tramp.*, first published by John Murray, London, 1911, re-published by EP Publishing, Yorkshire, Chapter IV page 81.

[9] B. Kelly, *Famous Advocates and their Speeches* London: Sweet and Maxwell, 1921, page 124.

Arthur Orton, was or was not the missing aristocratic heir, Roger Tichborne. Its outcome led to Orton's later trial for perjury. His manner in court tended to be less passionate than some of his more florid rivals such as Parry. Ballantine's voice, however, was notable for its hesitancy and drawling tone, said to be "*half infirmity, half affectation*".[10] It has been claimed that he was the inspiration for Anthony Trollope's Chaffenbrass in *Orley Farm*.[11]

Another prominently successful barrister of the time was Montagu Williams (1835–1892). Prior to being admitted to the bar, Williams, who at Eton had been a fine classics scholar with a particular enthusiasm (later to be heard in the courts) for Horace, had pursued a number of occupations including acting.[12] Before and after becoming a barrister he wrote for the stage, including two farces, *A fair exchange* and *Easy Shaving*. Williams had a ready address and was skilled in marshalling circumstances favourable to his client.[13] He mainly appeared in the criminal courts. His style, perhaps unsurprisingly, was artificial, theatrical and prone to purple passages.[14] In the Turf frauds case of 1877 three Scotland Yard detectives and a solicitor were tried for complicity in the frauds of two notorious criminals, Kurr and Benson, who had already been sentenced for defrauding an old French lady.[15] The two were produced from prison to give evidence against the detectives. Montagu Williams, defending one detective, said this of the criminals:

---

[10] J. R. Lewis, *The Victorian Bar* Robert Hale, London, 1982, page 63. Bernard Kelly, *ibid*, page 124, also noted a *certain hesitation* but also wrote of his *great charm of manner*.

[11] Law Times 82 (1886–8) pp. 198–199.

[12] Details of these and of his very early years are presented in Montagu Williams's memoirs, *Leaves of a Life being the Reminiscences of Montagu Williams QC*, Macmillan and Co., 1893, Chapters I–VI.

[13] B. Kelly, *Famous Advocates and their Speeches*, London: Sweet and Maxwell, 1921, page 127.

[14] Two good examples of his style are given in the Appendix to Williams's *Leaves of a Life*. The first (pp. 335–348.) is his address to the jury on behalf of Percy Lefroy, tried in 1881 for the murder of Frederick Gold on the London to Brighton Railway. According to Williams, this was "*the most sensational trial*" of his career. Lefroy was convicted and hanged. The second (pp. 348–363.) is Williams's jury speech, which he delivered over two days, for George Lamson, a surgeon tried, convicted and executed in 1881 for the murder by poison of his young brother in law. The case was very widely reported in the press.

[15] For an account of this case, in which Williams had defended another prisoner, one Murray, see Montagu Williams, *Leaves of a Life*, Chapter XXXIII, pp. 217–222.

Excellent in vice and exquisite in fraud – the cunning of a cat teeming from the eyes of one; the oily soft serpent-like treachery of deceit trickling down from the mouth of the other.

A few years earlier, in similar vein, Sergeant Vaughan had poured scorn on a witness by saying:

And then we come to Brown. Ah, there the impudent and deceitful fellow stands, just like a crocodile, with tears in his eyes and his hands in his breaches pockets.[16]

Montagu Williams prided himself on being able to assess how receptive jurors were to his advocacy and accordingly what more, if anything, was required. On this subject, in his *Reminiscences*, he wrote[17]:

An advocate who has had large experience (especially if that experience has been in criminal cases), can pretty well, when he has finished speaking, tell which way the jury incline. It was the custom of mine to try and make sure of two or three of the most likely men first, and then to devote my attention to the others. Sometimes one man in particular would present special difficulties. It would be easy to see that he had formed an opinion adverse to my client, and was resolved not to be influenced by what I was saying. There was nothing for it but to patiently hammer away. I found it was half the battle to rouse him from his indifference, and to thoroughly arrest his attention; while, of course, if he once opened his mouth to make an inquiry, and thus gave me an opportunity of addressing myself directly to him, I could usually count upon his allegiance. It was sometimes my experience, too, that, when it came to considering the verdict, one or two strong men would easily carry their fellow – jurors along with them.

In *Reminiscences*, Williams approvingly described Serjeant Ballantine's ability to delight jurors by *firing off a number of small jokes* in his speeches, something he had observed early in his career as a junior to Ballantine in

---

[16] Robert Walter, *Random Recollections of the Midland Circuit* (1869), Chiswick Press, page 13.
[17] Montagu Williams, *Leaves of a Life*, Macmillan and Co., 1893, page 87.

a case on a bill of exchange. Montagu Williams was noted for using humour in court to aid his persuasiveness. He recorded, "*I have noticed, indeed that jurors in a court of law, as also the ushers, are always convulsed with laughter on the smallest possible provocation*".[18]

The ill-fated Edwin James (1812–1882) QC, upon whose rather florid countenance it was said Charles Dickens based his description of the barrister Stryver in a Tale of Two Cities, and for a time Radical MP, was another with words. After his call at Inner Temple in 1835, he gradually built up a considerable practice in the criminal courts. He excelled in forcible address especially in cases where passion or prejudice might be relied on to sway the verdict of a common jury.[19] His most famous defence was that of the refugee Dr. Simon Bernard, tried, in 1858, for conspiring to assassinate Emperor Louis Napoleon III of France ("The Orsini Conspiracy"). Sir Fitzroy Kelly led for the prosecution. Edwin James's speech on behalf of his rather sinister client was a masterpiece of florid and rhetorical advocacy. It was laced with "glittering steel" and "mounted lancers" – the words had little to do with the issue in hand but, jurors passions aroused with fears of a French invasion, were rewarded by Bernard's acquittal, despite an unhelpful summing up by the judge, Lord Campbell, which led to frantic scenes of rejoicing at the Old Bailey and outside. Passionate advocacy by James, on another occasion, led to the judge suggesting, in view of comments made by counsel, that the Archangel Gabriel should be called to the witness box.[20] Three years after defending Dr. Bernard, the popular advocate was disbarred by the Benchers of Inner Temple for dishonourable conduct in financial transactions and was later declared bankrupt. Just before these events occurred it was said the government was contemplating appointing him as Solicitor General. James left London for New York where he put himself to work at the New York Bar, as well as appearing on the stage at the Winter Gardens Theatre.

---

[18] Montague Williams, *Leaves of a Life*, Macmillan and Co., 1893, pp. 50–51.
[19] Bernard Kelly, *Famous Advocates and Their Speeches*, Sweet and Maxwell, 1921, page 119.
[20] J R Lewis, *The Victorian Bar*, Robert Hale, London, 1982, page 120.

Digby Seymour (1822–1895) QC, an Irishman, also stands out for the use of flamboyant language which was successful before juries even in technical cases. As a member of the Historical and Literary Institution of Dublin he had produced an essay on the genius and study of rhetoric. Public speaking was regarded by him as a subject for careful cultivation and constant improvement. He was briefed in a compensation claim concerning some grass-fields near Neasden, where a large number of carriage horses had been allowed to graze. Digby Seymour made a colourful speech, not entirely empty of patriotic sentiment, about:

> *Arab steeds with flowing manes and panting flanks, careering over these fields as though they had been in the desert.*

His opponent, however, was a great expert in compensation cases like this and reminded the jury that they had to consider:

(a) the value of the land
(b) the number of years' purchase that should be given on it
(c) special principles of discount which applied, and so forth.

Out of his depth, a horrified Digby Seymour asked a junior counsel, who he was leading, what to say. His junior answered "*Don't worry about that rot.......just give them some more of those Arab steeds with their panting flanks*". This he did and won the highest compensation that had ever been awarded for land in the locality.[21]

Digby-Seymour's capacity for emotive denunciation was shown in his address to the jury in the Fenian Trial in Manchester, November 1st 1867.[22] Although instructed as one of the counsel for three Fenians, members of the Irish Republican Brotherhood, intent on ending British rule in Ireland, charged with murder of a police officer, during a successful attack on a police van to liberate two Fenian leaders being conveyed from court, Digby-Seymour was at great pains to disassociate himself with the Fenian cause:

---

[21] Arab Steeds. Viscount Alverstone's *Recollections of Bar and Bench* (1914), cited by Richard Hamilton, All Jangle and Riot, Professional Books, 1986, page 270.
[22] R v Allen, Larkin, O'Brien, Maguire and Condon 1867.

Of all the curses that ever fell on my unhappy country, Fenianism is the blackest and the worst. Famine may desolate and destroy; a pestilence may mow down its hundreds or its thousands, returning spring will renew the crops of the earth, and a refreshing atmosphere will subdue the pestilence. But Fenianism is a blighting curse, a cancer, fastening itself to the fairest spots of an otherwise fair island, and looking for its mischief and exerting its influence upon the most vital parts of my native country.

A little later he continued:

There is not a politician in my native land who has not denounced it; not a capitalist who is not afraid of it, nor an alter throughout the country which has not cursed it! The clergy have spoken of it as, in times of old, the Levitical priesthood and the priesthood of the East spoke: 'Go forth into the wilderness thou leprosy. Unclean! Unclean!...........'[23]

Another highly considered member of the bar was Henry Hawkins who, like Edwin James, had made his name as a criminal advocate in securing acquittals in the Orsini Conspiracy (1858) and also in the prosecutions that followed the collapse, in 1866, of the Overand Gurney discount house.[24] Like Montagu Williams, he had an interest in the stage. This assisted him to develop a graphic power of characterization which was frequently employed before juries in richly dramatic speeches. Lacking a classical education, and thus unable to make allusions to antiquity and the great oratory and literature of the past, he compensated by treating jurors with confidences, assuming them to be worldly men like himself, convincing them he was no different from them and making many references to horse-racing, then the leading gambling sport. Jokes were told by him to good effect. He had an extraordinary ability, by a wink or a gesture, to plunge courts, judge, jury, counsel and audience, into uproarious laughter, putting the jury into good humour and distracting them from damaging pieces of evidence.[25] Unlike some others,

---

[23] Reproduced by Kelly, *Famous Advocates and their Speeches*, London: Sweet and Maxwell, London, 1921, pp. 132–133.
[24] J. R. Lewis, *The Victorian Bar*, Robert Hale, London, 1982, pp. 70–71.
[25] J. R. Lewis, *ibid*, page 15.

who relied on a mixture of vanity, flair and memory, he was thorough in his preparation and worked hard, although on those occasions when he did not know his brief he appeared to manage competently.[26] Hawkins had a reputation as a rough cross-examiner. This was borne out in the case of *Tichborne v. Lushington* in 1871–72 where he behaved with such aggression towards the Claimant's witnesses that some of them refused to attend the later criminal trial for fear of facing him again. Repeatedly in Tichborne v. Lushington Hawkins used the weapon of selecting one small item from a witness's evidence and on which to concentrate his energies, examining it in minute, and often embarrassing detail. One of the issues in the case was whether the real Roger Tichborne had tattoo marks on his arm like those of the claimant. A man called Boyle claimed to have seen such marks when Tichborne pulled up his sleeve to rub his arm. Hawkins put these questions:

Hawkins: "Do you know why he rubbed his arm?"
Boyle: "I suppose it itched. I do not know".
Hawkins: "But what you think when you saw him rubbing his arm?"
Boyle: "I thought he had got a flea".
Hawkins: "A flea! Did you see it?"
Boyle: "No, of course not ".
Hawkins: "Whereabouts was it? Just show me (*The witness pointed to his upper arm*). What time was this?"
Boyle: "Ten past eleven".
Hawkins: "On the second occasion did you think it was a flea again?"
Boyle: "I suppose so...."
Hawkins: "What time was it? About the same time?"
Boyle: "Yes".
Hawkins: "Ten past eleven?"
Boyle: "YES".
Hawkins: "Then all I can say is, he must have been a very punctual old flea".[27]

---

[26] An aspect of Hawkins's abilities marvelled upon by Sir Edward Clarke in his unfinished short treatise on advocacy, published some years after his death as an Appendix to E. W. Fordham, Notable Cross-examinations, Constable, 1951.

[27] Reproduced by Richard Du Cann, *The Art of the Advocate*, Pelican Books, 1980, page 126.

It was said that Hawkins often rose to his feet with no firm ideas of the way his cross-examination should proceed; he had to rely on experience and instinct which was sometimes spectacularly correct.[28]

Hawkins, along with many other of his contemporaries, acknowledged that little children in court could rend the hearts of jurors in criminal and civil cases and indeed encouraged their presence.[29] In his *Reminiscences*[30] Hawkins describes how he defended a man who had suddenly, and without any apparent reason, killed his wife. Securing his acquittal was helped by the evidence of a Vicar, who explained he had regularly attended church for thirty five years. In his view even greater assistance had been rendered by the presence in court of the prisoner's intensely sobbing children. Henry Hawkins conceded that their excessive grief might not have been all it appeared to be after hearing that just a few days before the trial they were playing on an ash-heap in the village where they lived, swinging around a dead cat with a string about its neck, and singing:

This is the way poor Daddy will go!
This is the way poor Daddy will go!

Away from juries, Hawkins had little reputation in arguing law before the appellate courts. After seventeen years as a QC, Hawkins was elevated to the Bench in 1876.

Willie Mathews was another barrister with a sense of drama. He had been the pupil of Montagu Williams. A child of the stage, the son of the playwright Charles Williams, he had a flow of language and a passionate earnestness that juries found irresistible, despite an unusual habit, which was possibly cultivated to hold the attention of listeners, of beginning a sentence with an accusative case and ending on a preposition. J.A Foote,

---

[28] See Henry Hawkins, *Reminiscences of Henry Hawkins, Baron Brompton, Edited by Richard Harris, K C,* E. Arnold, 1904, republished by Kessinger Publishing, USA 2004, especially Chapter XIV: 'The case of Mr. Faker and the Welsh Will', in which, through testing his evidence in cross examination, Hawkins exposed a well-known dissenting clergyman, thus destroying the plaintiff's case, called as a witness by his opponent Edwin James.

[29] This was, of course, appreciated at least since the days of ancient Rome. See Excursus (Classical Rhetoric) available on the Internet: Historyadvocacy.wordpress.com.

[30] Chapter 5. J. Murray, 1911.

KC., who knew Mathews on the Western Circuit, in his book "*Pie Powder*" speaks of Mathews's "*fervid eloquence which became the admiration and despair of his rivals and contemporaries*" and adds, "*He was the only advocate I have ever known who could make a juryman shed tears, and on one occasion at least I have seen him perform the same operation in cold blood upon a reluctant judge*".[31] In his memoirs, Travers Humphreys, an eminent QC and later High Court judge, recounts how he had also seen a judge and jury being reduced to tears by Mathews.[32]

Signs of Change

Even though histrionics continued to thrive amongst these leaders of the bar and were copied by some juniors, signs of change began to appear. Men like Hardinge Giffard, who became Lord Halsbury and Lord Chancellor for a total of eighteen years,[33] John Holker, later to be appointed Attorney General, Charles Russell, a future Lord Chief Justice, and Edward Clarke began to significantly change the style of advocacy. Their approach, which was increasingly emulated by others at the Bar, was "*quieter, more learned and less inclined towards violent appeals to emotions and florid language and quoting widely from popular verse and literature*".[34] Less concerned with relying on the tricks of the Victorian stage, they also were developing a more dignified and controlled manner in their conduct towards each other and to witnesses. These barristers tended to select the best arguments from their client's case and to drive these home forcefully to jurors, rather than saturate them with rhetorical elaboration of all conceivable points. They also avoided tiring juries with needless repetition.

Hardinge Giffard (1823–1921), who narrowly escaped a pistol bullet fired by a deranged clergyman in the Old Bailey in 1854, was recognized

---

[31] *Pie Powder*, J. Murray, 1911, Page 32. On the following page, Foote wrote about hearing Mathews addressing a common jury in a "*torrent of burning eloquence, probably incomprehensible to most of them, but nonetheless impressive*".

[32] Travers Humphreys, Criminal Days, Hodder and Stoughton, 1946, pp. 68–69.

[33] See John Hostettler, *Lord Halsbury*, Barry Rose, 1998.

[34] J. R. Lewis, *The Victorian Bar*, Robert Hale, London, page 120.

for his judgement, power of expression, freedom from speaking non-sense, not talking for talking's sake and for his ability to grasp all the facts of complicated cases.[35] He accepted a wide variety of briefs and in London divided his time between the Chancery bar and the Old Bailey. His court-room demeanour was often understated, even stilted.[36]

Recalling his association with Hardinge Giffard, Sir Edward Clarke, in 1916, wrote:

It is now fifty years since I made his acquaintance at the Old Bailey where he had a most lucrative practice. It was then a rough place and some of the older men had habits of cruel and offensive cross – examination and violent and unscrupulous advocacy, which Giffard's influence and example did much to banish from our criminal courts. He was not a great defender of prisoners: Ballantine and Parry.......had the most important defences but.....Giffard was constantly appearing in important prosecutions. To listen carefully to the whole of a case when Giffard prosecuted with Poland for his junior and Russel Gurney was the presiding judge, was the best lesson a young barrister intending to practice in the criminal courts could possibly have.[37]

---

[35] Such qualities were praised by the eminent solicitor William Freshfield in a letter he wrote to Giffard in 1883, and cited in Lewis J. R. *The Victorian Bar*, page 163. He was said to be blessed with great powers of memory to such an extent that he could read a brief without making a single note and conducted one heavy case without taking the ribbon off the papers in court; they were later found to have only one thing written on the outside: a list of the trains back to London. Richard Hamilton, *All Jangle and Riot*, Professional Books, 1986, page 177. Another, although somewhat later, advocate, who was also renowned for a phenomenal memory was Sergeant A. M. Sullivan, the last Sergeant at the Irish Bar who died in 1959. It was said of him that he never needed to refer to papers in court. Brian Gibbens, *Elements of Modern Advocacy*, New Law Cassettes, Butterworths, London, 1979. Minimising the need to read papers, enabling barristers to maximize time looking at witnesses, judges and juries, was often seen as a valuable persuasive technique in advocacy, pro-jecting confidence and sincerity of belief in a client's case. Indeed in his short treatise on advocacy Sir Edward Clarke, *infra*, remembers being told by Harry Hawkins, *earlier*, to *never examine or cross-examine from your brief. Know your brief and examine from your head.* He recalled this *as one of the most useful pieces of advice I ever received.*

[36] R. F. Heuston, *Lives of the Lord Chancellors 1885–1940*, Oxford, 1964, 12. Hardinge Giffard, although generally eschewing them, did vividly employ theatrical emotion and drama, presumably for entirely tactical reasons, in his six hour speech before lay magistrates at Market Drayton in 1867. He was instructed to halt the prosecution of Edward Eyre, the former governor of Jamaica, for murder, arising from his bloody suppression of the Morant Bay uprising in 1865. At one stage, Giffard broke down in tears and called on God before resuming his appeal to the biases of rural magistrates. Eyre was not committed. (See Korstal, R. W. *A Jurisprudence of Power; Victorian Empire and the Rule of Law.* Oxford University Press, 2005, pp. 302–310.)

[37] Reproduced by J R Lewis, *The Victorian Bar*, Robert Hale, London, 1982, pp. 163–164.

John Holker (1828–1882) did not attend university and was articled to a Westmoreland solicitor before being called to the Bar at Gray's Inn, at the then comparatively late age of 26, in 1854. He began to specialize in patent cases and then commercial law more generally. The Tichborne cases, in which he was not involved, did much to promote his career: As they occupied many of the leaders of the bar, solicitors had to look elsewhere for forensic ability. This resulted in Holker being thrust to the fore. There he thrived, with a great knowledge of business and of how businessmen thought, suppressing all oratory, claiming little or no knowledge of law and always putting the most common place view of a case to a jury. "*A great getter of verdicts, the impression he made on a jury was that his client had a first – rate case and was to be pitied for having such a second rate advocate*".[38] A contemporary wrote of him; "*this tall plain Lancashire man never seemed to labour a case nor to distinguish himself by ingenuity or eloquence, but through whom the justice of his case appeared to shine through a somewhat dull but altogether honest medium*". He had *the art of never seeming to be cleverer than the people he was addressing.*[39] J. A. Foote, who had also encountered him, wrote, *he was massive and deliberate, with a hesitating delivery that amounted at times to a stammer, but he could address a jury as if he was one of themselves, and won their confidence by his apparent sincerity rather than by a parade of oratorical power.*[40] The appearance of great candour was his most valuable asset in advocacy. In court it was said he would accept suggestions from juniors and solicitors clerks,[41] marking him out from many barristers of the old school, who had much of the prima donna about them. Sir John Holker became Solicitor-General under Disraeli's administration in 1874 and was briefly Attorney General. After the fall of the Conservative government, he was appointed a Lord Justice of Appeal.

Charles Russell (1832–1900), born at Newry in Ireland, was admitted as a solicitor in 1854 and soon noted for vigorous advocacy in the county

---

[38] AW Cockburn QC. An Address on Advocacy to the Christ Church Law Club, May 15th 1952. Published by the University of Southampton.

[39] Mr. Balfour Browne K.C. Quoted by Francis Cowper, *Holker of Gray's Inn, Graya* 14, Easter 1934, page 71.

[40] J. A. Foote, *Pie powder from the Law courts*, John Murray, 1911, page 177.

[41] Francis Cowper, *Holker of Gray's Inn*, Graya 14, Easter 1934, page 72.

courts. He was called to the English Bar at Lincoln's Inn in 1859 and rapidly became established in the North of England. His chief rival on the Northern Circuit was John Holker. In his early days, perhaps keeping with the spirit of the times, flashes of temper were seen and many angry exchanges with opposing counsel, judges and jurors occurred. This was to change and as the years passed he won great admiration for his advocacy. Russell's powers of cross-examination were acclaimed as those of genius,[42] whilst in the art of forcibly stating a case to a jury he was extraordinary, said to be beyond every advocate in living memory.[43] In the opinion of John Alderson Foote, who heard him conduct cases, Russell was an *elemental force*. In similar vein Richard Travers Humphreys, who had also observed him, wrote:

> *What one remembered after witnessing one of his great performances was not the admission extorted from a witness, the astuteness of the questions put in cross-examination, or even the eloquence of speech to the jury, but the atmosphere which the man created. Whoever was the judge, from the moment Russell got going he dominated the court.*[44]

Unlike many of his contemporaries, he did not attach much importance to what he jokingly called "*rhetorical fireworks*", believing that juries were becoming increasingly suspicious of florid oratory and theatricality and preferred to base their decisions on what they believed to be solid facts.[45] Again, distinguishing himself from many others, Russell always

---

[42] Charles Russell's biographer, R. Barry O' Brien *wrote: It was a fine sight to see him rise to cross-examine. His very appearance must have been a shock to the witness, – the manly, defiant bearing, the noble brow, the haughty look, the remorseless mouth, those deep set eyes, widely opened, and that searching glance which pierces the very soul. "Russell", said a member of the Northern Circuit, "produced the same effect on a witness that a cobra produced on a rabbit".* R. Barry O'Brien, *O'Brien's Life of Lord Russell*, Smith, Elder, 1901, page 101. John Singer Sargent's large portrait of Charles Arthur Russell, Baron Russell of Killowen, painted in 1899, hangs in Lincoln's Inn.

[43] B. Kelly, *Famous Advocates and their Speeches*, London: Sweet and Maxwell, 1921, page 135.

[44] *Criminal days*, Hodder and Stoughton, London, 1945, page 91.

[45] R. Barry O' Brien, his biographer, said to Russell, "*Your methods are altogether different, you do not as a rule manoeuvre, you go straight at the witness.* Russell replied: *With an English jury it is different. They are busy and they want to go away quickly. Mere finesse they do not appreciate; go straight at the witness and at the point; throw your cards on the table. It is a simple method and I think it is a good method*". *O'Brien's Life of Russell*, Smith, Elder, 1901, pp. 100–101.

meticulously prepared his cases so that when he was in court he could watch the jury and the judge in everything they did, however trivial it might seem. He was always ready and alert and would not hesitate to stand up to any judge if he thought the rights of the advocate were being invaded.[46] Russell was made a Queen's Counsel in 1872. Such leaders of the Bar as Serjeants Ballantine and Parry and Henry Hawkins QC found in him a very formidable rival. Russell was engaged in many well known cases, but his most famous were the successful defence of the Irish Nationalist leader Charles Stewart Parnell, before the Parnell Commission in 1888, and the defence of Florence Maybrick at the Liverpool Assizes in 1889 who was convicted of murdering her husband by poisoning him with arsenic.[47] Sir John Russell was Attorney General in the Liberal Governments of 1885 and 1892 and was appointed Lord Chief Justice in 1894, the first Catholic to hold that office for centuries.

The late Victorian period saw a number of contests in court between Sir Charles Russell and Sir Edward Clarke. Edward Clarke (1841–1933) was not from a privileged background, beginning his working life as a shop assistant in a silversmiths run by his father. Although lacking money, influential friends, connexions with the law and social standing, he had a driving ambition to excel first by becoming a barrister and then by entering politics. After periods as a writer at East India House and a law reporter, he raised sufficient funds to enter Lincoln's Inn as a student and to be called to the bar in 1864, aged 23. Small criminal cases came his way. In time they were followed by weightier matters. Solicitors noticed his skill in persuasively presenting medical evidence and cross-examining doctors – both the result of vast preparation before trials.[48] The case which established him was that of Harriet Staunton in 1877, when Clarke was 36. He was briefed to defend Patrick Staunton on a charge of murder. The kernel of the Crown's case was that a woman of limited mental powers had been neglected and starved to death over months by her cal-

---

[46] Lord Norman Birkett, *Six Great Advocates*, Penguin, 1961, page 71.

[47] See Lord Norman Birkett, *ibid*, pp. 71–80. Also, for a highly readable account of the trial, F. E. Smith, *Famous Trials*, Hutchinson and Co, Ltd., 1930, *Mrs Maybrick*, pp. 399–412.

[48] Edgar Lustgarten, *R v The Stauntons*, part of the Old Bailey Series, broadcast in 1970 on Radio 4.; tape kindly lent by Mr. Leslie Blake, Senior Lecturer, Department of Law, University of Surrey.

lous husband, Patrick, and his relatives, to obtain her small inheritance. Public outrage and interest in the trial was intense. Despite much undermining by Clarke of medical evidence on behalf of the Crown, all four defendants were convicted and sentenced to death after a summing up by Mr. Justice Hawkins (Henry Hawkins, *earlier*) pointedly against the defendants.[49] Clarke's closing speech had a very great effect on the country and propelled him up to advocacy's top rank. His early desire for political fame was abandoned. During his remaining thirty seven years at the bar he appeared in many famous and sensational cases. Against Sir Charles Russell in 1886, he obtained a verdict of not guilty for Adelaide Bartlett who was charged with murdering her husband with chloroform. In 1890 he appeared in the Parnell Divorce suit. The following year Sir Charles Clarke represented the plaintiff in the Baccarat case in which the Prince of Wales gave evidence. He fought for Oscar Wilde in his three trials at the Old Bailey in 1895. And in 1896 he appeared for Dr. Jameson, who was prosecuted in London after the Jamieson Raid in South Africa.

Clarke was a fine speaker and had taken lessons in voice production and public speaking. He knew the value of pause and of a change in tempo.[50] Unlike others of the period, "*he had inherited few of the declamatory, lachrymose, resonant talents of the early Victorian Bar*".[51] Clarke relied on persuasion in his speechmaking, an appeal to logic that sprang from a deep sincerity, rather than almost wild appeals to emotion. Unlike many barristers, he seldom employed ridicule.[52] Juries found for him because they believed he believed. The extract below is part of a peroration from a closing speech at the Old Bailey in 1872 when he defended Police Chief Inspector of Police, also by the name of Clarke, charged with conspiracy to defeat justice. For the time, it shows a restrained use of emotion:

Gentlemen you, I know, will do your duty; but while it is part of your duty clearly and peremptorily to pronounce guilt where guilt is well established, it is

---

[49] Following a public outcry, and a petition signed by over seven hundred doctors that the cause of Harriet Staunton's death was not starvation but tuberculosis, they were reprieved.

[50] Travers Humphreys, *Criminal Days*, Hodder and Stoughton, page 92.

[51] J. R. Lewis, *The Victorian Bar*, Robert Hale, London, page 141.

[52] DuCann, Edward, *The Art of the Advocate*, Penguin Books, 1993, page 144.

the highest and best privilege that you to scout from the judgment seat the per-
jured witness, and to send out the innocent man with an unchallengeable ver-
dict of Not Guilty to hold up before his fellows. Judge in this case as you would
be judged. Use diligence, discretion, and discrimination in dealing with the
verdict; and I do hope confidently – I trust it is not the mere advocates feeling
that speaks in my words at this moment – that Clarke may go out from this
court, not discharged because a jury could not agree; not with some bastard
verdict of not proven to hang round his neck for the rest of his life, the irremov-
able stigma of suspicion of crime; but with the straightforward, honest Not
Guilty that sends him back to his friends an honoured man; that sends him
back, for the rest of his life, to enjoy the love, obedience, honour, troops of
friends, and all that should accompany old age; to leave his children when he
goes an heirloom richer than wealth can purchase, grander than power can cre-
ate – the splendid heritage of an unsullied name.[53]

Edward Clarke's unfinished short treatise on advocacy, only published
some years after his death,[54] shows he employed in both cross-examination
and speeches, the two forming what he called *"a combined address to the jury"*,
subtle psychology and close attention to those details his preparation and
management of the case in court led him to believe would concern jurors:

The cross-examination of the chief witness for the plaintiff is always of great
importance. It is the first opportunity which counsel for the defence has of indi-
cating, instead of presenting, because the most skillful and effective cross-
examination is that which interests the jury and sets them thinking what the
answer to the plaintiff's case, or the case for the prosecution, can possibly be, and
by the selection of and arrangement of the facts referred to, suggests the defen-
dant's case instead of stating it.

Presently comes the speech in which the defence is formulated; and if, listen-
ing to that speech, a juryman says to himself, "Why that is just what occurred
to me when the witness was in the Box," the verdict, so far as he is concerned,
is safe. The conclusion which his own intelligence has suggested must be right.[55]

---

[53] Quoted by Richard Du Cann, *The Art of the Advocate, ibid*, page 218.

[54] In the form of an Appendix to E.W. Fordham, *Notable Cross-examinations*, Constable and Company, 1951.

[55] Elsewhere in his treatise, Clarke criticizes Sergeant Parry, *earlier*, for often spoiling shrewd and powerful cross-examinations by *violence and harshness* to witnesses. John Duke Coleridge

In the assessment of Lord Birkett:

> *In an age when advocacy was held in great esteem, nobody ever equalled Clarke in marvellous persuasive power. Some of his learned brethren excelled him in some spheres. He lacked, for example, the overwhelming elemental force of Charles Russell and could not rival his incisive, persistent, penetrating power of cross – examination. Others perhaps had a greater sense of the dramatic or were more truly versatile; but Edward Clarke had the supreme gift – the advocate's pearl of great price – the gift of persuasion. This, when all is said and done, is the gift to which all other qualities of the advocate are subordinate: and it was by this gift that Clarke won his enduring fame.*[56]

Norman Birkett (1883–1962), was called to bar in 1913. He never saw Edward Clarke in action, but recalls that older barristers, whenever conversation turned at the Inns of Court or in the Bar Messes on circuit to great advocates, spoke of him with admiration and wonder. It is, therefore, very likely that his highly successful advocacy was an influence on them in the later Victorian period and after.[57]

It is perhaps not too fanciful to suggest that the more restrained advocacy before juries that was emerging may have been influenced by the style of an earlier barrister James Scarlett (1769–1844), Lord Abinger (1835), who was appointed Lord Chief Baron of the Exchequer in 1834. Invariably mastering each brief sent to him, not

---

(1820–1894), eventually Lord Chief Justice of England, was praised for his ingenious and painstaking cross-examination, in which the more closely a witness was entangled the more suave and gentle Coleridge's manner became. Clarke, however, described, as *"studiously unfair"*, Coleridge's *habit* of repeating a witness's answer or quoting it in a subsequent question but not exactly as it had been said, though insufficiently altered to attract comment from opposing counsel or judges, as a means of quietly getting the witness to give his or her case away.

[56] *Six Great Advocates*, Penguin, 1961, page 38.

[57] Sir Malcolm Hilbery, born in the same year as Lord Birkett, in a speech, entitled *Duty and Art in Advocacy*, at Gray's Inn, delivered in 1938 when he was a High Court judge, (*Graya* No XX, Easter), recounted how, as a young boy, he had seen, Sir Edward Clarke in the Kings Bench: *"It has remained a vivid memory and a model to this day"*. Travelling back in generations, and showing how young advocates may to some extent be influenced by older and outstandingly successful ones, Edward Clarke himself professed, in his short treatise on advocacy, Fordham, *ibid*, admiration for William Ballantine, Henry Hawkins and John Duke Coleridge.

taking more that he could really attend to,[58] having a deep knowledge of the law and consummate advocacy soon made him one of the leaders of the bar. A particular talent was getting witnesses to tell their stories as if for the first time. In marked contrast to many of his contemporaries, Scarlett's highly winning method of addressing juries did not involve rhetorical expedients but choosing the very best argument on his client's behalf and putting it with all his ability in a well modulated musical voice, paying strict attention to facts and good diction. His manner was relaxed and his tone conversational. Of Scarlett's achievements with juries a number of stories are told, some of which contrast him with Henry Brougham. One has it that at the end of a Yorkshire Assizes a lawyer found himself in the company of a juryman. The lawyer asked the juror what he had thought of leading counsel. "'*Well*' said the juryman 'that Lawyer Brougham be a wonderful man; he can talk, he can: but I don't think nowt of Lawyer Scarlett'. Indeed replied the lawyer, but you have given him all the verdicts. 'Oh, there's nothing in that said the juror, he be so lucky, you see, he be always on the right side'".[59]

In later Victorian and in Edwardian times Sir James Scarlett's accomplished advocacy was seen as instructive in a number of practical books for barristers beginning their careers. For example in 1894, on cross-

---

[58] It was said of James Scarlett, in contrast to many of his colleagues, that

> One of his great merits was that when he was engaged in a cause his services might always be relied on. He disdained to adopt the vicious practice of some barristers, then far too common, of wandering from court to court and taking contemporaneous briefs in all, to the damage of those whose briefs they had accepted.

Unattributed quote in Richard DuCann, *The Art of the Advocate*, Penguin Books, 1993, pp. 40–42. The habit, to the detriment of the quality of their advocacy, of leading silks to accept, when they were in court, as many small briefs as their clerks could collect is also mentioned by Sir Edward Clarke in his short unfinished treatise on advocacy, Appendix to E.W. Fordham, *Notable Cross-examinations*, Constable and Company, 1951.

[59] A. W. B. Sampson, *Biographical Dictionary of the Common Law*, Butterworths, 1984. For Scarlett's own assessment of his advocacy, in a biography written by his son, see Peter Campbell Scarlett, *A Memoir of the Right Honourable James, First Lord Abinger*, J. Murray, 1877, Chapter 18.

examination, Henry Hardwicke, (drawing on Edward W. Cox, *The Advocate: His Training, Practice and Duties*, published in 1852[60]) wrote:

> *In cross – examination he outstrips all that have ever appeared at the British Bar; not, perhaps, in one single quality – for while some have excelled him in strength and force, others have left him behind them in craft and wit. His superiority, however, as an accomplished cross-examiner – as one combining the best qualities for the office, and making the best use of them at the best time and to the best effect – must on every hand be admitted. His brow is never clothed with terror, and his hand never aims to grasp the thunderbolt; but with the gentlemanly ease, and the polished courtesy, and the Christian urbanity and affection, with which he proceeds to the task, do infinitely more mischief to the testimony of witnesses who are striving to deceive, or upon whom he finds it expedient to fasten a suspicion. He has often thrown the most careful and cunning off their guard, by the very behaviour from which they inferred their security. Seldom has he discouraged a witness by harshness and never by insult: and to put men upon the defensive by a hostile attitude, he has always considered unwise and unsafe. Hence he takes those he has to examine, as it were, by the hand: makes them his friends, enters familiar conversation with them, encourages them to tell him what will best answer his purpose, and thus secures a victory without appearing to commence a conflict.*[61]

On closing speeches before juries, Hardwicke said:

> *The advocate should address the jury just as he would address a friend in the street upon a matter of business. When he meets a friend he talks to him familiarly and uses plain language and homely illustrations, and does not leave him unless he makes himself understood. This is the way in which Lord Abinger dealt with his juries, and was the chief reason he almost invariably defeated the brightest ornaments of the English bar who were more eloquent and more learned than himself, but who did not have the faculty of communicating their knowledge in this way.*[62]

---

[60] J. Crockford, London.

[61] *The Art of Winning Cases, or Modern Advocacy: A Practical Treatise on Preparation for Trial and the Conduct of Cases in Court*, New York, Albany Banks and Bros, 1894, passage quoted in *The Examination of Witnesses in Court*, by F J Wrottesley, Sweet and Maxwell 1910, pp. 147–148.

[62] Hardwicke, *The Art of Winning Cases*, New York, Albany Banks and Bros, page 281.

6

Decline of Jury Trials in the Civil and Criminal Courts and Other Key Developments

Opportunities for passionate appeals to emotion, floral passages and theatrical gestures much reduced as trial by jury in civil actions declined. Juries were little used in the new county courts which were set up in all areas by the County Court Act 1846.[1] They were intended, in the words of the County Court Act 1846, which introduced them, *for the more easy recovery of small debts and demands, in England*. Solicitors, given full rights of audience in these courts, acted for the majority of persons represented there. Indeed from an early date, solicitors became established who specialized in advocacy before each county court.[2] Parties to disputes could give evidence and represent themselves. In 1867, 542,569 causes were determined in the county courts; only 856 of these were tried by a jury.[3] Foreshadowing the *bar wars* between barristers and solicitors in the later twentieth century about rights of audience in court, the Bar bitterly resented what they saw as a major intrusion by

---

[1] See A. H. Manchester, *A Modern Legal History of England and Wales 1750–1950*, Butterworths, 1980, pp. 118–120.

[2] H. Kirk, *Portrait of a Profession. A History of the Solicitor's Profession, 1100 to the Present Day*, London, Oyez Publishing 1976, Chapter 8, page 157.

[3] A. H. Manchester, *ibid*, page 95.

© The Author(s) 2019
A. Watson, *Speaking in Court*, https://doi.org/10.1007/978-3-030-10395-8_6

solicitors into their domain of advocacy.[4] In the legal press, favourably disposed to the interests of barristers, articles casting aspersions on the quality of solicitor advocates persistently appeared. One asked *"whether their loud shop – boy manner, sharp and incisive as it may be, would not be tolerated at the Bar? As attorneys they are eminent, as barristers they would collapse"*.[5] But by and large the bench and solicitors got on very well and the judges expressed their opinion that the solicitors managed highly competently.[6] The County Courts were a success. In their first seven years no fewer than 3,575,205 cases were entered there[7] and it was clear they were meeting a real need. Accordingly their financial jurisdiction was gradually increased: in 1850 to £50; and in 1903 to £100. Further, Parliament significantly added to the importance of county courts by giving them jurisdiction in bankruptcy in 1869[8]; in 1880 cases under the Employers' Liability Act,[9] which in 1897 became the Workmen's Compensation Act,[10] in its time a fruitful source of litigation; and in 1890 the winding up of companies with capital not more than £10,000.[11]

In 1854 the Common Law Procedure Act permitted issues of fact in the higher courts to be tried by judges alone, albeit with the consent of

---

[4] For example in *Advocacy in The County Courts, A Letter to Sir Alexander Cockburn, MP., Her Majesty's Attorney-General, by A Barrister of The Inner Temple*, London: S. Sweet, 1851, the anonymous author called for the exclusion of solicitors from the County Court, advocacy "*being no part of an attorney's business. With him lies the collecting of evidence and preparing all the preliminary and practical details in the action and the selection of the barrister who shall advise him on any questions of legal intricacy, and finally conduct the cause in court. The great principles of judicial practice, the deep research and knowledge of cases, the forms through which truth and argument are made to prevail, all lie beyond his province and rest peculiarly with the counsel, whose business it is to study and practically learn the most effective mode of marshalling the evidence collected, and the best course through which matters of fact may be presented to a jury, or points of law argued before a judge*". (pp. 9–10.) Further (page 14), the author severely criticized attorneys who had begun to specialize in advocacy in the county courts. They are described as "*an inferior class of attorneys, who find it worth their while to attend and to act, not only on their own account, but as agents to other members of the profession, who have not time to give their attention to county court practice, but who are willing to share the fees allowed under the Act*".

[5] Law Magazine and Review, vol4 (NS), page 89.

[6] H. Kirk, *Portrait of a Profession*, Oyez, London, page 158.

[7] Figure presented by H. Kirk, *Portrait of a Profession*, Oyez, London, 1967, page 158.

[8] The Bankruptcy Act 1869, Section 4

[9] The Employers Liability Act 1880, Section 6.

[10] See Workmen's Compensation Act 1897, Schedules 1 and 2 which confirm the jurisdiction of the County Court.

[11] Companies Winding Up Act, 1890, Section One.

the parties. Section One of the Act said that the "verdict" of the judge was to have the same effect as the verdict of the jury. Some judges were initially bewildered by the dual role placed upon them.[12] Judges under the new procedure adopted a discursive form of judgement in which findings of fact intermingle with comment, combining in one piece the trial judge's notes on the evidence, directions on the law, the court's decision and often the arguments of counsel.[13] Whilst the chief focus was on law and facts, the discursive nature of judgements permitted judges scope, where they were thought apt, for some references to the classics, Latin, works of English Literature and history, although few could possibly have approached the County Court Judge, on whom the lawyer and humourist Theo Mathew (1866–1939) based one of his Forensic Fables, who "*so often cited apposite extracts from the works of Cicero, Ben Jonson, Rabelais, Tennyson, and other authors both ancient and modern that in order to get them down correctly each of the reporters had been compelled to purchase a copy of the book of quotations in which the sound lawyer discovered them*".[14]

Prior to the passing of the Judicature Acts (1873–1881) trial by jury took place in well over 90 *per cent* of cases in the superior courts[15]; the period afterwards saw growing disuse of jury trial.[16] Unlike jurors, judges

---

[12] J. A. Foote, *Pie Powder*, John Murray, London, 1911, pp. 84–85 tells an amusing story of a judge who was unsure whether he should find the facts as he himself thought or as he thought a common jury would have found.

[13] J.H. Baker, *An Introduction to English Legal History*, Fourth Edition, Butterworths, 2002, page 93.

[14] *The Sound Lawyer Who Made A Good Resolution*, published in 1926 and reprinted in *Forensic Fables* (Complete Edition) 1999, Wildy and Sons Ltd., London, page 97.

[15] R. M. Jackson, *Incidence of Jury Trial During the Past Century* (1937–38) 1 Modern Law Review 132.

[16] The decline was steep. According to the *Law Journal*, cited by J. R. Lewis, *The Victorian Bar*, 1982, Robert Hale on page 128, some 94 per cent of defended cases in the 1879 Queen's Bench were before juries; by 1892 the proportion had fallen to 54 per cent. It has not been possible to locate this edition of the *Law Journal* in either the libraries of the Inns of Court or the Institute of Advanced Legal Studies London. Connor Hanley, *The Decline of the Civil Jury in Nineteenth Century England*, Journal of Legal History, Vol. 26. Number 1, April 2005, pp. 253–278, considers the seeds of the decline of jury trials in the superior courts were sown during the two decades that preceded the Common Law Procedure Act 1854. In his view three factors combined to undermine use of the civil jury: increased recognition of the integrity of the judiciary by lawyers; efforts made by lawyers to professionalise the practice of law; and the successful introduction of juryless trials by the County Courts Act, 1846.

sitting alone in the High Court or County Court, despite Lord Bramwell's dictum that "*one third of every judge is a common juror*"[17] had little taste for sensational appeals, flowery language and theatricality, but did have a high appreciation of law, fact and logical structure. Accordingly advocacy before them adjusted in style and shortened in length. Knowing when to press an argument, when not to and carefully gauging, by various subtle means, how submissions were being received by judges became essential. In his book of reminiscences on forty years of life at the Bar published in 1911 John Alderson Foote QC wrote[18] "*Evolution has produced a new type, and the common- law leader is no longer of a different type of species from his brother who practices in equity*".[19] The change was commented upon by George King, in a rather humorous piece written in 1896.[20] He informs readers of a former Scottish judge of former times who, on being offended by an advocate's lack of use of emotive language before him said:

> *Declaim Sir! Why do you not declaim? Speak to me as if I were a popular assembly.*

---

[17] Referred to by William Renwick Riddell, *Common Law and Common Sense*, Yale Law Journal, Vol. 27, No 8 (June 1918), page 996.

[18] *Piepowder*, John Murray, London, 1911, Chapter IV, page 83.

[19] Equity practitioners almost never addressed juries (Section 3 of the Chancery Amendment Act 1858 extended Jury trial to Chancery, but no such trial took place until 1867 and very few followed.) and consequently their style of advocacy, with its concentration on the law, had been markedly different from those appearing in common law courts; nor did they usually cross-examine witnesses or go on circuit – see Edward Heward *A Victorian Law Reformer. A life of Lord Selborne*, Barry Rose Publishers Ltd., 1998, page 44. For a less than flattering description of Chancery advocacy in Victorian times see Foote's memory of Sir Horace Davey (*Pie powder*, page 173). William Ballantine, the eminently successful common law Serjeant, wrote in his memoirs (*Some Experiences of a Barrister's Life*, R. Bentley, 1880, page 103) "*In the equity courts the notion of cross-examination is ludicrous; it has, however, the merit of being thoroughly inoffensive*". What was seen as ineffectual cross-examination in Chancery was criticized as well by Henry Hawkins, *Reminiscences of Henry Hawkins (Baron Brampton)* 1904, Reprinted by Kessinger Publishing, USA, 2004, page 310. Lawyers who conducted the very few cases that came before the ecclesiastical courts also did not do so before juries. Indeed much was done by affidavit and written submissions. (Interview with Dr. Charlotte Smith, of Reading University School of Law, after her paper, *The Judicial Committee of the Privy Council as the Final Court of Ecclesiastical Appeal*, delivered at the Institute of Advanced Legal Studies on 28th February, 2008.)

[20] *Lawyers and Eloquence*, William Andrews ed. *The Lawyer in History, Literature and Humour*, William Andrews and Co, 1896, page 260.

King goes on:

> *This love of declamation is not shared by judges of the present day, whose continual interruptions in cases tried without juries make it impossible for counsel to indulge in any taste for rhetoric. Non –jury cases have vastly increased in number, and, in conjunction with the growth of the technique of the law has brought into existence a race of severely argumentative advocates whose somber language never learns to stray outside the dry sequestered vale of the law.*

In strong agreement with this view, John Alderson Foote wrote:

> *The decadence of the orator is thus the natural consequence of the evolution of the modern trial. Judges sitting without juries, official referees, and professional arbitrators have curbed the fancy and emasculated the eloquence of the ambitious advocate; and* (perhaps influenced by the 18th Century verse of an *Elegy written in a country church-yard,* by Thomas Gray, whom he admired and sometimes employed in speeches before juries) *many a mute, inglorious Erskine has doubtless pined in obscurity, or withered speechless at the portals of the Commercial Court. A very learned official referee is reported lately to have said that the language of metaphor fatigued him; and even common jurymen, taught by their betters, yawn cynically when the poor flowers of present – day eloquence are offered for their delectation. Thus to find the ideal advocate, one would look for a chartered accountant, accustomed to read the lessons in his parish church.*[21]

Summary Trials Before Magistrates and Their Consequences

A key feature of the nineteenth century criminal procedure, was the growth of the summary trial, a non-jury criminal trial before justices of the peace. The speed of justice was greatly accelerated by the Criminal Justice Act in 1855,[22] which provided that in cases of simple larceny

---

[21] J. A. Foote, Pie Powder, John Murray, 1911, page 86.
[22] Described by A. H. Manchester, *A Modern Legal History of England and Wales 1750–1950,* Butterworths, 1980, page 161 as a *turning point in the history of the criminal process.*

(theft) not over five shillings, or attempted larceny from the person or attempted larceny, the defendant might be tried by magistrates, instead of a judge and jury – if they thought fit and the defendant agreed. This measure led to a big decline in jury trials.[23] Throughout the remaining years of the nineteenth century, there followed an expansion in the number of offences, previously only tried on indictment by a judge and jury, that were made "either way" matters, that is triable by magistrates with their consent and of the accused.[24] Prisoners often consented because of the lesser sentencing powers of magistrates, compared to those at the Assizes or Sessions, and to save time they might have to spend in prison waiting for their trial.[25] A consequence of these reforms in criminal procedure was a decrease in the overall scope for dramatic advocacy in front of jurors. Almost without exception, solicitors acted for the small proportion of defendants who were represented in summary trials. Their right to represent parties at petty sessions (magistrates' courts) had been given statutory backing in 1848.[26] The petty sessions became the base upon which many a young solicitor established his practice. Cases there were reported in detail in the local press and the solicitors whose names appeared most often with the most success had an advertisement previously only available to members of the Bar. Work at petty sessions began to grow substantially; the motor car making a significant contribution; control of the liquor became increasingly important after 1879; power to make separation and maintenance orders was given in 1878 and the enforcement of welfare and public health legislation of the period was a matter for the magistrates. The combined effect of the expansion of the jurisdictions of the county courts and petty sessions and of the social and economic changes of the time meant there was a vast amount of work in

---

[23] See R.M. Jackson, *Incidence of Jury Trial during the Past Century.* (1937–38) 1 MLR 132. In 1854 trials on indictment (jury trials) numbered 29,359 whilst in 1856 the figure was 19,437. (page 136.)

[24] The Criminal Consolidation Acts, 1861, which conferred yet more powers on magistrates, marked the beginning of this further movement. For other measures see, Jackson, *ibid.*

[25] A. J. Ashton, *As I went on my way*, Nisbet and Co, London, 1924, page 248.

[26] 11 & 12 Vic c43, section 12.

advocacy available to solicitors in the places where they practiced for which they had no need of the help of counsel or London agents.[27]

Because magistrates were more like judges, indeed stipendiary magistrates were professional judges, advocacy in their courts usually lacked the histrionics and powerful emotional appeals heard by juries. An advocacy handbook published in 1881 strongly advised solicitors to concentrate on the facts and the practical.[28]

Specialist Statutory Tribunals

Nineteenth century governments faced considerable challenges by the rapid, novel and profound changes in economic and social conditions resulting from the industrial revolution. From the 1830s specialist statutory tribunals were conceived and adopted as the principal method of both implementing new regulatory legislation and resolving disputes between the state and the subject, or between the subject and the subject. The tribunal's legal nature and its procedures were debated and refined during the Victorian period.[29] Tribunals were selected in preference to courts because they offered greater speed, less expense and could be locally based. Moreover, they could be staffed by lay members with specialist knowledge, as opposed to by judges who, although highly competent in law, procedure and evidence, lacked expertise in other complex fields, and capable of reaching decisions on questions of fact, often through a chiefly inquisitorial process, for example in assessing rateable value, income tax, liability, copyhold matters and the existence of boundaries. (A right of appeal to the Quarter

---

[27] H. Kirk, *Portrait of a Profession*, Oyez, London, 1976, page 162.

[28] Douglas Morley Ford, *Solicitors as Advocates*, London: Shaw and Sons 1881: Part I deals with summary matters and Part II with actions in the county court.

[29] See Chantal Stebbings, *Legal Foundations of Tribunals in the Nineteenth Century*, Cambridge University Press, 2007, Chapter one. The study focuses on four groups, each with prominent and formal adjudicatory functions: the fiscal tribunals, the oldest; the tithe, copyhold and enclosure tribunals, the most inquisitorial; the Assessment Committees (rates), the most administrative and the Railway Commissioners, the most judicial and court like. See, also, A. H. Manchester, *A Modern Legal History of England and Wales, 1750–1950*, Butterworths, pp. 150–159, *An alternative to courts*.

Sessions was available.) Some tribunals were presided over by judges. The Railway Commissioners, who dealt with compulsory purchase of land and compensation when railways were constructed, were the most judicial and barristers appeared before them. In effect they were a specialist court.

However most tribunals did not require legal representation – this was seen as one of their strengths – save in the most complicated matters. When they were called upon, lawyers' style of advocacy was not of the extravagant kind heard before juries but practical and generally unadorned.[30]

The Judicature Acts 1873–1881 and Their Effects on Advocacy

The years 1873–1875 saw the passing of the Judicature Acts, a landmark in English legal history and one which was to affect advocacy significantly. By this legislation the civil courts were reformed. Replacing twelve unco-ordinated courts with overlapping jurisdictions, a new Supreme Court was created consisting of the High Court, divided into five divisions, and the Court of Appeal. A further tidying up took place in 1880 when the three Common Law divisions were consolidated to produce the Court of Chancery, Queens Bench and Divorce, Probate and Admiralty. The 1873 Act also prevented the possibility of further clashes between law and equity and established a Committee made up of judges to draft procedural Rules of the Supreme Court. In 1876 the House of Lords was made the final court of appeal with judges chosen from the Supreme Court, or from members of the Bar of at least fifteen years standing.

The Judicature Acts 1873–75, and the new rules of court appended in the schedule to them, reformed written pleadings before trial. The law had previously been very rigid concentrating on their form rather than substance. Skillfully employed by parties' lawyers, it could be used to limit greatly matters of law and fact that could be heard. Victorian judges

---

[30] See J. A. Foote, who regretted this, *Pie Powder*, John Murray, 1911, page 86.

had inherited a tradition that lawsuits were like a sporting contest; a participant who deserved to win on merit but failed to follow the rules of the game could not in fairness be the winner.[31] Under the new rules, cases began with a *Statement of Claim* briefly stating the facts on which the plaintiff relied and the relief sought. The defendant then entered a *Defence*. This had to be more than a mere general denial of allegations in the *Statement of Claim*. The *Defence* could include a set off or counter-claim. After this the parties could either plead new facts or join issue with the whole or part of the previous pleading. Objections on points of law could also be pleaded. Each pleading was to contain, in numbered paragraphs, the material facts on which a party relied, but not the evidence by which they were to be proved. Parties were able to raise points of law by pleading or by applying to court to have a pleading struck out as disclosing no reasonable cause of action to answer. Very significantly, points of law could now be taken at trial even if not pleaded. Pleadings could be amended even, in some circumstances, at trial. Prior to the 1873–75 Acts few pleadings could be amended. Observing, in 1887, the consequences of the reforms Lord Justice Bowen, an appellate judge, approvingly said *law has ceased to be a scientific game that may be won or lost by playing some particular move.*[32] The practice of advocacy was considerably affected by these changes. Opportunities for winning cases by taking points concerning inadequacies and defects in opponents' pleadings, on which considerable expertise had developed, were much reduced. This necessarily led

---

[31] John Baker, *An Introduction to English Legal History*, 4th Edition, 2002, Oxford University Press, page 90. Some years after the Judicature Acts and the new rules of court, Lord Chief Justice Coleridge, who held this office between 1890 and 1894, wrote of the previous tradition and its effect on advocacy: *The old pleader attached more importance to the statement than to the substance stated..................It had become associated in the minds of many men with narrow technicality and substantial injustice. This was not the fault of the common law, but it was the fault, if fault it were, of the system of pleading, which looked at practically, was a small part of common law, but very powerful men had contrived to make it appear that it was almost the whole of it; that the science of statement was far more important than the substance of the right, and that the rights of the litigants themselves were comparatively unimportant unless they illustrated some obscure, interesting and subtle point of the science of stating those rights.* Reproduced in Richard Harris, K.C. *Illustrations in Advocacy*, Stevens and Haynes, 1915, *The Old School of Nisi Prius Advocacy*, Chapter XV, page 120.

[32] J. H. Baker, *An Introduction to English Legal History*, 4th Edition, Oxford University Press, 2002, page 92.

barristers to a greater concentration on matters of substantive law and the quality of evidence in trials. The possibility of amending pleadings, and raising matters of law at trial which had not been pleaded, gave them a greater flexibility to incorporate new evidence and freshly thought legal argument and also more of an ability to respond to opponents.

7

The Late Nineteenth Century and the Beginning of the Twentieth Century

Four years before the close of the nineteenth century, the barrister George King recounted how jury advocacy had changed in late Victorian England. After approvingly quoting "*The plainest words are the profitablist in weightiest matters*",[1] he wrote:

> *The average barrister of today though less addicted to florid declamation, to lavish imagery, is doubtless a more effective speaker than the average of fifty years ago. He does not compare the reputation of a cheesemonger in the City of London to the bloom upon the peach adding, in the inflated style of a famous serjeant, 'Touch it, gentlemen, and it is gone for ever', but the fair name of the tradesman is quite as safe, if not safer in his hands.*[2]

---

[1] From Thomas Fuller (1608–1661), the eminent churchman and historian. His works, including *The Church-History of Britain from the Birth of Jesus to the Year 1648* and *Ephemeris Parliamentaria, or a Faithful Register of Transactions in Parliament* [from 1627 to 1628], with a Forward urging law students and lawyers to purchase it, had been read by lawyers since both books were published in the 1650s and sold in bookshops near the Temple. Interview with Dr. Kate Loveland, School of English, Leicester University, held on 29th April, 2010.

[2] *Lawyers and Eloquence*, In William Andrews ed. *The Lawyer in History, Literature and Humour*, William Andrews and Co., 1896, page 261.

© The Author(s) 2019
A. Watson, *Speaking in Court*, https://doi.org/10.1007/978-3-030-10395-8_7

In contrast to earlier years, when advocacy to jurors was frequently marked by noise and almost endless declamation in very long closing speeches, King explained how effective cross-examination and organization of facts and argument had achieved greater importance:

> *The object of much of the fine talking of days gone was to plunge the jury into a turbulent sea of irrelevancies, to confuse rather than to convince the minds of twelve good men and true. What the present leaders of the Bar chiefly aim at is a keen cross-examination of the witnesses and an effective arrangement of the facts. Order is Oratory's as well as Heaven's first law.*[3]

He then recounted a story about the mid Victorian judge Mr. Justice Maule, who was renowned for pointed wit and (both as a barrister and as a judge) occasional sarcasm and sharp temper.[4] After tiring of his inability to understand the opening speech of a barrister he is said to have exclaimed:

> *I wish you would put your facts in some kind of order. Chronological order is one way and perhaps the best; but I am not particular: any order you like – alphabetical order if you prefer it.*

It was King's opinion that "*it is difficult to believe that such a reproof could with any degree of justice be administered now*".

He further explained[5] that judges "*deeper sense of the value of public time*" led them to intervene more frequently when dealing with "*barris-*

---

[3] Andrews, *ibid*, page 262.

[4] See Edward Manson, *Builders of Our Law During the Reign of Queen Victoria*, Horace Cox, London, 1895. Although as a judge critical of longwinded and unstructured advocacy, there is evidence that Edward Maule himself when a barrister was prone to these traits – J.B. Atlay, *The Victorian Chancellors*, Smith, Elder, 1908, vol 2, pp. 85–86, records the following outburst from Lord Tenterden, who strongly disliked repetition: "*You have told us that three times, Mr Maule.*" Maule replied, "*Only twice, my Lord.*" Robert Walton, *Random Recollections of the Midland Circuit*, Chiswick Press, 1869, pp. 150–151, recounts that at the end of a speech given by Maule in the Bail Court in Westminster Taunton J exclaimed "*Mr Maule, – Mr Maule you have been arguing for the last half hour, and like a child, like a child Mr Maule.*" Maule replied "*I am well content to be likened to a child, for a child, if spared, becomes, in process of time, a man; but once a bear, my Lord, always a brute.*" See also David F Pugsley, Mr. Justice Maule and the Western Circuit, *The Western Circuiteer*, Michaelmas Term 2000, pp. 14–17.

[5] *Lawyers and Eloquence* in William Andrews, *The Lawyer in History, Literature and Humour*, William Andrews and Co., London, 1896, page 264.

ters .... still to be found in the courts in whose mind there lingers the notion that the only way to emphasise a contention is to repeat it" and how they had become much more robust in ordering the removal of noisy parties and spectators from court.

Evidence Given by Prisoners and Its Effects

A change in criminal procedure in the late nineteenth century, intended as an additional safeguard for the innocent, had considerable consequences for advocacy. Subject to some judicial discretion, following the introduction of the Prisoners' Counsel Act 1836, the prisoner could not say anything to the jury. As Mr. Justice Coleridge told the accused in *R v. Boucher* (1837),[6] *"Prisoner, your counsel has spoken for you. I cannot hear you both"*. For several years counsel was permitted to state fully the defence which the accused had instructed them to make; then that practice was forbidden and counsel could only put such defence hypothetically with a result that was *often whimsical and ludicrous.*[7] The Queen's judges at different times met and laid down rules of procedure. The rule which endured until 1898 was that the accused, though defended by counsel, might make a statement before his counsel addressed the jury, but if he introduced any fresh facts in his statement counsel for the prosecution was entitled to a general reply. Perhaps mainly because of this right, the rule was very rarely used.

The Criminal Evidence Act 1898 permitted accused persons to give evidence on their own behalf, subject to cross-examination by the prosecution.[8] Although a defendant was not compelled to go into the witness

---

[6] (1837) 8 Car& P. 141.

[7] Edmund Purcell *Forty Years at the Criminal Bar*, Fisher Unwin, London, 1916, page 46.

[8] This practice was allowed earlier in the United States. In 1864 the state of Maine passed a statute making the accused and his spouse competent but not compellable witnesses. Others followed: Massachusetts (1867); New Hampshire and New York (1869) and New Jersey (1871). By 1878 no fewer than twenty eight states had enacted similar statutes. A survey, conducted by the Society for the Amendment of the Law in 1878, and published in the Irish Law Times of that year (12 Ir LT, 554, 563, 575 and 593), found the general view in those states was that reform had worked well, wrongful convictions had been prevented and that judges and lawyers originally hostile to the

box, and, at first, it seems, a number of judges tried to dissuade prisoners from so doing,[9] jurors soon became willing to draw adverse conclusions if he or she did not. Statements made by the accused affected the task of counsel as his closing speech to the court would be listened to the in the context of evidence given by his lay client. The reform of 1898 therefore loosened the control of advocates over the conduct of their client's defence.

Drawing on his experiences as a barrister before and after the Criminal Evidence Act 1898, Sir Travers Humphreys saw it as revolutionising the style of advocacy for the defence in criminal cases.[10] Humphreys recounts that during his first ten years at the Bar, when prisoners were not competent to give evidence, *"an advocate was free to suggest to the jury any story, in his closing speech, which his ingenuity could devise as a possible explanation of the proved facts or to insinuate into their minds that element of doubt which was sufficient to render a verdict of 'guilty' unsafe"*. Cases often turned into a controversy whether any explanation could be put forward by the defence consistent with the proved facts of the case. *"This was the chance for a skilful and eloquent advocate, and it was upon this topic that the energies of some of the most distinguished orators have been expended"*. On insinuation of doubt, he tells of the methods, at the London Sessions, of men such as Edmund Purcell, a man who would accept "I P" work ('In Person' signifying that no solicitor had been employed in the case, but that Counsel had received his instructions and fee directly from the prisoner or his relatives or friends), and Arthur Hutton, *"a superior and rather more expensive edition of Purcell"*, who declined to. E D Purcell is described as well educated, but with little knowledge of law, charming of manner, having a soft and pleasing voice and a persuasive style of address peculiarly his own. *"An astute cross-examiner, he never made the mistake of saying to the witness 'I put it to you that the fact is', thereby irrevocably pinning himself*

---

change, were now convinced of its advantages and utility. For the long campaign which led to the Criminal Evidence Act 1898 in England and Wales see David Bentley, *English Criminal Justice in the Nineteenth Century*, The Hambledon Press, London, 1998, Chapters 15, 16, 17 and 18.

[9] Purcell, *Forty Years at the Bar*, Fisher Unwin, London, 1916, page 47.

[10] *Criminal Days*, Hodder and Stoughton, 1945, pp. 46–49.

to a particular state of facts. Purcell would do no more than insinuate that there may have been a mistake and many witnesses would concede that, as they were not infallible, an error might have occurred, although they did not think it had". Such an admission would be given great emphasis by Purcell in his closing speech, where there would be much reference to the jury's duty to only convict if the case against the prisoner was proved beyond reasonable doubt. Humphreys explained how juries not infrequently acquitted when this device was used. However, he also tells of how prosecution minded judges sometimes responded by asking the witness – box warder to read out to the jury the acquitted person's record of previous convictions, thereby reducing the effect of counsel's strategy in later cases heard by them. For this reason solicitors and counsel would sometimes try hard to have their client's case heard early on a jury's first day.

After the Criminal Evidence Act came into force, Sir Travers Humphreys recalls how in the majority of cases the accused wished to give evidence and that counsel was reluctant to dissuade them because if the trial led to a conviction he would be blamed for the result. Persons convicted before were less keen, having unpleasant memories of past experiences in the witness box, and more inclined to accept the advice of their barrister. Although counsel could not comment on the fact that a defendant had not gone into the witness box, Judges could and did. It became usual for Judges, Recorders and Chairmen to "*point out, with more or less emphasis, that there is one person who knows a great deal which the jury would like to know and that is the prisoner*".[11] Whilst knowing what his client would say in examination in chief, counsel nonetheless frequently feared, often correctly, that this version, composed whilst awaiting trial, would crumble under cross-examination either from its own inherent weakness, or by it being incompatible with a statement made by the defendant to the police at the time of his arrest or shortly afterwards. Also if he gave evidence, a defendant casting aspersions on the honesty of prosecution witnesses ran the real risk that any previous convictions he had would go before the

---

[11] A. J. Ashton, *As I went on my way*, Nisbet and Co., London, 1924, page 255.

jury, usually with disastrous consequences. In short, it was an out and out pitfall for many defendants.[12] Honing skills in re-examination, which has to be done by nonleading questions, although latitude is sometimes allowed, to limit damage caused by prosecution cross-examination of defendants, became a necessity.

According to Humphreys, the main challenge for a criminal advocate became accommodating the evidence of his client, called as the first witness for the defence, which may have strayed from that in his instructions, particularly because of cross-examination, with the facts proved by the prosecution. He thought of this as a *"mundane task compared with the flights of imagination permitted to his predecessors"*: In this Humphreys was unlikely to have been alone.

As early as 1851 (1846 in the county courts) parties in civil courts were able to give evidence themselves, consequently influencing advocates' presentations of cases there.

Rules About Opening Speeches

Advocacy in both civil and criminal courts was affected by rules concerning opening speeches. At one time it was common for counsel to range at will among facts which could not be proved, but by the beginning of the twentieth century it had become established and applied by the courts that an advocate may not open any fact to a jury that he is not in a position to prove either by witnesses he is going to call or by documents that can be produced.

Edward Marshall-Hall infringed this rule in 1903. He appeared for the former secretary of an American lady. He had brought an action against her in defamation, based on what she had told her new secretary that the plaintiff was a disreputable person and was attempting to blackmail her. Marshall-Hall had been provided with much unsavory information about

---

[12] Sir Patrick Hastings, recognized as one of the first half of the twentieth century's most able advocates, wrote *many a murderer has stepped joyfully into the witness box and by his own eloquence has promptly hanged himself.* Patrick Hastings, *Cases in Court,* William Heinemann, 1949, page 11.

the lady and her sister, none of which he could prove. Nevertheless, in his opening he said, perhaps impulsively:

> *She* [the defendant] *cannot for one moment say that she does not know what it is to be accused of blackmail herself. I may afterwards, gentlemen, have the opportunity of asking her some questions with regard to her views on this particular subject. But be that as it may, she is a woman who knows exactly what she means by the word blackmail, and she cannot possibly have read all the American Press, dealing with her and her sister, without knowing what an accusation of blackmail really means.*

Marshall-Hall secured a verdict and substantial damages for his client. The defendant immediately appealed and the decision was reversed, partly because of the scandalous and irrelevant material in his opening speech.[13]

Expert Witnesses

By the closing decades of the eighteenth century, it had become established, as an exception to rules against witnesses giving hearsay and opinion evidence, both key parts of that century's "adversarial revolution" in court procedure, that opinions given by experts who had not personally observed the facts, instructed by parties to a dispute, not by the court itself as previously had been the case, was admissible as evidence.[14]

During the nineteenth century, expert witnesses increasingly began to appear in trials. Tremendous expansion of industry and the subsequent rise of professional expertise frequently turned the scientific expert witnesses into pivotal figures in the court-room. More traditional expert witnesses – physicians, clerics, navigators, sea captains, and merchants – were joined by chemists, microscopists, geologists, engineers, mechanists and other men of science. Embarrassing public displays from the witness box of eminent scientists in

---

[13] See Richard DuCann, *The Art of the Advocate*, 1993, Penguin, pp. 81–82.
[14] Tal Golan, *History of Expert Testimony in the English Court Room*, Science in Context 12,1 (1999), pp. 7–32.

zealous heated opposition to each other, sending jurors into utter confusion, were reported in the press, casting doubts on the honesty of their motives and the integrity of their science.[15] Calls for experts to be appointed by the court rather than the parties themselves were made but not accepted. Following formulation by the judges of the M'Naughton Rules in 1843[16] of insanity as a defence to murder, medical men, "insanity experts", sometimes disparagingly dubbed "mad doctors", entered courts in significant numbers to testify on the mental responsibility of defendants.[17] As the century wore on the ranks of medical expert witnesses swelled because of increasing numbers of accident cases, especially on the railways, and claims for secondary symptoms and disability resulting from injury. Appearance in court by medical experts held the possibility of raising their profile and establishing their authority within their profession. As with other expert witnesses, the drama of vehement disagreements was much reported in the newspapers.

Reflecting widespread concern about expert witnesses for what appeared to be their venality, Baron Bramwell, a rather outspoken judge, invented a classification of perverters of the truth which was frequently repeated, "*liars, d-----d liars, and expert witnesses*".[18] Shortcomings apart, the legal profession was content to employ experts as a means of establishing cases and casting doubt upon, if not undermining, those of their opponents. Advocates had to deal with, and accommodate, their evidence in examination in chief, cross-examination and closing speeches. This required familiarity with often complex and technical matters and, where necessary, the ability to rationally deal with such evidence that was unfavourable to their case: bombast and flamboyancy, in themselves, being insufficient. In a widely read practical book on advocacy, published in

---

[15] Tal Golan, *ibid*, page 16.

[16] Under the Rules, which were adopted throughout much of the common law world, but are now hardly used, the defence of insanity may only be established if clearly proved that, at the time of the committing of the act, the party accused was labouring under such a defect of reason, from disease of the mind, as not to know the nature and quality of the act he was doing; or if he did know it, that he did not know he was doing what was wrong. M'Naghten's Case [1843] All ER Rep 229.

[17] For an account of highly reported controversial cases concerning the defence of insanity in the decades following establishment of the M'Naughton Rules see Roger Smith, *Trial by Medicine*, 1981, Edinburgh University Press, Chapter 6.

[18] J. A. Foote, *Piepowder from the Law Courts*, John Murray, London, 1911, page 180.

1910, by Frederick John Wrottesley, who was later to become a Lord Justice, the author, drawing on experience accumulated over the years, wrote *"the ability to cross-examine professional expert witnesses well is rare"*. He continued:

> *The only safe way for an advocate who has an expert to deal with upon cross-examination, is to hold him down to the issues involved and not to allow him to cover too much ground, nor to argue the case of the party who has called his services into requisition. Experts are, as a class, shrewd and cunning, and are usually selected on account of their eminence in their professions, or skill in their advocations, and they are presumed to speak guardedly and carefully upon topics with which they have the greatest familiarity, for they often stake their reputations upon the result of the trial in which they are called to testify. Hence the advocate whose duty it becomes to examine witnesses of the kind, cannot come to the performance of his task with too much information upon the subject under investigation.[19]*

Examination of Witnesses: A Much More Precise Art

Just how far forensic advocacy had moved by 1910 from indiscriminately histrionic and instinctual performances, observed throughout the majority of Queen Victoria's reign towards something much more structured and subtle, rational and capable of being learned, may be seen by further reading of Frederick Wrottesley's practical book on advocacy. This work was designed to reflect the standards then expected by the bar and to be read by members freshly called.

The author sets out detailed rules and strategies to be followed for both examination in chief and cross-examination. In his chapter on the latter he mentions Sir James Scarlett (1769–1844, Lord Abinger from 1835)[20]

---

[19] Frederick John Wrottesley, *The Examination of Witnesses in Court*, Sweet and Maxwell, 1910, London, pp. 93–4.

[20] See Chap. 5 for suggestions of Scarlett's possible influence on barristers, including John Holker, Hardinge Gifford, Charles Russell and Edward Clarke, who did much to change the style of late Victorian advocacy.

who once said of an eminent early nineteenth century contemporary that his idea of cross-examination was putting over again every question asked in chief in a very angry tone. Wrottesley, who found this fault still afflicting certain barristers, wrote:

> *The objects of a cross- examination are three in number. The first is to elicit something in your favour; the second is to weaken the force of what the witness has said against you; and the third is to show that from his present demeanour or from his past life he is unworthy of belief, and thus weaken or destroy the effect of his testimony. We shall endeavour to give in this chapter clear and well-defined strategies for the accomplishment of each of these objects.*

He continued:

> *There are two modes of cross-examining a witness pursued by accomplished advocates. One is usually termed the savage, and the other the smiling method, and the latter is usually to be pursued. An adverse witness can often soften his narrative and modify or change many things when asked to explain them and will do so if approached in the proper way; but if the advocate makes an attack upon him he will strive to injure his cause as much as possible. Timid or diffident witnesses should not be frightened, if they are honest. With the dishonest witness, however, no severity of treatment can hardly be too great. But with the female, youthful, modest or aged witness the advocate should deal kindly. As a matter of policy, aside from the humanity and cruelty of an opposite course, it is better to pursue this plan, and even if it were not the best policy, an advocate can never afford to do anything unbecoming a gentleman in the discharge of his duties, whatever they may be.*[21]

After attending to relevant rules of evidence,[22] Wrottesley then states that: the art of cross –examination is not to examine crossly, although it

---

[21] F.W. Wrottesley, *The Examination of Witnesses in Court*, Sweet and Maxwell London, 1910, page 78. Similarly, Sir Cecil Henry Walsh, The Advocate, Pioneer Press, Allahabad, 1916, page 95 wrote the: *"method of cross-examination by direct attack, is as a rule the least successful. It is certainly, the least pleasant to hear, and the least edifying. The insidious, half friendly, half-confidential method is usually the more successful, merely because if a witness is attempting to deceive, it is more apt to put him off his guard"*.

[22] An important development in the law of evidence affecting advocacy had been the introduction, through case law (A.G. V Hitchcock. (1847) 1 Ex 91 and Palmer V Trower, (1852) 8 Ex. 247) and

acknowledged that this persisted; there should be a good reason for examining a witness and for each question asked and a prudent advocate will ask as few as possible; the object of cross-examination is not to produce startling effects, but to elicit facts which will support the theory intended to be put forward; it is highly important for the advocate to frame his questions in plain, simple language adapted to the understanding of the witness; many cases are lost by injudicious attacks upon the credit of witnesses; and that no advocate should allow himself to become an instrument of vengeance in the hands of his irate clients.[23] This more measured approach to cross-examination is worlds apart from that taken by the Irish barrister Charles Curran (Chap. 2), whose methods were recorded with approval by fellow Irishman, and leader of the English criminal bar, Charles Phillips (1787–1859), *Horticultural Phillips* (Chap. 4), and indeed emulated by him, and many of others, in the nineteenth century. In a speech on Curran, Phillips explained how he dealt with untruthful or unwilling witnesses:

> *He argued, he cajoled, he ridiculed, he mimicked, he played off the various artillery of his talent upon the witness; he would affect earnestness upon trifles, and levity upon subjects of the most import, until at length he succeeded in creating a security that was fatal, or a sullenness that produced all the consequences of prevarication. No matter how unfair the topic, he never failed to*

---

by statute (28 and 29 Vict. c. 18, s. 6.) of rules which meant, subject to two exceptions (the fact that a witness was convicted of a crime and the fact he was biased in favour of the party calling him), answers given by a witness to questions put to him in cross-examination tending to shake his credit by injuring his character were treated as final. See Sir James Fitzjames Stephen, *A digest of the law of evidence*. Macmillan, London, 1877, Chapter XVI, Article 130. Prior to these rules counsel could call witnesses to prove allegations made in cross-examination. When they did so, trials sometimes swelled to almost unmanageable proportions. For a modern exposition of the law concerning collateral facts see Colin Tapper, *Cross and Tapper on Evidence*, 11th Edition, Oxford University Press, 2007, pp. 343–345.

[23] That bullying, blustering and thumping the table in cross-examination was increasingly seen as out of place is confirmed by part of a speech delivered by Sir Walter Schwabe K.C., who became Chief Justice of the Madras High Court in 1921 and served until 1924, in London. He advised advocates to: "*Cultivate a pleasant manner and get on as friendly terms as possible with the witness. Reproving, lecturing, bullying were methods now recognized as belonging to a first generation. One should bring out the unpleasant facts with an air of condolence and regret rather than with an air of triumph, which might raise sympathy and one should never lose one's temper*". Reproduced in S. C. Sakkar, Hints on Modern Advocacy and Cross-Examination, S. C. Sakkar and Sons (Private) Ltd., 4th Edition, 1985, page 201.

avail himself of it; acting upon the principle that in law as war, every stratagem was admissible. If he was hard pressed, there was no peculiarity of person, no singularity of name, no eccentricity of profession, at which he would not grasp, trying to confound the self-possession of the witness by the, no matter how excited, ridicule of the audience.[24]

In the late nineteenth century the formulae in cross-examination 'I put to you' and 'I suggest to you' came into use, and remain much heard. There is no need to use these words provided the challenge is made clear to the witness and the court when an advocate wishes to challenge the truth of a witness's evidence, or to put to the witness what the advocate's client or witnesses will later swear happened (*putting the case*). The alternatives of 'I put' and 'I suggest' were resisted by some barristers at the time because they feared that the use of the personal pronoun would make it appear to juries that they were giving evidence, something which along with expressing personal opinions, had to be avoided.

In his recollections, starting in the 1870s, of forty years at the bar, John Alderson Foote, considered examination in chief of witnesses by counsel and recalled:

The young beginner used at one time to be taught to take a careful note of his leader's opening, and to examine the witness from that rather than from his proof of evidence. There are obvious dangers in taking this advice, especially if the leader has not had time to read his brief. It has been said with more apparent reason that it was to meet this possible contingency, that the practice of entrusting the first and most important witness to the hands of junior counsel originated.[25]

Wrottesley, deals with examination in chief (in the chapter of his work before that on cross-examination); the purpose of which being to *"lay before the Court and the jury all that the witness knows about the case which is relevant and material"*. Again reflecting a change in advocacy practice

[24] *A Character of Charles Curran, Esq.,* in *Speeches of Charles Phillips,* Williams, Mason and Co., Cincinnati, 1818, pp. 191–196.

[25] J.H. Foote, *Pie Powder from the Law Courts,* John Murray, London, 1911, pp. 196–197.

from that which existed throughout much of the previous century, and illustrated by Foote's memoirs, he attaches great importance to the skills necessary for this task, which he saw as demanding great care. Approvingly, Wrottesley[26] quotes from a report, in the Birmingham Daily Post in March 1893, of an address on the subject given by Sir Frank Lockwood (1846–1897), then one of the leaders of the bar:

> *He believed that the examination of a witness in chief, or the direct examination of witnesses, as it was called in Ireland, was very much underrated in its significance and its importance. If they had to examine a witness, what they had got to do was to induce him to tell his story in the most dramatic fashion, without exaggeration; they had got to tell him, not to make a mere parrot-like repetition of the proof, but to tell his own story as though he were telling it for the first time – not as though it were words learnt by heart – but it were a plaintive story, plaintively telling it. And they have got to assist him in the difficult work. They had got to attract him to the performance of his duty, but woe be to them if they suggested to him the terms in which it was to be put. They must avoid any suspicion of leading the witness while at all the time they were doing it. They knew perfectly well the story he was going to tell; but they destroy absolutely the effect if every minute they were looking down at the paper on which his proof was written. It should appear to be a kind of spontaneous conversation between the counsel on the one hand and the other, the witness telling artlessly his simple tale, and the counsel almost appalled to hear of the inequity under which his client suffered. It was in this way, and in this way alone, that they could effectively examine a witness.*

With approbation, Frederick Wrottesley recounts how Sir James Scarlett, who excelled in forensic success, attached great weight to the examination in chief and how in his cases he would always examine witnesses himself.

In accordance with what had then become established tactics, Wrottesley wrote that much care and attention should be given to the arrangement of testimony: both as to the order of questions asked of

---

[26] F.W. Wrottesley, *The Examination of Witnesses in Court*, Sweet and Maxwell, London, 1910, page 36.

individual witnesses and the order in which witnesses are examined advising putting the most intelligent and most honest witness first and saving one of the best for the close.

As mentioned in an earlier section, the Criminal Evidence Act 1898 allowed defendants in a criminal cases to give evidence on their own behalf in trials, often necessitating re-examination by counsel, in an attempt to undo damage done to his client in cross-examination. This clearly gave an incentive to develop skills in this area. To reach the desired standard of re-examination in criminal and civil trials, again illustrating the extent court advocacy had evolved into a much more planned, subtle and precise art, Wrottesley advised[27]:

> *great discretion in asking for explanation of what the witness stated on cross-examination. He should, before doing this, be satisfied that the witness can explain, satisfactorily, the apparent contradictions in his testimony, for it would be more hurtful to call for an explanation, and obtain one that is injurious, than to pass over in silence the point not susceptible of explanation.*

Drawing further on the report of Sir Frank Lockward's speech in Birmingham, the author gave an example of how not to re-examine a witness[28]:

> *Re-examination – the putting Humpty-Dumpty together again – was by no means an unimportant portion of an advocate's duty. Once, in the Court of Chancery, a witness was asked in cross-examination by an eminent Chancery leader, whether it was true that he had been convicted of perjury. The witness owned the soft impeachment, and the cross-examining counsel very properly sat down. Then it became the duty of an equally eminent Chancery Q.C. to re-examine 'Yes' said he, 'it is true you have been convicted of perjury. But tell me: have you not on many other occasions been accused of perjury and acquitted?'*

---

[27] Page 153.
[28] Page 154.

More Documents and Lengthening Civil Trials

In his memoirs of forty years of practice as a barrister, published in 1911, John. Alderson Foote, reported that many civil trials were lengthening, an important trend that was to continue for much of the twentieth century:

> *That an action should occupy a judge for a whole week is nowadays considered nothing extra-ordinary. Most seriously contested special jury cases last a couple of days; and on circuit one constantly sees the first common jury barely finished at the end of a long day's sitting.*[29]

The author considered the main reason for this was greater complexity in human affairs, rather than greater wordiness and lesser ability of counsel, leading to more documents, especially business correspondence, which had to be read by barristers and introduced as evidence, addressed in closing speeches and then dealt with by judges in summing up. In Foote's view, the requirement imposed to undertake this sometimes rather unexciting but essential practical activity further limited counsel's scope for flights of forensic eloquence.

Decline of Classics and Other Former Influences

Foote[30] noted that classical styles of oratory, which had much influenced Burke, Sheridan and Fox in the eighteenth century and Brougham in the 19th, were little used by advocates before juries and not in front of judges alone. On their power to persuade jurors he wrote:

> *"Who can read the Philippics, or the De Corona, or the denunciations of Cataline now, and say with truth that he would have recognized the authors as*

---

[29] J.H. Foote, *Piepowder from the Lawcourts*, John Murray, 1911, page 90.
[30] Foote, *ibid*, pp. 85–90.

supreme masters of eloquence if he had not been taught to think so. . . . . .the Orations have become dry bones and there is no breath in them."[31]

Knowledge and appreciation of Demosthenes, Cicero, and Quintilian had declined, even on special juries. It had been greater amongst special jurors rather than common jurors because many more of the former had been educated at public or grammar schools, where there had been emphasis on the classics. Although Latin remained strong – but had begun to be much less quoted in parliamentary debates by end of the nineteenth century[32] – compulsory Greek had already been abolished, much to the dismay of certain headmasters, who concluded it was an explanation for falling standards of eloquence in public life.[33]

Foote saw no value in using passages from the speeches of Burke, Erskine or Brougham before juries: "*Take, for instance, Brougham's speech in defence of Queen Caroline, or Burke's impeachment of Warren Hastings, or any of Erskine's incessant invocations of the Deity. Can we honestly say that any of these move us to pity, or quicken us with sympathy, or thrill us with indignation? . . . . .How turgid it all sounds to us now! How verbose! How unconvincing!*".[34]

However, casting a practical eye on their persuasiveness, Foote wrote approvingly of the "*legends of Troy, of Ulysses, of ancient Rome, of Olympus and Parnassus* and that *the stars of Milton and Shakespeare blaze for ever in the eternal sky*".[35] Greek legends, Shakespeare and Milton were very much part of the school curriculum for those fortunate enough to be able to pursue education beyond a basic level.

Certain barristers, especially those steeped in works such as Demosthenes, Lysias, Antiphon, Cicero and Quintilian, and who were

---

[31] J.H. Foot, *Piepowder from the Lawcourts*, John Murray, 1911, page 88.

[32] Christopher Stray, *Classics Transformed*, Clarendon Press, 1998, Chapter 3. This was principally because of the growing number of working class Members of Parliament who had not formally studied Latin, Greek and the Classics (Interview with Mr. Stray on 2nd July, 2010).

[33] Abolition of the compulsory Greek requirement by Oxford and Cambridge came immediately after the First World War: See Christopher Stray, *Classics Transformed*, Clarendon Press, 1998, Chapter 9.

[34] J. H. Foote, *Piepowder from the Lawcourts*, John Murray, 1911, page 88.

[35] Foote, *ibid*, page 89.

masters of metaphor and histrionic expression regretted what they saw as the decay of eloquence at the bar brought about by changed public appreciation of their merit and because of judges sitting without juries.[36] In some ways talk of the decline of bar oratory in England and Wales resembled theories about the fate of rhetorical advocacy in Rome during the Principate, after Quintilian, when judges became bureaucratized functionaries with long lists of cases and little regard for considerations other than law.[37] Parallels were drawn to Rome by some who lamented what had occurred in England. Others did not see alteration in advocacy as a deterioration, but rather evolution. They saw advocacy as pre-eminently the art of persuasion, not merely classical structures and allusions, purple passages and dramatic gestures. This demanded sensitivity to the tribunal, knowledge of law and procedure, choosing telling arguments, and ordering them tightly. Bernard Kelly,[38] for instance, appeared to reflect this view, albeit in his somewhat colourful way, perhaps betraying a certain nostalgia for a richer form of language at the Bar. To him the wisdom of the *"mighty soldier"*, the Duke of Wellington, who advised a young Member of Parliament *"to say what you have to say, don't quote Latin, and sit down"*, had come home to the present generation. Although the *"Graces* were *now usually silent amidst the groves of Theseus"*, there had been enormous gains as impassioned rhetoric had frequently been responsible for grave errors and miscarriages of justice. Kelly concluded:

> But if modern verbal address be less richly endowed with poetic similitudes and ornate figures of speech than heretofore, it is in many respects none the less worthy of our admiration. For as a rule, it is dignified, coherent, and even, at times, positively eloquent. The object of every sincere speech, after all, is not to arouse the passions or flatter the senses, but to convince the hearers of the truth.

---

[36] For humorous examples of this see Theo Mathew (1866–1939), *Forensic Fables*, Wildy and Sons, 1999, *The Blushing Beginner and The Bearded Juryman* (pp. 57–58) and *The Brilliant Person, The Vulgar Individual With A Cockney Accent And Two Malefactors* (pp. 305–306), both originally published in 1926.

[37] See J. A. Crook, *Legal Advocacy in the Roman World*, London, Duckworth, 1995, Chapters One and Two. The author seeks to controvert the view that advocacy decayed and sets out to show how it adapted to changed conditions, one of which was the fading away of by the second century AD of jury courts.

[38] *Famous Advocates and their Speeches*, London, Sweet and Maxwell, 1921, page 28.

8

A Spectacular Quartet of Leading Barristers

At the end of the nineteenth century and during the first quarter of the twentieth century, sensational trials still attracted intense public interest and remained an important source of entertainment. The advocacy of Sir Rufus Isaacs, Edward Carson, F. E. Smith and Edward Marshall Hall, who frequently opposed each other, was much reported. The advocacy that brought them triumph exerted important influence on other barristers then and after.

Sir Rufus Isaacs (1860–1935) became Solicitor General, Attorney General, Lord Chief Justice of England, Ambassador to the United States, Viceroy of India and Foreign Secretary.[1] The son of a prosperous Spitalfields fruit importer, Rufus Isaacs left school at 14 and tried his hand for some years in his father's business. Afterwards, he became a stockbroker. Unable, however, to meet his obligations, he was only saved from bankruptcy by loans from his mother, made on the basis he would read for the bar. Rufus Isaacs was called to the Bar in 1887 and made a QC in 1898, the same year as Marshall Hall. Knowledge of business helped him obtain many commercial cases. But soon he became

---

[1] For a very readable short biography of Rufus Isaacs, see *The Charmed Life of Rufus Isaacs*, Law Society Gazette, 14th December, 1988.

© The Author(s) 2019
A. Watson, *Speaking in Court*, https://doi.org/10.1007/978-3-030-10395-8_8

prominent in many memorable jury trials. The first in which he came to public attention, through mass newspaper reporting, was the high society Hartop divorce case in 1902. His very measured and effective cross-examinations were noted. In 1904 Isaacs was briefed to conduct a private prosecution of Whittaker Wright, a great financier whose vast empire suddenly collapsed. It was alleged he had published false balance sheets, knowing them to be false and with intent to defraud. The much publicized case, brought by stockbrokers, was enormously complicated. Isaacs distinguished himself by the clarity he explained it, in a melodious voice, to a special jury during a five hour opening speech and by breaking Whittaker Wright, a formidable figure, in a mighty cross-examination. The way he conducted this prosecution took him to the heights of the bar.

The following year he defended Sir Edward Russell, the editor of the Liberal newspaper the *Liverpool Daily Post*, who faced an indictment for criminal libel brought by eight Conservative members of the Licensing Committee of the Liverpool Justices. In an article written in the Daily Post, Russell criticized the Committee for failing to try to reduce the number of public houses in Liverpool, which it had powers to do under the Licensing Act of 1904, and said that this was to be expected of friends of the liquor trade. Before opening strongly for the defence on the theme of free speech, Isaacs again showed his remarkable ability to cross-examine by establishing the proceedings had been brought for political reasons. He also obtained a clear admission from Sir Charles Petrie, one of the Plaintiffs, that when he read the piece he had not seen it as imputing corrupt or dishonest motives to him. After Sir Edward had given his evidence, Isaacs made a powerful closing speech in which he invited the jury to follow the view of Sir Charles Petrie. They appeared to do this by acquitting Sir Edward Russell. Rufus Isaacs' advocacy made a great impression on a 21 year old listener in the Liverpool Assizes in St George's Hall – Norman, later Lord, Birkett, who wrote *it undoubtedly stirred some of those feelings which were ultimately to lead me to the Bar and the courts of law.*[2]

---

[2] Lord Birkett, *Six Great Advocates*, Penguin, 1961, page 62.

Rufus Isaacs, although he used to appear most in the civil courts, is often best remembered for his advocacy in prosecuting Frederick Seddon and his wife, charged with murdering their elderly lodger, Miss Barrow, by poisoning her with arsenic; the motive being said to obtain her small fortune. It was Rufus Isaacs's first and only murder trial. By this time, 1912, he was Attorney General. His opponent was Marshall Hall, who destroyed the Crown's identification evidence that Maggie, the Seddon's 16 year old daughter, had bought flypapers, from which arsenic could be extracted, from a chemists. Further, in a masterful cross-examination, demonstrating his understanding of scientific matters, he almost brought the Home Office expert to admitting a vital point he was contending. The case looked shaky for the prosecution; indeed an application by Marshall-Hall that there was no case for the defendants to answer nearly succeeded. However, Frederick Seddon, almost definitely against the advice of his counsel, decided to give evidence himself, as he was entitled to do under the Criminal Evidence Act 1898. He thereby presented himself to the most accomplished cross-examiner of his day.

Rufus Isaacs began[3]:

Mr Seddon did Miss Barrow live with you from July 1910 till September 1911?

Yes was the answer

He then asked: "*Did you like her?*" At first, perhaps taken aback by its subtlety, Seddon could only repeat the question, knowing he could not say "Yes", because the jury already knew of her extremely unpleasant character, and that if he said "No" that might strengthen the motive for poisoning her. With sharpness of mind, he said: "*She wasn't a woman you could have been in love with, but I sympathized with her deeply*".

Seddon was cross-examined for six hours during which time he revealed himself to be a mean, self-centred, cold and greedy man who responded to questions with a mixture of condescension and arrogance. By his answers it became clear he was the murderer. Rufus Isaacs, despite the fact that the Crown's evidence was not overwhelming (at best it was highly circumstantial), led Seddon, through his questions, to convict

---

[3] Proceedings of the Central Criminal Court, 27th February, 1912, page 737.

himself.[4] However, Mrs. Seddon, who was also cross-examined by Rufus Isaacs, impressed as a simple woman, dominated and used by her husband.

Rufus Isaacs' cross-examination of Arthur Seddon was cool, calm, incisive, tactful, searching, but never oppressive. He conducted himself throughout with an unfailing courtesy that was almost deferential.[5] His advocacy was very removed from the bullying and browbeating of much of that in the nineteenth century and in its precision, subtlety and cold planning, far apart from the almost indiscriminate use of theatrical technique and appeals to emotion then frequently resorted to. Rufus Isaacs was described as *the mildest mannered man who held a thousand – guinea brief, and one of the most effective.*[6] In his analysis of Rufus Isaacs's advocacy, Edgar Lustgarten, the noted broadcaster on crime and the law, attributed his success to a melodious voice, practical intelligence, insight into people, grasp of facts and great capacity for preparation. In cross-examination, he did not go in for a display of fireworks, or overwhelm, but could undermine. He was not a stirring orator, generally eschewing formal perorations in closing speeches, but lucidity and charm compelled an attentive audience.[7]

Edward Carson (1854–1935), advocate, politician and Law Lord (1921–29), was another leader of the late nineteenth and early twentieth century English Bar.[8] Already a QC in his native Ireland, as the leader of the Unionists he was later to do much to ensure that Ulster remained in the United Kingdom, Carson was called to the bar in Middle Temple in

---

[4] Lord Birkett, *Six Great Advocates* Penguin, 1961, page 62. It has been said Marshall Hall used Seddon's conviction as a warning to defendants of the risks of giving evidence on their own behalf.

[5] George Keaton, *Harris's Hints on Advocacy*, Eighteenth Edition, 1943, Stevens and Sons, London, page 9. For an analysis of the case by F. E. Smith, see First Lord Birkenhead, *Famous Trials, The Seddon Case*, Hutchinson and Co, Ltd., Edinburgh and London pp. 365–384. For additional analysis of Rufus Isaacs's cross-examination of Arthur Seddon's see Edgar Lustgarten, *Advocate Impeccable*, BBC Radio 4, 1970. Tape recording kindly made available by Mr. Leslie Blake, Barrister, Lecturer in Law, Law Faculty, Surrey University.

[6] Quotation from Denis Judd, *Lord Reading*, Weidenfeld and Nicolson, 1982, and used by Richard Hamilton, *All Jangle and Riot*, Professional Books, 1986, page 167.

[7] Edgar Lustgarten, *Advocate Impeccable*. BBC Radio 4, 1970.

[8] See H. Montgomery Hyde, *Carson: the life of Sir Edward Carson, Lord Carson of Duncairn*, Heinemann, London, 1953.

1893 and appointed a QC the following year. He established a reputation as a resolute fighter for his client, a master of the epigram and the verbal quip, the possessor of a voice that charmed all hearers and the taker of risks that generally came off.[9] Like Rufus Isaacs, his greatest strength was in cross – examination, in which he was pointed and persistent, but also generally measured, cool headed and polite, and was able to cope even with such masters of words as W. S. Gilbert and Oscar Wilde. In 1895 Carson was instructed on behalf of the Marquess of Queensberry, to lead his defence in Oscar Wilde's libel action against him; the evidence for which was a card inscribed by Queensberry: "For Oscar Wilde, posing as a somdomite(sic)".Carson had been Wilde's contemporary and rival at Trinity College, Dublin during their student days.

Wilde, with his rapier wit, managed to tease and torment Carson during a long cross-examination. Unperturbed, Carson continued and started to question Wilde about his acquaintance with a number of named young men. After a confident response by Wilde to an earlier question, Carson asked him about a young man, sixteen when Wilde knew him, called Walter Grainger.

"*Did you ever kiss that boy?*"

"*Oh dear no!*" Wilde replied dismissively. *He was a particularly ugly boy.* Ignoring the laughter in court, Carson took the answer seriously and swiftly asked,

"*Why did you say he was ugly? Is that the reason why you did not kiss him?*" Shaken and realizing his mistake, Wilde tried a haughty response; "*You are impertinent, Mr Carson*", but this was to no avail.

"*Why, why, why, why, did you add that?*" Carson demanded.

That afternoon, Oscar Wilde's counsel, Sir Edward Clarke, closed his case without calling, as was widely expected, Lord Alfred Douglas, as a witness. Nothing could have saved the case for him. Much, however, had been done for Carson as a cross-examiner.[10]

---

[9] Travers Humphreys, *Criminal Days*, Hodder and Stoughton, 1946, pp. 92–94.

[10] See, *The Trials of Oscar Wilde With an introduction by H. Montgomery Hyde*, Hodge, London, 1948.

Appreciating jurors carried with them into the jury room only a small fraction of the many words said in a trial, and were not usually used to listening to involved argument, Carson would fasten upon words with high impact they would retain. He also had considerable ability to condense a whole case into a single pointed question at the end of his cross-examination.[11] These aspects of his advocacy were strongly seen in his defence of the Evening Standard in a much reported action for libel brought by Cadburys, the chocolate manufacturers, in 1909.[12] The case arose from an article in the Standard which contrasted Cadburys well known Quaker benevolence and philanthropy with alleged toleration, and financial support, of a cocoa production and trading system, involving brutal slavery, in San Thome, Portuguese Africa.[13]

Carson's last questions in cross-examination to George Cadbury were:

Carson: *"Now I have come to the end, and I ask you only this one question. From 1901 down to 1908 when you ceased trading, was there anything effective you did at all?"*

Cadbury: *"I think so myself. I admit that my efforts resulted in a good deal less than I should have liked, but I do not admit that I did nothing at all"*.

Carson: *"Have you formed any estimate of the number of slaves who lost their lives in preparing your cocoa from 1901 to 1908?"*

Cadbury: *"No, no, no"*.

Carson's advocacy, like that of Rufus Isaacs was direct, did not rely on theatrical techniques or involve numerous quotations from poetry and

---

[11] Carson's gift of dramatizing long and complex episodes in a few masterly words may be compared with that of Demosthenes in his speech in defence of Ctesiphon and with speeches made by Winston Churchill.

[12] *Cadbury Bros Ltd v The Standard Newspaper* 1909 (Unreported in the law reports). See: Richard DuCann, *The Art of the Advocate*, Penguin Books, 1993, pp. 159–166; Edward Fordham, *Notable Cross-examinations*, Constable, London, 1951, pp. 95–96, and John Munkman, *Technique of Advocacy*, Stevens and Sons, London, 1951, pp. 101–102. The trial was in Birmingham. The plaintiffs were represented by Rufus Isaacs K. C. and John Simon K. C. The jury found for them but Sir Edward Carson's deadly cross-examination had the effect of reducing the damages awarded to one farthing. Also see Lowell J. Satre, *Chocolate on Trial: Slavery, Politics, and the Ethics of Business*, Athens: Ohio University Press, 2005.

[13] For a description of how the production and trading system functioned, see Kevin Grant, *A Civilised Savagery: Britain and the New Slaveries in Africa*, Routledge, 2005.

allusions to the classics; it was not the kind Sir Patrick Hastings less than flatteringly described as "*flatulent oratory*".[14] In the opinion of Lord Birkett, Sir Edward Carson's advocacy influenced Hasting's own forensic style.[15] Certainly he wrote approvingly of Carson in his memoirs, published in 1946:

> *Just as Gerald du Maurier sounded the death knell of the old-time school of thunderous declamation from the stage so Edward Carson put an end to forensic platitudes and passionate but irrelevant perorations from the bar.*[16]

The third leading barrister of the period to be considered is F.E. Smith, Lord Birkenhead (1872–1930). He was also a Conservative politician and like his friend Carson, attracted to the Unionist cause. Called to bar in 1899, after a period of teaching law at Oxford University, Smith was made the youngest Kings Counsel in the country in 1908 before later becoming the youngest Solicitor General, Attorney General and Lord Chancellor, from 1919 to 1922, who, in this capacity, was mainly responsible for the great reforms of property law in 1925; achieving all this before the age of 53.[17] He rapidly acquired a large practice after arriving at the bar, where he was recognized for his extremely quick grasp of the essential facts, knowledge of the law and very effective advocacy, Amongst many *causes celebres*, he was instructed: for the plaintiffs, in the Marconi libel case; on behalf of Ethel Le Neve, the murder's associate, who was acquitted in the trial of Dr. Crippen[18]; and for the co-respondent in the unwholesome Moosbrugger divorce trial in 1913 which was said to have been won by his eloquence.[19] In 1916, as Attorney General, he prosecuted

---

[14] A phrase of Hastings quoted by David Pannick, *Advocates*, Oxford University Press, 1992, page 229.

[15] *Six Great Advocates*, Penguin, 1961, page 29.

[16] *Cases in Court*, William Heineman, 1949, page 11.

[17] See R. F. V. Heuston *Lives of the Lord Chancellors, 1885–1940*, Clarendon Press, 1964, pp. 354–402.

[18] For F. E. Smith's own accounts of the Marconi case and that of Ethel Le Neve, see First Earl of Birkenhead, *Famous Trials*, Hutchinson and Co, Ltd., Edinburgh and London, 1930, *The Marconi Scandal*, pp. 267–276, and Ethel Le Neve: Crippen's Mistress, pp. 277–286.

[19] See: R. F. Heuston, *Lives of the Lord Chancellors 1885–1940*, Oxford, 1964, pp. 362–368 for details of these and other cases in which he appeared.

the Irish nationalist Sir Roger Casement, captured attempting to ship German arms to Ireland. Before the First World War, in a series of notably successful libel actions, beginning in 1906, Smith acted for the industrialist William Lever, later Viscount Leverhulme, against Lord Northcliffe and his various newspapers, who ended up paying nearly a total of £220,000 in damages and costs, then an enormous amount.

"F E"'s style of advocacy, both before judges sitting alone and with juries, was said to be clear, direct and "unceremonious", confidently delivered with an almost "lackadaisical air".[20] Like Rufus Isaacs and Edward Carson, it was not prone to histrionics and blatant general appeals to emotion, frequently intensified by generous quotations from literature or verse. Like theirs, his advocacy resembled Sir Edward Clarke who, a generation or so before, had broken with the profuse, declamatory, melodramatic and meandering style heard throughout much of Victorian Britain. Indeed F. E. Smith, after he retired as Lord Chancellor, dedicated his book written about famous trials to Sir Edward Clarke and recommended "*his standards and methods of advocacy to young gentlemen fitting themselves for practice at the Bar*".[21]

His talent to arrange material in cases to its best effect and ability to argue law, the result of meticulous preparation, was astounding. Despite his reputation as a witty, ruthless and agile cross-examiner, he never sought to score off counsel on the other side, except in self-defence.[22] An instance of his wit in cross-examination is given by his biographer, Bechhofer Roberts:

Smith asked "*Is my client a friend of yours?*" "*Him*" sneered the witness. "*Why, he is the village idiot*". "*I see*", retorted Smith, "*a relation*". Smith's sharpness, presence of mind and ability to lull unsuspecting witnesses onto the rocks, for which he was renowned, is illustrated by the story, well known to barristers at that time and long afterwards, of when he was

---

[20] C. E. Bechhofer Roberts, *Lord Birkenhead*, Newnes, London, 1936, page 114.

[21] Earl of Birkenhead, *Famous Trials*, Hutchinson and Co, Ltd., London, 1930, Dedication. Cases in the book are described concisely, and it is written in clear, assured, largely unornamented, absorbing and usually short sentences, a literary style similar to the author's approach to advocacy in court.

[22] C. E. Roberts, *Lord Birkenhead*, Newness, London, 1936, page 109.

appearing for a bus company against whom damages were claimed for a young man whose arm was said to be permanently disabled after an accident. *"How high can you lift your arm?"* Smith asked the youth. With a show of great pain he raised his arm to the level of his shoulder *"And how far could you raise it before the accident?"* The plaintiff thrust his arm high into the air – and lost his case.[23]

Whilst generally polite to judges and accepting of their authority, Smith was not always so, especially in his early career, and in this it might be said he was closer to Marshall Hall than Rufus Isaacs and Carson. His exchanges with Judge Willis, at Southwark County Court, were reported in the newspapers. One case involved a boy who had been knocked over and injured by a tram. Smith appeared for the company. The judge, perhaps allowing sympathy to overrule his independence, requested that the boy, who had been blinded by the accident, be seated on a chair in front of the jury. When hearing this, F E Smith sarcastically remarked that perhaps the boy should be passed around the jury box. *"That is a most improper remark"*, exclaimed the judge.

"It was provoked by an improper suggestion" was the reply.

Judge Willis paused to think of a trenchant retort and said *"Mr Smith, have you ever heard of a saying by Bacon, the great Bacon, that youth and discretion are ill-wedded companions?"*

"Yes I have", came an instant reply *"and have you ever heard of a saying by Bacon, the great Bacon, that a much talking judge is like an ill tuned cymbal?"*

"You are offensive sir!" said the judge.

"We both are", Smith replied: *"the difference is that I am trying to be, and you can't help it. I, who have been listened to with respect by the highest tribunal in the land, am not going to be browbeaten by a garrulous old county court judge"*.[24] On another occasion, after a long argument on a point of procedure, Judge Willis asked sarcastically *Whatever do you suppose I am on the Bench for Mr Smith?*

---

[23] Roberts, *ibid*, page 112.

[24] It may be that F E Smith was reacting against the devise, much used by barristers in the nineteenth century, of bringing into court small children, who were often far from discouraged to hide their distress, for sentimental effect on juries.

"*It is not for me, m'lud, to attempt to fathom the inscrutable workings of Providence* was the reply".[25]

F E Smith attracted a good deal of criticism later in his career, when Attorney General, for exceeding bar etiquette, requiring restraint by prosecutors, by the vigour with which he sought the conviction of Sir Roger Casement, tried for treason before three High Court Judges in 1916.[26] Sir Roger, previously a distinguished British diplomat, was of Irish descent. He visited Germany on several occasions seeking to persuade Irish prisoners of war to join the Irish Brigade. The intention was to land them and supplies of guns in Ireland to help fuel a rebellion. He was arrested in Ireland after landing from a German vessel. Smith's opening speech concluded with the words:

> *The prisoner, blinded by a hatred for this country, as malignant in quality as it was sudden in origin, has played a desperate hazard. He has played it and he has lost. Today the forfeit is claimed.*

When Casement made a statement from the dock, immediately before being sentenced to death, Smith walked ostentatiously out of Court. After the Court of Appeal subsequently dismissed Casement's appeal there was great controversy about the correctness of the judgement.[27] However an appeal to the House of Lords could only lie with the permission of Smith, as Attorney General, which was refused.[28]

---

[25] C. E. Roberts, *Lord Birkenhead*, Newnes, London, pp. 112–113.

[26] R v Casement 1916 32 TLR 601 K.B. Div; 1916 32 TLR 667 (C. C.A.). Unable to find an English King's Counsel who would accept his instructions, Sir Roger Casement was represented by Sergeant A. M. Sullivan, the last of the Irish sergeants. The case has been seen as a low point in the cab rank rule, adopted since the eighteenth century as a moral justification for advocacy, Chap. 2.

[27] A monumental, and highly detailed, painting, by Sir John Lavery, recording Sir Roger Casement's appeal before five judges in the Court of Appeal against his conviction for treason, may be seen in the King's Inns, Dublin, capital of the Irish Republic.

[28] See: R. F. V. Heuston *Lives of the Lord Chancellors*, 1885–1940, Clarendon Press, 1964, pp. 370–381. F. E. Smith, First Earl of Birkenhead, *Famous Trials*, Hutchinson, Edinburgh and London, 1930, *Sir Roger Casement*, pp. 237–246, said he was placed in a "singularly delicate position" but was convinced there was no substance in the principal point made by Casement's defence that treason could only be committed by a person physically present in the country (Page 244). As Attorney General, F E Smith's fairness as a prosecutor has also been severely questioned in a case which took place the following year that of the trial of Alice Wheeldon, a seller of second hand

Edward Marshall Hall: A Contrasting Advocacy and Attachment to the Old

In the closing of the nineteenth century and first quarter of the 20th, before radio and television, when sensational trials were still such an important source of national entertainment, members of the public would be enthralled by the cases of Edward Marshall Hall, following them in daily newspaper reports and queuing for hours to enter the courts where he appeared. His earlier career, built on dramatic handling of matrimonial, defamation and murder cases, was nearly ruined in the Chattell libel case. Hetty Chattell was enjoying a successful career at the age of 28 when the Daily Mail said that a Gaiety Girl called Rosie Boote was her daughter. It was not true; Miss Chattell had never been married. The Daily Mail therefore implied she had an illegitimate daughter and must be a lot older than she gave the impression. The newspaper never apologized. Marshall Hall won £2500 damages for her. The Daily Mail appealed to the Court of Appeal where Lord Justice Mathew, who disliked him much, bitingly criticised Marshall Hall for remarks to the jury about the Daily Mail's conduct of the case. Lord Justice Mathew's comments were printed with gusto by the newspapers, many of whom had lost defamation cases to plaintiffs represented by Marshall Hall. His confidence was shattered and regular clients deserted him. Only by selling his large collection of silver was he able to survive the down turn in work.[29] Marshall-Hall's

---

clothes, two of her daughters, both school teachers and her son–in–law, a lecturer in chemistry, who were charged with and convicted of conspiracy to murder the prime minister, David Lloyd George. At their committal and trial, Smith employed highly prejudicial, emotive and venomous language and, it is alleged, deliberately suppressed harmful evidence to the Crown in what was in effect a show trial against elements hostile to continuing the War; a view confirmed by the release of MI5 papers eighty years later. See John Jackson, *Losing the Plot*, History Today, May 2007. Interview with Mr. Jackson held on 26th November, 2007.

[29] A. E. Bowker, *Behind the Bar*, 1949, Staples Press, New York, page 27. Harry Furniss's caricature portrait of Marshall – Hall, drawn in the 1890s, kept at the National Portrait Gallery, London, shows him inspecting a piece of silverware and pockets full of others. The latest biographer of Marshall Hall charts the ups and downs of his life and career, and shows how his own experiences and personal losses helped develop his understanding of human nature and enabled him to enter into the minds of a jury. Sally Smith QC, *Marshall Hall: A Law unto Himself*, Wildy Simmonds and Hill Publishing, 2016.

spectacular defence, in 1907, of Robert Wood, an artist on trial for the Camden Town murder, however, fully restored his practice. Wood was accused of the murder of a girl called Emily Dimmock, a part time prostitute who was found in her room naked and with her throat cut.[30] The evidence against him appeared strong. A postcard making an arrangement for them to meet was found in Emily's room, and Wood had been identified as both being in Emily's company on the night of her death and leaving the scene of the crime. Marshall Hall managed to devalue much of the identification evidence, but a major problem was whether to call Wood himself to give evidence, since both Marshall Hall and his instructing solicitor agreed that he would make a dreadful witness. When called, he was, but this worked in his favour, since he impressed as a gentle, talented, rather foolish and somewhat effete young man. Indeed he made his own examination by Marshall Hall as difficult as possible.[31] Marshall Hall asked at the beginning: "Did you kill Phyllis Dimmock?" (*No reply. The witness cast his eyes to Heaven.*)

Wood: Ridiculous (*Arms spread wide*)
Hall: "You must answer straight. I will only ask you perfectly straight questions. Once again, did you kill Phyllis Dimmock?"
Wood: "No, I most certainly did not".

Wood was acquitted by the jury who believed him incapable of murder. He was the first prisoner who successfully gave evidence on his own behalf under the Criminal Evidence Act.[32]

It was said of Marshall Hall had he not been a brilliant advocate he would have been an equally brilliant actor. He himself said:

---

[30] The case of Robert Wood received huge publicity. A little later, in 1908 and 1909, Walter Sickert, important in art in the transition from Impressionism to Modernism, produced, under the title *The Camden Town Murder*, a series of etchings and paintings depicting a clothed man lying next to a naked woman. *The Camden Town Murder*, or *What shall we do about the Rent?* may be seen at the Yale Center for British Art, New Haven, Connecticut, United States.

[31] Du Cann, Richard, *The Art Of The Advocate*, Pelican Books, 1980, page 88. See also Edward Marjoribanks, *For the defence: the life of Sir Edward Marshall Hall*, New York: The Macmillan Company, 1929, Chapter VIII.

[32] For an assessment of Marshall Hall in this case see Basil Hogarth, *Robert Wood, 1907, Famous Trials*, Edited by John Mortimer, Viking Books, 1984, pp. 170–212.

My profession and that of an actor are somewhat akin except that I have no scenes to help me and no words are written for me to say. There is no backcloth to increase the illusion. But out of the vivid, living dream of somebody else's life I have to create an atmosphere; for that is advocacy.[33]

His style of advocacy was certainly florid, emotional and theatrical.[34] It included passionate pleading, mentions of the Almighty (in earlier life Marshall Hall had been a preacher), weeping, allowing tears to stream down his cheeks as he spoke, and a variety of methods to distract the attention of jurors from unhelpful evidence being given by witnesses for the prosecution such as blowing his nose loudly, inflating a rubber cushion, used to ease his suffering from haemorrhoids – a condition unkindly said to be an occupational hazard for lawyers – and knocking over a glass of water. He favoured grand stage like entrances into courtrooms accompanied by junior barristers and attendants to heighten his dramatic affect on the jury. It was said when Marshall Hall came into court everybody was conscious of his presence:

There was a subtle change in the atmosphere, a tightening of the tension, an air of expectation, due in some measure to the extraordinary power of reputation, but mainly to his physical presence.[35]

In his closing speech on behalf of Edward Lawrence, indicted in 1909, for the murder of his lover with a gun, Marshall Hall stood with his arms outstretched and asked the jurors to imagine "*a great statue of justice holding those two scales with equally honest hands*". He then started to consider the evidence for and against the defendant. First one side, and then the other, he told them – swaying all the while – might appear lower and at times it might be impossible to tell which side was closest to the ground. As the captivated jurors watched he said:

---

[33] Quoted by Mark Lewis, *The Great Defender: Sir Edward Marshall Hall*, The Law Society Gazette. No 27, pp. 35–37, July, 13th, 1988.

[34] In the opinion of George Keaton, *Harris's Hints on Advocacy*, London, Stevens, 1943, page 9, Marshall Hall's style *recalled some of our great tragedians*.

[35] Lord Birkett, Presidential Address to the Holdsworth Club of the Faculty of Law, Birmingham University, 7th May, 1954.

Then in the one scale, in the prisoner's scale, unseen by human eye, is placed that overbalancing weight, the weight of the presumption of innocence...... it is your duty to remember the invisible weight of that invisible substance.[36]

He then let one arm drop with a thud to the bench.[37]

Although it is a fundamental rule of advocacy that no advocate may state his own belief in the innocence of his client, Marshall-Hall, was renowned for an ability to completely identify himself in court with his clients, said to flow from a sympathy and understanding of human frailty. He once wrote:

...if an advocate for the defence can legitimately in his advocacy convey to the jury the impression of his belief in his client's case, he has gone a long way towards securing their verdict[38]

He was also known for his audacious court reconstruction of crimes to emphasize to the Jury the importance of seemingly insignificant pieces of evidence. This technique was seen early in his career, when he acted the part of Marie Herman, an alleged murderess, with an iron bar, to show what he suggested actually took place. Famously, 30 years later at the Old Bailey, when he defended Madame Fahmy on a charge of shooting her husband, a rich Egyptian bey who had ill-treated her for many years, Marshall Hall, in his closing speech, crouched in front of the jury with the pistol in his hand and pretended to be her in her room at the Savoy Hotel. He next imitated the approach of her husband, who was intent on injuring her, and then Madame Fahmy's raising of the pistol as he came in. When he reached the moment the pistol went off and the husband fell, Marshall Hall let the gun fall to the floor with an enormous clatter, breaking the intense stillness of the court and greatly effecting all present.[39] The jury accepted her plea of self-defence.

---

[36] *Charge of Murder. Prisoner's Evidence*, The Times, 8th March, 1909, page 5.
[37] Edward Lawrence was acquitted. Edward Marjoribanks, *For the Defence: the Life of Sir Edward Marshall Hall QC*, New York: The Macmillan Company. 1929, pp. 256–64.
[38] Quoted by Richard Du Cann, *The Art of the Advocate*, Pelican Books, 1980, page 61.
[39] Lord Birkett, *Six great advocates*, Penguin Books, 1961, pp. 15–17.

Keeping alive the tradition of many nineteenth century advocates, he liberally used poetry and literature; a notable example being in the case of Harold Greenwood, a solicitor on trial in 1920 at Carmarthen Assizes for murdering his wife with arsenic. After dropping his voice to a whisper in his closing speech, Marshall Hall quoted to the jury the passage in full from Othello when he entered Desdemona's chamber which begins: "*Put out the light, and then put out the light*. Still in a low voice, he continued: *Are you going by your verdict to put out that light?* Then in a clear loud tone he said *No gentlemen of the Jury, I demand at your hands the life and liberty of Harold Greenwood*". He was acquitted.[40]

His most famous defences were of the Seddons (1912), George Smith, the "Brides in the Bath" murderer (1915), and of Ronald Light in the "Green Bicycle Case" (1920). Knowledge and ability to argue law, it has been said, were of secondary importance to him, his being an instinctual rather than planned performance. Marshall Hall, himself, admitted he was no great lawyer and when, during the course of a trial, a point of law arose he would mutter, in a stage whisper, to his junior "*You had better deal with this point it has some law in it*". A famous example of acting instinctively on the spur of the moment, and very effectively, was at the end of his defence of Marie Hermann in 1894.[41] Marie Hermann was a 47 year old Austrian born prostitute, much devoured by the life she had been forced to lead, who was accused of murdering an elderly client, Henry Stephens, whom she had solicited when he was drunk, with a poker in her room, after a dispute over payment. Marie Herman was prosecuted by Charles Mathews QC, who, earlier in his career, had established a reputation for brilliant cross-examination, by asking what appeared to be harmless questions but when taken together were quite deadly and also, when prosecuting murder, for dwelling on blood shed by victims; this case was no exception[42] At the end of his closing speech, as he was about to sit down, Marshall Hall saw Marie Hermann hunched in

---

[40] Winifred Drake gives a full account of this case in *The Trial of Harold Greenwood*, in the *Notable British Trials* series, W. Hodge and Co, Edinburgh and London, 1930.

[41] See, Richard Whittington – Egan, *God never gave her a chance – will you?*, New Law Journal, April 17th, 2000, page 522.

[42] Richard Hamilton, *All Jangle and Riot*, Professional Books, 1986, pp. 170–171.

the dock weeping. Seizing the moment, and without the slightest hesitation, he then said to the jury:

> *Remember that these women are what men made them. And do not forget, even she at one time was a beautiful and innocent child.....Look at her, gentlemen of the jury, look at her. God never gave her a chance, won't you?*

The jury did, returned a verdict of manslaughter and called for leniency.[43]

Another striking example of apparent spontaneity, and willingness to jettison carefully laid plans when opportunity presented itself, may be seen much later in Marshall Hall's career in 1924. He was briefed to defend a newspaper in a libel action brought by a woman MP who alleged the paper had implied she had entered parliament purely to win the title of the best dressed woman member of parliament. Whilst on his feet, he stopped in the middle of his speech to the jury because of the two minutes' silence then observed in all courts on Armistice Day. After it had finished he said:

> *Members of the Jury, we have just been celebrating the anniversary of the greatest national sacrifice which the world has ever seen. We have all suffered loss in the war; you have suffered.....And now, turning from this great national ceremony, we find ourselves in this court, and have to address ourselves to the trifling grievances of this lady.......*[44]

Marshall Hall gained the verdict sought by his client. Interestingly, opinion about his speech divided between those who considered that he had done what was necessary to win, and hence acceptable, and others who thought it was a nauseating display of emotion. The latter view, perhaps, reflected how sensibilities to the use of strong appeals to emotion by advocates had changed from Victorian times.

He was criticized, since the very beginning of his career, for being too ready to quarrel with judges, although it was said some of the judges were

---

[43] Mr. Justice Wells was hardly receptive to their plea and sentenced her to six years penal servitude.
[44] Reproduced by Richard DuCann, *The Art of the Advocate*, 1993, Penguin, page 70.

equally at fault and that at least one of them may well have been driven by malice.[45]

Sir Norman Birkett acknowledged that Marshall Hall: "*On his good days could dominate the Court and everybody in it, judge, jury and spectators alike, by the mere splendour of his presence and the compelling power of his forensic oratory*".[46] However, he rather qualified Edward Marjoribanks, Marshall Hall's rather eulogistic biographer[47] – who likened him to the great Roman forensic orator Hortensius, remembered because of his splendid physical presence, public adulation and powers of eloquent and persuasive speech – recalling Marshall Hall "*to be the strangest mixture of perfections and imperfections that I ever knew at the Bar*". A little further he said:

> *Sometimes with his quick and almost uncanny perception of the important point in a case, he would seize it, throw away every carefully conceived plan, and win victory against all the odds; and then, at other times, when he was at the most important stage of some other case, he would be suddenly blind to the most obvious considerations. His judgment would desert him, and he himself would become quite bewildered and lost.*

To illustrate his point about the unpredictability and flawed genius of Marshall Hall, Sir Norman Birkett told how when Sir Douglas Hogg, then Attorney General, was asked in 1923 to recommend counsel in the Russell divorce case he said, "*There's only one man at the bar who might pull it off for you. He might win you a brilliant victory or he might make a terrible mess of it; but I believe that he is the only man who can do it – get Marshall Hall*". In that case he was successful.

He then compared him to Patrick Hastings (1880–1952), a somewhat later barrister, "*who was made in quite another mould. There was nothing flamboyant about him. He was exceedingly scornful of some forms of forensic oratory and never attempted any flights himself.........The strength of*

---

[45] Sir Norman Birkett, *Six Great Advocates*, Penguin, 1961, page 20.

[46] Holdsworth Address in 1954, *ibid.*

[47] Edward Marjoribanks, *For the defence: the life of Sir Edward Marshall Hall*, New York: The Macmillan Company, 1929.

Hastings lay in quite another direction. He was, I think, the greatest cross-examiner I ever heard. He could destroy a witness with quite shattering power with his direct, incisive and penetrating questions, that came from him with the precision and speed of a machine gun. Remorselessly and relentlessly he broke down all defences, and when the triumph was complete he would make the briefest possible speech and sit down".[48]

An Assessment of the Advocacy of the Four Leaders and the Influence They Exerted

In Chap. 5, it was described how in the later Victorian period men like Hardinge Gifford, John Holker, Charles Russell and Edward Clarke began to alter significantly the general style of advocacy towards being quieter, more learned and inclined less to violent appeals to emotions, florid language and quotations from literature and popular verse. These barristers tended to select the best arguments from their client's case and drive them home forcibly, rather than saturate jurors with rhetorical elaboration of all conceivable points. Less concerned with relying on the tricks of the Victorian stage, they also conducted themselves in a more dignified manner towards judges, each other and witnesses. Their triumphs in cases, particularly famous ones, consciously or unconsciously, influenced other, often more junior, members of the bar to copy their methods increasingly. Painting with a broad brush, and aware of its limitations, it might validly be said that Rufus Isaacs, Edward Carson and F E Smith, save for the occasional disrespect he showed to certain judges, were their successors in advocacy. They were, however, heirs who took the art further, especially in their use of conversational language and in refining skills of careful and precise cross – examination, at the expense of long closing speeches; the quieter, but nonetheless more deadly, small snipers rifle with accurate sights was replacing loud, but often inaccurate, weaponry.

---

[48] Sir Norman Birkett, *Six Great Advocates*, Penguin, London, 1961, pp. 9–11.

Marshall Hall's record of victories before juries in murder trials during three decades, his intensity and passion, spell binding oratory, capable of sweeping jurors off their feet, ability to speak simply and attractively to ordinary people, and his dramatic reconstructions place him uniquely in the history of English advocacy in court. It can also be said that he fell within the tradition of histrionic advocacy, often declaimed and sometimes sprinkled in tears, with its blatant appeal to emotion, that had been witnessed so much in the nineteenth century.[49] Indeed Marshall Hall could be said to be almost its final deep gasp. Sir Norman Birkett described Marshall Hall as one of the "*last great forensic orators*".[50] In a similar vein, George Keeton appraised him "*the last of the dramatic criminal advocates*".[51]

Although overwhelmingly successful before juries, to whom he always really spoke even when addressing the judge or cross-examining a witness, Marshall Hall often failed to convince the Court of Criminal Appeal and other courts where there was no jury. An inability to adapt to these courts by following a more restrained form of advocacy, and in presenting clear factual and legal arguments,[52] led to uncomplimentary comparisons being drawn with his contemporaries, not of the "*histrionic school of advocacy*", including Sir Edward Carson, Sir Rufus Isaacs and F E Smith who appeared equally at home in any court with or without a jury. They instinctively tailored themselves to the tribunal and in Keeton's opinion "*their advocacy was on that account more universal in its appeal*" and of greater influence on the development of court advocacy than that of Marshall Hall. There can, however, be no doubt that the legendary "Great

---

[49] Edward Marjoribanks, *ibid*, page 29, describes how Marshall Hall, in 1884, during his first year of being a barrister, went to the Old Bailey and observed Sergeant Ballantine and Montagu Williams, both exemplars of florid and theatrical advocacy, Chap. 5, although very much in the advanced stages of their careers. It may be reasonable to speculate that Marshall Hall was much influenced by what he saw.

[50] Sir Norman Birkett, *Six Great Advocates* Penguin, London page 21.

[51] *Harris on Advocacy: The Conduct of Cases Civil and Criminal*, 18th Edition, Stevens and Sons, 1943, page 9.

[52] See Sir Norman Birkett, *Six Great Advocates*, Penguin 1961, pp. 19–20. Also Richard DuCann, *The Art of the Advocate*, Penguin, 1993, page 120, "*Marshall Hall was a supremely good jury advocate, but he was no lawyer*".

Defender's" exaggerated and exuberant style, which had brought him staggering success before juries and immense affection from the bar and public at large, did effect the conduct of criminal trials before juries by some barristers for years to come. His memory, unlike that of his contemporaries, never disappeared from the public being revived in the form of a television series in the 1970s, radio adaptations by John Mortimer of some of his trials in 1996[53] and during the early 2000s and, to an extent, through Mortimer's fictional creation, "Rumpole".[54]

---

[53] In his introduction to the radio adaptations, broadcast in 1996, John Mortimer began by saying that if you asked barristers of his generation what had made them buy a wig and gown they would say it was not they thirsted after justice it was because they had read the life and cases of Marshall Hall. "*Tall, handsome, silver-tongued, he could dominate a courtroom and woo a jury as no one has before or since*". Michael Vestey, *Murder most gripping.* The Spectator, November 23rd, 1996. In an interview a retired barrister, approximately ten years younger than John Mortimer, ventured that that perhaps the most enduring legacy of Edward Marshall Hall observed in his career was the adoption by some counsel in closing speeches of the scales of justice and the invisible weight of the presumption of innocence devise, made well known by Marshall Hall in the Edward Lawrence case. Some barristers in dealing with the evidence would perform the scales, whilst others would talk about the scales of justice and the presumption. (Interview with John Downing, 2nd April, 2007.)

[54] Horace Rumpole, who first appeared on television in the late 1970s, was said to be composed of fragments of real barristers, admired by John Mortimer, including his blind father, the quick tempered Clifford Mortimer, remembered for quoting much Shakespeare, and early nineteenth century English poetry, James Burge, a flamboyant Old Bailey junior, perhaps most recalled for his defence of Stephen Ward during the Profumo scandal in 1963 and Jeremy Hutchinson QC, renowned for his fearlessness, independence and total dedication to often unprepossessing clients. Geoffrey Robertson QC, *Rumpole of the Bailey: the very incarnation of English liberty.* The Times, January 17th, 2009.

9

The Silent Revolution in Methods of Advocacy

In 1943, during wartime Britain, G. W Keeton, then Professor of English Law and Dean of the Faculties of Laws in The University of London and at the University College, London, wrote about "*a silent revolution in methods of advocacy as practised by the English Bar*"[1] that had taken place over the previous 50 years. He observed that changed standards of professional etiquette and steadily greater dignity of the judiciary[2] had led to a

---

[1] G. W. Keeton, *Harris's Hints on Advocacy*, Stevens and Sons, 1943, page 10.

[2] Certainly by the latter part of the nineteenth century most judges exerted authority over advocates in court, something not all of them had been able to do sufficiently earlier. (See George King, *Lawyers and Eloquence*, In William Andrews ed., *The Lawyer in History, Literature and Humour*, William Andrews and Co, 1896, page 264.). Contributing to deference and courtesy shown to judges by barristers was greater respect for their intellectual and practical abilities as lawyers. Beginning in the 1860s both Conservative Lord Chancellors (Cairns) and Liberals (Hatherley and Selborne) sought to professionalise the judiciary and to make merit the consideration for appointment to the bench. (Robert Stevens, *The English Judges*, Hart Publishing, Oxford and New York, 2005, Chapter One) The movement towards meritocracy was to some extent impeded by Lord Halsbury (Hardinge Giffard) in the seventeen years he was Lord Chancellor between 1885 and 1905. His appointments were much criticised on the grounds "*he appointed to the High Court, and to a lesser extent the county court, men of little or no legal learning whose previous career in public life had been largely in the service of the Conservative Party or else were relations of his own*" (R. F. V. Heuston, *The Lives of the Lord Chancellors 1885–1940*, Oxford: Clarendon Press, 1987, page 36.). From Lord Haldane's Chancellorship (1912–15) legal and professional qualifications firmly became the criteria, though at first the change was not extended to the most senior appointments.

© The Author(s) 2019
A. Watson, *Speaking in Court*, https://doi.org/10.1007/978-3-030-10395-8_9

vast increase in courtesy between the court and counsel and between counsel. Quarrels in court were rare and when they did occur was regarded as a departure from professional good manners rather than a normal incident of litigation.[3] All barristers who practised in the common law courts were required to choose a circuit in which to work and, by convention to dine frequently in the circuit mess. In the last decades of the nineteenth century messes grew stronger in maintaining accepted professional standards of behaviour; the expulsion of Dr. Kenealy, for his conduct in criminal Tichborne Claimant case, from the Oxford Circuit Bar mess in 1874 is an early example of their willingness if necessary to take severe sanctions. Institution of a bar mess at the Old Bailey in 1891, a step spoken about since the 1840s to improve standards, may well have contributed to better behaviour there.[4] The conduct of prosecutions had also improved. Unlike in the previous century, they were no longer carried out in a "*sneering hectoring manner with witnesses mercilessly browbeaten and bullied if the occasion warranted*".[5] The idea of the prosecutor acting as a minister of justice, and therefore not striving for a conviction at any cost, was now firmly part of the etiquette of the Bar. This limited, if it did not eliminate, appeals by prosecutors to jurors' emotions.

It was widely held that Sir Richard Muir (1857–1924) was responsible for much of the improvement, especially at the Old Bailey – practice there influencing other courts – and introduced an atmosphere of fair-

---

However, a little later, Lord Sankey, Lord Chancellor from 1929 to 1935, when resignations occurred, replaced five Law Lords who had political backgrounds by others whose reputations rested on their professionalism as lawyers. (J. A. G. Griffiths, *The Politics of the Judiciary*, Fifth Edition, 1997, Fontana Press, Page 16. Also see, Shimon Shetreet, *Judges on Trial*, 1976, North Holland Publishing Company, pp. 70–71.)

[3] Great shock was felt when two barristers fought in court in 1907. The incident is described by David Pannick, Advocates, Oxford, 1993, page 54.

[4] Allyson May, *The Bar and the Old Bailey*, 1750–1850, University of North Carolina Press, Chapel Hill and London, 2003, page 242.

[5] William Cornish, *The Jury*, Penguin Books, 1971 (revised edition) page 168. See also Leo Page *First Steps in Advocacy*, Faber and Faber, 1943, pp. 127–128: "*Years ago the name 'Old Bailey lawyer' was a term of reproach. It indicated the man who was out to get a conviction even if it meant that he had to descend to any trick or unworthy expedient for the purpose…………… There has been a complete revulsion from those days when conviction was the object and the methods by which it was gained were immaterial*".

ness and impartiality in prosecutions which had never been seen before.[6] Underhandedness or trickiness in the task was said to be alien to him.[7] As a prosecutor he was regarded as the greatest of his time and represented the Crown in every trial of note in the Old Bailey from 1901 until his death. Born in Scotland, the son of a shipping broker from Greenock, he went to London with intentions of becoming an actor but, after a period working as a parliamentary reporter for *The Times*, abandoned his earlier ambition, turned to law and was called to the Bar at Middle Temple, where he later became a Master of the Bench. Muir was known to be hard working with little apparent need for conviviality. He usually spent half the night preparing for his cases and made notes on small cards with coloured pencils – one colour for examination in chief, one for cross-examination and another for possible re-examination. It was reported Muir could check up in a moment upon any contradiction or alteration between evidence given by one witness and another at the trial and what he had said when at the police court.[8] These cards were noticed in court and became known as Muir's "playing cards". He asked for painstaking thoroughness from the police in obtaining evidence. When presenting cases he placed much weight on physical evidence and little on eye witness testimony, except if it would bolster more concrete evidence. It was Muir who conducted the first prosecution involving finger print evidence in 1902.[9] Whilst Richard Muir deliberately avoided raising the emotional temperature, it was said that the "*lucidity of his argument and the clarity with which he stated the facts in his opening speeches wove a net so tightly round the prisoner in the dock that he could never afterwards escape from it*".[10]

---

[6] Richard DuCann, *The Art of the Advocate*, Revised Edition, 1993, Penguin Books, page 115.

[7] See Travers Humphreys, who knew him well, *Criminal Days*, Hodder and Stoughton, 1946, page 81.

[8] Travers Humphreys, *ibid*, page 80.

[9] Harry Jackson was found guilty at the Old Bailey of a charge of burglary of a house and stealing billiard balls. He received seven years penal servitude. The implications of the new technique were quickly realized in prosecutions. The attitude of some judges to fingerprints was one of distrust, but the value of this evidence was placed beyond doubt when, in 1910, the Court of Criminal Appeal upheld a conviction based solely on fingerprint evidence (R v Castleton (1909) 3 Cr App R 74).

[10] Richard DuCann, *The Art of the Advocate*, Revised Edition, 1993, Penguin Books, page 72.

Such was his reputation for meticulousness and great diligence that Dr. Crippen, on hearing that Muir was to prosecute him, said "*I wish it had been anybody else.... I fear the worst*". Muir's cross-examination of Crippen, before Lord Chief Justice Alverstone in Court No 1 at the Old Bailey, was a masterpiece of clear, direct and polite questioning, in simple language, each question dealing with one fact at a time, which conveyed to the jury the strength of the case for the prosecution. Characteristically, he saved all comment on the answers until his closing speech.[11]

Dramatic types of nineteenth century advocacy, in which counsel was prepared to adopt mannerisms, tricks of speech and gestures, parodied in Gilbert and Sullivan's *Trial by Jury*, to heighten the effect of their plea, Professor Keeton reported in 1943 had become almost obsolete:

> *A visitor straying into our courts (with the possible exception of the Central Criminal Court) might be forgiven if he imagined himself to be witnessing some unusual kind of company meeting. The tone of counsel is conversational and matter of fact. There is a somewhat misleading air of casualness about the proceedings.*[12]

---

[11] Richard DuCann, *The Art of the Advocate* Revised Edition 1993, Penguin Books, pp. 126–128. For that part of Muir's cross-examination of Dr. Crippen which concerned whether the human remains found in his house were those of Mrs. Crippen, a vital question for the jury, see E.W. Fordham, *Notable Cross –Examinations*, Constable, 1951, Chap. XI. The influence of Edward Muir endures. Over a hundred years later his cross-examination of Crippen is still held, by authors of text books on acquiring the skills of advocacy, to be a model of cross-examination techniques for both prosecution and defence. See, David Ross QC (*Advocacy*, Cambridge University Press, 2007, pp. 69–70.), who quotes passages from it and Robert McPeake (*Advocacy Manual*, Oxford University Press, 2009, pp. 179–188.), who reproduces a sizeable part. Richard Muir's preparatory notes for his prosecution of Crippen, commended by David Ross as "*an example to us all*", page 18, were found and published. They appear in Louis Blom-Cooper, *The Law As Literature*, The Bodley Head, London, 1961, pp. 14–33. Also see a commentary on them by Mr. Justice JH Phillips, *Practical Advocacy*, (1988) 62 Australian Law Journal 627–629.

[12] G.W. Keeton, *Harris's Hints on Advocacy*, Stevens and Sons, 1943, page 10. Nearly three decades before, in 1915, in the Foreword to *Illustrations In Advocacy by Richard Harris K. C*, Fifth Edition, a book mainly for aspiring and newly qualified barristers, George Elliot, K.C. wrote: "*It is said by many that eloquence is not now encouraged in the courts, that the artifices of advocacy are discouraged, that a plain brief statement of fact, as concise and succinct as the nature of the case will permit, is the style which best commends itself to the Bench, and the exigencies of time, whether in civil causes or in criminal trials, do not permit of those methods of advocacy which were so effective in days gone by*".

Sir Norman Birkett, an eminent advocate of the first half of the last century, in an address delivered in Gray's Inn Hall said of the altered style of advocacy: "*There may have been days when a flowery speech was effective, but it is no longer effective. Times change; manners change; all things change. Though the advocate of today does not seek to commend himself by flowery speech, he does seek to be persuasive*".[13] Advocates now sought to be persuasive by a conversational matter of fact advocacy making points earnestly, and if necessary, with persistence but rarely indulging in rhetoric in its pejorative sense of artful bombast and verbal chicanery, and normally avoiding the sorts of tricks and effects that were used previously.[14]

Giving the Haldane Memorial Lecture, in the same year that Keeton wrote about advocacy in court, Sir Gervaise Rentoul, the Chief Stipendiary Magistrate of London, stated "*… anything in the nature of theatricality should be avoided*, although, *in a criminal trial some dramatic licence may be permissible when the emotions of the jury are highly charged*".[15] On cross-examination he said: "*The old idea that to cross-examine means the same as to examine crossly has long disappeared. The successful advocate nowadays no longer thumps the desk with his brief; the rapier has taken the place of the broadsword: Sergeant Buzfuz is dead*".[16]

In 1917 the governing body of the Bar, the Bar Council, adopted a number of rules to control barristers when faced with making suggestions of fraud or dishonesty or attacking the credit of witnesses they had to cross examine. Subject to minor amendments they continue today.

---

[13] July 1st, 1957, entitled "*The Advocate*", published in Graya, No 46, pp. 89–96. Viscount Simon, in his forward to Leo Page's *First Steps in Advocacy*, Faber and Faber, 1943, pp. 7–8, wrote: "*A plain accurate statement arranged in the right order is worth tons of rhetoric. Juries, no less than magistrates and judges, want to do right; they are not impressed, any of them, by blather and pomposity, but are grateful for clear exposition*".

[14] Leo Page, *First Steps in Advocacy*, Faber and Faber, 1943, pp. 20–27, considered advocates would most likely achieve success by "*simplicity, sincerity* and *moderation*" in manner and matter and that persuasiveness would be much assisted by audibility, clear articulation, inflection to avoid monotony and for emphasis and absence of studied gesture (Chapter 5).

[15] On eschewing theatricality, Leo Page, *First Steps in Advocacy*, Faber and Faber, also published in 1943, page 24 wrote: "*A law court is seldom a fit place for stage business. Incidentally, the highly dramatic manner is a treacherous tool in inexpert hands. A first-class tragedian moves us with horror and emotion, but a second – rate performer excites only our ridicule. So it is in court*".

[16] Sir Gervais Rentoul, *The Art and Ethics of Advocacy*, Haldane Memorial Lecture, 1943, page 9.

Under the rules barristers could not suggest that a witness, or other person, is guilty of a crime, fraud or misconduct of which their client is accused unless such allegations go to a matter in issue (including the credibility of a witness) which was material to their client's case and which appeared to them to be supported by reasonable grounds.[17] Also they were prohibited from asking questions which were merely scandalous or intended or calculated only to vilify, insult or annoy either a witness or some other person.[18]

Serjeant Buzfuss's spirit of heavily belabouring witnesses in cross-examination had not entirely expired and appeared in a case before a High Court judge and a jury in 1934. The higher judiciary, however, showed a determination to send it on its way. The chief protagonists on either side of the cause, Mr. Lehwess and Sir Herbert Austin respectively, were cross-examined. Measured by the shorthand note Mr. Lehwess's examination occupied 80 pages; his cross-examination 265 pages. The examination in chief of Sir Herbert Austin occupied 39 pages and his cross-examination 148 pages. On matters of law, the case went to the Court of Appeal and on further appeal to the House of Lords.[19] The Lord Chancellor, Viscount Sankey, agreed with the censure of Lord Hanworth, Master of the Rolls, in the Court of Appeal, who had said "*There is a tedious iteration in some of the questions asked, and prolonged emphasis is laid on some matters trivial in relation to the main issues. Cross-examination is a powerful and valuable weapon for the purpose of testing the veracity of a witness and the accuracy and completeness of his story. It is entrusted in the hands of counsel in the confidence that it will be used with discretion; and with due regard to the assistance to be rendered by it to the Court, not forgetting at the same time the burden that is imposed upon witnesses. We desire to say that in our opinion the cross-examination in the present case did not conform to the above conditions, and at times it failed to display that measure*

---

[17] Now contained in Bar Code of Conduct para 708(j) and Written Standards para 5.10(h). Also, concerning advocacy by solicitors see Law Society's Code for Advocacy, Part VII para 7.1 (h).

[18] Now embodied in Bar Code of Conduct para 708(h) and Written Standards para 5.10. See also Law Society's Code for Advocacy Part VII para 7.1 (e).

[19] *Mechanical and General Inventions Co. and Lehwess v. Austin and the Austin Motor Co.* [1935] A.C. 346.

of courtesy to the witness which is by no means inconsistent with a skilful, yet powerful, cross-examination".[20]
The Lord Chancellor then went further in his criticism:

> *It is right to make due allowance for the irritation caused by the strain and stress of a long and complicated case, but a protracted and irrelevant cross-examination not only adds to the cost of litigation but is a waste of public time. Such a cross-examination becomes indefensible when it is conducted, as it was in this case, without restraint and without the courtesy and consideration which a witness is entitled to expect in a Court of law. It is not sufficient for the due administration of justice to have a learned, patient and impartial judge. Equally with him, the solicitors who prepare the case and the counsel who present it to the Court are taking part in the great task of doing justice between man and man.*[21]

In the course of a lecture on advocacy at Gray's Inn in 1938, Sir Malcolm Hilberry, then a King's Bench judge, considered the place of emotion in jury trials. In contrast to blatantly emotional advocacy, often short on analysis of the facts – or indeed sometimes almost completely replacing it – which was much heard in the preceding century, he observed that triumphant jury advocacy now made an appeal to reason combined with a subtle, restrained and focused appeal to emotion:

> *You will notice............ that the successful jury advocate always gives his address to a jury in the form of a well built argument, while the emphasis and appeal are all the time strongly emotional. The facts are marshalled to form the steps of the argument leading to the conclusion that is sought, but the nervous force of a controlled emotion passes all the while from the advocate to the jury, first to arrest their attention, then to hold it, and finally to dominate their judgment. It is in such work that rhetoric has its place and the sense of the dramatic.*[22]

---

[20] *Mechanical and General Inventions Co. and Lehwess v. Austin and the Austin Motor Co.* [1935] A.C. 359.

[21] *Ibid*, page 360.

[22] *Duty and Art* in *Advocacy*, a lecture delivered at Gray's Inn in Hilary Term 1938, Graya NoXX, Easter, page 11. Largely reproduced in Sir Malcolm Hilberry, *Duty and Art in Advocacy*, Sweet and

In a small profession where, until the end of the 1980s, there was very little formal instruction on advocacy, the views of judges and their ability to act on them by the way they received advocates in court, and those held by senior barristers, were influential, especially on newly called members of the bar, whose main method of learning was studying more senior barristers -watching *big men* in court[23]-, following the techniques of the successful and avoiding those of the unsuccessful.

Continued Decline of Jury Trials

In addition to changes in professional etiquette and rules and readier acceptance by the Bar of judicial control over legal proceedings, already mentioned, a number of other reasons also account for the transformation in style that had occurred. Continued fall in civil jury trials undoubtedly played a significant part. Reduction in the use of civil juries begun in the nineteenth century (by the end of that century only half of civil trials in the High Court were by a jury) gathered pace during the first half of the twentieth century. After 1935 it could be asserted that the jury trials in county courts had practically ceased to exist.

At High Court level, the judicature commissioners and a departmental committee which reported in 1913 favoured a more restricted right to trial by jury in civil cases. No changes were made until the Juries Act 1918, which was principally enacted because of shortages of jurors in wartime. The Act provided that all cases in the High Court should be before a judge without a jury unless the Court saw fit to order one, subject to the right to jury trial in cases alleging fraud, libel, slander, malicious prosecution, false imprisonment, seduction, breach of promise to marry, contested matters in divorce and heir – ship in

---

Maxwell, 1946. Concerning the use of controlled emotion, Leo Page, *First Steps in Advocacy*, Faber and Faber, 1943, pp. 128–129, wrote: "*It is legitimate for defending counsel to use pathos in order to move a jury in the interests of his client. But it is not considered to be the duty of counsel for the prosecution to be vindictive or to attempt to excite the indignation of a jury against a defendant by rhetoric*".

[23] As regularly observing the performance of distinguished barristers in court was described by Leo Page *First Steps in Advocacy*, Page 73.

probate actions. The pre - Juries Act 1918 position regarding juries was, however, restored by the Administration of Justice Act, 1925. Complaints about the cost and delays in proceedings at common law led to the re-introduction of restrictive legislation in the form of the Administration of Justice Act (Miscellaneous Provisions) Act 1933.[24] This Act, which encountered very little public opposition, removed an absolute right to jury trial in the King's Bench Division of the High Court. Trial by jury was to be ordered in cases of fraud, libel, slander, malicious prosecution, false imprisonment, seduction or breach of promise of marriage unless the court was of the opinion that the trial required any prolonged examination of documents or accounts or any scientific or local investigation which could not be conveniently made with a jury. In other cases the Court had a discretion to order a jury. This was applied narrowly.[25] Jury trial became more and more of a rarity as litigants, forsaking the traditionally rehearsed arguments in its support, increasingly opted for trial by judges alone to avoid delay and expense. Indeed seeking trial by jury came to be regarded with suspicion: it suggested the hope of confusion in a weak case, or the expectation of exorbitant damages in cases involving distressing details or high feelings.[26] Decline of trial by jury amounted to *a revolution in practice*.[27] Persuasiveness in front of Judges with no jury needed advocates to concentrate clearly on the facts in issue, an ability to argue relevant law, and a brisk unrepetitious delivery. It did not require oratorical

---

[24] For a closely contemporary analysis of the Act's provisions for civil jury trials see R. M. Jackson, *Incidence of Jury Trial During the Past Century*, Modern Law Review, Volume 1, No 2, Sept. 1937, pp. 141–142.

[25] Under the present law, Section 69 of the Supreme Court Act 1981, the right to jury trial is limited to only four specific areas: fraud, defamation, malicious prosecution and false imprisonment (Similar provisions are contained in the County Courts Act 1984.) Even in these matters, the right is not absolute and can be denied by a judge, under Section 69 (i) where *the case involves any prolonged examination of documents or accounts or any scientific or local investigation which cannot conveniently be made with a jury.*

[26] The temporary prohibition on civil jury service in the Second World War was a later blow from which civil juries never recovered. J. H. Baker, *An Introduction to English Legal History*, Butterworths, 2002, page 92.

[27] A. H. Manchester, *A Modern Legal History of England and Wales 1750–1950*, Butterworths, 1980, page, 95.

embellishment. A view from the judiciary on this point was clearly put by Mr. Justice Hilberry in his address on advocacy at Gray's Inn Hall in 1938:

> *A Judge is rendered uneasy by oratorical flourishes. Let the language there conform to the standards of the best prose. In the words of Robert Louis Stevenson "Beware of purple passages". Wed yourself to a cold "austerity".* Continuing, Hilberry then told an amusing story about Mr Justice Swift[28]:
>
> *A counsel, much given to emotional rhetoric began to open a case before the learned Judge sitting alone. He had not gone far before he was giving full rein to his oratory. Mr. Justice Swift tapped his desk; "Mr. Blank", he said, "there is no jury." There came the appropriate apology but again counsel was soon indulging in rolling periods and high-flown declamation. For some time the judge suffered it, then there came the tap of his pencil on the desk. "Usher", he said, "switch on the light over the jury box – Mr. Blank does not believe me".[29]*

Opportunities for criminal trials before juries lessened in 1925 when the Criminal Justice Act of that year brought a large number of offences previously triable only by a judge and jury within the jurisdiction of magistrates at petty sessions.[30]

---

[28] For more on Rigby Swift see E. S. Fay, *The Life of Mr. Justice Swift*, Methuen, 1939.

[29] In similar vein, though from the perspective of the Bar, Sir Patrick Hastings wrote: "*The judge has been at the game too long. His every instinct struggles against the possibility that he may be influenced against the true letter of the law by a speech however artistically or impressively it may be phrased. The decision is to be his and his alone; he knows the law, and he desires to know the facts; and after that he infinitely prefers to be left alone*". Patrick Hastings, *Cases in Court*, William Heinemann 1949, page 10. Lord Bingham, before his retirement as Senior Law Lord, in *The Role of the Advocate in a Common Law System*, The Inaugural Birkenhead Lecture Given in Gray's Inn Hall in 2008 (seventy years after Mr. Justice Hilberry's lecture on advocacy), *Graya*, No 122, Hilary 2009, pp. 17–24, said whilst "*an advocate might reasonably hope to touch the heartstrings of the jury more readily than those of a judge..... even judges were not the unfeeling decision-making machines they might sometimes appear; they responded to considerations of justice and injustice, right and wrong, human frailty and human need; there was often treasure there, which understated eloquence could unlock*". When interviewed at the House of Lords on 23rd October, 2007, Lord Bingham said it would be wrong to think that judges in earlier times were never influenced by such considerations, carefully and subtly put by advocates.

[30] Sir Thomas Skyrme, *The Changing Image of the Magistracy*, Macmillan Press, London, 1979, page. 5. See, also, R. M. Jackson, *Incidence of Jury Trial During the Past Century*, Modern Law Review, Vol. 1, no 2, September, 1937, page 137.

Impact of Leading Members of the Bar

G. W Keeton saw the more restrained and conversational advocacy that had emerged in criminal jury trials to have been influenced by the style of advocates in civil cases: "*In as much as the most influential members of the bar who set fashions in advocacy appear most frequently in civil cases, the methods followed by them tend to become general*".[31] As an example of this, he mentions the effect of Rufus Isaacs, the great majority of whose cases were civil. When he was a Law Officer and appeared in criminal cases, Sir Rufus was never rude to the prisoner in his cross-examination. Rather, he was courteous, almost deferential, but the effect of his questions was to build up a case of deadly significance, as was clearly seen in his prosecution of the poisoner Arthur Seddon in 1912 (Chap. 8). Keeton saw these traditions being carried over to the present day and "*being firmly established in our advocacy*".

Two influential and fashion setting members of the Bar during the first half of the twentieth century were Patrick Hastings and Norman Birkett, each will now be discussed.

Sir Patrick Hastings and His Effect on Advocacy

Sir Patrick Hastings (1880–1952), who was made a King's Counsel in 1919, became one of the leading barristers of his time, and, at the top of his profession, earned very considerable fees.[32] In 1912 he led for the defence of John Williams in the Eastbourne "*Case of the Hooded Man*", which made national headlines. Although Williams was convicted, Hastings's highly intelligent and focused defence strategy was much admired. His practice afterwards was almost completely in the civil courts in divorce, libel and fraud cases, often before juries. Mostly unlike other barristers, his style of advocacy, may, to some extent, have followed

---

[31] G.W. Keeton, *Harris's Hints on Advocacy*, Stevens and Sons, London. 1943, page 11.

[32] Hastings's biographer, H. Montgomery Hyde: *Sir Patrick Hastings. His Life and Cases*, Heinemann, 1960, stated that for many years he earned more than £40,000.

Charles Russell and Edward Carson, at least in cross-examination.[33] He was known to be contemptuous of the passionate appeals made to juries by advocates like Marshall Hall. Hastings was a master of direct forcible speech without any embellishments or ornamentation and recognized the immense value of brevity. According to Sir Norman Birkett, a friend and who frequently opposed him in court, Patrick Hastings was not a great speaker in the conventional sense:

> "*He was certainly not in the tradition of Sheridan, Charles James Fox and Edmund Burke. He was not a great reader and his mind was not stored with the riches of English literature or the great speeches of orators in ancient and modern times*". (This may, partly, have been because of an interrupted public school education at Charterhouse. When the Second Boer War, 1889–1902, broke out he had enlisted in the British Army) "*It was quite characteristic of him that he should affect to be scornful of forensic oratory of the flamboyant range because it was quite alien to his style of advocacy, and really outside his range; for in all that he did he seemed to want to put himself in a category of his own*".[34]

In his openings, whether for the plaintiff or the defendant, he was never long and rarely stylish. In print, the words chosen would appear to be random. Such an impression would have been entirely false as they were selected with great care to bring the case within the limits that Hastings wished to be set for it. He was able to do this by having complete mastery of his brief.[35]

Hastings stood straight and still in court, kept his eyes fixed on whoever he was speaking to, very rarely gestured with his hands, and avoided distractions, sometimes made deliberately by other barristers, such as jangling coins in pockets, fiddling with the ribbon on a brief or taking numerous drinks of water from a tumbler. He always spoke in a good clear voice. Great preparation ensured he was in complete command of

---

[33] N. Birkett, *Six Great Advocates*, Penguin, page 23.

[34] Birkett, *ibid*, pp. 23–24.

[35] Richard DuCann, *The Art of the Advocate*, Penguin, Revised Edition, 1993, pp. 84–85.

his brief, had no need to refer to papers during trial and could carefully observe the jury for small but significant signs.[36]

His examination in chief, resembling much that favoured by Sir Frank Lockwood (Chap. 7), appeared to be a conversation with the witness. Hastings would smile at some answer as though it had come to him by surprise, when it was really the answer he wanted and expected.

The outstanding strength of Hastings was in cross-examination. His frequent opponent, Sir Norman Birkett, recalled:

> *He could destroy a witness with quite shattering power with his direct, incisive and penetrating questions that came with the precision and speed of a machine gun. Remorselessly and relentlessly he broke down all defences, and when the triumph was complete he would make the briefest possible speech and sit down.*[37]

Hastings regarded cross-examination as *"the great, perhaps the final, test of advocacy"*. Although he said that he selected the one essential element, *without which all others are completely useless*, he wished to deal with, Hastings claimed that he did not prepare specific questions beforehand. He preferred to wait until such time he had carefully decided, by listening to examination in chief, whether a witness, *"was truthful or dishonest, stupid or cunning, intelligent or foolish"*.[38] The ability to assess accurately and almost instantaneously the personality and mentality of the witness facing him was to him the key skill in cross-examination; very different to the indiscriminate and loud "blunderbuss" approach in cross-examinations, much heard in Victorian times and earlier.

---

[36] Brian Gibbens QC, who, early in his career, watched Patrick Hastings in court, compared him with other advocates who *perpetually turned to the jury* when they were examining witnesses. He recounted that the intensity of Hastings's gaze and manner towards hostile witnesses was devastating. Brian Gibbens, *Elements of Modern Advocacy*, New Law Cassettes, Butterworths, London, 1979.

[37] Norman Birkett, Address to the Holdsworth Club of the Faculty of Law, University of Birmingham, 7th May, 1954.

[38] Sir Patrick Hastings, *Cases in Court*, Pan Books, 1954, pp. 252–254.

On his experience of being cross-examined by Hastings, in the libel case of *Laski v The Newark Advertiser and Parlby* in 1946,[39] in which he sued the Nottinghamshire paper in libel for a report that he advocated violence to achieve socialism at a public general election meeting in Newark, in 1945, Harold Laski wrote:

> *He performs his war dance about you like a dervish intoxicated by the sheer ecstasy of his skill in performance, ardent in his knowledge that, if you trip for one second, his knife is at your throat.......He moves between the lines of sarcasm and insult. It is an effort to tear off, piece by piece, the skin which he declares no more than a mask behind which any man of understanding could have grasped the foulness of your purpose. He treats you not as a human being, but as a surgeon might treat some specimen he is demonstrating to students in a dissecting room.*[40]

Like Sir Edward Carson, whose style may well have consciously or sub-conscientiously shape his own, Patrick Hastings excelled in the arts of denigration, especially ridicule.[41]

Writing in the 1960s, the eminent barrister and writer on advocacy Richard DuCann QC (1929–1994) considered Patrick Hastings was the finest cross-examiner before the English Courts in the twentieth century. Nonetheless, he strongly criticized him for ruthlessness and gross discourtesy which was unfair to witnesses and on occasions led to courts drawing the wrong conclusions.[42] Concerning this behaviour, which went un-rebuked wherever he practiced, DuCann gives the example of Hastings's cross-examination of Air Marshall Sir Hugh Vivian de Crespigny, who had been the Labour candidate for Newark and present

---

[39] Unreported in the law reports, but see a verbatim account published by the Daily Express London, 1947.

[40] Richard DuCann, *The Art of the Advocate*, Revised Edition 1993, Penguin Books, 1993, page 21.

[41] Marshall Hall, from whose style and approach Hastings wished to distance himself, employed this weapon only very infrequently.

[42] At one point DuCann describes his style as *brusque and tyrannical, The Art of the Advocate*, Penguin, 1993, page 154.

when Laski spoke at the meeting. DuCann presents the whole of the short cross-examination[43]:

Hastings:	*"Do you recognize this expression: 'It did not lie in the mouth of any member of the Tory party, who helped to organize the mutiny in the British Army over Home Rule in 1914, to discuss the question of violence? Do you remember anything like that being said by anyone'"?*
Sir Hugh:	*"No I do not. That does not mean it was not said".*
Hastings:	*"Many things may have been said that you did not hear?"*
Sir Hugh:	*"Sir Patrick......"*
Lord Chief Justice Goddard:	*"Will you try and answer the question Yes or No. We really must try and get on with this case".*
Sir Hugh:	*"There was nothing vital that I would not have heard".*
Hastings:	*"If you did not hear it, how did you know whether it was vital or not?"*
Sir Hugh:	*"I must ask your permission to elucidate this so as not to give the wrong impression..."...*
Hastings:	*"No thank you"* (sitting down)
Slade:	*"I have no questions in re-examination".*[44]

In effect, Hastings had refused to let the witness give the evidence he wanted to and also, of course, the jury the opportunity of hearing it.[45] Remarkably, Gerald Slade KC, leading counsel for Laski, and later a Judge of the High Court, did not seek to rectify this in re-examination, nor did Lord Chief Justice Goddard intervene.

Sir Patrick Hastings was invariably short in cross-examination, partly, perhaps because of a realization that a jury may quickly spot an advocate's failure to undermine a witness and as a result attach a disproportionate importance to his or her evidence. He also had the gift, possessed by

---

[43] DuCann, *ibid*, pp. 116–117.
[44] For a verbatim account of the case see *Laski v Newark Advertiser Ltd and Parlby.* Published by the Daily Express, London, 1947.
[45] Richard DuCann, *The Art of the Advocate*, Penguin, 1993, pp. 116–117.

Carson (Chap. 8), of crystallizing in a few questions the whole of the case he wished to advance and the bravery to do so:

> *The ability to pick out the one real point of a case is not itself enough; it is the courage required to seize upon that point to the exclusion of all others that is of real importance. Painstaking solicitors will place before counsel perhaps fifty different points, all of them prepared with skill and care; it must indeed cause bitter disappointment to find them disregarded and the whole trial proceeding as though there was only one solitary element that was really worthy of consideration. It requires some courage in an advocate to stake his own opinion perhaps against that of all who are assisting him; it is a great risk. But in a proper case he must be prepared to take it.[46]*

Infelicitous or inappropriate replies of witnesses were quickly seized upon. A distinctive feature of Hastings's style of cross-examination was use of comment after a witness had answered a question. Many of his contemporaries refrained from any comment on answers given in cross-examination until their closing speech. (Unlike Sir Edward Carson, greatly admired by Hastings and was said to be an important influence on him, who almost always put his comments within the framework of his questions.) Hastings was different and showed this clearly, in 1913, soon after being made a Kings Counsel, when he was called upon to cross-examine Bob Sievier who had brought an action in libel against Richard Wootton, a race horse owner and trainer.[47] Sievier, a pugnacious, witty and flamboyant character, represented himself. Carson, who had been leading Hastings, was called to Ireland in the middle of examining the plaintiff. In cross-examining Sievier, Hastings matched every jest with biting comment as this brief extract shows:

---

[46] P. Hastings, *Cases in Court*, William Heinemann London, 1949, page 252. An indication of Patrick Hastings's attitude in court towards solicitors' views on how cases should be run was given in an interview with Angela Delbourgo, a barrister and then a lecturer at the College of Law in London. She had known an elderly solicitor who, in his youth as an articled clerk, once accompanied Hastings in court and sat in front of him. The young man was told by Hastings he had one, and only one, function – to push a big pile of precariously balanced books onto the floor when given a dig in the shoulders, so as to make sure the judge was awake when he put his best point. Interview on 31st October, 2007.

[47] Sievier v. Wootton, 1913. 3 KB 499. See also H. Montgomery Hyde, 1960, *Sir Patrick Hastings, his life and cases*, London, Heinemann, pp. 76–77.

Hastings: *"Did you marry your first wife in 1882"?*
Sievier: *"Unfortunately for me, I did".*
Hastings: *"Unfortunately for her, too. Did she divorce you in 1886, four years later?"*
Sievier: *"She did".*

Another vivid example, much later in his career, is provided by Hastings's treatment of one of the witnesses in the Harold Laski libel case:

Hastings: *"Did you hear anything of this sort: 'Great changes were so urgent in this country that if they were not made by consent they would be made by violence?' Did you hear him [Laski] say that"?*
Witness: *"No, not in those words".*
Hastings: *"Dear, oh dear, Mr Laski seems to be so unfortunate. He must have been very good at hearing himself; he said that is what he did say…".*

Richard DuCann considered the *"modern fashion"* for advocates to include comment either direct or indirect in cross-examination was largely due to the influence of Hastings style.[48] Hastings, almost without exception, made his last question in cross-examination a comment. This, too, was copied by other barristers.

In his closing speeches to juries, Hastings spoke in a simple conversational narrative, no tortuous sentences or elegance of expression, analysed the facts and made no attempt at passionate persuasion. At all times he was able to convey to jurors he was in earnest, not merely playing a part, and that he respected their independence and judgement. Lecturing, cajoling or flattery was never resorted to. The closing speech was the main place for him to use his great ability to capture the essence of a case in just a few words.

It was a device of Hastings, before juries, to lay claim to the virtues of plain speech, straightforwardness and brevity. This is prominently illustrated in his closing speech in the Laski case when he began by saying:

---

[48] *The Art of the Advocate*, Penguin, Revised Edition, 1993, page 128.

May it please Your Lordship: Members of the Jury, I can start what I have to say to you with perhaps the only bit of good news you have heard so far. That is that I am only going to address you for a few minutes. I want to explain why, because I do not want you to think, and I hope you will not think, that the value of anything that is to be said to you is to be measured by the number of words.

In order to create the impression that he was about to make an appeal to their reason, rather than the sort of emotional address which had once been popular in courts, he continued:

You may remember in the old days it was the habit of advocates sometimes to make long and eloquent speeches on all sorts of subjects, including comments on the Goddess of Justice who sits with scales above the court.......

The technique of emphasizing to jurors, early in a closing speech, that reason would be engaged became much used, especially after the triumphs of Hastings and other leading advocates who employed it. The reality, though, is that emotion is frequently disguised by advocates as reason.

Three quarters through his speech Hastings said:

I told you I was only going to be a few minutes. I have been fifteen, and I am afraid that is too long. I wish you good luck that Mr Slade will not be four times as long. Whether you will get that good luck or not, I do not know. I doubt it.

In the event Slade spoke for two hours. In contrast to the tight, well constructed and stylish speech of Hastings, his was spiritless, diffuse and very repetitive. Given the jury's decision against Laski, which left him with enormous costs, Slade's performance came to be seen as a lesson how not to make a closing speech.[49]

Whilst the rather cheap gibe against opposing counsel was not widely used, the practice of promising to be brief, keeping it, thus creating the

---

[49] Richard DuCann, *The Art of the Advocate*, Revised Edition, 1993, Penguin Books, London, page 201.

impression of a reliable guide through the evidence, and drawing a comparison, usually implicitly, with the greater length of an opponent's closing speech, hoping to create resentment for the time taken, was a well tried method and one that was reinforced by Hastings's successes in major cases.

A further tactic, frequently employed by him, to gain advantage over opponents by blunting the effect of theirs, was to claim (falsely) that final speeches had little or no effect on the outcome of cases. Again this is illustrated in Laski, when towards the start of his speech, Hastings told the jury:

I may say after long experience that I have never known a case in which anything I have said has had any affect on a jury one way or another, and therefore I have come to the conclusion that the shorter the time I take in saying it the better for everyone.

According to Richard DuCann, an unfortunate legacy of Hastings was that many modern advocates took him seriously in doubting that closing speeches had any effect on the outcome of cases. They treat it as *"the advocate's eleventh commandment that* they do not and *stumble through the odious task of addressing the Judge or jury, boring themselves almost as much as their audience"*.[50]

Whilst Patrick Hastings did much to distance himself from the forensic approach of Marshall Hall they shared, despite being supremely good jury advocates, not being especially learned in the law.[51] In this he was not seen as a model at the bar. Nor was he for his occasional losses of temper and display of personal sensitivity; traits also in common with Marshall Hall. This is perhaps best illustrated by another passage from the Laski trial. During his cross-examination of Laski, then the Chairman of the National Executive Committee of the Labour Party, Hastings, who had been appointed Attorney General in the first Labour Government in 1924, but left active politics a few years later, broke off in the middle of a question:

---

[50] DuCann, *ibid*, pp. 191–192.
[51] Richard DuCann, *The Art of the Advocate*, Revised Edition, 1993, Penguin Books, page 199.

Hastings:	" ....are there any privileged in the Labour Party?"
Laski:	"Why indeed, Sir Patrick, when you were a member........."
Lord Chief Justice Goddard:	"No, Mr Laski".
Hastings:	"Do not be rude".
Laski:	"That is the last thing I want in the world".
Hastings:	"It may be difficult for you to be courteous, but do not be rude".
Laski:	"Not in the least".
Hastings:	"You are rude to everyone are you not?"
Laski:	"I do not think so".

Sir Patrick Hastings, in the introduction to his memoirs, published in 1949, wrote[52]:

For my part, the greatest change that I have noticed during the past 40 years lies amongst members of my own profession. Ponderous oratory, once so popular, and based undoubtedly upon Cicero's orations, has completely disappeared. Just as Gerald du Maurier sounded the death knell of the old time school of thunderous declamation from the stage[53] so Edward Carson put an end to forensic platitudes and passionate but irrelevant perorations from the bar. That such a change is an improvement no wearied juryman would deny.

There can be little doubt that Patrick Hastings, through his numerous triumphs at the Bar, influenced advocacy in a number of ways including: the practice of cross-examination and closing speeches: the need for carefully chosen words, to support a well thought out strategy, and to use them with economy and without unnecessary repetition; forcible and direct delivery without adornment; and an emphasis on an appeal to reason, rather than apparent emotion. His plain, conversational and highly concentrated, rather than diffuse, form could well be seen as taking advo-

---

[52] *Cases in Court*, London: Heinemann, pp. xi–xii.

[53] To support himself through his studies at the Middle Temple Hastings worked as a journalist specializing in theatre gossip and reviews and in 1925, whilst contemplating an alternative career as a playwright, wrote *The River*, which was produced in London that year.

cacy further than had been begun by Edward Carson, Rufus Isaacs, and F E Smith. The success of Hastings before juries, it is argued, indicates not only how he was able to speak in the language of his time but also his ability to understand the sensibilities of jurors, who were now so very different, for a variety of social factors, from those in earlier times. It is possible to speculate that his association with drama criticism and writing plays himself may have aided his comprehension of the contemporary mind.

Norman Birkett

Lord Birkett(1883–1962), more widely known during his lifetime as Norman Birkett, K. C. was called to bar in 1913, took silk in 1924 and became a judge in the Kings Bench Division in 1941. He was one of the British judges at the trial of major war criminals at Nuremberg. Afterwards, he was made a Lord Justice of Appeal. When at the Bar he established a great reputation as an advocate in the civil and criminal courts and was much in demand.[54] Notable civil clients included Lady Gladstone, Lady Mountbatten and Mrs. Wallace Simpson. He appeared either for the prosecution or the defence in a number of murder trials and sensational criminal cases. Shortly before his appointment to the High Court Bench, as was the custom, at least until the 1960s, for eminent QCs about to be elevated to the judiciary to be given a notorious murder case, he was presented in 1931 with the brief to prosecute Alfred Rouse,[55] a motorist alleged to have murdered his passenger and then set fire to his car to destroy the body and the evidence. An expert engineer for the defence gave evidence about the fusion of two bits of metal, thereby establishing a powerful point for the accused. Birkett rose to cross-examine.

"*What*" he asked in his precise, musical way, "*is the co-efficient of brass?*" The witness replied "*I do not know*".

---

[54] Whilst as KC, his income averaged £30,000 annually: H. Montgomery Hyde, *Norman Birkett: The life of Lord Birkett of Ulverston*, Hamish Hamilton, 1964.
[55] At Northampton Assizes commencing on the 21st November, 1931.

The question had taken the expert completely unaware. It made him so wary of Birkett, that when he was asked: *"You are an engineer, aren't you?"* he said *"I suppose so!"* Quickly and devastatingly, Birkett had destroyed his credibility entirely.[56]

Birkett and Hastings were regularly pitted against each other much in the same way as Edward Carson and Rufus Isaacs in the previous generation and more recently Edward Marshall Hall and Henry Curtis Bennett had been. Birkett's biographer, H. Montgomery Hyde, described how differences in forensic methods employed by the two advocates were reflected in their respective styles of cross-examination, each equally effective and produced similar results:

> *Hastings, with his beetling eyebrows, would fix an unfortunate witness with a severe look. 'Now, let me see, Mr A.' he would say and proceed to fire questions at him in such quick succession that he sometimes laid himself open to the charge of bullying. His friend Roland Pertwee, with a euphemistic touch, has described his manner in handling witnesses in court as 'cool, concise and gently cynical'. Birkett on the other hand, had a more suave and polished approach, as well as perhaps a deceptively friendly one. 'I wonder if you can help me, Mr. A.?' he would usually begin. But the admissions which he gradually and eventually elicited, ..., could pulverize a prevaricating or untruthful witness as completely as Hastings's more robust methods of questioning.[57]*

Later in his life he lectured, broadcast and wrote about advocacy. It can be said with certainty that he too influenced other advocates in the first half of the twentieth century and beyond.

---

[56] Birkett's destruction of the engineer's credibility in *R v Rouse* (Unreported), by asking a very basic question an expert may not remember, became famous at the Bar and the technique subsequently emulated, with varying degrees of success, in cross-examining experts in numerous fields. Indeed it is still influential. Keith Evans, in his book, *Advocacy in Court*, Blackstone Press, 1995, which is widely read by bar students, and recommended reading at a number of colleges where the Bar Professional Training Course is taught, uses it as an example of how to challenge a witnesses' expertise by making an in-depth study of just one tiny area on which to question at the beginning of cross-examination: *"Nobody – perhaps not even the ultimate leader in the field – knows everything about his subject"*, pp. 165–166.

[57] H. Montgomery Hyde, *Norman Birket: The Life of Lord Birkett of Ulverston*, London, Hamish Hamilton, 1964, page 221.

In an address to the Holdsworth Club of the Faculty of Law in the University of Birmingham in 1954,[58] Lord Birkett outlined much of his views about the advocacy he had delivered and liked to hear as a judge. He acknowledged the vast importance of: mastering the facts of the case; knowledge of the relevant law; the special qualities needed for examination in chief[59] and cross-examination and re-examination; the selection and formulation of the arguments; the widely differing styles of advocacy required for particular tribunals, whether they be judge alone, or judge and jury, or appellate courts; and the construction and arrangement of opening and closing speeches. However, Birkett considered the overriding quality to be – command of language:

> *If the argument of the advocate is presented in clear and choice language which seems to come naturally and easily from the speaker, and if in addition the advocate can make use of what appears to be quite natural gesture, the very argument itself seems more persuasive.*

Differing somewhat from Sir Patrick Hastings, who spoke forcibly without elegance of expression, ornamentation and embellishment, Birkett believed that:

> *in the main task of advocacy, the exposition, the narrative, the summing-up, the persuasion,* the advocate may use, and I think ought to use, the full range of our wonderfully flexible English speech. *For there is no speech to equal it in its amazing richness of expression..........*

Therefore, he held the advocate should be a student of words, knowing something at least of their history, sound, meaning, associations and, above all, the uses great masters of English had made of them. In this respect Birkett considered it well to know the Authorised Version of the Bible, the Book of Common Prayer, and have a knowledge of *"the great*

---

[58] Delivered on 7th May, 1954.
[59] Birkett excelled in the ability to obtain convincing evidence from witnesses by speaking to them plainly and in simple sentences. Edgar Lustgarten, Sir Norman Birkett, BBC Radio 4, broadcast in 1970.

triumvirate, Chaucer, Dryden and Shakespeare – who did so much to mould and fashion the language", and of writers like Swift, Sterne and Defoe, *"the great stylists"*.

To him, even in casual conversation, natural and graceful English was a desirable accomplishment, which most people found pleasant and a surprising number secretly wished to attain themselves *"And how much more is it to be desired when the whole purpose of the advocate is to gain the ends he seeks by the impression he creates upon the particular tribunal before which he appears"*.

Factors Influencing the Style of Advocacy That Became Established

Other, deeper reasons, contributed to the mainly conversational and matter of fact advocacy that had become established. Taste for melodrama, strong sentiment and froth, much represented in Victorian literature and drama had waned in the late nineteenth century to be replaced by a more restrained and reflective aesthetic with an emphasis on realism. Stories lay deep in society's psyche and most educated people read contemporary novels. For much of the century these were expansive, sometimes sprawling, narratives that sentimentally charted private fates often against great issues of the day. However, by the century's closing years, they were largely superseded by novels that were limited in scope and structured by greater self-reference and inner coherence. In the 1890s drama in Britain, through George Bernard Shaw and others including Henrik Ibsen, the pioneer of modern realistic drama, became a forum for considering moral, political and economic issues.[60] Somewhat earlier in 1882 a newspaper article said that while *"our forefathers delighted in plays that were full of tears they did not appeal to fashionable members of modern*

---

[60] In an address, entitled *Advocacy and Acting*, to the Oxford University Law Society, delivered in 1966, Sir James Stirling, then a High Court Judge in the Probate, Divorce and Admiralty Division, saw changes in styles of advocacy paralleling styles of acting: in both spheres the grand manner and the purple patch becoming unfashionable at roughly the same time. However he does not develop his thesis further. *Verdict*, VOL. 2. NO. 1.1966. pp. 7–9.

audiences: It is not difficult to move pit and gallery to tears but stall and box occupants are less easily worked upon".[61] (With the property qualification for jury service, jurors were most likely to have occupied those more expensive parts of the theatre.) In this book's brief excursus,[62] it is explained that almost since rhetoric began there was disagreement between those who saw it as a means of authenticating truth and those who saw it as a method of deception, sometimes termed "false rhetoric". Although the nineteenth century was a deeply oratorical age, as the century wore on, rhetoric came to be popularly seen in a negative light. Two instances perhaps best illustrate this. As early as the 1860s, Thomas Huxley ("Darwin's Bulldog") accused the opponents of Darwin's theory of evolution of hiding behind rhetoric. In a famous speech in 1879, Disraeli, in possibly an example of the pot calling the kettle black, said of Gladstone, then the Prime Minister, that he was:

A sophistical rhetorician, inebriated with the exuberance of his own verbosity, and gifted with an egotistical imagination that can at all times command an interminable and inconsistent series of arguments to malign an opponent and to glorify himself.[63]

From the world of drama, and indicative of feeling towards rhetoric at the beginning of the twentieth century, Harley Granville-Barker, in his 1905 play, *The Voysey Inheritance*, about the effects of corruption in a family firm of solicitors, has the bluff army major, Booth, say on a number of occasions, *Do not speak rhetoric to me!*, when he thinks others are not being straight forward with him.

Dramatic types of advocacy, in which counsel adopted mannerisms, tricks of speech, gestures, aggression, sometimes insults and even tears, became seen as a part of rhetoric, in the pejorative sense of artful bombast and verbal chicanery, and for that reason were widely disapproved. Jurors became far better informed than before, capable of seeing through it and

---

[61] "Weeping Plays", *The Era*, 8th April 1882, p 14. Quoted by Thomas Dixon, *Weeping Britannia*, Oxford University Press, 2015, p. 180.
[62] Please find at www.Historyadvocacy.wordpress.com.
[63] Quoted in The Times, London, July 29th, 1879.

resentful when empty rhetoric was tried on them. It may well be that the success of men such as Hardinge Giffard, John Holker, Charles Russell, and Edward Clarke was partly because they recognised the change in the mood of the public towards rhetoric and altered their advocacy accordingly in the later nineteenth century.

The developing field of emotional history identifies in Britain a shift, driven by many different reasons, from the 1870s to the run up to the First World War, in the prevailing emotion style from sentimentalism towards stoicism, discipline and restraint. In this context the ideal of the "stiff upper lip", not so much eliminating feeling but restricting where and ways it might be expressed, arose and remained a characteristic until it began to decline after the Second World War.[64] Given this it would have been surprising if advocacy before jurors had not become more calm, measured and austere.

As a consequence of nineteenth century reforms, education was available to more people.[65] Universal elementary school education, with its emphasis on the "3 Rs" (reading, writing and arithmetic), was introduced in the 1860's. Although teaching ended at an early age, the basic literacy and numeracy provided by it gave many the means of obtaining further knowledge.[66]

Parliament's decision in 1857 to create public lending libraries provided an important source. The growing number of national and municipal museums and galleries helped stimulate intellectual curiosity. Working

---

[64] Thomas Dixon, *Weeping Britannia*, Oxford University Press, 2015, Chaps. 14–20.

[65] See Michael Hyndman, *Schools and Schooling in England and Wales, a documentary history*, Harper and Row, 1978, especially Chapter 10, with a chronology of principal educational reforms in the nineteenth and twentieth centuries.

[66] In assessing factors which led to a general improvement in educational standards in the nineteenth century, Professor Rosemary Ashton (University College London, Department of English Language and Literature, interviewed on 13th November, 2007) considered publication and wide circulation of pamphlets, magazines and books, with the purpose of educating persons of modest learning, was of significance. Such works were produced cheaply by commercial publishing houses, including *John Murray*, exploiting contemporary advances in printing technology and distribution. Informative and sometimes entertaining, works were also published by noncommercial organisations whose aim was to promote education amongst the masses. Prominent amongst these was the Society for the Diffusion of Useful Knowledge which operated during the first half of the century.

class self-improvement, though unevenly spread, was another significant cause of increase in overall educational standards.[67]

Dozens of new private schools, often modelled on Thomas Arnold's Rugby School, to cater for the sons, and some daughters, of the growing middle class were opened in the latter part of the nineteenth century. These added to the general level of education in society. (Even before the advent of the "stiff upper lip" ideal, and not confined to public schools, self-control and emotional restraint had been instilled in boys and men by the nation's educational institutions).[68]

Beyond elementary education, the content of many school curriculums expanded to encompass the burgeoning sciences with their rational enquiry. As early as the 1860s a self-conscious scientific community had been forged that successfully challenged the intellectual authority of religion and metaphysics. Increasing amounts of knowledge were disseminated in newspapers and, in the next century, by wireless. By the 1880s Darwin's theory of evolution had entered popular culture.[69] Religious certainty, because of scientific explanation – succinctly put, *Darwin's books drove a cart through an older book* – began to lessen from mid Victorian times. For this and other reasons, it diminished still further in the remaining part of the century and afterwards.[70] The sort of impassioned appeal before juries to the

---

[67] Jonathan Rose, *The Intellectual Life of the British Working Classes*, Yale University Press, 2001, based upon the evidence of almost two thousand published and unpublished memoirs from nineteenth and twentieth century Britain, portrays a picture of a working class determined to achieve self-education by reading literature, including the Roman and Greek classics, going to concerts and the theatre – Shakespeare and other classical dramatists attracted enthusiastic and rowdy working class audiences, learning to play musical instruments, setting up mutual improvement societies and establishing the Workers Educational Association in 1903. In an interview, held at the Royal Society, London, on 2nd July, 2010, Professor Rose agreed with the thesis that jurors drawn from a more educated society than previously could reasonably be supposed to have expected more of an appeal to reason and to examine evidence more closely than before. He saw working class and lower middle class self-education contributing to this.

[68] Thomas Dixon, *Weeping Britannia*, Oxford University Press, 2015, pp. 204–206.

[69] *On the Origin of Species by Means of Natural Selection* (1859), *The Descent of Man and Selection in relation to Sex* (1871) and *The Expressions of the Emotions in Man and Animals* (1872) were read by a large section of the public. Many more people would have absorbed Darwin's key ideas from reports in the press.

[70] See J. F. Von Arx, *Progress and Pessimism: Religion, Politics and History in late 19th Century Britain*. Harvard University Press, 1985.

deity, quotations and stories from the bible, so much used earlier, could no longer be relied upon. In short, jurors with broader perspectives expected more of an appeal to reason from advocates in a conversational and matter of fact manner, rather than one histrionically directed at their emotions and faith.[71] From the 1920s it has been suggested that distaste for the continental European demagogues, such as Hitler, Mussolini, and Franco, with their power by oratory and theatre to move audiences in terrible directions, may also have contributed to jurors suspicions of obvious rhetoric.[72] The advent of radio broadcasting led to widespread abandoning of grand declamatory forms of public oratory in favour of a more personal "fireside" approach. It may be reasonable to suggest that this further helped the cause of conversational, rather than declamatory, advocacy before juries.

In the first capital defence case he conducted on his own, that of Marie Herman in 1894, an Austrian prostitute charged with killing a client, Marshall-Hall, with tears streaming down his face, told the jury in his peroration: "*Remember that these women are what men made them; even this woman was at one time a beautiful and innocent child*". Flinging an arm in the defendant's direction in the dock he continued: "*Look at her, gentlemen of the jury. Look at her. God never gave her a chance – won't you?*". Just a few decades later, because of jurors' different expectations, this approach would have been received with embarrassment rather than anything else: no longer dazzlingly effective oratorical pyrotechnics; at best a damp squib.[73] Along similar lines, John Alderson Foote recounted how Montagu Williams defending a prisoner charged with fraud in 1877 (Chap. 5), said of two witnesses against his client:

---

[71] Touching on this subject, George Elliot K.C., in his Forward to *Illustrations in Advocacy by Richard Harris K.C. Fifth Edition, 1915*, a work intended mainly as a guide to effective court advocacy for newly qualified barristers, wrote: *Further it may also be remembered that the development of education amongst all classes of the people has rendered juries much less susceptible to mere tricks of advocacy and less easily diverted from the real issues before them.*

[72] See Andrew Watson, *Changing Advocacy, Part Two*, Justice of the Peace, Vol. 165, 13th October, 2001, page 808.

[73] Very much to the surprise of counsel for the co-defendants in the much publicised Mary – Ann Leneghan case, which took place in 2005 and involved the murder by a gang of a teenage girl and an attempt to kill her friend, Gilbert Gray QC used the words *God never gave* him *a chance – won't you?* in his closing speech for a defendant. He was convicted. Interview with Anthony Arlidge QC, who represented another defendant, held on 30th October, 2007.

"Excellent in vice and exquisite in fraud – the cunning of a cat teeming from the eyes of one; the oily soft serpent-like treachery of deceit trickling from the mouth of the other". Foote, speculating on how jurors would react in 1910, said:

"Few indeed are the advocates nowadays who could venture upon such flights without exciting derision".[74] In 1921, Bernard Kelly explained how juries now seemed to have a higher appreciation of facts, usually little regard for mere graces of language and almost none for sentimental appeals: *"….. cynical yawns, and not higher emotions, more often than not greet the most pathetic efforts of counsel to create a sentimental leaning towards their clients at the expense of actual fact"*.[75]

Amusingly, drawing on recollections from his career, A W Cockburn Q C described a case when "grandiloquence" and "idle histrionics" did not commend itself to a jury; the implicit message being that a more conversational style might have done so:

I cannot forget hearing an extraordinary peroration in a very ordinary case some years ago which finished up with, 'Members of the Jury, the moving finger writes, and having writ moves on……' Then came a slight misquotation, and with a flourish of his coloured handkerchief, the exhausted orator sat down. It had all been very moving; and after a short breath-taking pause, came the summing up, in which the empyrean level was not even aimed at; and in a few seconds an earth-bound jury were in their own simple way recording what they thought about coloured handkerchiefs and moving fingers.[76]

---

[74] *Piepowder*, J. Murray, 1911, page 176.

[75] *Famous Advocates And Their Speeches*, London, Sweet and Maxwell, London, Sweet and Maxwell, 1921, page 27. Thirty eight years before, certainly not followed then by all barristers in criminal trials, more a call for it to be so, Sir James Fitzjames Stephen, wrote of advocacy: *"It is impossible to be eloquent in the sense of appealing to the feelings without more or less falsehood, and an unsuccessful attempt at passionate eloquence is of all things the most contemptible and ludicrous, besides being usually vulgar. The critical temper of the age has exercised an excellent influence on speaking in the courts. Most barristers are justly afraid of being laughed at and looking silly if they aim at eloquence, and generally avoid it by keeping quiet"*. Sir James Fitzjames Stephen, *A History of the Criminal Law of England*, Macmillan and Co., London, 1883, page 454.

[76] *In Limine*, An Address on advocacy to the Christ Church, Oxford, Law Club, May 15th, 1952, Published by the Faculty of Law, University of Southampton.

By changing their style of advocacy before juries towards the conversational and matter of fact, barristers consciously, or sub-consciously, followed Cicero's cautionary advice given centuries ago and avoided the *"very cardinal sin in oratory,* that is *to depart from the language of everyday life and usage approved of by the sense of the community"*.[77]

A possible further explanation for the transformation to a more conversational and matter of fact advocacy may have been the reduction of court reporting in newspapers, removing much of the gallery from the stage. Attempting to catch the eye of the press for words spoken in court, aiding a barrister's reputation, (sometimes also very useful to fulfill political ambitions) was an important contributory factor behind the emotive, theatrical, florid, and aggressive advocacy of the early Victorian period and after.[78] As late as the 1930s proceedings in court were still much reported, making barristers household names.[79] For instance in a popularity poll organized in 1935 by William Hickey, the Daily Express columnist, who invited readers to write to the newspaper naming the public personalities they most liked reading about, Norman Birkett got into the first twenty.[80]

After the War there were fewer reports from the courts, partly because of a shortage of paper and newsprint which led to cuts in the size of papers generally (For a time newspapers were restricted to only eight pages.). Sir Patrick Hastings, in 1949, compared the situation with *"not*

---

[77] De Oratore (translated by E W Sutton and H Rockman, Loeb edition, 1942) 1.iii.12.page 11.

[78] J R Lewis, *The Victorian Bar*, Robert Hale, London, Chap. 1. A tradition of courting the press appears to have survived until the late twentieth century. A Court of Appeal judge, interviewed on 11th July, 2007 (Lord Justice Sedley), spoke of how some barristers, at least up until the end of the 1970s, would try to cultivate interest amongst journalists in their achievements by drinking and dining with them in public houses in Fleet Street, then the centre of the newspaper industry, or sending their clerks to do so.

[79] In the one man show he performed in the years before his death in 2009, John Mortimer would reminisce about how his father, Clifford Mortimer, a blind divorce barrister who freely quoted poetry in court, drawing on a vast store, would demand that his wife read out detailed news reports of current divorce trials when they were traveling together in crowded railway carriages, often to the embarrassment of other passengers.

[80] Daily Express, February 1st, 1935. Lloyd George headed the list closely followed by Winston Churchill and Lord Beaverbrook. The other popular favourites included Gracie Fields, Bernard Shaw, Franklin Roosevelt, Mussolini, Rudyard Kipling, Greta Garbo and the Aga Khan, with whom Birkett tied for the final place amongst the first twenty.

very long ago when every trial of the slightest importance was reported in the public press". He continued: "*Morning papers had a page devoted to Law reports; evening papers displayed posters announcing every detail of so-called important trials and possibly even of the persons mainly concerned; there were murder cases, libel cases, cases about old ladies disputing over garden walls, even breach of promise cases. Every tribulation known to human life was brought before us and its appropriate remedy displayed. When the Courts were closed, the papers were half empty, and people knew that the silly season had arrived; something was missing from their daily lives*".[81]

The decline in volume of reports from court, and hence attention given to the efforts of advocates, continued throughout the 1950s and a further falling away of press coverage was noted by Lord Birkett at the start of the 1960s.[82]

---

[81] P. Hastings, *Cases in Court*, Heinemann page 12.
[82] *Six Great Advocates*, Penguin, 1961, page 9.

10

Changes and Influences on Jury Advocacy in England and Wales During the Second Half of the Twentieth Century

The previous chapter sought to explain, broadly in the five decades preceding the early 1940s, profound changes, that occurred in advocacy before the courts in England and Wales. In this chapter an attempt is made to describe how jury advocacy altered during the rest of the long twentieth century. Reasons, each of which will be considered, for this included: falling away in the use of Aristotle's ancient order of closing speeches, which usually ended with an emotive peroration; a huge expansion in eligibility to serve on juries, amounting to a "*democratization*", following the Juries Act 1974, resulting in considerable adjustment to ways jurors were addressed and use by advocates of different allusions and references; reduction, and eventual abolition, by the Criminal Justice Act, 1988, of peremptory challenge of jurors; prosecutions conducted in greater measured tones and more methodical and less aggressive defences, although the latter was not always present in sexual offences cases; decline in weight attached by juries to police evidence; less heavy drinking, a subject seldom discussed, by some barristers and the positive consequences of this on their performance in court; a rise of plea bargaining and the need to mitigate effectively after guilty pleas; introduction of Social Enquiry Reports and their effect on pleas in mitigation; the need to make, and respond to, submissions arising out of key changes in

© The Author(s) 2019
A. Watson, *Speaking in Court*, https://doi.org/10.1007/978-3-030-10395-8_10

evidence and procedure concerning the exclusion of confessions, when adverse inferences can be drawn from silence to questions put to the accused and from admission of a defendant's bad character. Finally advocacy in cases of defamation during this period, at first sight a remnant of an earlier less restrained and more exuberant age, is briefly considered.

Closing Speeches and Perorations

Traditionally, the structure of a speech to a jury followed Aristotle's ancient order of: Exordium (introduction); Statement (of the issues before the court); Proof (argument supporting one's case and the refutation of one's opponent); and the Peroration, an emotional appeal, which stood quite apart from the rest of the speech.[1] Richard Du Cann QC, writing in 1964, commented on how many modern advocates had appeared to abandon that conventional structure *"and followed no order at all to avoid an obvious display of these divisions, which might interrupt the sequence of thought the advocate was trying to induce on his or her listeners"*.[2] He also speculated that a reason for doing this was to avoid deciding whether the most important point in the speech should be put first or last. On the diminished use of the peroration, Du Cann wrote: *"…until quite recently it was possible to see counsel winding themselves up into the majestic spontaneity of their carefully prepared final onslaughts on the emotions of the jury"*. Perorations in capital punishment cases were often long and highly emotional. The

---

[1] From observation of surviving counsel's notes, it seems it was common for Victorian and Edwardian advocates to write out perorations in long hand before delivering them. In *Forensic Fables*, first published between 1926 and 1932, based on observations made during his career, Theo Mathew, tells a fable, the moral of which was that barristers for the defence should *perorate* (*The Brilliant Orator Who Won Fame As A Defender* pp. 321). It may well have been based on Marshall-Hall. He does, however, seem to advise, depending on the audience, that peroration, and the traditional division of a closing speech, may not always be effective (See *The Blushing Beginner and The Bearded Juryman*, pp. 57–58 and *The Brilliant Person, The Vulgar Individual With A Cockney Accent And The Two Malefactors* pp. 305–306). *Forensic Fables*, Reprinted by Wildy and Sons, London, 1999.

[2] *The Art of the Advocate*, Pelican, Pelican, First Edition, 1964, page 180.

abolition of the death penalty (effectively in 1965), according to one senior barrister, author and part – time Crown Court Recorder interviewed,[3] was important in the overall reduction of blatant appeals to the emotions and theatricality in jury advocacy. Another factor mentioned by him was the closure of many Victorian built courts in the 1960s and 1970s. Acting in small modern rooms, well illuminated by electric strip lighting, rather than poorly lit cavernous rooms built in the gothic revival, which were almost stages for melodrama, seemed incongruous and dated.[4]

A junior barrister interviewed,[5] undertaking criminal work and mainly instructed to defend, explained that, in her experience, barristers, both for the prosecution or the defence, now order their closing speeches similar to judges in their summing up to juries. The divisions followed are: informing the jury of the role of the judge and the jury; an explanation of the burden and standard of proof; setting out the law and what it is necessary for the prosecution to prove; addressing legal points of evidence, if necessary; and dealing with the evidence. The barrister explained that, when defending, she would conclude by re-iterating the standard and burden of proof. She reported the approach almost always taken was strict concentration on the facts which were interpreted and commented upon, sometimes liberally. Barristers spoke for themselves rather than relying on theatrical and emotional perorations.[6] In her view, overt appeals to emotion in perorations, and elsewhere in closing speeches, rather than engaging jurors' powers of reasoning, would be badly received by jurors who increasingly saw themselves as possessors of facts and

---

[3] Geoffrey Robertson QC interviewed 18th April, 2000.

[4] Some of the courts closed in the 1960s and 1970s were appreciably older than the nineteenth century, for example the Grand Hall at Winchester, built in the Thirteen Hundreds. On the effect of courtroom design on proceedings in court see Linda Mulcahy, *Architects of Justice: the Politics of Courtroom Design*, School of Law, Birkbeck College. A paper delivered at the W G Hart Legal Workshop 2006 at the Institute of Advanced Legal Studies, University of London.

[5] Interviewed on 7th September, 2007. She had eight years of experience in criminal work.

[6] The description of modern closing speeches made corresponded with observation of cases made at Blackfriars Crown Court, London between 3rd and 5th July, 2007.

knowledge through very easy access to computer data bases such as *Google*, social media books and papers. The possibility of somebody involved in the administration of justice sitting on the jury who would very rapidly see through what was going on, was also mentioned as a reason not to employ what could be seen as theatricality.[7] A leading barrister, specialising in criminal defence work and who has practiced since 1962, also confirmed that open appeals to emotion and blatant histrionics had disappeared. Advocacy had come to require the much more subtle accomplishment of being able to appeal to widely held stereo typical opinions which might not correspond with the letter of the law. It was often necessary to do so almost subliminally and always essential not to go beyond propriety. Ability to assess what the jury would take was vital. A number of examples of broadly held social attitudes, to which messages could be directed by stealth, were given. *"Buttons which could be pressed"*, included women who drink excessively and dress immodestly invite attention and persons assaulting others have only themselves to blame when the response they get from their victims may be more than the violence they used, provided it is not entirely out of proportion. Mention was made of a number of prosecutions that had taken place some years ago under the Obscene Publications Act 1959 for producing pornographic films. Most of these failed before the courts, except where children were involved. As a result, proceedings brought by the police are now very rare. Barristers for defendants had successfully appealed to the broadly held view amongst jurors that, whilst they would not want to view such films themselves, what adults wanted to watch in private was their business.[8]

---

[7] In April, 2004, lawyers judges and police officers became eligible to serve as jurors as a result of Schedule 33 of the Criminal Justice Act, 2003 coming into force.

[8] Interview with Anthony Arlidge QC on 30th October, 2007. Mr. Arlidge also stated even before judges sitting in appellate cases, without a jury, it was sometimes possible to subliminally appeal to concerns going beyond the limits of the immediate case.

Democratization of Juries

After 1919 both men and women could serve as jurors.[9] However the number of females was limited by the need to meet the property qualification applied to both sexes.[10] Consequently, as one judge, Lord Devlin, recognized, juries were predominantly male, middle aged, middle minded and middle-class. Following the 1965 Morris Report,[11] which concluded that a jury should as far as possible be a genuine cross-section of the adult community, the Juries Act of 1974 swept away the property condition for jury service. The only general qualification for inclusion on the jury panel became registration on the parliamentary or local government lists of voters. This led to a huge change in the makeup of juries. The average age of jurors fell and persons became eligible to sit on a jury at 18 years of age. The proportion of women increased, as did that of the working classes. It is estimated that the Act increased the number of potential jurors from eight million to thirty million.[12] Faced with juries of a wider social composition, some of the barristers interviewed said they had deliberately altered their approach in addressing jurors and were careful to use plain words wherever possible. In the opinion of one barrister, who recalled the reform, this had enhanced the clarity and effectiveness of advocacy, rather

---

[9] Probably expressing contemporary widespread views of counsel and judges on the effect of female jurors, A J Ashton, then the Recorder of Manchester wrote in 1924: *Cases seem to take longer when women are on the jury. There is a class of case, which lasts an hour or two, which men dispose of promptly. But women seem to want to talk it over and hear other views, so that they often go out to consider their verdict. The men never object to this, as they can smoke in the jury room. But we are often well into the next case before they come back with an obvious verdict. Women are less willing than men to find a man guilty, and inclined to be hard on a woman, especially if she is good-looking. They seem to have a curious difficulty in accepting the evidence of a constable. Perhaps it seems too good to be true....... I have noticed that the unmarried woman is often too nervous to do more than agree with the majority; and this is often useful.* (*As I went on my way*, Nisbet and Co., London, 1924, pp. 254–5).

[10] A juror from the City of London had to be a householder, or the occupier of premises, or the owner of land or personal estate valued at £60 per year. Jurors in the County of London had to reside in premises of net annual value above £30. Elsewhere they had to live in premises with a £20 net annual value.

[11] Lord Morris Committee on Jury Service. (1965) Cmnd. 2627.

[12] John Hostettler, *The criminal jury old and new: jury power from early times to the present day.* Waterside Press, 2004, page 125.

than reduced it.[13] A former House of Lords Judge interviewed,[14] said that many, though not all, barristers who changed their style in the 1970s were anxious to avoid appearing patronizing to jurors or of under-estimating their intelligence.

Following what might be described as the democratization of the jury, more barristers began speaking in ways that less resembled Received English Pronunciation ("RP"). The aim, as one put it, was to appeal more to the common man and woman. The trend continued. That RP is used less today, although still perhaps the most frequent pronunciation heard, reflects both a widening of the Bar's social base, which broadened in the 1970s accompanying increased numbers of barristers, and a general decline in that form of speech. This accelerated in the 1990s particularly amongst younger people, many of whom, especially in the South East of England, preferred "estuary English", the use of which makes it more dif-ficult to identify the class and geographical origin of the speaker.[15] The great increase in ethnic diversity in Britain, especially in London and the other large cities, led to more accents being heard in court advocacy. A solicitor interviewed[16] reported that certain barristers, who recognize jurors from similar minority backgrounds to their own, occasionally use

---

[13] Richard DuCann, *The Art of the Advocate*, Penguin, Revised Edition, 1993, page 29, assessing the consequences of the abolition of the property qualification, wrote that juries became much less susceptible to advocates "*whose weapons, words, and the use they make of them, have not changed at all*". A Queen's Counsel who was interviewed on 19th May, 2007, said that it had certainly con-signed to history the approach taken by the prosecution during the trial, in 1960, of the publishers of D. H. Lawrence's *Lady Chatterley's Lover*, who were charged under the Obscene Publications Act 1959. In a closing speech, which was considerably criticized at the time for being out of touch, leading prosecution counsel, Mervyn Griffith – Jones, asked the jury if this was the sort of book *you would wish your wife or servants to read?*. Not only did he count the number of times sexual inter-course had taken place in the novel but translated Phallus "*for those who had forgotten your Greek*".

[14] Lord Woolf, 27th June, 2007.

[15] On the fall in RP generally, see Kirsten Sellars, *We wanna talk like common people*, Daily Telegraph, 21st June, 1997; *Where are the gels who can talk proper?* The Times, July, 23rd 2007 and also the Leading Article of that date; and Melvyn Bragg, *RPRIP*, BBC Radio 4, 6th August, 2011, which observed the decline of R P alongside an increasing pride in regional accents. One barrister inter-viewed said of a younger recent opponent in a criminal jury trial that *her voice slid from Home Counties English down to the lower reaches of the Thames estuary and back in the course of a single sentence*.

[16] Interviewed on 12th March, 2006. She appeared in magistrates' courts in central London and instructed counsel to appear in the Crown Court.

words and phrases, speech patterns and rhythms in their closing speeches to strengthen their appeal to them. She also spoke of a decline in use of RP by advocates in the magistrates' court and a rise in accents originating overseas.

Barristers of senior call, said that they deliberately used briefer sentences than earlier in their careers when addressing juries and, whenever possible, avoided subordinate clauses and parenthesis. They explained this was because short sentences are by far the most used in newspapers, magazines, contemporary novels and, above all, in television and films. Perhaps exaggerating somewhat, one barrister spoke of the imminent arrival of almost "sound-bite advocacy". There was general agreement that the average person's concentration span had fallen, mainly because of the effect of television.[17] Some commented that this was an important reason why final speeches had shortened and why more emphasis is now placed on cross-examination in jury trials. A retired Circuit Judge[18] said that juries, like judges, prefer it *"clear and concise"*. Jurors wanted to go home. He hazarded that, in many cases, an advocate who took 20 minutes for a closing speech would succeed over an opponent whose lasted an hour.

The movement, earlier in the century, towards conversational, rather than declamatory, advocacy in closing speeches continued. Over the last two decades the practice of reading a prepared speech to a jury has been abandoned almost entirely: Spontaneity, or the appearance of it, and *chattiness*, though necessarily one way, became popularly equated with sincerity.[19]

In an episode of the BBC series *Brief Encounters*,[20] the broadcaster and legal commentator, Marcel Berlins, emphasized how much the modern jury differed from that of earlier times. In his view people were more

---

[17] Mr. John Cooper, a criminal barrister and a member of the Bar Council, in an interview in the *Times*, October 21st, 2009, said: *There is no doubt that the ability of the public to appreciate lengthy speeches and oratory has declined over the years. As a society we no longer listen to sermons and speeches at public meetings in the way that we would 100 years ago, before the advent of multimedia. As a result, advocates had to alter their style and the fashion for florid and colourful advocacy of even two decades ago had diminished.*

[18] Interviewed 25th July, 2007.

[19] Interview with Anthony Arlidge QC held on 30th October, 2007.

[20] Repeated on Radio 4, shortly after the death of George Carman QC in 2001.

educated about events because of television. They are also less deferential. It is said that society in general is now less respectful of status and office than formerly. Some identify this change as originating in the 1960s.[21] Ann Rafferty QC, a distinguished criminal barrister who contributed to the BBC programme, said jurors were drawn from the *I know what I am entitled to culture*; metaphorically they no longer look up to barristers but peer across at them. This appears to be widely appreciated by modern advocates who consciously avoid any appearance of looking down at and patronising juries.

References and Quotations

References to, and quotations from, Shakespeare,[22] the Greek and Roman myths and classics, poetry, Dickens, Sir Walter Scott and other famous authors of English literature seem to have been quite prevalent as late as the 1960s, as was mention of historical events by advocates. In an interview, one retired barrister said that Shakespearean quotes and references would have been comprehended by *40 per cent* of those serving on a pre – 1974 jury, whilst the others would pretend that they understood. Greco-Roman classics and myths on the other hand would in his estimation have only reached about *10 per cent* of jurors.

A short article in the *Criminal Law Review* in 1967 cited press reports in which judges and counsel had variously likened defendants and other parties to Macbeth, Lady Macbeth, Iago, from "*Othello*", and John Ridd, from R D Blackmore's historical novel "*Lorna Doone*". Observations had

---

[21] Anthony Arlidge QC considered that satirical television programmes, which gripped Britain in the 1960s, such as the hugely popular *That was the week that was*, much eroded almost automatic respect and deference for politicians. This spread to other figures in the establishment including judges, seen before as wise but terrifying figures, and barristers, previously held in awe. Mr. Arlidge was of the view that this had been replaced by public fascination in barristers and an expectation they would be good with words. Interview on 30th October, 2007. On the decline of deference and increased questioning of authority in Britain see Samuel H. Beer, *Britain Against Itself: The Political Contradictions of Collectivism*, Norton, New York, 1982, Chapter 3. The phenomenon, though its causes may have differed somewhat, was not restricted to Britain.

[22] On lawyers' allusions to Shakespeare, see O. Hood Phillips, *Shakespeare and the Lawyers*, Methuen and Co., 1972, Chapter 11.

also been made that certain parties had not been brought up in accordance with the principles of Dr. Arnold of Rugby School and their standards were not those defined by the nineteenth century public school headmaster and writer Dean Farrar in *"Eric"*, *or "Little by Little"*. As it appeared that the average juryman required a fair measure of literary erudition, the article, perhaps a little humorously, asked whether in addition to being predominantly "male, middle-aged, middle-minded and middle class jurors" ought also to be well read.[23]

If Richard DuCann can be seen as representative, even before the composition of juries was reformed, barristers seem to have been aware that references and quotations could be overdone, as could other oral seasonings. In the first edition of his book, *The Art of the Advocate*, published in 1964, Du Cann wrote: *the use of hyperbole, metaphor, simile, inversions of language, parallels, and allegories should be carefully controlled. Arguments should seem to rely more on force of logic than extravagancies of language.*[24]

Socially inclusive juries, where the educational backgrounds and literary interests of many members were not at all similar to those of counsel and the judges, and changes in the curriculum of schools, which gained

---

[23] 496 [1967] Crim L.R. In a concession to contemporary times, it was reported that a reference to James Bond had also been made. Judges dealing with pleas in mitigation, especially if advocates knew they had an interest in literature and Shakespeare, occasionally might encounter quotes or allusions to Portia's speech from the Merchant of Venice (Act IV Scene 1) with its appeal to mercy and praise for who shows it. A QC, interviewed on the 4th February, 2010, said that, in his opinion, many pre-1974 Juries Act jurors, who were often more socially deferential, and received less formal education than barristers, expected to be entertained by a display of literary erudition from an educated person, presumed to be from a superior social class, and would have been disappointed if they did not.

A 1940 survey of reading in nonacademic high schools, where pupils would have left at 14 showed that 62% of boys and 84% of girls had read some poetry: their favourites included Kipling, Longfellow, Masefield, Blake, Browning, Tennyson and Wordsworth. 67% of girls and 31% of boys had read something by Shakespeare. (See Jonathan Rose, *The Classics in the Slums*, City Journal, August, 2004.)

The survey suggests the suitability of literary allusions made by barristers to middle aged jurors, as reported in the Criminal Law Review article of 1967. Many jurors, because they were usually middle class and remained at school longer, would have had greater knowledge of English literature than those in the 1940 survey. On the importance at elementary school between 1870 and 1940, of reciting poetry, as part of English instruction, see Catherine Robson, *Everyday Life and the Memorized Poem*, Princeton University Press, 2011.

[24] Richard DuCann, *The Art of the Advocate*, Penguin, 1964, pp. 179–180.

momentum from the 1960s,[25] even in private and public schools attended by many advocates, led to a decline in allusions to and quotations from literature, references to historical events and other garnishments. A retired barrister interviewed said the last thing he wanted to do was to appear elitist or remote in front of the jury. Whereas before the reform of the jury their use may have helped jurors identify with him, afterwards they became a barrier. To a limited extent, he recalled, that they could still be used for some years before juries in more middle class London suburban areas such as Kingston.[26]

Whilst verbal condiments offered by lawyers to juries became rarer, they continued to be served for years to certain stipendiary magistrates, who appreciated them, in London, and possibly other large cities. Thirty or forty years ago most stipendiary magistrates were barristers, who had often attended public school and many at Oxford and Cambridge Universities. Occasionally it was said that some owed their appointments to being well connected, rather for outstanding talent at the bar. Some would make quotations in Latin; Greek was not unknown but was highly exceptional. References to literature, poetry and sport were also heard. Why they did this can possibly be explained by their backgrounds, boredom after a few years on the bench, and, as was suggested by a Lord

---

[25] Robert Graves in the Introduction to his *The Greek Myths*, first published in 1955, wrote ....*the Classics have lately lost so much ground in schools and universities that an educated person is now no longer expected to know (for instance) who Deucalion, Pelops, Daedulus, Oenone, Laaocoon, or Antigone may have been.* (*The Greek Myths*, Combined Edition, Penguin, 1992, page 11.) The National Curriculum, introduced in England and Wales in 1988, made no reference to classics, once at the heart of British high culture. Jeremy Paxman, author and television interviewer, reviewing *University Challenge*, a quiz programme screened since 1962 and for which he had been question master for 16 years, considered that today's students know less about classics: *It's interesting to see how, as years go by, they know less and less about classics and the Bible and more and more about science and computing.* (Daily Telegraph, 11th August, 2010, *Students have lost touch with classics, says Paxman*.)

[26] Interviewed 2nd April, 2007. Five years after the Juries Act 1974, Brian Gibbens QC advised young advocates against *straining to introduce literary allusions*. Brian Gibbens. *Elements of Modern Advocacy*, New Law Cassettes, Butterworths, London, 1979. Very unusually these days, Anthony Arlidge QC, a noted scholar and author on Shakespeare, said that he occasionally used quotes from Shakespeare and Oscar Wilde but would go to great lengths to make sure jurors comprehended them and why he was doing so. Interview on 30th October, 2007. Gilbert Gray QC (1929–2011), an eminent and eloquent advocate before juries, who sometimes appeared in the same cases as him, never shrank from theatrical courtroom gestures and would often quote poetry or Shakespeare.

Justice of Appeal,[27] in an attempt to differentiate themselves from defendants in their courts.

The legal historian and writer, James Morton,[28] who as a criminal solicitor regularly appeared before the Magistrates' Courts in inner London, described how one stipendiary had a great regard for Horace and Virgil. As a result, lawyers might have excerpts from their works snapped at them. Extravagant mitigation, for example, could be met with *"Vitae summa brevis spem nos vetat incohare longam"* (life's short span forbids us entering on far-reaching hopes). Another spoke, in English, of the *"sword of Damocles"*,[29] when dealing with a suspended prison sentence, of the *"labour of Sisyphus"*[30] when court orders, such as probation and community service, had failed and of a frustration rivaling that of *"Tantalus"*.[31] One stipendiary had a deep interest in poetry and often quoted John Betjeman. Allusions to horse racing, and even hunting, were made by an Irish stipendiary, whilst another, fluent in the language, used Italian whenever any opportunity arose. In order to be as persuasive as possible, solicitors and barristers would try to adopt the language, quotes and allusions made by stipendiary magistrates. James Morton described how some would go beyond that by learning replies in Latin or Italian that could possibly be made and suitable references to the classics and poetry, ancient and modern. Their efforts were very often welcomed and in some instances, he was sure, affected decisions made and sentences passed, even to the extent of influencing whether someone went to prison. Mr. Morton recounted how a new generation of stipendiaries (now referred to as District Judges) appointed in the 1980s had no interest in ornate advocacy from lawyers, preferring plain words throughout. The last of the *old school* retired at the beginning of the 1990s. With them went what remained of the flamboyant advocacy employed by solicitors and barristers in the London Magistrates courts.[32]

---

[27] Interviewed on 18th July, 2007.

[28] Interviewed on 16th July, 2007.

[29] See Cicero: *Tusculan Disputations V*, XXI [61].

[30] Robert Graves, *The Greek Myths*, Combined Edition, Penguin, 1992, pp. 216–220.

[31] Robert Graves, *The Greek Myths*, Combined Edition, Penguin, 1992, pp. 387–393.

[32] It was reported, by a solicitor interviewed, on 12th March, 2007, that advocates then, as in the past, adopted somewhat different approaches to magistrates who were District Judges (Stipendiaries, professional judges) and the great majority who are not. Most often, District Judges do not require

Allusions are still made in court but before juries are mostly likely to be from up-to-date culture such as television, films and newspaper stories. This is hardly surprising when the power of the mass media in everyday life is considered. As it was put in an American article on the subject:

> *Mass media has brought its stories into our homes and into our hearts. Contemporary mass media provides the central frame of our cultural reference for our conversations and our fantasies. When we tell our own stories, they often involve encounters with media celebrities. When we recount our fantasies, they often involve fictional characters from our favorite films or television shows. When we start to speak with our friends catch phrases from contemporary sitcoms and commercials roll off our tongues, much as Shakespeare and the Bible fell easily to the lips of an earlier generation Let's face it—media culture is our culture.........* [33]

From what he had observed, a retired Circuit Judge [34] said, advocates needed to be very careful, when going beyond the common denominator of contemporary mass culture, in making allusions to and quoting from literature. This was particularly so because of the diverse ethnic mix of many juries in London and other large cities. Danger lay in some jurors, because of their different back grounds and education, (they may well have been educated abroad and in languages other than English) being completely bewildered, distracted and left feeling apart. Thought had also to be given to references to history which might not be understood, [35] or even found offensive.

---

opening speeches from the prosecution in trials. Closing speeches by advocates for the defence (prosecutors are not normally allowed one in summary trials) concentrated on the facts in dispute rather than the law, which it is assumed is more than understood by the District Judge. In front of lay magistrates, the pace of examining witnesses was slower and closing speeches concentrated on the law and the evidence. They may also be somewhat more susceptible to restrained appeals to emotion. Many advocates structured their closing speeches in the order that magistrates deliver their judgements: the offence; areas of evidence not in dispute; areas in dispute and findings upon them.

[33] Unidentified author, published on Massachusetts Institution of Technology website: http//web.mit.edu

[34] Interviewed 25th July, 2007.

[35] One the conclusions reached by Sir David Cannadine, who led a two year research project at the Institute of Historical Research, London University on the teaching of history in English state

Peremptory Challenges

For most of the twentieth century barristers on behalf of defendants could challenge potential jurors without giving any reason in an attempt to obtain a sympathetic jury. In 1925, the number of such challenges, known as peremptory challenges, was reduced from 25 to 12. The number was limited in 1949 to seven (or seven for each defendant where two or more were tried together) and in 1977, by the Criminal Law Act of that year, fixed at three. The long standing right of peremptory challenge was abolished altogether by the Criminal Justice Act, 1988,[36] on the grounds that it ran against the important principle of random selection of juries.[37] Senior barristers interviewed[38] explained that being able to assess potential jurors, which could have a great bearing on the verdict, was considered an important part of being an advocate. Up until 1991, when the provision in the 1988 Act came into effect, if there were four defendants, in a 'multi-hander' it was possible to change the entire composition of the jury. Full exercise of the right by both counsel where two defendants were concerned could alter it by half. In many cases the object of using peremptory challenge appears to have been to remove people thought of as middle class in the stereotypical belief they might be more prosecution minded. The way people dressed was important in making decisions, as were any newspapers or books they were carrying. Some barristers looked as closely as they could at a potential male juror's hands. If they were smooth this was an indication that he was not in manual employment. One senior barrister interviewed recalled one of the first cases he defended before a jury in the 1960s. A co-defendant was represented by another somewhat more experienced counsel who, when he saw a smartly dressed man with a copy of *The Times*, said, very firmly, "*at all costs we have got to get rid of*

---

secondary schools during the past century, is that since changes in history teaching in the 1960s and 1970s away from the subject as a national narrative, and because history is no longer compulsory from the age of 14, many adults today would struggle to recognise characters from British history. (*The Red Bits Are British*, October, 15th 2011, BBC Radio 4, Archive on 4.) This may well help to explain why they are no longer usually referred to by advocates in speeches to jurors.

[36] Section 118.

[37] The prosecution still has the right to 'stand by' a juror without showing cause and with no upper limit, subject to guidelines issued by the Attorney General in 1988.

[38] On June 21st, 2006 and on 2nd April, 2007.

him. He looks far too intelligent![39] Proposals to abolish peremptory challenge were resisted by many barristers at the criminal bar and it was missed when the right was taken away in 1991.

Less Ferocity

Senior barristers and a Lord Justice of Appeal interviewed agreed that prosecutors had become less ferocious. Even in the 1970s they recalled that it was not unusual for defendants to receive a savage onslaught from counsel. In the opinion of a Lord Justice of Appeal,[40] counsel acting for defendants were now generally less aggressive and more methodical.[41] However a distinction was drawn with rape cases where some barristers still humiliated alleged victims and witnesses. He spoke of having to reprimand a barrister six times during one trial for such behaviour. In his opinion, a sub-culture persisted in which local solicitors briefed counsel known to be aggressive. This contrasted with the practice of the Crown Prosecution Service who frequently instructed sympathetic barristers, principally for the sake of the alleged victims.

Decline in Weight Given to Police Evidence

There was agreement amongst senior lawyers and judges interviewed that juries, and also many magistrates, examine evidence given by police witnesses much more intensely than they did some decades previously, when there was much confidence in the police. Police officers were seen as public

---

[39] Interviewed on June 21st, 2006.

[40] Lord Justice Sedley, interviewed on the 11th July, 2007.

[41] Judge Case, a Circuit Judge and Treasurer of the United Kingdom Women Judges' Association, who had begun her career as a barrister in the early 1970s, interviewed on the 15th May, 2009 at the College of Law Bloomsbury, expressed a similar view. When asked if he had observed a like change in Scottish criminal advocacy, Lord Mackay (Lord Advocate of Scotland 1979–1984 and Lord Chancellor of England 1987–1997), who began appearing in courts from the mid – 1950s, said it was his impression that advocacy had always been less aggressive, hectoring and blustery than south of the border and in this respect had not changed greatly. He said advocates and solicitors preferred to show a witness was untruthful by their line of questioning rather than calling him or her a liar (Interview at House of Lords, 10th December, 2008).

servants who gave evidence dispassionately and neutrally in court. Decline in weight attached to police evidence was said to be principally caused by police mal-practice and fabrication of evidence revealed in successful appeals arising from a number of high profile cases. Defendants convicted in the 1970s, but not acquitted on appeal until many years later, included the "*Guildford Four*"[42] and the "*Birmingham Six*".[43] In preparing and running cases on behalf of defendants advocates would once try to depart from police evidence as little as was absolutely necessary, mindful of the credibility given to it. Because jurors and magistrates grew increasingly likely to approach testimony of police officers with caution, their evidence became challenged more frequently in trials. In response, advocates for the Crown, less confident of securing convictions on police evidence, began to give emphasis to other evidence, especially in closing speeches.[44]

Plea Bargaining

Senior barristers interviewed recounted how it became necessary for counsel to become proficient in plea bargaining, a practise hardly acknowledged to exist in English and Welsh courts until an important

---

[42] See Robert Kee, *Trial and Error, the Guildford pub bombings and British Justice*, Hamish Hamilton Ltd., 1986.

[43] See Louis Blom – Cooper, *The Birmingham Six and other cases*, Gerald Duckworth and Co Ltd., 1977. Pressure on suspects to confess, and other illegal activities carried out by the West Midland Serious Crime Squad, were much reported in the 1980s. Geoffrey Robinson QC recalled another source of skepticism about police evidence: The popular television series *Rumpole of the Bailey*, written by John Mortimer QC and first shown in the 1970s. Alerted in many episodes to the possibility of it occurring in interviews that were then neither tape recorded or videoed, Old Bailey juries began to throw cases out where they suspected police forensic trickery. *The buzz in the Old Bailey robbing room was that Rumpole was the reason.* Geoffrey Robertson, *Rumpole of the Bailey: the very incarnation of English liberty.* The Times, January 17th, 2009.

[44] Lord MacKay, interviewed at the House of Lords, 10th December, 2008, described increased skepticism towards police evidence, a feature he saw as common to both Scotland and England, as a very major change during his career and one which has had major effects on the way advocates conduct trials. Lord Justice Goldring, interviewed at the Royal Courts of Justice on the 30th April, 2009, considered an important reason why juries now often retire for longer periods before announcing their verdicts than they did when he began his career as a barrister in the late 1960s was that jurors became less trusting not only of police officers but also of the Crown Prosecution Service, barristers acting for the Crown and judges. Reflecting society more generally, he saw jurors as less willing to make judgements on the conduct of others.

and controversial study at the Crown Court in Birmingham during the 1970s.[45] In England and Wales, plea bargaining has three meanings: an agreement between the judge and the accused that if a defendant pleads guilty to some or all of the offences charged against him the sentence will or will not take a certain form; the prosecution agreeing with the defence that if the accused pleads guilty to a lesser offence they will accept the plea; and the prosecution agreeing not to proceed on one or more counts in the indictment against the accused if he or she will plead guilty to the remainder.[46] Plea bargaining in the last two meanings became a frequent occurrence, approved by the courts. The bargain is usually struck by prosecution counsel and defence counsel outside court before the start of the trial. In practical terms plea bargaining led to fewer trials for advocates and more emphasis on delivering persuasive pleas in mitigation.

Social Enquiry Reports and Pleas in Mitigation

The introduction of Social Enquiry Reports in the late 1960s[47] had an effect on pleas in mitigation. Produced by the Probation Service (or social services departments if a juvenile was involved), they were intended to assist judges and magistrates, who had power to order them, in deciding how to deal with an offender. They contained much about a person's home life, work history, previous offending, attitude to present offences

---

[45] John Baldwin and Michael McConville, *Plea Bargaining and Plea Negotiation in England*. Law and Society Review, Vol. 13, No 2 Winter 1979, pp. 287–307.

[46] John Sprack, *A Practical Approach to Criminal Procedure*, 11th Edition, Oxford University Press, 2006, pp. 284–287.

[47] Under Section 57 of the Criminal Justice Act 1967 – see David Haxby, *Probation a changing service*, Constable, London, 1978, Chapter 6. About this time the entitlement of a defendant to speak before he or she was sentenced was abolished. Following extensive reforms of court sentencing brought into being by the Criminal Justice Act 1991, Social Enquiry Reports became known as Pre-Sentence Reports. Their content and format became more prescribed, as did the circumstances when they were ordered.

and often included a recommendation for sentence. Judges usually read the reports before coming into court or, if they had not, would do so before counsel started to mitigate.

Reports gave barristers and solicitors additional information. Sometimes this led to clients being asked to clarify certain areas and to give their views about recommendations made in them. Consideration of reports often suggested lines to follow in making pleas. Information presented in a report could result in pleas being shortened. When judges agreed with recommendations contained in a report they would indicate to counsel that their pleas could be brief. Counsel and solicitors interviewed said that some judges and magistrates would become irritable if they felt lawyers were merely reading out what was in the report and would say things like, "*I have read that*" or, even, "*I can read too!*". To avoid this, it came seen as wise to refer judges to the relevant paragraphs rather than quote from them, unless there was a very good reason to do so. A senior counsel interviewed[48] spoke of problems that arose when a Social Enquiry Report made an unrealistic recommendation, usually for a non-custodial sentence. In these circumstances counsel had to use what was useful in the report whilst carefully keeping away from that which, if pressed, could well have been harmful.[49]

On pleas in mitigation, a junior barrister interviewed, who specialised in defence work,[50] said that the scope for creativity – suggesting certain courses of action and asking for credit for aspects of a person's history – had been reduced when dealing with some offences where minimum sentences had been introduced in recent years.

---

[48] Interviewed on 10th April, 2007.

[49] As advocacy in the criminal courts adjusted to Social Enquiry Reports, from the 1960s practitioners in the civil courts dealing with family matters had to have regard to reports written by social workers on the welfare and custody of children.

[50] On the 7th September, 2007.

Accommodating Key Changes in Law and Procedure

When asked about other major influences on advocacy in the closing decades of the last and the beginning of this century, a number of barristers mentioned the need to accommodate three key changes in the law of evidence and procedure.

Under the Police and Criminal Evidence Act 1984 a criminal court must exclude from evidence a confession by an accused if it has been obtained by oppression, or as a result of something said or done which is likely to render it unreliable.[51] Also under the Act evidence generally, including confessions, may be excluded, in the court's discretion, to ensure a fair trial.[52] The ability to make submissions on these sections became crucial in advocacy before the magistrates and Crown Court.

Submissions under the Criminal Justice and Public Order Act ("CJPO") 1994 also became essential. Before the CJPO 1994, silence of an accused in an interview could not be used as evidence against him or her at trial. The Act weakened the right to silence by providing that adverse inferences may be drawn against the accused in certain circumstances from his or her failure to mention certain facts, to account for possession of certain objects, substances or marks, or to account for his or her presence at certain places.[53]

The third change cited as greatly affecting criminal advocacy was the Criminal Justice Act 2003. Prior to coming into force of this legislation, a defendant could be cross-examined on his or her previous convictions only if he or she attacked the character of the prosecutor or his or her witnesses. The circumstances in which an accused's bad character may be admissible were expanded under the Act.[54] Given the generally accepted negative consequences of revealing a defendant's bad character, especially

---

[51] Section 76.

[52] Section 78.

[53] Sections 34, 36 and 37. See Peter Murphy, *Murphy on Evidence*, Ninth Edition, 2005, Chapter 10.

[54] Section 101. See Murphy, *ibid*, Chapter 6.

to a jury, submissions on admissibility are of great importance in trials. If admitted, advocates for the defendant now have to consider calling evidence about previous convictions that would reduce their relevance to offences presently alleged and also how to minimize their impact by comment in closing speeches.[55] These, and other changes, led to more preliminary applications to judges on points of law, before a jury was empanelled.[56]

Traditionally in England and Wales, prosecutors put their witnesses in the witness box without speaking to them in advance about their evidence or any of the issues in the case. The rule arose in the eighteenth century when prosecutions were largely brought by private persons. Judges at the time did not trust private people to deal honestly with their witnesses because a widespread trade existed in bribing them.[57] To reduce this, the judges developed a rule that people who prosecuted privately must not speak to witnesses they were to call.

In a speech delivered in 2006[58] the Director of Public Prosecutions ("DPP"), and head of the Crown Prosecution Service, Mr. Kenneth MacDonald QC made the point that public prosecutors today were not private citizens but members of professional legal bodies, and of a public prosecuting authority subject to codes of conduct and rules that status implies. When speaking about the rule to colleagues abroad, the DPP said they were astonished to hear a criminal justice system existed in which prosecutors are forbidden from speaking to witnesses before a trial begins. Indeed he recounted how a Supreme Court Judge in Canada had told him she would report a prosecutor to his professional body for

---

[55] Anne-Marie Critchley, interviewed 7th September, 2007.

[56] In the opinion of Lord Bingham of Cornhill, then Senior Law Lord, the increase in preliminary applications on points of law, including abuse of process, was a notable development in advocacy during the closing decades of the twentieth century. Interview on 23rd October, 2007. Lord Justice Goldring, interviewed on the 30th April, 2009, explained that applications concerning admission into evidence of bad character have risen while the number of application to exclude confessions have fallen because of audio taping or videoing interviews in police stations.

[57] See J. H. Langbein, *The Origins of Adversary Criminal Trial*, Oxford, 2003, pp. 148–150. One aspect of this trade was that 'men of straw', identified by pieces of straw tucked into their shoes, hung about outside courtrooms, available to act as witnesses – for a fee.

[58] 23rd May, 2006.

incompetence if he or she was to call a witness in a serious criminal case without testing that evidence before proceedings started.[59] To the DPP, the rule, preventing prosecutors speaking to alleged victims, was at its most unsupportable where the Crown Prosecution Service had to decide whether to bring cases when it was one person's word against another, as in rape where the defence of consent is run. In what can only be described as a fundamental change in the legal system and the practice of advocacy, Mr. MacDonald announced: *So we are now in the business of interviewing witnesses and I suspect that in areas like serious sex crime there will be a very significant improvement in prosecutions and prosecution decision making.*

After consultation with the judiciary, the Bar Council and the Law Society, to allay concerns that witnesses would be coached or evidence contaminated, a pretrial witness interview pilot scheme was introduced in in Greater Manchester, Merseyside, Lancashire and Cumbria in 2006. Before it began the Bar agreed to change its professional code of conduct to facilitate the scheme and a Code of Practice was drawn up for Crown Prosecution Service lawyers.[60] Interviews were recorded on audio or, in some circumstances, videotaped and made available to the defence,[61] Two years later pre-trial interviews were permanently extended across England and Wales.

Very shortly before its national implementation, an experienced prosecution barrister put forward that pre-trial interviews might considerably affect the task of advocacy in some cases. As it was not unusual for the defence to suggest that a witness's account was influenced by questions asked by a police officer taking his or her statement, he considered, where

---

[59] The rule preventing prosecution advocates interviewing their own witnesses was much questioned in Britain following the acquittal of four youths charged with manslaughter of the south London school boy Damilola Taylor in 2002. The judge ruled that the evidence of the main prosecution witness, a 12 year-old girl, could not be relied on. The then Attorney General, Lord Goldsmith QC, in 2003, began a process of consultation on whether CPS lawyers should interview witnesses before trial. In 2004, the Attorney General concluded that prosecutors should be able to interview key witnesses about their evidence.

[60] Polly Botsford, *Early warnings*, Law Society Gazette, 105/12, 28th March, 2008, pp. 12–13.

[61] In an interview with the Director of Public Prosecutions, held on 23rd May, 2006, Mr. McDonald expressed confidence that sufficient safeguards would exist against coaching witnesses and "improving" evidence.

pre-trial witness interviews take place, potential exists to suggest in cross-examination that questions asked by a prosecution lawyer were improper and may have influenced the witness.

"That puts the prosecution lawyer in a very difficult position since, whereas the police officer who took a witness statement can go into the witness box and answer any such accusations, it is not convenient for the lawyer who is conducting the prosecution to be presenting the case one minute and then stepping into the witness box to defend him or herself the next." [62]

Heavy Drinking and Boredom

An impression existed amongst lawyers interviewed that heavy drinking by barristers, an aspect of the Bar for generations, but seldom discussed, had declined over the last two decades. Excessive consumption of alcohol had, in their view, impaired the quality of some advocacy, especially after lunch, and reduced time for effective preparation of cases, particularly those received the night before.

It was said in an interview with a solicitor,[63] who frequently instructed counsel in the Crown Court, that sometimes barristers, to relieve boredom in some cases, decided on a theme for the day, for example golf, and competed with each other as to who could make the most references to it in proceedings. It is impossible to say how widespread this practice is.

More Hastings Than Birkett?

Some years ago a former Attorney General, said that much forensic oratory was now delivered like a chartered accountant reading a Sunday church lesson. Whilst many would regard this as an exaggeration, it is beyond doubt that advocacy to persuade juries, for a number of reasons,

---

[62] David Allan, 23 Essex Street Chambers. Interviewed by Polly Botsford for article, *Early Warnings*, Law Society Gazette, 105/12, 28th March, 2008. pp. 12–13.
[63] Interviewed 20th August, 2007.

chief amongst them being the need for advocates to speak in the language of time, was shorter, plainer and more direct at the start of this century than it was at the beginning of the last. Broadly speaking, and usually without the bullying sometimes associated with him, the direct and forcible style favoured by Sir Patrick Hastings earlier in the century, eclipsed that of Lord Birkett, with its greater concern for the graces and literary heritage of English. This does not mean, however, that some histrionic ability amongst advocates came to be considered unnecessary. Speaking about modern jury advocacy a retired High Court judge[64] said that in his experience jurors expected a bit of style, not dreariness, and wanted to be charmed, without being patronized. In his view, as much care as an actor should be taken in pitch, speed of delivery and pauses to accentuate points, convey and invite interest. According to him, constant movement of the eyes to scan the jury to make each member feel important was vital. His views echoed those of Sir James Stirling, then a judge in the High Court, written in 1966 in *Verdict*, the Journal of the Oxford University Law Society:

> *To some extent the same technical equipment is necessary to both professions. Voice, diction, variation of pace, stress, the effective pause, are necessary weapons in both armouries. The actor studies these things deliberately; the advocate is largely let to make use of them by instinct and acquired experience. A too conscious artifice on the part of counsel would probably distract him from the main task, which is to marshall his material: but even good material can be reduced to excruciating dullness by poor delivery or a complete lack of dramatic instinct. Even a wholly juristic argument must be given some "bite" if it going to be listened to easily.[65]*

Later in this article Sir James Stirling advanced the thesis that changes in advocacy curiously corresponded with those in styles of acting. This view was put to Anthony Arlidge QC who said that parallels could certainly be

---

[64] Interviewed 24th July, 2004.

[65] *Verdict*, Oxford University Law Society, Hilary, 1966, VOL 2. NO 1. page 8. On ability through voice to convey and invite the interest of jurors, it was said of the late Richard Ferguson QC "*that he had the kind of voice that could read the jury the telephone book and they would listen*". Obituary, Times, 30th July, 2009.

drawn with the stage over the last three decades which had seen the falling away of *Lawrence Olivier* Shakespearian acting, with its unevenly paced and highly stylised delivery, involving hard emphasis on selected words, and the rise of a more naturalistic and conversational form.[66]

Advocacy in Defamation Cases: A Remnant of an Earlier Age?

Trials of civil defamation actions before a jury number very few each year but they often attract much publicity. It is probably correct to say that more vivid and entertaining advocacy, frequently with heaps of sarcasm and ridicule, is employed in these matters than anywhere else.[67] These trials, in some respects, appear as survivors from an earlier, less restrained and exuberant period. However, beneath the forensic extravaganza usually lies much greater preparation in cross-examination and closing speeches than in earlier times. George Carman QC, who died in early 2001, was recognized as the outstanding advocate in defamation trails.[68] When asked, he stressed that real spontaneity in addressing juries was a thing of the past. To him, painstaking effort beforehand to coin phrases and choose words carrying emotional over-tones and great attention to detail was crucial. In this, his admirers compared him with Cicero and Quintilian. He also had theatrical ability. Like the playwright Harold Pinter, George Carman in court, according to Marcel Berlins *"was a master of the pause, allowing a witness's dubious answer in cross examination to remain in the air for a while, giving the jury a chance to savour it, before pouncing on it and exposing its shortcomings"*.[69]

---

[66] Interviewed on 30th October, 2007.

[67] Judges, to the delight the press, are sometimes said to go along with these spectacles by asking barristers to explain things, sometimes of an embarrassing nature, that they already know. Interview with retired Circuit judge, 25th July, 2007.

[68] See Dominic Carman, *No Ordinary Man: A Life Of George Carman Q. C.*, Coronet Books, Hodder and Stoughton, 2002.

[69] Marcel Berlins, *Writ large*, The Guardian, January 8th, 2001. Commenting on the style of George Carman, Anthony Arlidge QC said it was surprisingly declamatory in an age of conversational advocacy. Interview on 30th October, 2007. When interviewed at his chambers, on 30th July,

Further Considerations

This Chapter aimed to outline changes to advocacy in jury trials in England and Wales during the last half of the twentieth century. Additionally in the first two decades of this century advocacy has also had to accommodate: increased employment of expert witnesses in trials; the use of special measures for vulnerable and intimidated witnesses and of witness protection orders in trials of serious and violent offences; submission of written skeleton arguments to judges on complex questions of law; victim impact statements; the prospect of trials without juries in complex frauds and where there is a risk of jury tampering; and the danger of jurors unlawfully conducting research on the internet, thus undermining their role as fact finders bound by rules of evidence.

2009, Michael Beloff QC, spoke of cases in which he had appeared in defamation trials against George Carman. He said it was noticeable that when matters of law arose George Carmen would hurriedly turn to his juniors for advice. At first Michael Beloff was mystified by this, knowing that his opponent had obtained a first class degree in law and generally shone brightly at Oxford University, but then concluded he had *deliberately purged himself of his knowledge of law in order to find the same wavelength as his audience of jurors.*

11

Developments in the Second Half of the Twentieth Century Influencing Advocacy in the Civil Courts

Availability of Legal Aid

Before the Legal Aid and Advice Act 1949, part of the postwar Labour Government's programme of radical social reform, little legal advice or representation in court was available to those who could not pay for it.[1] The Act, described by the then Attorney General, Hartley Shawcross, "*as*

---

[1] For an outline of what existed previously, and its very limited nature, see Harry Kirk, *Portrait of a Profession*, London: Oyez Publishing, 1976, Chap. 8 and A. H. Manchester, *A Modern Legal History of England and Wales 1750–1950*, London, Butterworths, 1980, pp. 99–104. See also Steven Hynes and Jon Robins, *The Justice Gap: whatever happened to legal aid?*, Legal Action Group, 2009: Chapter 1 describes the origins of legal aid, developments in the scheme established in 1949 and controversial reforms made by the New Labour government, 1997–2010, which critics maintained much reduced its availability in civil courts. Public funding for cases much further diminished as a result of the Coalition government's considerable retrenchment of legal aid, set out in the Legal Aid, Sentencing and Punishment of Offenders Act 2012. Fewer people now have access to free legal representation than at any time since legal aid was introduced. For criticism of these reforms see House of Commons Justice Select Committee Report, *Impact of changes to civil legal aid under Part 1 of the Legal Aid, Sentencing and Punishment of Offenders Act 2012*, Printed 4th March, 2015. http://www.publications.parliament.uk/pa/cm201415/cmselect/cmjust/311/31102.htm. In protest against continuing cuts to legal aid fees for barristers more than 100 chambers refused to take on new legal aid work for two months in 2018. Also in that year, because of what it saw as huge underfunding of legal aid, the Law Society predicted criminal defence solicitors were heading for extinction. Law Society Gazette, 6th August, 2018, p. 10.

© The Author(s) 2019
A. Watson, *Speaking in Court*, https://doi.org/10.1007/978-3-030-10395-8_11

the charter of the little man to the British courts of justice", introduced means tested legal aid, administered by the Law Society, but funded by the government, for a wide range of civil, including family, and criminal cases. This meant professional advocacy before the courts was available to greater numbers of people and, consequently, for solicitors and barristers work became more abundant. The quality of advocacy for clients who before the 1949 reform would have instructed lawyers on limited funds, but after the Act qualified for legal aid, increased as greater resources became available to prepare their cases and to represent them in court.

The abolition, in 1965, of the Bar's rule that required a client to pay a special fee if he or she wanted to be represented by a barrister from another circuit made a further, albeit much smaller, contribution to access to counsels' services. This former restrictive practice, introduced in late Victorian times, also made it necessary to pay an additional fee for a barrister from within the circuit to attend at court.[2]

Relaxation of the Rules Against Hearsay Evidence

A retired Queen's Counsel, who had specialized in commercial law, reflecting in an interview on changes in advocacy during his career, considered the Civil Evidence Act 1968 was of great importance Together with the later Civil Evidence Acts of 1972 and 1995, this legislation swept away some two centuries of jurisprudence concerning the circumstances in which hearsay evidence could be adduced in civil trials. The hearsay nature of evidence became primarily a question of weight rather than admissibility.[3] Advocates were no longer required to fill their minds with complex law on hearsay and to make often long submissions in trials on why such evidence should be admitted or excluded. This contrasts starkly with the United States, where hearsay, and other rigid rules relating to admission of evidence,

---

[2] See J. R. Lewis, *The Victorian Bar*, Robert Hale, London, 1982, pp. 127–128.
[3] See *Murphy on Evidence*, Ninth Edition, Oxford University Press, Chapter 7.

continue to apply in civil trials, even though the majority of cases are now decided by judges, not jurors, for whom rules of admissibility were intended.

Less Angular Judges

A former solicitor interviewed, who had briefed and attended many counsel during the 1960s and 70s, especially in the Chancery Division of the High Court, recounted that judges could be pompous, aggressive and unpleasant to barristers applying for court orders who did not know the particular way they managed their court and cases. The slightest mistake was seized upon and could result in a case being put at the bottom of the cause list, or even not being heard at all that day. It seemed then that knowing the way a judge operated and looking the part was sometimes more important than the substance of an advocate's case. The solicitor, who later became a Master in the Chancery Division, the Queen's Bench Division and the Family Division of the High Court and a circuit judge, explained that the following years saw a marked improvement. Judges became much more civil and constructive to counsel. He mainly attributed this to younger judges remembering what they had gone through earlier as barristers.

A solicitor who had appeared in the County Courts since the early 1980s and also sat as a deputy district judge, said that certain judges at the beginning of his career were more attentive and polite to barristers than solicitors and to solicitors who had briefed them in the past when they were barristers. They were least civil to young solicitors, especially females. He reported that such behaviour had disappeared. However, although plain rudeness from the bench appears to be the exception rather than the rule, and advocates of yesteryear faced worse, some instances of belittling and undermining behaviour are still reported by young advocates and new measures are called for to deal with it.[4]

---

[4] *Bullying advocates is not a judicial prerogative*, Law Society Gazette, 14th October, 2017 and *Judicial Behaviour: Bullying in the Court Room*, Law Society Gazette, 13th November, 2017.

Changes in Civil Procedure and the Transformation of Advocacy

Civil procedure changed enormously in the closing years of the twentieth century and led to a transformation in advocacy.

The Picture Before Reform

Civil litigation at common law rested on an adversarial system in which the parties themselves set the agenda and the pace of proceedings, culminating in a trial where all the business was conducted orally, even documents and legal authorities were read out in public.[5] Even in the appellate courts, the idea of written advocacy was abhorrent. This was illustrated by the case of Rondel v Worsley,[6] concerning the immunity of counsel from being sued in negligence. The Court of Appeal was presented with a litigant in person with a lengthy and closely argued document. Lord Justice Dankwerts described this *"as wholly irregular and contrary to the practice of the court"* and added *"in my opinion it should not be allowed as a precedent for future proceedings"*.[7] In appeals to the Court of Appeal the judgement below was read out in its entirety, often adding much to the length of the hearing. If they wanted to draw attention to its inadequacies, appellants would seek to have the judgement read towards the beginning of their case. Respondents, if satisfied by the judgement usually preferred it be read later.

Little exchange of information by the parties took place before a trial, save for pleadings, discovery and following orders for interrogatories (questions asked by one party to the other about his or her case). Opening speeches were made and could, in cases of high value and or importance, be very lengthy set pieces of advocacy lasting days. If done well they could be highly persuasive. A former judge in the House of Lords interviewed,

---

[5] For a picture of the traditional approach to civil litigation see Mr. Justice Lightman, *The case for judicial intervention*, New Law Journal, December 3rd 1999, pp. 1819–1836.

[6] [1967] 1 QB 443.

[7] *Ibid*, page 509.

who began his career in the mid-1960s, said there was often great advantage for an advocate to make the first opening speech giving an opportunity to shape the case favourably before judges, who had little other information, although this disappeared if evidence was not as said to be or legal argument considered wanting.

Each side called witnesses as to fact who were examined, cross-examined by the opposing advocate and then re-examined. Whether witnesses would *come up to proof*, i.e. give as evidence what they said in their statement to solicitors, was of major concern to advocates who could generally only ask them non-leading questions (essentially those that did not suggest their answer). Before 1995 barristers were prevented by their professional rules from discussing evidence with lay witnesses. Techniques to steer witnesses back to what they had said in their proof of evidence were essential, as was quick thinking about how to manage cases when witnesses failed to come up to proof.

Expert witnesses were called, with little or no notice to the other side. A valued tactic was ambushing and surprising opponents. This was often done by suddenly producing new witnesses. Provided their evidence did not fall outside matters set out in the pleadings this was permitted. To be able to cross-examine surprise witnesses was an esteemed skill demanding considerable mastery of the case. By and large at trial Judges asked advocates and their witnesses few questions and only intervened to insist that rules of evidence and procedure were obeyed. The outcome of litigation very often depended upon whom parties could afford as their advocates and experts. Costs, ordered by the court, were unpredictable and often disproportionate to the matter in dispute. They might be swelled by the use of pre-trial injunctions, freezing orders and orders to preserve evidence which were sometimes used, as were onerous orders for discovery, to harass opponents and added unnecessarily to delay. There were hardly any limits on the length of examinations and submissions by lawyers, who were allowed to get on at their own speed. A former Court of Appeal judge, recounted it was *like a slow bicycle race – the view was you could take as long as you wanted.*

The length of many trials was prolonged by advocates introducing more exhibits into evidence, much assisted by the rise of the photocopier in the 1970s (A High Court judge interviewed observed "*that some solicitors lived by their photocopiers*".)

As early as the 1950s problems of delay and disproportionate expense in High Court litigation had been debated. The best way to end them was seen with the judge rather the parties. The Evershed Committee recommended more intervention by the court, and a stronger line on the "summons for directions" before trial, but little came of this.[8] Increasingly from the late 1960s, the traditional judicial position of "hands off", giving almost free reign to barristers in court, and the approach of revealing as little of a party's hand before trial as possible, became recognized as contributing much to the slowness and inefficiency of civil justice, which almost seemed an expensive sport favouring those with deepest pockets, rather than an effective, swift and just way to solve disputes. Calls for radical change mounted and began to be met in the 1980s.

Changes Begin to Occur

The Report of the Review Body on Civil Justice in 1988[9] proposed a "cards on the table" approach to civil litigation and set in chain a series of reforms. In 1992 compulsory exchange of witness statements between parties before trial was introduced. This shortly followed on from a requirement that they disclose expert reports to each other. Judges ordered more interrogatories to elucidate issues in cases. A High Court Practice Direction in 1995[10] carried things further. Under the Direction judges were to exercise greater control over the preparation for and conduct of hearings. This was to be achieved by a number of measures: limiting discovery; imposing time limits on oral submissions and the examination of witnesses; more narrowly defining issues to be addressed; abandoning the practice of counsel in court reading aloud documents and authorities; written witness statements were to stand as examination in chief unless otherwise ordered so oral evidence would usually begin with the cross-examination; counsel were to provide the court with skeleton argu-

---

[8] Final Report of the Committee on Supreme Court Practice and Procedure (1953) Cmd 8878.
[9] Cmnd 394.
[10] Practice Direction [1995] 1 All E. R. 385.

ments (These had already been introduced for the Court of Appeal in 1989 under Lord Donaldson, the then Master of the Rolls); parties supplying the court with bundles and written evidence to read in advance of trial; and in heavy cases permitting the court to require written submissions as well.

The effect of these reforms was that judges became much more informed about the cases they were to try. They were freed from being almost completely in the hands of counsel. No longer had they to sit, as Mr Justice Lightman put it, *"silently like sphinxs, but rarely smiling"* gradually absorbing what the application or case was about. Judges could, and did, take greater control of cases and began to steer them. The reactive judge of the past was replaced by the proactive judge. *"Informed judicial intervention was born"* in the courts of first instance.[11] Prior to its arrival there, judicial intervention had long come of age in the appellate courts, particularly the House of Lords, where judges could read reports and documents from cases decided in courts below. Active judicial intervention by Registrars (now District Judges), although seldom informed beforehand of the cases they were to deal with, previously also existed under the highly informal small claims procedure, where parties were only rarely represented by solicitors or counsel, which was introduced in 1973.

After the introduction of witness statements standing as evidence in chief, the function of barristers in relation to witnesses became somewhat more complicated. This is because solicitors began to send draft witness statements to barristers for their approval or, increasingly, instruct them to draft witness statements. Both activities may involve a barrister requesting a solicitor to ask the witness more questions for the purpose of elaborating certain parts he or she has dealt with, and to turn the witness's attention to other evidence with which it apparently conflicts. Guidance on the role of the barrister in preparing witness statements, principally to guard against anything approaching witness coaching, was set out by the General Council Of the Bar.[12]

---

[11] Mr. Justice Lightman, *The case for judicial intervention*, New Law Journal, 3rd December, 1999, pp. 1819–1836.

[12] *Preparing Witness Statements for Use in Civil Proceedings*, Bar Standards Committee. First Issued January, 2001 and Reviewed September, 2008.

The Woolf Report, the New Civil Code and Stages in a Usual Trial

One year after the 1995 Practice Direction, Sir Harry Woolf, now Lord Woolf, published *Access to Justice*, the report of a committee of inquiry into civil litigation, which proposed more changes to simplify litigation and reduce its cost. The recommendations in the report were mostly adopted and embodied in new Civil Procedure Rules, which replaced both the Rules of the Supreme Court in the High Court and the County Court Rules in the County Courts.

Under what was intended to be a completely new civil code, courts were directed to give effect to the "overriding objective" of dealing with cases justly.[13] This included ensuring parties are on an equal footing and in ways that are proportionate to the amount of money involved, the importance and complexity of the case, and the means of the parties.[14] The Court must further the overriding objective by actively managing cases which includes fixing tight timetables, or otherwise controlling progress of the case, and, where appropriate, encouraging the use of alternative dispute resolution procedure.[15]

"Hands on" judicial participation in trials was a central element in the CPR reform of civil procedure. Pre-reading of papers by the judge, particularly of the parties' skeleton arguments, and his or her active participation in the hearing are distinguishing characteristics of a modern civil trial under the new Civil Procedure Rules. Time limits, placed by Judges on the length of speeches and cross-examinations, are also frequently present, especially in cases allocated for trial under the "Fast Track" procedure. Subject to some exceptions, notably minor personal injury and housing disrepair cases, which can only be heard in this track if they do not exceed £1000, claims with a value up to £5000 are allocated to the

---

[13] CPR, r. 1.1.
[14] CPR, r. 1.2.
[15] CPR, r.4.2

small claims track which replaced the small claims procedure, introduced in 1973. Like what it superseded, strict rules of evidence do not apply in small track claims hearings. Unless there are compelling reasons not to do so, claims worth between £5000 and £15,000 were allocated to the fast track; and claims exceeding £15,000 were sent to the multi-track. Following acceptance of the proposals of a review published in 2007 the £15,000 limit was raised to £25,000 for claims commenced on or after 6th April 2009.

After a judge has read the bundle of trial papers, skeleton arguments very important amongst them, the stages of a typical trial are[16]:

Some discussion between the judge and the advocates, but, unlike before, no formal opening speeches;

Witnesses confirm the content of their witness statements; one or two questions may be asked of witnesses of fact, at the behest of the judge, but examination-in-chief as previously known, is now rare (even before the Civil Procedure Rules judges had been given the power, which they often used, to order that witness statements stood as examination-in-chief);

Cross-examination limited by the trial timetable; discursive cross-examination is stopped by the clock and irrelevant cross-examination not allowed to prolong the trial;

Parties' final submissions in which they develop their skeleton arguments, but unlike pre-Civil Procedure Rules cases, these usually take the form of a discussion of issues with the Judge rather than a formal closing speech (In multi-track cases there may be an adjournment for both parties to submit written submissions);

And, following judgment, submissions about costs which may be more lengthy than formerly.

---

[16] See Judge Frenkel, *The New Advocacy*, The Law Society Gazette 96/24, June 16th, 1999, page 141.

Combined Impact on Advocacy

The fundamental changes brought about by the Civil Procedure Rules and earlier reforms, diminishing the oral element in civil trial procedure, had a major effect on advocacy. Only cross-examination, probably its most important and defining aspect, continues from the traditional form of common law civil trial, which best now survives in the United States. Reportedly, insistence on skeleton arguments/case summaries gave rise to initial complaints from some counsel who objected that they had come to the Bar to be court advocates and not to draft documents. They became, however, a fact of life, the impact of which cannot be over-stated. In effect, a skeleton is now a party's first "speech" which he or she is allowed to deliver without any interruption from the Judge, who may rightly assume it is the advocate's best effort. As Mr Justice Lightman put it in 2004, "*It may properly enable the judge to form a provisional view of the case on which the Judge is asked to make at least a provisional judgment on the case as a whole and the merits of some or all of the issues, and it is perfectly legitimate for the judge to do so and so inform the parties, putting them on notice of the hurdles to be surmounted: see Costello v Chief Constable of Derbyshire [2001] 1 WLR 1437 at page 1440, para 9. In a word cases can be won or lost on skeleton arguments*".[17] It has been advanced that at appellate level some cases are decided before oral argument is heard.[18]

Because judges delivered more and more reserved judgements, both at trial and appeal level, skeleton arguments became, in a sense, advocates' closing speeches, available to members of the court long after the oral argument finished. Originally they were conceived as "skeletal" and succinct documents to identify and summarise the relevant issues of fact and law, not to argue them fully in writing. The essential minimum requirements are a chronological account of relevant facts, a statement of the

---

[17] Mr. Justice Lightman: lecture to the Chancery Bar Association entitled *Advocacy – A Dying Art?*, January 2004.

[18] Andrew Goodman, *Influencing The Judicial Mind – Effective Written Advocacy in Practice*, XPL Publishing, 2006, p. xvii. In support of this, Mr. Goodman stated that in about 40 percent of appeals heard since 2000, either one side or the other was not called upon to make an oral presentation.

issues of law and fact and an evaluation of the rival answers to those issues. Indicative of the growing importance of written advocacy, it was said in the mid first decade of the century courts were unconcerned with their length where material provided was necessary, persuasive and assisted the court to solve the problem before it. A Court of Appeal judge, interviewed in his chambers showed examples of skeleton arguments submitted to him. The shortest was 25 pages and the longest 47 pages. Whilst he agreed that skeleton arguments concentrate minds on a case, the judge thought that some might be too long because they attempted to deal with peripheral matters which might arise. Another Lord Justice of Appeal said some were almost like speakers' notes. A former law lord spoke of needless repetition when advocates merely repeated almost verbatim what had been written. They agreed that *quality* advocates are those who strike a good balance between written and oral presentation, appreciating that the purpose of advocates' speeches is to elaborate and supplement the skeletons.

In modern civil trials witness statements stand as evidence in chief, although judges may direct that a witness be examined in chief. A Lord Justice of Appeal interviewed, said when he had tried cases at first instance, he insisted that counsel should ask a witness a few questions in chief on evidence that was not in dispute, so as to help him assess his or her general credibility. He understood that this practice, which he considered helpful, was now very rare, mainly because of a desire to save court time. Consequently, he believed, that in civil cases many young barristers had lost the ability to examine in chief. This view was shared by a Central London County Court judge who usually only ordered some examination in chief of witnesses, to assist him in assessing their credibility, in cases where fraud is alleged. He contrasted advocates' lack of accomplishment in conducting examination in chief with the past when skill in this area was an essential part of civil law advocacy.

Judges interviewed were of the opinion that witness statements had greatly expanded in length to cover almost any conceivable issue. Time taken in cross-examination had much increased on the basis that unless challenged what was in a witness statement would be accepted by the court as evidence. It was explained that both these developments were to avoid the possibility of being sued in negligence by clients and referred to the landmark House of Lords case of *Arthur JS Hall and Co v Simons*, decided in 2000.[19] This established that an advocate could be sued for negligent conduct in court. Before lawyers could only be sued for negligent preparation of a case outside court. In his view, clients in the High Court were much more critical of and aggressive towards their lawyers than earlier, "*Everyone now has a view*". This may be connected with the high cost of litigation. Because of the growth in size of witness statements and correspondingly prolonged cross-examination, two Lord Justices of Appeal interviewed thought that in some cases the previous system of oral examination in chief and cross-examination might have been be quicker. On the matter of judges imposing time limits for cross-examination and closing speeches, they reported most advocates observed them. However, when advocates did not, there was a great variation in how judges reacted. Some were very keen to enforce limits, whilst others, particularly those who had not conducted trials themselves as advocates (in other words they had previously been solicitors rather than barristers), were very reluctant to intervene. It was certainly useful for advocates to have knowledge of their judge and how much latitude they would be given.

Encouragement, backed by sanctions in costs, of disputants to jointly appoint a single expert witness, whenever possible, is an important component of the civil procedure reforms. The single expert's report covering matters in dispute usually carries much weight in court. Dealing with these reports in submissions, either to persuade or, more difficultly, to dissuade judges to follow their conclusions, has become as important aspect of civil advocacy.

A premium in contemporary advocacy is put on being flexible to deal with issues raised, not as the advocate may have calculated, but as they are brought up by the Judge, sometimes at the beginning of the case, but more frequently in closing submissions. In the opinion of Mr. Justice Lightman[20] civil advocacy now requires a far greater knowledge of the facts and law by advocates than when Judges were "*generally tame and on a tight lead*" and seldom intervened during proceedings. Now they "*may*

---

[19] [2000] 3AER 673.
[20] *The case for judicial intervention*, New Law Journal, 3rd December, 1999, pp. 819.

be found barking – on occasion perhaps biting at the ankles of advocates". He saw *"confidence not to he overawed, resilience to respond, tenacity to challenge, tact to mollify and the authority to inform and persuade"* as indispensable qualities in advocacy when dealing with judicial interventions, which should be made for the purpose of directing both parties advocates to essential issues so as to save time and costs. As with enforcing time limits in cross-examination and closing speeches, he identified differences between judges in the extent they intervene with questions. Again, those who had been advocates appeared more likely to intervene than those who had not.

After judgement has been delivered, or following a decision on an interim matter, a vital part of advocacy is making persuasive submissions on whether costs incurred, which may in some cases exceed the amount of a claim, are proportionate and reasonable. According to a senior barrister interviewed this requires advocates to have a much greater grasp of the principles upon which costs are calculated, and how they have been accumulated in cases they are involved, than before the introduction of the Civil Procedure Rules.

Speaking shortly after the Civil Procedure Rules came into effect, Lord Justice Sedley predicted that *"greater weight placed on co-operation between lawyers in getting the real issues before court, more general emphasis under the Civil Procedure Rules on compromise and settlement, and the qualities of preparation, organization, and sensitivity now required of advocates would further advance reasoned persuasion in advocacy at the expense of whatever remains of rhetoric and bombast"*.[21] Interviewed eight years later,[22] he considered that in civil advocacy this had largely come true. In the early 1990s, Richard DuCann wrote about the practice then emerging in some tribunals of requiring summaries of speeches, which were somewhat similar to skeleton arguments, in advance of a hearing: *"It may flatten the language which is used, rhetoric cannot survive in print, but it does concentrate the mind wonderfully"*.[23] Lord Justice Sedley strongly agreed with this quotation.

---

[21] The Lord Morris Memorial Lecture, Cardiff University, September 28th, 1999.

[22] 11th July, 2007.

[23] *The Art of the Advocate*, Penguin Books, 1993, page 189.

A retired Queen's Counsel said that in commercial law cases rhetoric and bombast had gone long before skeleton arguments and the Woolf reforms. He explained that practitioners in that area of law were usually highly educated in law and of considerable intellectual calibre (His chambers demanded that pupils had a first class degree). Commercial cases, especially those on appeal, were frequently very complicated and of great financial value. Much preparation and research on the law was necessary. In short it was a very serious business and one in which there was simply no room for distractions of rhetoric and bombast, which would certainly not be appreciated by highly paying clients. A similar opinion was offered by Michael Beloff QC in an interview. In his view, the decline of rhetoric, the use of "*borrowed plumage*" from literature and history, and of bombast was also much linked to what he termed "*fragmentation of fora*", particularly during the last three or so decades of the twentieth century. Rather than being, as in past times, generalists in many areas of law appearing before a variety of courts, advocates, because of law's increasing technicality, tend to be restricted to practising law in specialist courts and tribunals. The language employed there was very much that required by the specific setting and simply did not lend itself to what might be described as the more grand and universal forms of address heard when advocates appeared before many courts.[24]

Interviewed, Lord Justice Sedley considered skeleton arguments and the Civil Procedure Rules had speeded trials up and this was beneficial. Whilst recognizing advantages in these reforms, Mr. Justice Lightman considered trials were being slowed by advocates, orally and in writing, bombarding judges with judgements from superior courts. This, in his opinion, was the result of publishers reporting more and more cases without making efforts to distinguish between extempore and considered judgements to avoid duplication: "*The practising lawyer is obliged to expend ever increasing resources and time (paid for by clients) on obtaining access to and studying these reports*".[25] Barristers interviewed agreed that they often

---

[24] Interview conducted on 30th July, 2009.
[25] The 6th Edward Bramley Memorial Lecture, Sheffield University, 2006 and in interview 8th March, 2007.

did cite more law than they did before. One said that this was because internet legal data bases had made cases more available, with new ones arriving very quickly.

The internet has made easier the task of researching foreign law which is increasingly cited by advocates as persuasive authority, especially before appellate courts. There have been a few occasions when courts, concerned that domestic authorities appeared to give an inadequate answer to an acute human problem, have invited counsel to explore civil law authority in addition to Commonwealth and United States authority already cited to them.

Facility in civil advocacy is no longer measured in the planning and delivery of long speeches: Preparation of persuasive skeleton arguments/case summaries and chronologies, responding to interventions from judges with in depth knowledge of the relevant facts and the law at their fingertips and the ability to make pertinent submissions on costs are now highly prized. To adjust to these crucial requirements of modern advocacy law colleges, teaching vocational courses for barristers and solicitors, increased their instruction to students on drafting skeleton arguments/case summaries, responding to interventions by judges and submissions on costs and it is anticipated more will be taught about them in future.

The Tradition of Oral Advocacy Under Threat?

The new style of civil advocacy stressing persuasiveness on the page and adhering to time limits on questioning and the length of speeches, led some lawyers, albeit a minority, to believe the fundamental tradition of oral advocacy itself in the English courts was endangered. In 2000, delivering the Margaret Howard Memorial Lecture at Oxford University, Michael Beloff, a leading public law Queen's Counsel and President of Trinity College, Oxford, expressed the view that, as well as limiting opportunities for future specialist advocates to incrementally develop and improve their skills in smaller cases, which had become less numerous, the changes could also affect the quality of Judges' decisions. In his opinion dialogue between counsel and the bench sometimes *"forces new thinking not hinted at in the skeleton"* argument. Verbosity was to be deplored but the pendulum has swung the other way with the danger that "*brevity may be seen as an end in itself*".

Some four years later Michael Beloff, in an article entitled *England's dying art* written for the New Statesman[26] returned to the theme that oral advocacy was under threat and with it the quality of justice. He explained that oral address had little role in the European Court of Justice, where British lawyers had appeared for more than three decades, often just occupying fifteen or twenty minutes, and that it was not uncommon for more energy to be spent on negotiating the length of the speech before the hearing begins than on delivering the speech itself. Interrogation from judges is rare and rights of reply better not exercised, he reported. Oral advocacy, he conceded, at the European Court of Human Rights, served a greater function, but time for it is measured in hours rather than days. Mr Beloff remarked: "*A case that migrates from the Strand to Strasbourg will undergo a process of miniaturization*".[27]

Turning to skeleton arguments, Mr Beloff stated that what were intended to be a mere platform for oral presentation had developed *obese proportions* and, rather than a support, they had become a snare: "*With some judges, fidelity to the skeleton prompts the retort 'I have already read this' with others any departure from it risks the testy question 'Where is this in your skeleton'?*". He contrasted 2004 with 1967, when he was called to the Bar. In those days "*some judges made it an article of faith never to read any of the papers before they entered the courtroom in case doing so prejudiced their minds. They expected — indeed, wanted — counsel to shape the analysis for them*". (In an interview Lord Bingham, then Senior Law Lord on the Judicial Committee of the House Of Lords, explained that whilst this was accurate, most judges in appeal cases would have read the law reports from the courts below and in the House of Lords the majority would have considered the Case, the jointly produced document setting out agreed facts and issues of law between the parties.)

---

[26] 16th February, 2004. Special Supplement: *Are they off their Trolleys? The Future of Legal Services* pp. xxvi–xxvii.

[27] Beloff, *Ibid*, page xxvi.

Mr Beloff identified a further threat to oral advocacy coming from an increasing unwillingness on behalf of some judges to hear it, following Lord Templeman who, in a series of observations in the Appellate Committee of the House of Lords,[28] strongly criticised, *"torrents of words"*. He said that it *"was not the duty of counsel to advance a multitude of ingenious arguments in the hope that out of ten bad points the judge will be capable of fashioning a winner"*.[29] Where written advocacy is substituted for oral, two assumptions were made, which according to Mr Beloff, were not always justifiable. The first is that the judge has read the argument and the second is that he or she has understood it. On the basis that both are correct, he was troubled that advocates would have insufficient opportunity to engage with judges who disagree with their arguments. He continued:

The development of the common law – like the English language, one of England's major contributions to civilization – has been the product of a constant dialogue between Bar and Bench. No experienced advocate doubts that cases can change shape, sometimes dramatically, when what seemed an impeccably logical submission is tested to destruction, or not, by the judge. As Lord Justice Laws said in a recent decision: 'That judges in fact change their mind under the influence of oral argument is not an arcane feature of the system; it is central to it'. Or as Mr Justice Megarry put it, still more succinctly, three decades ago: 'Argued law is tough law'.

Elsewhere in his article, Mr Beloff asserted, polemically, that relegation of oral advocacy to the margins would be a victory for the solicitors' profession in the so-called "Bar Wars" about solicitors' rights of audience in the higher courts: *"Having won from Lords Mackay and Irvine* (previous Lord Chancellors) *advocacy rights in the highest courts but made (with a few exceptions) little impact there, solicitors are thinking, if you cannot join them, beat them. And their weapon of choice is the written page. Is this to be the last hurrah, not only for silks, but for the Bar itself?"*.

---

[28] Notably in the case of *Ashmore v. Corporation of Lloyds* [1992] 2 All ER 486.
[29] *Ashmore v Corporation of Lloyds* [1992] 2All ER486 at page 493.

Some of Michael Beloff's views were put to judges interviewed. One Lord Justice of Appeal said skeleton arguments were certainly not a snare or a tyranny. Admitting that he could not speak for all judges, he thought considerable tolerance was shown when departures occurred from what skeletons contained. This sometimes happened, he explained, when another counsel, who did not draft the skeleton, appeared as an advocate in court, or a leading counsel decided to run a case differently from that indicated by a junior in his skeleton. In those circumstances he considered it is not perhaps surprising that comments may be heard from judges. He wondered whether the remarks by judges reported in Mr Beloff's article had been made in such contexts, but emphasised efforts were not made to stifle new submissions. Particularly in appeal cases, judges may give a steer to counsel on what they consider to be best points in a skeleton and those in which they are least interested in. This, in his opinion, was where skeleton arguments were of considerable value. If, however, barristers do not go in the directions hinted, they were not stopped from developing their arguments. The Lord Justice of Appeal disagreed with Mr Beloff that the greater role of written advocacy had inhibited oral presentation and debate. He recognized the latter's worth in making *the penny drop* and giving fresh insights. In his view many barristers were still addicted to oral advocacy and it was something that most judges, at present, put up with. However, advocates had to accept greater intervention from judges who were now much better informed about cases before them. That skeleton arguments did not preclude other points being raised; that time limits, although generally abided by, were not always rigidly enforced; and that there was considerable variation between judges in the extent they intervened with questions indicated that civil advocacy was in a time of transition. He said that there were still many long winded advocates. In the future, as written advocacy became more accepted as the norm by younger advocates, he thought there would be fewer of them. Regarding English appellate cases, on matters of law, he said that he would like to see the United States Supreme Court model adopted. Written argument is presented and limited time exists, thirty minutes, for oral presentation by advocates of key points only and for them to answer questions asked by judges. He recognized that such a shift would involve much greater work for judges and advocates outside court. Another Lord Justice of Appeal described how skeleton arguments, particularly in appellate courts, had expanded from two pages to a full argument in writing. Whilst useful in focusing minds and enabling judges to reach provisional views, he did not want them to replace oral argument. In apparent agreement with Mr Beloff, he said that the *dialectic* between barristers and judges was crucial and could lead to a better decision than would have been taken purely on paper. Oral argument, in the higher courts, was a great strength of the English legal system and one which, he reported, was much admired throughout the world.

Five years after publication of *England's dying art*, Michael Beloff was interviewed[30] to see whether he still held the views expressed in his article. He said that experience as an advocate, and as Senior Ordinary Appeal Judge in the Channel Islands, led him to modify his position. He now accepted oral advocacy could exist harmoniously with written advocacy as long as a role for the former was preserved, allowing an essential dialogue between advocates and judges so that arguments could be clarified and tested,. There was much left to be done to calibrate the balance between the two and to organize better written advocacy. Like members of the senior judiciary interviewed, he was concerned about the size of many skeleton arguments which, in many cases, could resemble the length of briefs submitted to courts in the United States. Mr Beloff suggested two pieces of written advocacy should be submitted to judges. The first would be a very skeletal document setting out the matters in dispute and the law involved, whilst the second would be fuller giving the background to the case and additional details of relevant law. The latter document would be of assistance to judges writing their judgements. In drafting paper advocacy, Mr Beloff urged advocates to follow the six specific points listed by Lord Bingham in his lecture *The Role of an Advocate in a Common Law System*, given in Gray's Inn Hall in 2008[31]: set out the facts in a clear, accurate, fully referenced and neutral way; be clear in your own mind exactly what you want to say: make it as simple

[30] On 30th July, 2009 at Blackstone Chambers, Temple, London.
[31] Summarised in *Graya*, No 122, Hilary 2009, pp. 17–24. The lecture was the first in an annual series on advocacy, known as The Birkenhead Lecture, inaugurated in 2008 by Mr. Beloff, then Treasurer of Gray's Inn.

as possible, but no simpler; cite authorities sparingly and without extensive verbatim quotation; be brief; and use clear and simple language.

Mr Beloff agreed that modern oral advocacy in the civil courts, where judges, largely as a result of written advocacy, had a grasp of the facts and issues and a sense of points they thought were crucial, demanded advocates were not thrown when judges asked them questions and made comments before they could fully deploy their carefully prepared orderly and logical arguments. Closely allied to the key skill of entering readily into dialogue with any member of the tribunal was the ability to resume the thread of the argument when the judges had finished.

Because of pressures and expense of court time, Mr Beloff recognized that the days when *"the judge danced at the speed of the tune of the litigants had gone"*. Instead it is now the judge who is the *"conductor"*. In this task paper advocacy has a value.

Accepting his views on written advocacy had altered and were now similar to those more widely expressed, Mr Beloff said that his principal opposition to it had been because of romantic nostalgia for unhurried oral advocacy in English courts which was pleasing to listeners in court, had good, as opposed to negative, rhetorical qualities and was a form of art.

Perhaps the greatest, though little commented upon, curtailing of the principle of oral advocacy took place in social security law, mainly for reasons of economy. Before Regulations in 1996 were implemented persons dissatisfied with benefit decisions could appear in person at a Social Security and Child Benefit Tribunal, or be represented there by an advocate (usually from a law or advice centre), although only a small minority of claimants were. Claimants, alternatively, if they chose, could make written submissions to the tribunal. This was rare. The government department responsible for the decision was always represented by a Representing Officer. After expressing concern about wasted expense because nearly one in three appellants failed to appear before Social Security and Child Benefit Tribunals, the government, introduced Regulations providing appeals to Social Security and Child Benefits Appeal Tribunals should only be dealt with by written submissions, unless one of the parties expressly requests an oral hearing, or the tribunal directed oral procedure should be followed.[32]

---

[32] Social Security (Adjudication) and Child Support (No. 2) Regulations 1996.

Decline of Allusions in Advocacy to the Classics, Poets, History and Latin

A former solicitor, who frequently accompanied counsel instructed by his firm to the Chancery and Queen's Bench Divisions of the High Court of Justice in the 1960s, recounted use of Latin words by barristers and judges was common then. Greek words were very occasionally heard, although not by him. To him this was hardly surprising given the classical education of most judges at the time and the central place of Roman Law in law degrees at Oxford, where he had studied, and Cambridge Universities. The former solicitor said that allusions to, and quotations from, literature were frequent, especially in the Chancery Division; Shakespeare, Milton, Walter Scott and Homer (in English) were the favourites. References to historical events were also made. A retired House of Lords judge, reflecting on his early career as a barrister in the same period, recounted quotes and allusions from literature and historical references were a feature of the courts but emphasised that many barristers and judges, perhaps even the majority, did not use them. A similar view of their frequency was taken by a Lord Justice of Appeal. Both thought, because of the particular audience to whom they were addressed, counsels' purpose in using them had been to aid persuasiveness and clarify meaning, but was also intended to show their erudition.

A Central London County Court judge spoke of other reasons why allusions and quotations were made by advocates. Counsel would sometimes deliberately slightly misquote or make an allusion that was not entirely apt before a judge known to be fond of the classics or English literature. This was done to give him the opportunity of correcting what had been said. Usually he would begin: "*Surely Mr ... do you not mean?*" Counsel would then earnestly agree. The judge, confirmed as the most educated person in court and possibly thrilled, might then feel more disposed to counsel and his submissions. Certain judges, however, possibly because as barristers they had used the device themselves, were entirely unmoved.

Even when Shakespeare, Milton, Scott, Homer and others were quoted and alluded to in abundance during the early twentieth century, their persuasive value before judges had been doubted. Sir John Simon, who served as Attorney General and later Lord Chancellor, considered such efforts as embellishment; ornamenting an advocate's speech rather than achieving practical results.[33] According to Sir Norman Birkett, Sir John Simon's particular strength lay "*in his no-nonsense ability to turn what otherwise may well have been a dry recitation of facts supported by authorities into a fascinating and enthralling narrative and to tell it with great skill. In the process the facts were marshalled and arrayed; the important ones emphasized and the less important lightly touched on. His mastery of law made complicated matters sound clear and simple and convincing*".[34] In contrast to Sir John Simon's estimation of it, Lord MacMillan, in an address given in Birmingham in the early 1930s,[35] valued literary knowledge highly in persuasion: "*I believe that no advocate can be a great pleader who has not a sense of literary form and whose mind is not stored with the treasures of our great literary inheritance upon which he may draw at will. The fortune of an argument depends much more than is commonly realized on the literary dress in which it is presented. A point made in attractive language sticks in the judicial memory*".

Sir Norman Birkett in 1954 also spoke approvingly of counsel reenforcing their arguments by appropriate quotations from literature.[36]

In an interview a House of Lords judge said the demise of flowery language and flamboyance in court was one of the two greatest changes in advocacy that he had witnessed (the other was the rise of paper advocacy). He had no regrets about it. A former Lord Chancellor, who had been a distinguished advocate in Scotland, considered, advocates in Scotland, save for a very few, had *always been less flamboyant, flowery and poetic* in their words than many in England.

Literary quotations and allusions and references to historical events in Crown Courts declined swiftly after the Juries Act 1974 widened very considerably the composition of the jury. They endured longer at the

---

[33] In an address during a visit to Canada in 1921. Reprinted in Graya No VIII, Easter 1931, pp. 32–35.
[34] Sir Norman Birkett, Presidential Address to the Holdsworth Club, Faculty of Law, University of Birmingham, 7th May, 1954.
[35] Quoted by Birkett in his Presidential Address, above.
[36] Presidential Address to the Holdsworth Club.

appellate criminal level and in the higher civil courts, in part reflecting similarities in the social and educational backgrounds of most judges and barristers. Nonetheless, over the decades, these features in speech became increasingly rare as did Latin words and phrases. The retired House of Lords judge interviewed described how judges had shown less appreciation of their use by barristers. He agreed that opportunities for them had further diminished with the arrival of the Civil Procedure Rules. Written skeleton arguments, time limits and interventions from judges, replacing many aspects of the traditional trial, meant plain, unornamented, direct, and precise advocacy was required.

Two Court of Appeal judges interviewed, one of whom studied classics, said that, even if they wanted, few judges would feel confident today in quoting from them. One said that judges had become hesitant about referring to historical events or figures in judgements lest they might be considered controversial or a distraction. To explain this, he pointed to what Lord Justice Simon Brown had said at the beginning of his judgement in Rv Ministry of Defence ex parte Smith and other Applicants[37]: *"Lawrence of Arabia would not have been welcome in today's armed forces: homosexual men and women are not allowed to serve"*. This led to many articles and letters in the newspapers about whether T. E. Lawrence was homosexual. The two Court of Appeal judges concurred in thinking that because few judges make allusions to literature, quote from it and refer to historical figures and events in their judgements, few advocates do so in seeking to persuade them. The then Senior Law Lord, Lord Bingham, agreed it had become rare for advocates, as well as judges, to quote from literature and to allude to history. However, he continued to refer to them when it aided clarity of understanding. A similar approach was taken by Lord Justice Wall in the Court of Appeal. Warning of the damage done by warring parents in a custody dispute before the Court, he quoted a stanza from Philip Larkin's hard-hitting and very direct *"This be the Verse"* in a postscript to a judgement:

---

[37] QBD 1995 4 All ER 427.

Indeed, as I read the papers and the expert report and the oral evidence…, I was
powerfully reminded of the first four lines of Philip Larkin's This be the Verse.
They fuck you up, your mum and dad.
They may not mean to, but they do.
They fill you with the faults they had
And add some extra, just for you.
The rest of the poem seems to say more about Philip Larkin himself than it does
about the human condition, but these four lines seem to me to give a clear
warning to parents who, post-separation, continue to fight battles of the past
and show each other no respect.[38]

The Civil Procedure Rules 1998, which replaced the Rules of the
Supreme Court and the County Court Rules, removed many Latin (and
Law French) words and phrases. They were followed by a Statutory
Instrument in 2004 which swept away the former Latin names of the
prerogative remedies. Mandamus, prohibition and certiorari became
known instead as mandatory, prohibiting and quashing orders respectively. The message, though never officially delivered, to judges was stop
using Latin in court altogether. Although not obliged to do so, most
have. One of the Court of Appeal judges interviewed said that he would
still use Latin for technical terms, the meaning of which was understood
exactly, where there was no simple English translation. He did not think
he was alone in this. Indeed Lord Bingham, a year before his retirement
in 2009, in the Birkenhead Lecture in Gray's Inn, urged advocates to
employ clear and simple language in both oral and written advocacy.
However he continued *"this was not an argument against the use of Latin*
where appropriate: a host of Latinisms had survived over the centuries pre-
cisely because they had a well understood meaning and there was no conve-
nient synonym- such as prime facie, ab initio, pro bono, a fortiori, de facto,
ad hominem and de minimus and more technical expressions such as ratio
decidendi, per incuriam, forum conveniens, lex fori…".[39]

---

[38] R(A child) [2009] EWCA Civ 358, paras. 124–125.
[39] Inaugural Birkenhead Lecture at Gray's Inn Hall on 6th October, 2008, *The Role of an Advocate*
in a Common Law System, Graya, No 122, Hilary 2009, pp. 17–24.

Now, partly as a result of judges using very few Latin words or phrases, if any, advocates generally avoid them. It is reported that some judges will ask them not to use Latin, while others, particularly older judges, are more tolerant.

Despite much removal of Latin and updating of English legal terms, the language of the law, a highly specialized form of speech, still remains substantially apart from that in common use. Expressions, for example, like *"balance of probabilities"* and *"beyond reasonable doubt"* have distinct technical meanings. Language differences do not end there. They extend to language used daily by lawyers in court. *"With great respect"* addressed to another means strong disagreement. *"May it please your honour"* is frequently used to open a party's case. Other court language includes *"I put it to you that..."* and *"I suggest"*, both often employed by advocates in putting their client's case in cross-examination; *"I hear what you say; Sir will see"* and *"If I may trespass upon your honour's patience"*.

Changes in Advocacy in the County Court

A retired County Court judge recalled that when he was appointed to the bench in 1979 advocacy was still very formal. A lot was also verbose. Some was flamboyant. Many judges were pompous and idiosyncratic in their approach. Knowing how particular judges liked to run their courts and about their likes and dislikes was an important aspect of advocacy. A number of advocates would try and mirror the language, on occasion including Latin, used by them. Literary allusions, metaphors and similes, for example to cricket, calculated to please, although not always achieving their object, were frequently made. Most judges, in his opinion, realised what they were trying to do; some had attempted it themselves as advocates.

This style of advocacy was changed by increasing numbers of cases arriving in the County Court, as a result of legislation passed in the 1970s, about housing and domestic violence. Particularly in the latter, especially in emergency applications, judges needed counsel and solicitors to explain the facts rapidly. They were not occasions for long ornamented and formal speeches. In his view this plainer, shortened, direct and more business like advocacy spilled over into other areas of the court's jurisdiction. The judge's view was corroborated by barristers whose County Court practices extended back to the early 1980s. The judge said that the second major influence on advocacy he had observed came with the introduction of skeleton arguments, written witness statements standing as evidence in chief and fast track trials within time limits. In his view much advocacy previously practised was not needed now. Skill in cross-examination, though, remained indispensable and always required thorough planning. Being on top of the law, especially cases cited in skeleton arguments, was vital, as was anticipating and responding to questions from judges on facts. A clear mind and concision was necessary. He had no regrets that the type of advocacy, though sometimes more colourful, heard when he was first appointed to the bench had become history. Few other County Court judges, he thought, missed it either.

The New Realities and Clients' Perceptions of Advocacy

It was reported that some clients whose cases were heard soon after the Civil Procedure Rules were introduced in 1999 found the more abbreviated role occupied by oral advocacy to be surprisingly different to what they were expecting and were rather disappointed.[40] Some even went as far as saying they had felt deprived of "a proper day in court". To allay concerns, and forestall complaints, many solicitors, barristers and solicitor advocates found it necessary to explain to clients about the new procedure, the purpose of skeleton arguments, the role of spoken advocacy to augment and support what was written and about time limits. A High Court judge reported the gap between popular expectations of advocacy in civil disputes and reality took some years to close.

---

[40] See Mr Justice Lightman, *The case for judicial intervention*, New Law Journal, December 3rd, 1999, page 1836.

Conditional Fees and Behaviour in Court

Most civil cases have been removed from the scope of legal aid.[41] In its place are "no win no fee" conditional fee agreements ("CFA"). They are marketed on the basis that a lawyer will not take a fee if a client's claim fails. If the client wins they may charge a "success fee" of up to 100 *per cent* more than their usual fee. This, and the cost of after the event insurance (to cover a CFA client's liability for the opposing side's costs if he or she loses at trial) was normally paid by the unsuccessful party. However since the Jackson reforms introduced in 2013, solicitors can no longer recover their success fees or insurance premium from the losing side but must take it from the client's award, lessening the distinction between CFAs and contingency fees where lawyers take a share of whatever their clients receive. Concerns were expressed that giving solicitors and barristers, who may be instructed by the former on a no win no fee basis, a direct financial interest in the outcome of disputes might lead to more aggressive advocacy, less civility towards each other in court and even worse. The Royal Commission on Legal Services,[42] which reported in 1979, rejected the idea of contingency fees. It stated that such a scheme, giving lawyers a clear stake in what happened to a case, might lead to undesirable practices including *"the construction of evidence, the improper coaching of witnesses, the use of professionally partisan expert witnesses, especially medical witnesses, improper examination and cross-examination, groundless legal arguments designed to lead the courts into error and competitive touting"*. Judges and barristers, questioned about them, reported little change in behaviour in court as a result of conditional fees, but could not exclude the possibility that some advocates might be tempted to act unethically.[43] Supporters of conditional fee agreements have commented

---

[41] Access to Justice Act, 1999, Schedule 2 and Legal Aid, Sentencing and Punishment of Offenders Act 2012, Part I.

[42] CMND 7648. Volume 1.

[43] Although not specifically directed at advocates, the Legal Services Ombudsman reported in 2014 that: "The no win, no fee market has become increasingly aggressive, with many law firms competing for cases and sometimes prioritising sourcing a large number of customers over a careful selection process," and that "A business model which consistently overvalues the chances of success can

that the prospect of receiving no payment if cases are lost has led advocates to prepare more thoroughly and sometimes this may be reflected in
higher standards of advocacy. In the United States, where contingency
fees often give lawyers a large personal interest in whether cases are won
or lost, it was reported they have no noticeable effect on manner and
performance in court. One law professor colourfully put it "*if an attorney
is a pitbull, he will be just that, no matter the arrangements for payment*".

After the introduction of conditional fees, the Bar Council removed
cases under this arrangement from the cab-rank rule.

Litigants in Person

Litigants in person increasingly form part of modern, especially civil,
court life. Limited research has been carried out into their experience of
court processes and their impact on proceedings. However a study published, in 2005 of four first instance courts[44] found that, although there
was little evidence of an explosion in numbers of litigants in person,
unrepresented parties in cases were common. They were usually defendants. Obsessive and difficult litigants formed a very small minority of
litigants in person, but posed considerable problems for judges, lawyers
and court staff. Although the study did not consider the Court of Appeal,
it was known to have a large population of unrepresented litigants.

The study concluded some litigants in person dealt with matters well;
others were totally without confidence, whilst some began confidently
but ended poorly. Litigants seemed to cope particularly poorly with procedural, as opposed to substantive, hearings and also where new or unpre-
dicted issues arose. Judges had a range of ways to deal with hearings with
unrepresented parties. They included directing opposing lawyers to sum-
marize their case and make very clear submissions on it. Some judges, the

---

drive lawyers into unethical practice in order to avoid financial meltdown." Guardian, 6th January,
2014.
[44] Richard Moorhead and Mark Sefton, Cardiff University, *Litigants in person: Unrepresented litigants in first instance proceedings*, Department of Constitutional Affairs, DCA Research Series 2/05,
March, 2005.

study revealed, would intervene in hearings considerably more than others. A number would intervene quite modestly, telling litigants in person that they should get legal advice, rather than saying precisely what was wrong with their case, or what needed to be done to put it right. Others much more directly engaged with the substantive issues before them, making explicit references to legal positions (sometimes, in effect, advising litigants) or cross-examining on their behalf. These judges were seen to abandon the role of neutral arbiter in favour of the *neutral advocate*, or that of the *inquisitorial judge*.

As a result of the Legal Aid, Sentencing and Punishment of Offenders Act 2012, Part I, which removed means-tested legal aid from private family and other areas of law, numbers of litigants in person rose substantially, although the precise extent is unclear. More significant has been the shift in the nature of litigants in person, who are increasingly people with no option other than to represent themselves and who may therefore have some difficulty in effectively presenting their cases. According to Sir James Munby, President of the Family Division, in evidence to the House of Commons Justice Select Committee in 2015[45]:

Previously we had a lot of litigants in person who were there through choice. They tended to be people who had a particular point of view, but who understood the case, were articulate and had the confidence to appear in court. We now have a lot of litigants in person who are there not through choice and who lack all those characteristics.…

The result is that the courts are expending more resources to assist litigants in person and require more funding to cope. In 2013 the Bar Council produced a *Guide to Representing Yourself in Court* for persons who do not qualify for legal aid, but cannot afford representation. Two years later the Bar Council, Chartered Institute of Legal Executives and the Law Society introduced guidelines for lawyers who find themselves opposed to litigants in person.

---

[45] House of Commons Justice Select Committee Report, *Impact of changes to civil legal aid under Part I of the Legal Aid, Sentencing and Punishment of Offenders Act 2012*, Printed 4th March, 2015. http://www.publications.parliament.uk/pa/cm201415/cmselect/cmjust/311/31102.htm

Some litigants in person are assisted in court by *McKenzie* friends. *McKenzie* friends originate from a 1970 divorce case *McKenzie v McKenzie*,[46] in which Mr. McKenzie, who was no longer publicly funded and had no representation, was refused a friend to come into court and sit with him during proceedings. The case went to the Court of Appeal where it was held that Mr. McKenzie's friend should have been allowed to remain and "*sit quietly beside the husband and give him from time to time some quiet advice and prompting*".[47]

The function of McKenzie friends has since grown. Whilst lacking rights to conduct litigation or act as an advocates, courts may, in the interests of justice, on a case by case basis, grant them audience. Four types of McKenzie friends now exist: "traditional", such as a family member or friend providing a supportive presence in the courtroom and limited non-legal assistance; "volunteer", belonging to an institution or charity; "fee-charging", offering the conventional limited service understood by this role; and, more numerous since the removal of much of civil legal aid, "fee-charging providing a wider range of services", including general legal advice and, where permitted speaking on behalf of clients in court.[48]

Concerns about the variable quality of professional McKenzie friends, many of whom widely advertise their services, have been expressed by the Bar Council and the Law Society[49] and calls made for them to be regulated or self-regulated, although this would present significant challenges given their wide range of roles.

Quite clearly a requirement placed on modern advocates is to be able to deal with litigants in person, the different ways judges react to them, and with McKenzie friends.

---

[46] [1970] 3 W.L.R. 472.

[47] Lord Justice Sachs, at page 477, paragraph H. The judgment also cited a comment made by the Chief Justice, Lord Tenterden, in a case in 1831, that *any person, whether he be a professional man or not, may attend as a friend of either party, may take notes may quietly make suggestions, and give advice, Collier v Hicks* [1831] 2 B.& A. p. 669.

[48] Legal Services Consumer Panel, *Fee Charging McKenzie Friends* (April 2014).

[49] House of Commons Justice Select Committee Report, *Impact of changes to civil legal aid under Part I of the Legal Aid, Sentencing and Punishment of Offenders Act 2012*, Printed 4th March, 2015. http://www.publications.parliament.uk/pa/cm201415/cmselect/cmjust/311/31102.htm

A Specialist Form of Advocacy: Mediation and Collaborative Law

The Woolf reforms in the late 1990s introduced a range of measures to further a more co-operative approach to civil justice. One of these was positive encouragement to use mediation so that disputes, wherever possible, should be resolved without court hearings. Pre-action protocols and cost sanctions, as well as the over-riding objective of the Civil Procedure Rules, promote recourse to mediation by parties to litigation as have cases in the courts.[50]

Alternative Dispute Resolution ("ADR"), of which mediation is one technique, is less common in the United kingdom than many other common law countries, notably the United States, Canada and Australia, but has increased and is widely predicted to rise further. A number of lawyers have qualified as mediators. Particularly in cases of high monetary value or other importance, persons going to mediation are accompanied by lawyers to advise them and speak on their behalf. Advocacy skills necessary for mediation representation differ from those required in the more formal setting of court. Ability to project the strength of a party's case at the outset of a mediation is seen as particularly important and key to reaching a settlement. In 2010 Mediation Advocacy became a compulsory part of the Bar Professional Training Course, which replaced the Bar Vocational Course.

As an alternative to traditional divorce practice, collaborative law arrived in this country from North America in the first decade of this century. In essence this involves parties and their lawyers entering into a binding commitment to resolve all matters without involving the Courts. There then follows a series of meetings in which everyone – the individuals and their lawyers – are present. During the course of these *Four Way* meetings lawyers, help to ensure all relevant information is on the table, advise when necessary and aim to move their clients towards workable and fair agreements. Creative acceptable solutions tailored to particular

---

[50] For example in *Dunnett v Railtrack* [2002] 2 ALL ER 850, *Halsey v MiltonKeynes General Hospital NHS Trust* [2004] 1 WLR 302and *Burchell v Bullard and others* [2005] EWCA Civ 358.

domestic circumstances are sought. Once every one is in agreement the lawyers draft a formal document which is submitted to the court for approval and made into a binding Order. The informal, but carefully chosen, speech, a hybrid of advocacy and negotiation, employed in this process, strongly contrasts with the stylized and rigidly structured advocacy in the divorce courts, still with some room for rhetorical flourishes, especially by counsel.

Greater Use of the Welsh Language

Welsh is now heard more in the courts of Wales. Indeed trials may be conducted in it. The Laws in Wales Acts 1535–1543, annexing Wales administratively into England, created a single state and legal jurisdiction. The Acts contained measures to restrict and discourage the speaking of Welsh. Section 20 of the 1535 Act decreed English was the only language to be used in courts of law. However until the late nineteenth century the vast majority in Wales spoke Welsh. A high percentage of them had little or no English. This necessitated evidence being given in Welsh which was translated into English, mainly for the benefit of judges and lawyers who frequently did not speak Welsh. The Welsh Courts Act 1942 officially allowed use of Welsh in courts provided the Welsh speaker was under a disadvantage in having to speak English. This was very narrowly interpreted by subsequent case law. These cases were effectively overturned by the Welsh Language Act 1967, which introduced the concept of 'equal validity' between the Welsh and English languages. The Welsh Language Act 1993 went further and established that 'in the course of public business and the administration of justice, so far as is reasonably practicable, the Welsh and English languages are to be treated on the basis of equality.' Specifically it stated that Welsh may be spoken in court by any party, witness, or other person who wishes, subject to prior notice required by rules of court, and that provides any necessary interpretation will be obtained.[51] Court Rules embodying rights of court users, including

---

[51] Welsh Language Act, 1993, Section 22. Special rules apply in Magistrates Courts.

advocates, in Wales to speak Welsh in both the criminal courts and civil and family courts have been introduced.[52]

The number of cases heard in Welsh has risen. In 2015–16 there were 570, including one judicial review. It was anticipated that this would go to up to 700 by the end of 2017.[53] Partly as a result of adaptations to the recruitment processes, the number of Welsh-speaking judges has grown, with a third of all Circuit Judges, a third of District Judges and just under a half of District Judges (Magistrates' Courts) being able to conduct cases in Welsh. The Welsh Language Act 1993 does not enable empanelling bi-lingual juries where evidence is presented in Welsh, or for translators to retire with the jury. The consequences of this, especially potential for injustice through misunderstanding, are debated and calls have been made for reform.[54]

Not only is Welsh increasingly spoken by judges, barristers, solicitors, parties and witnesses in court, but, as a result of establishing the National Assembly for Wales (*Cynulliad Cenedlaethol Cymru*) in 1999[55] and subsequent additions to its powers[56] both primary and secondary legislation may be passed in Wales. Indeed a body of law, already by 2017 comprising 50 pieces of primary legislation and more than 4000 Welsh statutory instruments, is accumulating. More and more barristers and solicitors appearing as advocates in Wales have to be aware, as a vital aspect of their practice, of differences in law and procedure from England.

---

[52] *Cynllun Iaith Gymraeg*, Welsh Language Scheme 2018–2021, HM Courts and Tribunals Service, 2018, pp. 19–25.

[53] Lord Chief Justice's Report, Judiciary of England and Wales, 2017, page 28.

[54] Sir Roderick Evans, then Presiding Judge of the Wales Courts Circuit, *Bi-lingual Juries*, Address to Centre for Welsh Legal Affairs, University of Aberystwyth, 22nd November, 2006.

[55] Government of Wales Act 1998.

[56] Government of Wales Act, 2006. This legislation gave the Assembly primary legislative competence in 20 devolved areas. Its powers in these areas were enhanced by the result of a referendum in 2011.

12

The Teaching of Advocacy: An Important Influence

When assessing influences on advocacy, the introduction of systematic and rigorous training in the late twentieth century, must be considered an important factor.

In Sir Patrick's day

Sir Malcolm Hilbery, reflecting a widely held view at the time, in his address on advocacy in Gray's Inn in 1938, was doubtful whether advocacy could be systematically taught except, perhaps, by observing successful practitioners in court.[1] Similarly Patrick Hastings, whose style in his great forensic successes did much to influence that of other barristers, wrote in 1954 "*There is no school of advocacy, in all probability no such school would be any value even if it could exist......*".[2]

Sir Patrick was of course absolutely right in as much as no school of advocacy existed in his time. The bar examinations, introduced in 1852

---

[1] Graya XX, pp. 11.
[2] *Cases in Court*, Pan Books Ltd., 1954, page 252.

© The Author(s) 2019
A. Watson, *Speaking in Court*, https://doi.org/10.1007/978-3-030-10395-8_12

and made compulsory in 1872, covered only the law. This was eloquently criticized in 1943 by Leo Page, a stipendiary magistrate, previously a highly successful barrister, who wrote:

If, for example, the student intends to be called to the Bar, amongst other esoteric knowledge he must master the matrimonial system of the Roman Empire and the Institutes of Justinian, to which in all probability he will never again have occasion to refer and which the day following his examination he will make every effort to forget. Until recently, if he desired to be admitted a solicitor he was required to ground himself in ecclesiastical and Admiralty jurisprudence which almost certainly for the remainder of his professional career would be completely useless to him. Towards whichever branch of the profession he may incline the law student will, therefore, be necessarily equipped with a vast amount of learning of which much is of dubious value, if, indeed, it is of any value at all. Yet it is a singular reflection that in the training of an advocate neither the Benchers of his Inn nor the Council of his Law Society include Advocacy as an essential study.[3]

Since medieval times, when apprentices would sit in 'the crib' at the royal courts at Westminster, the principal way for young lawyers to learn about advocacy was to go and watch it in the courts, especially the efforts of acknowledged masters. Early in a barrister's career briefs often came only very slowly allowing ample time to do so. Discussion about what was observed between contemporaries and with more senior barristers in chambers also took place.

An understanding of advocacy could be supplemented by reading a small number of practical books on the subject, for example, corresponding with Sir Patrick's early career, Robert Harris's *Hints on Advocacy* and works by Frederic Wrottesley (later Lord Justice Wrottesley) might also be studied. In 1943 they were joined by Leo Page's *First Steps in Advocacy*, with a foreword written by Viscount Simon, the Lord Chancellor. A retired Circuit Judge, interviewed in 2010, described this short book as a *vastly important work* that had influenced heavily the post war generation of barristers, including Richard Du Cann, with whom he was a contemporary in chambers. In turn Richard Du Cann, through his successes and

---

[3] *First Steps in Advocacy*, Faber and Faber, 1943, pp. 10–11.

widely read book, *The Art of the Advocate*, first published, by Penguin, in 1964, affected advocates later in the twentieth century.

During this period, and certainly in earlier times, those who had studied the classics, might have recalled, and seen some value in, the methods of Demosthenes (whose oration *On the crown* was still seen as instructive to prosecutors as late as 1943 by George Keeton in the 18th Edition of Harris's *Hints*), Lysias, Cicero and Quintilian although the worth of studying classical masters as a preparation for the bar was increasingly questioned by the 1920s and before then, as is indicated in Theo Mathew's *Forensic Fables*.[4] Patrick Hastings, himself, was certainly no enthusiast for classical influences on modern forensic advocacy.[5]

Young barristers may additionally have gained advice on techniques of advocacy by reading biographies and autobiographies of judges and lawyers, the number of which had much increased from the nineteenth century.[6] Two barristers called to the Bar in the late 1960s, before bar students received formal training in advocacy, said that they, and most of their contemporaries, had read Norman Birkett's *Six Great Advocates*, Patrick Hastings's *Cases in Court* and biographies written on Marshall Hall, F. E. Smith and others. The methods and techniques they found in them were discussed amongst students and pupil barristers.

Some barristers might have acquired skills in public speaking and debating through membership of debating societies, especially at Oxford and Cambridge Universities and, earlier at school. However, Leo Page, in *First Steps in Advocacy*, page 21, described speeches in many university debating societies as *"concerned to display the speaker's own brilliance, prepared in advance, sparkling with epigrams, but with the merest semblance of advancing a case or of dealing with an argument, and as such should be avoided by young men who wish to earn their living in the courts"*.[7]

---

[4] See the *Blushing Beginner And The Bearded Juryman* pp. 57–58 and *The Brilliant Person, The Vulgar Individual With A Cockney Accent And The Two Malefactors* pp. 305–306 in *Forensic Fables*, Reprinted in 1999 by Wildy and Sons, London.

[5] See *Cases in Court*, London, Heinemann, 1950 pp. xi–xii.

[6] See Philip Girard, *Judging Lives: Judicial Biography from Hale to Holmes*, Australian Journal of Legal History (2003) Vol. 7.

[7] Page 21.

Formal Advocacy Instruction for Bar Students and Barristers Early in Their Careers

Six decades later, the quote from Sir Patrick no longer holds good: The teaching of advocacy is considered not only worthwhile but essential.

Limited formal instruction in advocacy for bar students began in the 1970s when the Council of Legal Education ("CLE") required whose who had declared an intention to practise at the bar to undertake practical exercises. The element of advocacy training in the programme was not extensive and largely consisted of small groups of students, during the early evening, visiting barristers in chambers for instruction on how to conduct straight forward submissions. One or two students might attempt exercises that they had prepared beforehand and then receive comments upon them from the barrister. Court visits, when students had the opportunity of talking to judges and magistrates, were also arranged. Judges and senior barristers would often advice intending barristers to go on a public speaking course. For advice on conducting trials, students were strongly urged by tutors, and by practicing barristers they met in chambers, to read *The Art of the Advocate* by Richard Du Cann, who was invited to the CLE each year to give a lecture of about one hour's length. Students could also see themselves, albeit very briefly, on film performing a short plea in mitigation.

Following extensive research, at the behest of the Bar Council, mostly amongst the junior bar, about what a full time course to bridge the academic stage of training and pupillage should comprise, the Council of Legal Education introduced the Bar Vocational Course ("BVC") in 1989. It replaced the previous rather academic Bar Finals course which had been slightly shorter. Delivered exclusively at the Inns of Court School of Law ("ICSL") in Grays Inn, the new course taught knowledge of criminal and civil procedure, evidence and sentencing. The greatest concentration, however, was on the teaching of skills in opinion writing and drafting, conducting conferences with clients and, above all, advocacy. A retired Law Lord, who in 1989 was Chairman of the Council of Legal Education, the body which then governed the Inns Of Court School of Law, said in an interview, twenty years later, that structured advocacy teaching was introduced as sensible *consumer protection* at a time when a number of solicitors did not exercise *sufficient quality control* of barristers they instructed in the lower courts. This had led to complaints of *some pretty shocking performances.*

The educational philosophy which informed instruction was that the successful performance of any skill could be broken down into a number of elements. From these elements, it was possible to identify performance criteria. These criteria can be used for assessing how good a particular performance is, and as the basis for providing constructive 'feedback', to improve it if necessary.[8] Some years after the inception of the BVC at the ICSL, the Bar Council gave permission for the course to be taught at a number of other institutions in the country. The ICSL, however, remained the biggest provider of places. In 20,007 the ICSL ceased to exist as an independent entity and was incorporated into City University Law School.

Advocacy skills, defined as "*skills necessary to prepare, manage and present a case or legal argument, both orally and in writing,* [reflecting the rise of paper advocacy] *before a court or other tribunal, whether formal or informal*"[9] were key on the BVC. Instruction in advocacy was to the level sufficient to prepare students for later advocacy training during pupillage. The Bar Standards Board specified that each student was to undertake at least 12 advocacy exercises in class under the supervision of a tutor and that advocacy would be assessed six times on the course, three times on a formal basis. Advocacy assessment contained: submission of a written argument; interventions from the bench; knowledge and application of legal principle; and witness handling, including examination in chief and cross-examination. Witness handling came in the later stages of the course and legal submissions might be dealt with in mooting. The amount of teaching needed to complete the advocacy element of the BVC varied between approved establishments. At the College of Law (which became the University of Law in 2012), for instance, instruction in civil advocacy, required students to act as barristers in: opposed applications to set aside default judgements; injunctions, unopposed and opposed; summary judgements, for which

---

[8] Peter Hungerford-Welch, *Advocacy*, New Law Journal. 150 NLJ 1532, 20th October, 2000.
[9] Bar Council: BVC Specification Requirements and Guidance. Revised 2006.

they had to draft skeleton arguments; submissions on costs; and personal injury submissions. There were also two trials, one fast track and the other multi-track, where, in addition to being counsel, students played witnesses. Judges and senior practitioners, some of whom had retired, acted as judges in the multi-track trial where three parties were represented.

Criminal advocacy training at the College of Law, which was embedded in the teaching of criminal procedure and evidence, included: making applications for adjournments, and bail; summary trials; submissions of no case to answer based, amongst other things, on identification evidence; pleas in mitigation and drafting indictments and defence statements for Crown Court trial. There were also sessions devoted to practising opening and closing speeches, examination in chief and cross-examination and applications to exclude evidence.

Students' advocacy was often video recorded so that, together with tutors comments made, it can be reflected upon later. In addition to instruction during the day, there were a number of practitioners evenings when students were obliged to perform exercises before practising barristers who appraise them. Most students involved themselves in mooting competitions, judged by members of staff and external barristers.

In 2001 the Bar Council declared that all teachers of advocacy on the BVC should be qualified as instructors by the Inns of Court Training Committee (IATC) and use its methods. Loosely based on techniques pioneered by the American National Institute of Trial Advocacy, the IATC approach, developed to train pupil barristers, is strict. One aspect of the student's performances is identified by the instructor who explains to him or her what they did, why it is inappropriate and how to avoid the problem. The instructor then seeks to demonstrate to the student how to improve before asking him or her to replay that aspect of his or her performance. Observations, performances and the feedback from instructors are short. It was reported that a number of BVC lecturers at the ICSL considered the IATC method was too narrow and unsuitable for students, yet to acquire the resilience of pupil barristers, who may require constructive feedback and sensitive encouragement on more than one selected point. Strong feelings were aroused; some lecturers approved of it wholeheartedly, considering it introduced students to harsh realities of life at the bar; others resolved to use it sparingly or not at all.

As in the past, there was an expectation that pupils would spend the first six months of their pupillage, during which they have no rights of audience, accompanying their pupil master or mistress in court and the watching advocacy there. (known in earlier times as *standing by Nellie*). In 1992 the Bar Council, in order to higher standards, made it a requirement that before their second six months of advocacy expired all pupil barristers must attend an of advocacy programme at their Inn of Court, lasting the equivalent of three days. These subsequently evolved and developed. At Gray's Inn, for instance, pupils must now take a two part short course on practice management which includes guiding them through the transition from academic student to independent advocate and a discussion on ethical issues of practice. They are also obliged to attend two workshops about witness handling which together deal with case analysis and then give students the opportunity to practice examination in chief and cross-examination. Pupils are further required to participate in a course on interlocutory applications. After a short discussion with trainers in their chambers, in which they have the chance to discuss their skeleton arguments, pupils perform before a real judge sitting in the Royal Courts of Justice, who afterwards offers some advice. A fuller appraisal is later given by the trainers. Finally pupils must take part in a trial exercise held at the Royal Courts of Justice. Each party to a case is represented, before a real judge, by a pair of pupils. Witnesses are played by members of the Inn. Trainers critique pupils' performances at various stages.

Pupils may also attend two voluntary courses. The first of these is on legal argument and involves pupils in an opposed injunction application. Their performances are reviewed by trainers. The second non-compulsory course covers handling costs applications. Courses are run by volunteers, either barristers or judges belonging to the Inn, and the IATC method is used extensively. Usually six pupils are instructed by two trainers.

The Bar Council in 1998 introduced a rule that all barristers in their first three years of practice must complete a minimum of 45 hours of continuing professional development including at least nine hours of advocacy. Gray's Inn began a weekend programme to satisfy the advocacy requirement, an important feature of which is handling expert witnesses in court. Bar Circuits also introduced formal advocacy training courses for barristers during their early years. One such is the intensive week long

Advanced Advocacy Course held annually by the South Eastern Circuit at Keble College, Oxford. The faculty, which constructively critiques participants, consists of senior juniors, silks, and judges, all of whom have undergone teacher training for the course. Participants work on either a criminal of civil case. After interlocutory matters have been dealt with and participants have devoted one and a half days of working with experts in a trial setting, the course culminates, on the last day, with a full trial. In the civil case this is before a High Court Judge or Deputy, whilst the criminal case is heard by a judge and jury. The jury's deliberations are filmed: each participant receives the film. Jurors also complete a confidential questionnaire on each advocate's performance.

In an interview, held in 2007, the Vice Chairman of the Grays Inn Advocacy Committee believed the greater attention to teaching advocacy that arrived with the Bar Vocational Course, and the efforts made in advocacy training for pupils and for barristers in their first three years practice, had led to greater proficiency by newly admitted barristers in court. This was a great plus, an opinion shared by most senior barristers and judges. The days of the fledgling barrister asking the court usher to put his or her case at the bottom of the court list, so he or she could listen to similar cases to fathom out what to do, had largely gone. The Vice Chairman agreed that the introduction of formal advocacy training marked a great shift away from the long held belief that competence in advocacy was innate – you either have it or you do not – towards recognizing that it can be taught and later improved upon by work and experience. BVC lecturers also interviewed strongly sympathized with the latter position The Vice Chairman doubted whether increased formal training had resulted in more uniformity of barristers' style, as had been predicted by the less enthusiastic about it. He said that the nature of much work in early years of practice did not permit too much of a distinctly individual approach which, in his view, developed later and with more heavy work. A Lord Justice of Appeal agreed that BVC and Inns of Court training in advocacy, which concentrated on the *basics*, did not prevent acquiring more personal forms of advocacy afterwards. He added that his son had recently qualified as a barrister and had reached a standard much higher than when he had done some thirty years before. Instruction in advocacy then did not sufficiently equip barristers to practice advocacy: "*It was of little help*".

Reflecting on the growth of advocacy training, Michael Beloff QC, reputedly the highest paid silk at the English and Welsh Bar and Treasurer of Grays Inn in 2008, considered, in an interview, that first class advocates excelled because they came to the Bar with gifts and experiences of public speaking, rather than as a result of what is learned on courses and workshops. Whilst he thought they did not create great advocacy, they did however have clear value in reducing errors and mistakes that could be made in early days and it was very noticeable how much people attending advocacy workshops at Grays Inn rapidly improved.

In September 2010 the Bar Vocational Course was replaced by the Bar Professional Training Course ("BPTC"). Essentially the core of the BVC course, including training in advocacy, was retained, but the BPTC curriculum is broader.[10] In particular it includes a "resolution of disputes out of court" module, comprising negotiation, mediation, arbitration, early neutral determination, expert determination and other processes of alternative dispute resolution. Students are instructed in the specialist skills of advocacy necessary and are required to perform a mock mediation.

Entrance requirements to the BPTC have become more rigorous. An internal report conducted by the Bar Standards Board, in 2008, found poor standards in English amongst some BVC students; both native and non-native speakers of the language. Inability was identified both to speak fluently, with close attention to grammar, vocabulary and syntax, and to write clear, correct and well structured prose. Concern was expressed about how standards of advocacy could be damaged. As a consequence, a new aptitude test for admission, concentrating on critical reasoning and clarity in expression, was introduced for BPTC applicants.

Advocacy Training for Solicitors

Advocacy for solicitors, as James Morton, the distinguished criminal solicitor, historian and former editor of the New Law Journal, put it, was *"very hit and miss: no courses, no lectures, get on and do it. So of course, some*

---

[10] See Marcus Soanes, *Enhancing Legal Education*, Counsel, January, 2010, pp. 14–16.

advocates were better than others......".[11] It was not covered by the professional examinations or courses until the Legal Professional Course ("LPC") was introduced in 1993.

Mr. Morton, whose career began in London in the early 1960s, described in an interview how newly qualified solicitors instructed to appear in the magistrates court sought advice from those more experienced in their firm and, crucially, from others present at court, who were generally very helpful. They would ask the clerk to the justices about the procedure to be followed, which sometimes varied considerably from court to court. Requesting cases be called on later, so that applications and submissions could be observed, was common. Books on advocacy were occasionally consulted, but sometimes disappointment was felt by readers as few had direct relevance to the business of the magistrates. There is little to believe that preparation for appearances in other courts, such as the County Court was very much different.

Nowadays there is formal training in aspects of advocacy. The Law Society LPC written standards state: "*Students should be able to formulate a coherent submission based upon facts, general principles and legal authority in a structured, concise and persuasive manner. The student should understand the crucial importance of preparation and the best way to undertake it. The student should be able to demonstrate an understanding of the basic skills in the presentation of cases before various courts and tribunals.........".*[12]

They do not prescribe the amount of teaching time to be devoted to advocacy, although institutions that provide the course typically spend between 7 and 12 hours teaching it. This is usually divided between large and small group sessions. (Some providers, such as the largest, the University of Law (formerly the College of Law), also use e-learning such as web casts, permitting students to study at their own pace). Teaching can be in the context of either criminal or civil litigation. At the University it is mainly in civil. The prime focus of LPC advocacy rests on presentations and applications. There may or may not be some discussion of the principles of witness handling (examination in chief and cross-examination) but not practice. This contrasts with the BPTC where wit-

---

[11] Morton's Musings: *Kings of the Court*, Law Society Gazette, James Morton, 22nd February, 2007.
[12] LPC written standards 10vs – September 2004.

ness handling is seen as a key skill. Also unlike the BPTC, advocacy is assessed only once and on a simple competent/non-competent basis. In recent years, examination at the University of Law involved submissions in summary judgement or setting aside a decision made in default.

There is no requirement for trainee solicitors to undertake any advocacy as part of their work, although some do at tribunal or civil interlocutory levels, where rights of audience are not necessary. Before the end of their two year training contract all trainees must undertake the Professional Skills Course ("PSC") of which three days is devoted to advocacy training. The advocacy element of this course, provided by a number of institutions, varies considerably in content. Some include witness handling at an introductory level.

All solicitors spoken to considered formal advocacy training, introduced by the LPC and PSC, was very positive for the profession and contributed to greater confidence and competence amongst newly qualified solicitors. Some, however, wanted more instruction, especially in conducting trials. This was thought urgent because of the arrival of higher rights of audience.

In 2017 the Solicitors Regulation Authority announced plans to introduce a new independent centralized form of assessment, the Solicitors Qualifying Examination ("SQE") that everyone who wishes to become a solicitor must pass. This radical, and controversial, change in professional legal education will be introduced in 2020, although for some years afterwards transition arrangements will enable those who have started the process of qualification under the previous system to complete it. Details of what will be required under the form of assessment are not yet available, but it is safe to assume advocacy will form an important element and that institutions preparing students for the SQE will teach it.

Fellows of the Institute of Legal Executives

In 2006 the Institute of Legal Executives ("ILEX") was approved by the Lord Chancellor to grant greater rights of audience to its Fellows. ILEX issues certificates in civil proceedings, family proceedings and criminal proceedings.[13] Fellows certified as eligible, on the basis of their knowledge

---

[13] See Chap. 14: "Rights of Audience".

and experience, attend a six day course, which they must pass.[14] Interactive tuition in small groups takes place using case studies and practical exercises. The final day consists of assessing performances in advocacy and knowledge of procedure and evidence.

When assessing influences on advocacy, the introduction of systematic and rigorous training in the late twentieth century, must be considered a most important factor.

---

[14] Baljeet Basra, Professional Development and Regulation Department, Institute of Legal Executives, interviewed on 17th July, 2007.

13

Appearances: Broadcasting and Dress

Broadcasting of Court Proceedings

The extent of broadcasting court proceedings varies between jurisdictions. Most Australian states allow television cameras into courts and their activity is controlled solely by the discretion of judges or officials.[1] Similarly, in California filming is permitted in trial and appellate courts at judicial discretion.[2] In England and Wales, by comparison, all electronic media in courts, save the Supreme Court, was prohibited before 2013. Now, subject to strict requirements, cases from the Court of Appeal may be broadcast and will soon be joined by Crown Court sentencing remarks. The new law and the steps toward it are described. Views expressed before the change in the law about court broadcasting and its effect on advocates and advocacy are recounted.

---

[1] Daniel Stepniak, Paper produced for Department for Constitutional Affairs Broadcasting Courts Seminar held on 10th January, 2005.
[2] *Broadcasting Courts, Consultation Paper*, CP28/04, Department for Constitutional Affairs, November, 2004, Annex E.

© The Author(s) 2019
A. Watson, *Speaking in Court*, https://doi.org/10.1007/978-3-030-10395-8_13

The Road to Change

Before the Criminal Justice 1925 Act, photographs of participants in court proceedings were a popular subject for newspapers and were often taken by portable and discreet cameras by a growing band of news photographers. The infamous Dr. Crippen was photographed in the dock in 1910. During the debate in the House of Lords on the Criminal Justice Bill specific reference was made to "*a photograph ...... taken at the Old Bailey of a judge passing sentence of death... A most shocking thing to have taken, or to have published, dreadful for the judge, dreadful for every body concerned in the case*".[3] In the House of Commons some arguments were heard against "*trying to censor the press*", but the majority view was that "*Everybody has suffered for a long time by prisoners in the dock and witnesses being pilloried by having their photographs taken, and this is to prevent that happening*".[4]

Section 41 of the 1925 Act, made it an offence an offence to take photographs, or sketch judges, jurors, parties or witnesses in the courts of England and Wales and within the precincts of the building accommodating them. It never applied in Scotland although before 1992 courts there prohibited cameras.

Parliament has been televised since 1989. This included the Judicial Committee of the House of Lords, then the highest domestic court.[5] Judgements and live proceedings of its successor, the United Kingdom Supreme Court, may be viewed on a dedicated YouTube channel and a Sky News website. Broadcasting of inquiries[6] has been allowed with leave of the chairman. In 1999, for example, the Chairman of the Southall Rail Accident Inquiry, Professor John Uff QC, granted permission to televise all its proceedings. In 2004, Lord Hutton, who chaired the Inquiry Into The Circumstances Surrounding The Death of Mr. David Kelly C.M. G.

---

[3] House of Lords Debates, Vol. 56, column 313.

[4] House of Commons Debates, Vol. 183, column 1599.

[5] To allow proceedings in its successor, from October, 2009, the United Kingdom Supreme Court, to be televised, the Constitutional Reform Act 2005 amended Section 41 of the Criminal Justice Act 1925 to exclude them. Cases may be watched live on the court's website: http://www.supremecourt.gov.uk

[6] Save for those held under the Tribunals and Inquiry (Evidence) Act 1921 which are covered by Section 9 of the Contempt of Court Act 1981, restricting sound recording.

("The Hutton Inquiry") in 2004, allowed opening and closing statements to be broadcast and publishing of a rolling transcript of the inquiry on the internet and on 24-hour news channels, but refused permission to allow television pictures of witnesses giving evidence to be filmed. The Shipman Inquiry, under Dame Janet Smith, held in the early 2000s into the activities of the mass serial killer, Dr. Harold Shipman, permitted some filming. The Leveson Inquiry into press conduct, during 2011 and 2012, was broadcast more or less in full, including witnesses' testimony.

Since the banning of photography in English and Welsh courts in 1925, and particularly during the past thirty years, the question of broadcasting court proceedings has been raised several times. An argument put strongly in this country, and abroad, for broadcasting is that justice should be "seen to be done". Those who make it sometimes quote Jeremy Bentham, *"Publicity is the very soul of justice. It is the keenest spur to exertion and the surest of all guards against improbity"*.[7] In addition, it is argued by some, showing court proceedings would bolster public confidence in the criminal justice system and, as regards civil justice, make courts less daunting for lay people to use.

In 1989, a working party of the Bar Council chaired by Jonathan Caplan QC published a report, *"Televising the Courts"*, into the feasibility and desirability of televising court proceedings in England and Wales. The report advocated amending the law to enable televising of courts on an experimental basis. Its recommendations were put in to a Private Members Bill, the Courts (Research) Bill 1991, but this fell on its Second Reading in the House of Commons.

In neighbouring Scotland, Lord Hope, then Lord President, allowed a strictly limited experiment, in 1992, which let cameras to courts. Their access afterwards was controlled by means of a practice note. A number of BBC documentaries involving courtroom film were produced. These included *The Trial*, a series of five programmes showing scenes from first instance Scottish criminal trials. Broadcasts in the 1990s on British television of the trials of William Kennedy Smith (1991), O. J. Simpson (1995), and Louise Woodward (1997) from the USA were much deplored as prurient soap

---

[7] The Works of Jeremy Bentham: Volume 9, page 49, Russell and Russell, New York, 1962. This passage was quoted by Lord Shaw in Scott v Scott [1913] AC 417.

opera and media circuses.[8] They were cited by opponents of court filming in this country, although the BBC ten part documentary series "*Boston Law*", shown in January 2001, depicting many court scenes, was widely praised for explaining the Massachusetts system of criminal justice.[9]

In 2002 the BBC was granted permission to televise Abdel Baset Ali Mohmed Al-Megrahi's appeal, under Scots Law in the Netherlands, against his conviction for the Lockerbie bombing. The coverage was under strict guidance laid down by the Scottish Courts, including a prohibition broadcasting any witness giving evidence.[10]

The question whether court proceedings should be broadcast, and if so how they should be regulated, did not disappear. In 2004 Lord Falconer, the then Lord Chancellor, issued a Consultation Paper in 2004 entitled *Broadcasting Courts.*. Although there were concerns about filming full trials, the majority of respondents supported the filming of judges' decisions and sentencing remarks.

The following year a pilot filming exercise of appeal cases in the Royal Courts of Justice took place. Footage was never broadcast but was studied for possible use as material for news reports, documentaries and educational programmes.

The Labour Government did not reach a decision whether to accept broadcasting but the former Justice Secretary, Lord Falconer QC, set out his thinking in a speech to the Press Gazette and Newspaper Society Media Law Conference in 2007[11]:

> *The test must be, in allowing television access to courts, will this add unnecessarily to the distress of victims and witnesses and separately, will knowledge that the TV cameras are there make people less willing to give evidence? Open justice may lead to the removal of justice. Something no one wants to see.*

---

[8] Jonathan Caplan QC, *From Pen to Lens*, Counsel, April, 2001, page 10. For a mixed opinion, which acknowledged filming may have helped educate viewers about courts and criminal procedure, see Notes of the Week, *The Trial of Louise Woodward*, Justice of the Peace, Vol. 161, November, 15th, 1997, page 1051.

[9] For example by John Cooper, *Boston Law*, The Times, February 13th, 2001.

[10] *Abdelbast Ali Mohmed Al Megrahi v Her Majesty's Advocate* SCCR [2002] 509. See *Broadcasting Courts, Consultation Paper*, CP 28/04, Department for Constitutional Affairs, November, 2004, page 19.

[11] Held on the 17th May, 2007 at Reuters Building, Canary Wharf, London.

There is no easy answer. As I have said, I am in favour of moving forward in ways I have already set out. No to filming witnesses and victims, yes to judges when for example they are making their sentencing remarks. But the way forward must be one .... which does not deliver openness at the price of individual protection.

Broadcasting in courts does not have to be a binary decision cameras or no cameras. In the US, for instance, there is a variegated pattern of when and where cameras are allowed in. A simple yes or no, would not serve anyone's best interests.

In 2011, Mr. Kenneth Clarke QC, then Justice Secretary in the Coalition Government, announced his intention to amend existing legislation to allow broadcasting from the Court of Appeal and also of sentencing remarks by judges at the Crown Court, though not of trials, jurors, witnesses, defendants or victims. Giving evidence to the House of Commons Justice Select Committee, the Attorney General, Dominic Grieve QC, said there were no plans to extend broadcasting beyond what was announced. Any further expansion could, in his view, lead to "theatricals" from lawyers and defendants and cause "ethical and practical difficulties".[12]

Leading figures such as the former Director of Public Prosecutions, Keir Starmer QC, and the President of the Supreme Court, Lord Neuberger, added to the debate in favour of broadcasting in some circumstances, subject to appropriate safeguards for victims and witnesses.

Legislation introduced in 2013[13] allowed the Lord Chancellor, with the concurrence of the Lord Chief Justice, to disapply s 41 of the Criminal Justice Act 1925 preventing photography in court. The Act states that the decision on filming rests with the judge, not the parties or the broadcasters. A judge may in the interests of justice, or to prevent undue prejudice, direct that filming is not allowed. No appeal exists against such a direction.

Permission to film in the Court of Appeal was granted by Statutory Instrument[14] the explanatory memorandum to which states its aim is "*to*

---

[12] Daily Telegraph, 8th August, 2011.
[13] Section 32 of the Crime and Courts Act 2013.
[14] The Court of Appeal (Recording and Broadcasting) Order 2013.

increase public engagement with, and understanding of, what happens in courts by allowing judgments to be filmed and broadcast in certain circumstances".

Broadcasters are subject to strict controls. The statutory instrument confines filming to submissions of the lawyers, exchanges between the lawyers and the court, and the court giving judgment. Where a person is not legally represented, recording is only allowed of the judgment. The defendant may not be filmed. Where there is a possibility of a retrial arising from a criminal conviction appeal, or an application to appeal against conviction, a recording must not be broadcast until the court gives permission. Like the filming of Parliament, the footage can only be used for news and current affairs. Any use of the film in a light entertainment programme is forbidden.

In 2016 a pilot scheme was announced by the Ministry of Justice and the Lord Chief Justice to film, although not broadcast, sentencing remarks from senior judges in eight Crown Courts across England and Wales, including the Old Bailey. Cameras will film only the judge. Filming court staff, victims; witnesses, defendants and advocates will be prohibited. The impact of cameras in court will be assessed. The then Justice Minister, Shailesh Vara, considered broadcasting sentencing remarks would allow the public to hear judges' decisions in their own words and the numerous factors they have to take into account and that this would contribute to more openness and transparency about what happens in courts.

Views and Opinions on the Effects of Court Cameras on Advocacy

In years preceding the 2013 legislation to allow limited broadcasting of court proceedings, findings of research undertaken in other countries was examined and a variety of opinions were expressed about what effect televising the court room would have on the administration of justice and upon advocates and advocacy.

International evidence on the effects of broadcasting on advocates was not extensive. Civil and appellate court proceedings in United States Federal Courts were televised for an experimental period between 1991 and 1994. The experiment was evaluated by the Federal Judicial Centre using questionnaires, interviews and analysis of broadcasts. It found that judges believed there had been no adverse effect on counsel due to cameras and some even reported an improvement in their performance.[15] Following the O.J. Simpson trial in 1995, a judicial task force was set up in California to survey the views of trial and appellate judges and attorneys about televising cases. The task force found little evidence of lawyers *playing to the camera*.[16] These findings markedly diverged with what was said in conversations in the early 2000s with American legal academics and lawyers and judges[17] who were decidedly of the opinion that televising court proceedings did encourage attorneys to act theatrically and diminished the standing of the courts.

Somewhat alarmingly, in 1997, the New York State Committee, established to study a ten year experiment of televising courts in that state, recorded that 37 per cent of judges surveyed said that television coverage caused judges to make rulings they otherwise might not have. This may be most acute in jurisdictions where judges are elected or confirmed by vote after appointment. The Committee said cameras in court could have an effect on decisions reached by juries. If there was a very strong tide of public opinion in a case as a result of television or radio coverage, it might be very hard for a jury to remain unbiased, making the task of advocates acting for the defence more difficult.

Reviewing televising cases in Commonwealth countries, Geoffrey Robertson QC found there was little to show lawyers "hammed up" their advocacy. On the contrary, he reported, television "*produced greater prepared lawyers, better behaved judges and a more informed public*".[18] It was said that *The Trial*, a series of programmes made under the controlled experiment in Scotland, *earlier*, represented an accurate picture of the

---

[15] Research summarized in *Broadcasting Courts, Consultation Paper*, CP 28/04, Department for Constitutional Affairs, November, 2004 on pages 49 and 101.

[16] Report summary of the Californian Judicial Task Force on Photographing, Recording and Broadcasting in the Courtroom.

[17] At Harvard Law School Trial Advocacy Course Winters 2000 and 2001; admittedly not a statistically significant sample of academics, lawyers and judges in the United States but not a small number.

[18] *Court on Candid Camera*, The London Evening Standard, September 29th, 2000.

courts and that cameras had not led participants, including lawyers, *playing up to the cameras.*[19] In his Report, in 1999, Professor John Uff QC, the Chairman of the Southall Rail Accident Inquiry, wrote[20]: "*The experience of televising the inquiry gave no support whatever to fears expressed by many parties that witnesses would be prejudiced or that advocates would play to the cameras. The extent of serious television coverage was, however, disappointing*".

In contrast suggestions were made that broadcasting would tempt lawyers into histrionics, playing to television audiences to further their reputations, as some had done to newspaper reporters in earlier times, when there was intense press interest in court cases. There was anxiety the serious business of justice would be turned into entertainment, much as it was in the nineteenth century *cause celebre.*

Speaking in 2001, Lord Irvine of Lairg, then Lord Chancellor, believed *There is a great risk that the behaviour and judgements of lawyers, witnesses and the jury might be affected by the knowledge that they were participating in a live media event.*[21] Some years later, a former Master of the Rolls and Lord Chief Justice,[22] said, subject to safeguards, he agreed with experimental broadcasting of court proceedings but recognized a possibility some lawyers would behave theatrically. However he considered that in trials before judges and on appeals, which almost completely turn on law, this would be entirely unappreciated by judges and therefore be wholly counterproductive for their clients. In the same year the Senior Law Lord, explained that although his principal objection to televising court proceedings was the additional stress it might impose on parties involved, danger also existed some lawyers would act to the audience behind the camera.[23] Two Lords Justices of Appeal interviewed also thought some barristers would play to the gallery if cameras were present.[24]

---

[19] *Broadcasting Courts, Consultation Paper*, CP 28/04, Department for Constitutional Affairs, November, 2004, page 15.

[20] Quoted by Jonathan Caplan QC, *From pens to lens*, Counsel, April 2001, page 10.

[21] Quoted by Bob Marshall-Andrews QC, *Court on camera*, Legal services, New Statesman, 16th February, 2004, page xv. He suggested that Lord Irvine should have added "judges" as "it is difficult to see why they would be immune from the process".

[22] Lord Woolf, interviewed on 27th June, 2007 at the House of Lords.

[23] Lord Bingham, interviewed on 23rd October, 2007.

[24] Interviewed respectively on 11th July and 18th July, 2007.

Robert Marshall Andrews QC, MP. claimed, writing in 2004, that the vast majority of practicing barristers opposed cameras in court.[25] A barrister, interviewed in 2007, doubted broadcasting trials would have a healthy influence on advocacy.[26] He feared for the cab rank rule. Some advocates might find reasons to decline cases because they would not want to be seen on screens across the length and breadth of the country associated with particularly unpopular defendants or parties who might, therefore, be deprived of the best and most skilled representation. The same barrister feared publicity seeking barristers would be more concerned with their images than with effectively representing clients, resulting in failure to put unpleasant, but highly probative, questions to particular witnesses. Further he considered there was a risk that prosecutors might behave in a more aggressive way so as not to attract public criticism for *being soft*.

Apprehension about witnesses was raised. It is widely accepted that testifying as a witness, especially as an alleged victim in a criminal matter, can be very nerve-racking. Research from abroad was cited that indicated cameras may deter people acting as witnesses and affect the quality of their evidence.[27] In the event of a trial being filmed, advocates would have to take into account that witnesses may be more reluctant, nervous and self-conscious. It was broached that if witnesses watched coverage of other witnesses giving evidence earlier they could, either deliberately or subconsciously, alter their testimony and also some might be tempted to

---

[25] *Court on camera*, New Statesman, Special Supplement: *The future of legal services*, 16th February, 2004.

[26] Alexander Hewitt, 14th September, 2007.

[27] A committee set up in 1995 to evaluate a ten year filming experiment of civil and criminal trials and appellate courts in New York found, in a poll of voters, that 54 per cent of those surveyed said they would be less willing to testify if cameras were present (Cameras in New York Court Rooms. Marist Institute for Public Opinion Poll, December 1996). In a similar poll held in New Zealand, 58 per cent said cameras would affect their willingness to appear as a witness in a criminal trial. (UMR Insight Ltd., Media Coverage of Court Proceedings: A Summary Report, February 1998). This evidence contrasts with that from the 2001 Committee of the New York Bar Association and the Federal Judicial Center, which analysed the US Federal Court filming experiment. The former showed that, in the many cases they investigated, only two witnesses had been lost because of cameras in court (Report of the Special Committee of the New York State Bar Association on Cameras in the Courtroom), while the latter discovered only one of the 110 counsel who responded to its survey reported losing a witness because of filming. (Molly Treadway Johnson, Electronic Media Coverage of Courtroom Proceedings, November 4th, 1993).

tailor their evidence to make it more acceptable to the viewing public. Again advocates would have to deal with both these possibilities.

The prospect of filming litigants in person, whose numbers had grown, caused concern. The quality of their "self advocacy" could be affected if they felt intimidated by cameras.[28] A risk was felt some might behave in a dramatic way. Judges and lawyers facing litigants in person would be forced to take these considerations into account.

As it was put by Lord Justice Laws, *before the current debilitating forms of mass entertainment were available the leading barristers were pop stars.*[29] F. E. Smith, Edward Carson, Rufus Isaacs, Marshall Hall, Norman Birkett and Patrick Hastings were household names due to intense reporting of court cases in newspapers. Save the late George Carman, with his defamation practice, no advocate has since remotely had a public profile approaching theirs. It was speculated that if trials were to be televised it was possible barristers might once again become very well known. However, the barrister, and former MP, Robert Marshall-Hall QC. described most crimes in court as *generally sad, tragic or dull* and questioned how long the popular appetite for real, as opposed to fictional, court cases would last.[30] Perhaps supporting this view it is noteworthy that research during the last decade shows a reduction in court stories and a dramatic fall in space given to them in national, regional and local newspapers.[31]

The law in England and Wales to permit limited televising Court of Appeal cases and sentencing remarks in the Crown Court is a long way off from allowing broadcasting first instance trials, and the theatricals, ethical and practical difficulties that might accompany them. However it is possible that the Act of 2013 may be a milestone along a road to much more broadcasting of proceedings with considerable consequences for advocates and advocacy.

---

[28] See *Broadcasting Courts, Consultation Paper* CP 28/04, Department for Constitutional Affairs, November, 2004, page 50.

[29] John Laws, Epilogue: *Cicero and the Modern Advocate*, in Jonathan Powell and Jeremy Paterson Ed, *Cicero the advocate*, Oxford University Press, 2004, Chapter 15, page 413.

[30] *Court on camera, Ibid.*

[31] Brian Thornton, *The case of the disappearing court reporter*. Proof No. 2, January, 2017, pp. 92–93.

Dress in Court

Wigs and Gowns

Judges and barristers appear dressed both in gowns and wigs in the criminal courts, and in gowns in civil courts and also some family hearings. They are not worn in the Supreme Court (nor were they in its predecessor, the House of Lords), the Commercial Court, the Magistrates' Court and most family hearings. It is probably true to say that many throughout the world closely associate British courts with wigs and gowns. The wearing of wigs, although somewhat different to present ones, by judges and barristers dates from the late seventeenth century. Barristers' black robes, which replaced those in other colours and designs, also originate from that time. Judicial robes, worn today, can be traced to the fourteenth century, but have much evolved in style since then.[32]

Whether wigs and gowns should be worn is an issue that has reared its horsehair head over many decades and has usually been accompanied by a flurry of correspondence in *The Times* and elsewhere. Opponents believe they *"epitomize all the defects of English law, its remoteness, its uncritical reverence for tradition, its absence of rationality, and its inability to see obstacles in the way of the understanding of the legal system by laymen"*.[33] The opinion that it may intimidate victims and witnesses, especially the young and the vulnerable, has also been voiced. Further, some assert that that the wearing of wigs and gowns encourages self-importance and pomposity of speech. It has been claimed they can result in unnecessary flamboyance amongst barristers. A critic of wigs and gowns said: *"Dress affects manner. People tend to act the part they look. Theatrical costume is fine for drama productions, but do we really need dramatic behaviour in our courtrooms? It may be good for the tourist trade, but does it fit the seriousness of the work in hand?"*.[34]

---

[32] J.H. Baker, *A history of English judges' robes*, SN 1978.

[33] Ursula Riniker, *Wigs, robes and other paraphernalia*, Justice of the Peace, 9th September, 2000. An early critic was Thomas Jefferson who wrote, during a debate in 1790 about whether wigs should be worn in the new American federal Supreme Court: *"For heaven's sake discard the monstrous wig which makes English judges look like rats peeping through benches of oakum"*. Quoted by Charles Warren, *The Supreme Court in United States History*, 3 Volumes, Boston: Little Brown, 1924, Volume 1, Page 48.

[34] Adrian Turner, *Time For A New Look*, Justice of the Peace, 30th September, 2006.

Arguments for retaining traditional court dress include[35]: that it: symbolizes the authority of office holders; helps instil a respect for the law; reminds judges and barristers that theirs is a solemn role; emphasizes the impersonal and disinterested approach of the judge; assists people in court identify who is who; and provides some security to wearers through anonymity, especially in criminal cases. Another point made is that it helps create a level playing field by preventing barristers from competing with each other in dress, with the object of winning favour with jurors, which it is said has happened in the United States, and other countries, between attorneys. Wigs and gowns, it is also claimed, help to reduce discrimination on grounds of age, race and gender Whether wigs and gowns should be retained was publicly consulted upon by the Lord Chancellor's Department in 1992.[36] A clear majority of respondents backed continued wearing of them and it was announced by the Lord Chancellor and the Lord Chief Justice that no changes would be made. In 2002 practising members of the Scottish Faculty of Advocates voted decisively to retain wigs and gowns.[37]

The matter was revisited in England and Wales by the Lord Chancellor's Department the following year when it produced another consultation paper[38] which contained the result of a preliminary survey of 1500 members of the public and 500 court users, defined as victims of crime, witnesses, jurors and defendants in the criminal courts, as well as claimants and defendants in the civil courts. More than 60 percent of respondents thought court dress should be modified in some way.[39]

---

[35] *Court catwalk*, Counsel, June 2003, page 5.

[36] *Court Dress*, a consultation paper, was issued in 1992. 520 responses were received from organizations and individuals – 67 percent favoured retention of court working dress; 15 percent were for abolition in all respects; and the remainder supported some simplification, including 14 percent who advocated abolishing the wig.

[37] *The Wigs Have It*, Law Society Gazette, 2002.

[38] *Court Working Dress in England and Wales*, May, 2003.

[39] 53 percent of respondents believed dress should be changed for criminal judges, 64 percent for civil judges and 61 percent for barristers. A survey conducted by the journal *Counsel* amongst barristers attracted 3751 responses. It showed that the bar was willing to embrace change in certain areas but there were others, most conspicuously criminal work in the Crown Court, where it was not. For a detailed breakdown of the results see *Counsel*, July, 2003, page 22.

Very probably mindful of this research, the Lord Chief Justice, Lord Philips, announced in 2007 reforms of court working dress, ending centuries of tradition. From 1st January, 2008, judges ceased to wear wigs, wing collars and bands when sitting in open court in civil and family proceedings. Circuit Bench judges continued to wear the same gown as before, but all other judges now appear in a new simply designed gown.[40] Other than having a single set of robes throughout the year, there is no alteration in court dress worn by judges in criminal proceedings. Advocates follow a similar dress code to that of the judge. Accordingly what is worn by the Bar in criminal proceedings has not changed, but in civil proceedings wigs, wing collars and bands are no longer worn; robes, however, still are.[41] Solicitor advocates, who had long fought for parity with barristers, are now permitted to wear wigs, wing collars and bands in circumstances where these are worn by the Bar.

The Niqab and Burqa and Advocacy

At least for the foreseeable future, the question of traditional court dress appears to have been settled. The same cannot be said of some items of clothing that reflect Britain has become much more ethnically and religiously diverse. Little, if any, controversy arose about the wearing of Silk turbans and the Moslem head-scarf-hijab, instead of wigs, in court by advocates and judges.

The full-face veil with a slit for the eyes, the niqab, is worn by a small minority of Moslem women in the United Kingdom. It entirely hides the woman's face, head and hair from view. The burqa is the most radical veiling. This is a loose garment that completely conceals the wearer apart from her hands with a gauze panel or slit for the eyes. It is worn by many fewer women than the niqab. However the wearing of both garments

---

[40] The simple continental-style black gown, with slicks of red extending to the chest from the collar, was first revealed on 13th May, 2008 and modelled by the Lord Chief Justice, Lord Philips. It was designed by Betty Jackson, a former designer of the year, who made no charge for her work. *The Guardian*, 13th May, 2008. The gown is made of a dark navy gabardine and wool mix, trimmed with velvet on the cuffs and facings. The version for women has a pleated white removable ruff.

[41] For the bar's divided reaction to the Lord Chief Justice's announcement concerning court dress see Elizabeth Davidson, *Time to Dress Down?* Counsel, October, 2007, pp. 18–19.

appears to be increasing. In November 2006 an advocate in a full-face veil was asked to stand down at an immigration tribunal hearing. The judge said that he could not hear what she was saying. This case sparked a debate on wearing the niqab and burqa in court.[42] The Judicial Studies Board ("JSB") issued guidelines that veils should be accommodated in court unless judges, on a case by case basis, think otherwise.[43]

Wearing clothes that obscure the face raises issues for advocacy in courts where hearings remain predominantly oral and open. Dealing first with advocates, any difficulties of audibility could be relatively easily overcome by microphones. The face, however, in seeking to persuade judges, magistrates and especially jurors is a fundamental. It is of great importance in cross-examination and for encouraging witnesses in examination in chief. An advocate who chooses to cover her face, it could be argued, is disabling herself and not acting in the best interests of her client. In matters which are concerned with questions of law and do not involve witnesses this view may be of less weight. Also, when considering witnesses, it may be that some would find it daunting, or even intimidating, to be cross-examined by a veiled advocate.

Veiled judges, magistrates and tribunal members would be challenging for advocates accustomed to receiving facial clues, which can, of course, on occasion be misleading, as to how their submissions are being received. However it must be said that some judges and magistrates give little or nothing away by non-verbal communication.

The facial gestures of witnesses when examined and cross-examined are often of use to fact finders in assessing their credibility. Behind the veil the impact of questions is hidden. When dealing with witnesses it may be possible to reach a compromise: Evidence might be given unveiled, but in a court emptied of spectators and possibly behind a screen making the witness visible only to the judge, a jury if there is one, and the advocates. The use of a video-link may also be of assistance. (Finding acceptable solutions in each case is emphasized much by The Judicial Studies Board.)

---

[42] See Barbara Hewson, *Let us see your face. Counsel*, June 2007 pp. 10–12. and Fatim Kurji, *Justice for all*, same issue of *Counsel* pp. 14–16. On the veil generally, see Jennifer Heath, *The Veil: Women Writers on its History, Lore and Politics*, University of California Press, 2008.

[43] Equal Treatment Bench Book, Chapter 3.3. In Pakistan a different approach has been taken. The Chief Justice of the Peshawar High Court issued a directive in November, 2006 that veils were not to be worn, reported in the *Pakistan Daily Times*, 4th November, 2006.

In a case heard at Blackfriars Crown in 2013, the judge, His Honour Peter Murphy, ruled that the defendant was allowed to stand trial wearing a niqab, although she would have to remove it before giving evidence so that she might be seen by him, the jury and counsel. A screen to shield her from public view would be offered, or alternatively her evidence could be given via a live TV link. Addressing Article 9 of European Convention of Human Rights, Freedom to Manifest Religion, the judge said it was necessary for a democratic society to restrict the rights of a defendant to wear a niqab during court proceedings.

Balancing the right of religious manifestation against the rights and freedoms of the public, the press and other interested parties such as the complainant in the proper administration of justice, the latter must prevail over Defendant's right to manifest her religion or belief during the proceedings against her to the extent necessary in the interests of justice.

No tradition or practice, whether religious or otherwise, can claim to occupy such a privileged position that the rule of law, open justice and the adversarial trial process are sacrificed to accommodate it.

That is not a discrimination against religion, it is a matter of upholding the rule of law in a democratic society.

Keith Porteous Wood, executive director of the National Secular Society, severely criticised the ruling. He said:

It is vital that defendants' faces are visible at all times, including while others are giving evidence, so we regret the judge's decision not to require this. We will be complaining to the Office of Judicial Complaints and also be asking senior legal officers to make visibility throughout court hearings mandatory, and not subject to judges' discretion.

It is predicted that challenges for cause will be made at the Crown Court by counsel on the inclusion of a woman wearing the full veil as a member of the jury. The JSB reminds judges that, as in all such challenges, there must be a genuine and legitimate basis for it, based on the particular circumstances of the case.

These, and other concerns about the niqab and burqa in court will affect advocates and judges in the future. It may be that some will have to be resolved by Parliament or by higher court decisions, which weigh the right to manifest one's religion or belief against the interests of justice and the rule of law.

14

Developments with Consequences for Advocacy

Rights of Audience

Extension of rights of audience in the higher courts to solicitors, represented an important break with the past when they were principally confined to barristers. This change, driven by ideas, accepted by governments, of market competition, raised questions about what criteria should be met, and training undertaken, by solicitors seeking higher court rights. The effect of solicitor advocates on the quality of advocacy overall is highly important. Issues arose with large firms of solicitors conducting in-house advocacy in the higher courts including, rather fundamentally, whether this is always in the interests of their clients. The Crown Prosecution Service's greater use of its own advocates with higher rights of audience to prosecute in the Crown Court instead of members of the independent bar proved controversial, as has deployment of nonqualified lawyers but with limited rights of audience in the magistrates court. The number of advocates has further been expanded by Fellows of the Institute of Legal Executives obtaining extended rights of audience in the lower courts. With more people able to act as advocates, maintaining standards of advocacy has assumed greater significance. New formal

© The Author(s) 2019
A. Watson, *Speaking in Court*, https://doi.org/10.1007/978-3-030-10395-8_14

quality control mechanisms are planned. These and other developments are considered in this section.

Barristers and Solicitors: The Present Position

Currently, barristers enjoy rights of audience in all courts after completing the first six months of their pupillage. Solicitors, apart from those granted higher rights, are limited to the lower courts. They have full rights to be heard in the Magistrates Court, Small Claims Court, County Court and the Coroners' Court. Solicitors have rights of audience at the Crown Court in sentencing hearings, appeals from the Magistrates Court in specified circumstances and certain preliminary hearings. In the High Court they have rights in chambers and may represent a client in open court in an emergency with the leave of the judge. No automatic rights exist in the Court of Appeal. Save before the Appeal Committee, there are none in the Supreme Court. In Europe, English and Welsh solicitors have the same full rights as barristers to be heard in the European Court of Human Rights, the European Court of First Instance and the European Court of Justice. It is not always appreciated that the greatest volume of advocacy in this country is performed predominantly by solicitors in the Magistrates Court and the County Court. Indeed, beginning in the 1980s, more solicitors began to specialise in advocacy before the lower courts, either as members of firms or as free-lance advocates, sometimes operating from the equivalent of barristers' chambers, instructed by firms or by the Crown Prosecution Service.

Calls for a Greater Role for Solicitors and the Granting to Them of Higher Rights of Audience

Historically, the courts determined which advocates had rights of audience before them. Concerning litigation in the higher courts, it was considered that the interests of justice were best served by the solicitor meeting the needs of clients, developing a rapport with them, taking full and proper instructions, advising on likely outcomes and thoroughly preparing cases for barristers at trial.

This traditional view came to be questioned by those who maintained that clients would gain if solicitors conducted every stage. It was argued that clients would benefit from a representative with a deeper understanding and familiarity with their case than a barrister who may have been instructed at short notice, especially if the barrister originally instructed could not appear at court because he or she was "part-heard" (occupied in another case which had "over –run"), or just for an isolated hearing. Savings in costs might also be made with a solicitor being paid on an hourly rate, as opposed to paying a barrister a brief fee; this being particularly relevant if a case settled before trial.[1]

The Conservative government was receptive to these points and, principally in the name of increasing choice and competition between lawyers in the interests of consumers of legal services,[2] made provision for solicitors to achieve higher rights of audience in the Courts and Legal Services Act 1990.[3] The means by which this was to be implemented was through Regulations. In discussions about the introduction of the Higher Courts Qualification Regulations 1992 the Lord Chancellor's Advisory Committee on Legal Education ("ACLEC") put forward that training of trainee solicitors in advocacy, higher court procedures and evidence did not equate with that received by trainee barristers. This analysis was shared by the Lord Chancellor and the judiciary. The consequence of these discussions was the introduction of rigorous training and assessment requirements for solicitors who wanted to acquire higher rights of audience in the criminal courts, civil courts or both.[4] Partly because of the toughness of examinations, which many candidates failed, the num-

---

[1] For a summary of these arguments see Kate Henley, *Higher Rights: Access all areas*. Law Society Gazette, 25th January, 2007.

[2] Speaking about widening of rights of audience, Lord MacKay, Lord Chancellor at the time, said that to him it did not matter if advocates were called barristers or solicitors. What was important, however, was that they were proficient for the task. Interview on 10th December, 2008.

[3] Section 17.

[4] See *Higher Rights of Audience Discussion Paper*, Solicitors Regulation Authority, 2007, page 3. Representatives of the judiciary and the bar on ACLEC were criticised in some quarters, for example in the *Lawyer*, Comment, 10th August, 1996, *Give solicitors equal rights of audience*, for discriminating against solicitors and for trying to protect the bar's dominance of higher court advocacy at all costs.

ber of solicitors who sought and who acquired higher rights was low.[5] The operation of the scheme to acquire higher rights was the subject of a review in 1995 from which came the Higher Courts Qualification Regulations 1998 intended to provide greater opportunity for solicitors to obtain them. Solicitor advocates became a part of the Scottish legal landscape earlier in the 1990s when solicitors in Scotland were given the ability to seek extended rights of audience, entitling them to plead before the Court of Session, High Court, UK Supreme Court and Judicial Committee of the Privy Council.

The Access to Justice Act 1999 introduced the radical principle that, on full admission to the profession, all solicitors would have full rights of audience in all courts but required them to comply with the training requirements and rules laid down by the Law Society. The government, now Labour, again justified this change in who could perform higher court advocacy on the basis that more competition between lawyers would advantage consumers of their services. Following the Access to Justice Act, the Higher Courts Qualification Regulations 2000 amended the existing route leading to the Higher Courts Qualification and added two others. The three are now: the development route, for more junior solicitors who complete thorough training and assessments in advocacy, evidence, procedure and ethics, and present a portfolio of their experience; the exemption route, for solicitors or barristers with at least three years' post-qualification experience who can demonstrate a track record of advocacy in the higher courts; and the accreditation route, again for solicitors with at least three years post-qualification experience who can show litigation experience (not necessarily advocacy) in the higher courts and who complete advocacy training and assessment.

At the time of passage of the Access to Justice Act 1999 there was worry, mainly among barristers,[6] but also some judges, that standards of

---

[5] Figures contained in the Lord Chancellor's Consultation Paper *Rights of Audience and rights to conduct litigation in England and Wales: 'The Way Ahead'*, Lord Chancellor's Department, June 1998, para 1.11, showed that in May 1998 only 624 solicitors, out of more than 70,000, had obtained the Law Society higher courts qualification. Of these many were former barristers. See *also Solicitor advocates: reluctant Rumpoles – only a tiny number of solicitors has qualified to work as advocates in the higher courts.* Law Society Gazette, 93/24 5th June, 1996.

[6] See Julian Gibbons, *Those same old arguments*, Comment, New Law Journal, October, 23rd 1998, and Robert Verkiak, Nick Murray and Stephen Ward, *Focus rights of audience: Changing Advocacy*,

advocacy could fall if considerable numbers of solicitors chose to exercise their new rights. In the 1999 Cardiff University Lord Morris Memorial Lecture[7] Lord Justice Sedley explained that advocacy can be accomplished by many people, "*but at its higher and highest levels it involves unique skills of preparation, learning and sensitivity which requires as many years of single-minded practice as make, for example, a first class conveyancing solicitor or corporate contract negotiator. If solicitors continue to function as solicitors, rather than devoting themselves entirely to advocacy, the nature of their work will prevent them from expanding their competence in advocacy to that of the best barristers*". A further related concern expressed by Lord Justice Sedley about greater involvement by solicitors in advocacy was how early acquisition by barristers of essential skills might be limited. He argued that if solicitors absorbed all but the heaviest cases the incremental experience, which makes a reliable barrister, would evaporate causing the Bar to eventually whither, impoverishing clients of a specialized resource and removing from the courts a source of assistance on which they rely. Skills in forensic advocacy, for which this country has been renowned for generations could, he feared, be lost forever.[8]

Others, who welcomed greater participation by solicitors in advocacy, made known their belief that these apprehensions were either unfounded or greatly exaggerated, perhaps in an attempt to keep as much of a restrictive practice as possible, and took little account both of the capacity of solicitors to adapt rapidly to the higher courts and of the additional train-

---

Law Society Gazette, 95/36 23 September 1998, pp. 20–23.

[7] 28th September; entitled *The Future of Advocacy*.

[8] Eight years later, the same Court of Appeal judge, asked about solicitor advocates, still maintained that in order to be proficient in the higher courts frequent practice is necessary. Difference in the amount of experience generally explained why standards of advocacy were usually higher amongst barristers than the solicitor advocates who appeared before him. He drew a comparison with an orthopaedic surgeon performing a neurological operation. Expressing a candid view, he said that whilst sometimes encountering poor advocacy from barristers, he seldom saw a good solicitor advocate. Interview, 11th July, 2007. Lord Bingham considered, with notable exceptions, few were very good. Before his appointment as Senior Law Lord, in 2000, he had been addressed by some in the Court of Appeal. Appearances by solicitor advocates were very rare in the House of Lords. Like Lord Justice Sedley, he considered that advocacy at the highest levels required repeated experience. Some solicitors, though, might acquire this. Interview, 23rd October, 2007.

ing they would receive before appearing in them.[9] They pointed overseas to the majority of countries that do not have the division between barrister and solicitor. Asserting standards of advocacy do not suffer there on that account, they maintained that trial lawyers in these jurisdictions accumulate more than adequate competence through experience. (With reference to the United States, where opportunity for trial advocacy by attorneys is decreasing, this argument may now be less than compelling).

There was speculation about whether significant numbers of solicitors would act as advocates in the higher courts.[10] Whilst it was predicted that solicitors in the Crown Prosecution Service and other government bodies and those with a real taste for advocacy would do so, a major factor was said to be economic circumstances. If the economy continued to be buoyant then, in most cases, it was thought that it would usually be more profitable for solicitors to remain working in their offices and instruct barristers to appear, rather than themselves attending court, which might consume an uncertain and considerable portion of the day.

From the Rule amendments in 2000 to 1st January, 2007 the number of solicitor advocates rose to 3663, an increase of 212 percent. Of these 889 solicitors held Higher Courts Qualification in all proceedings; 777 solicitors obtained the qualification in civil proceedings; and 1997 had acquired it in criminal proceedings.[11] In the context of approximately 5000 barristers engaged in criminal work, it is in this last category that solicitor advocates made the most impact.

A sore point with a number of solicitor advocates was that they were instantly recognizable as such because, unlike barristers, they did not wear a wig in court. Some said that this could have placed them at a disadvantage, especially before juries who might have considered them inferior. One solicitor – advocate interviewed said the solicitors' gown he had to wear, different in design to those worn by barristers, made him

---

[9] For example Thomas Lawson-Cruttenden, holder of a higher courts qualification in the civil courts, *Advocacy –The power of speech-solicitor advocates should not be intimidated by their Bar brethren as preparation, not oratory, is the key to winning.* Law Society Gazette, 92/16 29th November 1995.

[10] See Nick Murray, *Focus rights of audience: Advocating Change,* Law Society Gazette, 95/36 23 September 1998, pp. 21–22.

[11] Source: The Solicitors Regulation Authority ("SRA") The total number rose to 4995 by 2008 (SRA) and further increased to 5200 in 2012 (Law Society Gazette 2nd February, 2012.).

look like a court usher. Differences in dress were removed as from 1st January, 2008 when a Practice Direction issued by the Lord Chief Justice came into effect.[12]

The Criminal Bar Association in a discussion paper[13] expressed concern that increased use of solicitor higher court advocates by the Crown Prosecution Service and defence solicitors, coupled with the government's intended reforms of legal aid from 2008, thought likely to encourage law firms to handle more advocacy,[14] would reduce the amount of work available to criminal barristers and lower standards of representation. Whilst welcoming competition from highly qualified solicitor higher court advocates, it was claimed there was a danger that the market would be abused by ones that were under-qualified and inexperienced.[15]

---

[12] Practice Direction (Court Dress) No. 4. Made by the Lord Chief Justice in accordance with procedure laid down in Part 1 of Schedule 2 of the Constitutional Reform Act 2005. The first wig to be worn by a solicitor advocate was in Doncaster Crown Court. Law Society Gazette, 10th January, 2008.

[13] Published on 12th February, 2007.

[14] The Chairman of the Bar Council 2008/2009, Timothy Dutton QC, interviewed on the 8th May, 2008, after he had delivered an address at the College of Law, Store Street, London, thought that solicitors firms would keep more advocacy in publicly funded criminal and civil work in house when reforms recommended by Lord Carter's Review of Legal Aid Procurement were implemented. The Carter Review envisaged firms doing publicly funded work would amalgamate into larger ones and then competitively tender for funds from the Legal Services Commission for blocks of cases in their area. Bids would be on the basis of a set amount for a case. In all but exceptional circumstances, the lowest tender could be expected to obtain a contract to supply legal services. The Chairman of the Bar expressed his fear that concern by firms to put in low bids could badly affect the quality of work performed, not least in advocacy in court with less preparation and fewer instructions sent to more experienced advocates be they barristers or solicitors.

[15] The Criminal Bar Association returned to the theme of reduced quality of advocacy in a speech made by its chairman at the Bar Conference in 2008. Peter Lodder, QC, accused solicitor advocates of keeping the conduct of serious trials for themselves instead of instructing more experienced barristers and of being unfit for the task. He said: *There is a huge increase in the use of higher court advocates. The Bar does not say such an advocate is bad by definition. Some are good, but there are many who are truly appalling – defence solicitors who have never before conducted a crown court trial and have very little experience in the magistrates' trials now appear as junior advocates to defend in murder trials.* (Reported in The Times, 3rd November, 2008.) More criticism was directed towards solicitor advocates in the Crown Court in April, 2009 when Judge Gledhill QC openly in court criticized the performance of three of the four solicitor higher court advocates in the case he had tried. Concerned about the competence of one of them, he said he came close to discharging the jury. Further, Judge Gledhill alleged the advocates' firms had *chosen to keep the trial within the company* for financial reasons. *Judge slams solicitor-advocates*, Law Society Gazette, 23rd April, 2009. A spokesman for the Law Society expressed dismay that the judge made his comments without giving the advocates concerned an opportunity to comment or respond, causing them substantial harm. The Law Society sought an assurance that what it termed *judicial misconduct* would not be repeated.

Numerous exchanges, some heated, involving barristers, solicitors, judges, the Law Society and the Bar, followed throughout subsequent years, about the quality of work provided by solicitor advocates.

By 2014 the number of solicitor advocates had expanded to 6426, of whom 52 percent were qualified in the criminal courts, 24 percent civil court qualified and 24 percent qualified to practice in both courts.[16] The growth of the number of solicitor advocates in the criminal courts was substantially caused by the effects of Lord Carter's review of publicly funded legal services in 2006 which paved the way for a fixed fee payable to solicitors covering all defence costs, including advocacy, making practice in the Crown Court as a higher court advocate more attractive financially. Also legal aid cuts in criminal cases led to a shortage of barristers prepared to undertake them and to firms saving on the costs of instructing counsel. The slower rate of increase in civil court solicitor advocates with higher rights was attributed to the raised financial jurisdiction of the county court and more use of alternative dispute resolution, limiting the need to practice in the High Court. However reforms of civil litigation funding and costs are now said to be providing solicitors with greater incentives to represent clients directly before the higher courts and interest in higher rights of audience has grown.

Following criticism of their conduct in an appeal arising from a murder trial by solicitor advocates, the Society of Solicitor Advocates in Scotland held an extraordinary meeting at which it was agreed objective advice should be given at all times to enable clients to make an informed choice of representative. *Society 'dismayed' by Gledhill*, Law Society Gazette, 30th April, 2009. Because of what it described as unfair competition from solicitor higher court advocates, who have direct access to clients and can pay referral fees for work, the Bar Council established a working group in May, 2009. The group considered mounting a campaign in police stations, magistrates' courts and prison newspapers to explain entitlement to a barrister and also to press solicitors to inform clients, in their initial correspondence with them, of their right to a barrister. Also in May, 2009 the president of the Council of the Inns of Court, Lady Justice Smith, wrote to presiding judges, resident judges and circuit leaders asking if work done by solicitor higher court advocates is being done satisfactorily and sought their views on whether defendants were being offered a proper choice of representative. The letter was rapidly withdrawn after the Law Society expressed concern that it appeared biased against solicitor advocates and employed lawyers and seemed to support a campaign against them by the self-employed criminal bar. In the wake of the criticisms made against solicitor higher court advocates, June Venters, the first female solicitor QC and an experienced solicitor advocate, alleged that prejudice from some members of the bar and some judges was "*a fact of life*". (*Law Society Gazette*, 2nd July, 2009.)

[16] Source: The Solicitors Regulation Authority. In 2014 there were 129,552 practising solicitors and over 15,000 barristers.

A report on criminal advocacy by Sir Bill Jeffrey in 2014,[17] found 'a marked shift' in the distribution of advocacy work in the Crown court away from the bar, with 'many more solicitor-advocates than there were in the years following the liberalisation of the rights of audience'. Between 2005/06 and 2012/13, the percentage of publicly funded cases in which the defence was conducted by a solicitor-advocate rose from 4% to 24% of contested trials, and from 6% to 40% of guilty pleas. Both statistics were described as on a rising trend. In 2012–2013, Crown Prosecution Service (CPS) in-house lawyers, many of whom were solicitor advocates, led the prosecution in approximately 45% of Crown Court trials. The report noted a substantial reduction in demand for both barristers and solicitor advocates. There were many more criminal advocates, barristers and solicitor advocates, than work for them to do because recorded and reported crime was down, fewer cases reached the criminal courts, more defendants pleaded guilty and court procedures had become simpler. On the question of quality of advocacy between barristers and solicitor advocates the Report identified "undeniably an element of inter-professional rivalry at play" but was also concerned solicitors, by keeping work within their firms, were not fulfilling their professional obligation to choose advocates best able to represent their clients' interests, and that this should be addressed by the Law Society.

A view strongly expressed by the judges in the Jeffrey Report was that although the best advocacy remained very good, general standards amongst both barristers and solicitor advocates had declined. Judges were particularly concerned about relatively inexperienced solicitor advocates sent to court by their firms and those who operated beyond their competence. Removing the growing number of solicitor advocates from Crown courts was not put forward, but measures to improve their quality were recommended including: more consistent training and accreditation framework for all criminal advocates; common minimum expectations for continuous professional development; and introduction of something similar to pupillage for solicitor advocates. The Jeffrey Report highlighted 'the disparity in mandatory training requirements' with barristers required

---

[17] Independent Criminal Advocacy in England and Wales, Ministry of Justice, 2014.

to complete 120 days of advocacy training before appearing in the Crown court while solicitors could do so after just 22 hours of training.

In discussions that followed publication of the Jeffrey Report there was much agreement the main shortcomings in solicitor advocate training lay in post-qualification training, which was far less developed than that for the bar, rather than in the Legal Practice Course and the training contract.[18] A prominent solicitor advocate said he would like to see the Inns of Court assisting training solicitors.[19]

Whilst clear it would neither be feasible or desirable to turn the clock backwards on rights of audience, the Jeffrey Report warned that the supply advocates skilled to conduct complex trials would be in doubt if the current trends towards the use of solicitor advocates and away from the bar continued.

Higher Rights and Large Firms

As a part of a more general move to provide a total service for clients, a "one stop shop", larger firms of solicitors have made great efforts over the last years to supply full "in-house" litigation services for their clients. This involved training partners and other solicitors to carry out roles generally undertaken by barristers including drafting pleadings, settling evidence, preparing skeleton arguments and acting as advocates. Advocacy is performed by solicitor advocates with higher rights of audience, some of whom are former barristers who have converted to become solicitors, and

---

[18] In 2010 a report commissioned by the Law Society, written by Mr. Nick Smedley, after interviewing 45 persons, including the Lord Chief Justice, the Chief Executive of the Legal Services Board, the Chairman of the Bar Council and the President of the Council of the Inns of Court, found that unless the training of solicitor advocates improved they would continue to be viewed as *second class citizens*. Training arrangements were "*not fit for purpose* and that the *quality and quantity of training is inadequate to set and maintain standards*". It concluded training on the Legal Practice Course and during training contracts fell short of what was required; post –qualification continuing professional development must be improved; a compelling case existed for improving training in the lower courts; and a new Advocacy Accreditation Scheme and an academy for solicitor advocates should be established. The report recommended solicitor advocates should be mentored during their first three years in practice and mandatory continuing advocacy skills training with an annual minimum of hours' requirement introduced to prevent practice by what were described as *occasional* solicitor advocates.

[19] See *Solicitor – advocates: raising the bar*, Law Society Gazette, 22nd September, 2014.

who because of the Access to Justice Act 1999 have been able to retain their rights of audience, and by employed barristers. Since the 1999 Act barristers employed by firms are permitted to keep their rights to be heard in all the courts. They were not, however, eligible to become partners with solicitors. However the Legal Services Act 2007, finally put into force in 2011, which introduced legal disciplinary partnerships, now allows them to do so. The trend for barristers to work in solicitors firms has gathered pace.[20]

The city firm Herbert Smith, with a large litigation practice,[21] established an advocacy unit, or "in house chambers," in 2005 to undertake advocacy in general commercial matters brought to it by other departments in the firm. The unit had three partners of whom two were Queens Counsel. One of their roles was to monitor the quality of advocacy services provided in house. In addition three associates were permanently attached to the unit, while another three or four were seconded from other practice areas. Skills that they gained were carried back to their own practices. The advocacy unit maintained clients were offered freedom of choice. If an advocate is required, a client can select in house counsel, one of the firm's 57 solicitor-advocates, or an independent barrister from external chambers.

The big firm Eversheds also pioneered a dedicated advocacy unit. The extent to which the "Herbert Smith model" of an advocacy unit could be emulated was thought to be limited to all but the biggest firms with their large sized litigation practices from where cases can be referred.

Advantages of in-house advocacy for clients are said to include greater familiarity with cases, speed of service, a significant savings in cost because fees are calculated on an hourly rate instead of a fixed barrister's brief fee, paid even if a case settles, and greater transparency in accounting for work done. Not all welcomed unreservedly the rise of in house representation. In a lecture delivered at Sheffield University[22] in 2003,

---

[20] Law Society statistics showed that in 2012 62 mixed solicitor/barrister practices existed providing advocacy services in courts and tribunals where a member or employee of a practice has rights of audience. Law Society Gazette, 2nd February, 2012.

[21] See Advocacy Unit. Herbert Smith. http://www.herbertsmith.com and Herbert Smith brochure *International Advocacy*, 2012.

[22] *The Civil Justice System and the Legal Profession – The Challenges Ahead*, The 6th Edward Bramley Memorial Lecture.

Mr. Justice Lightman said: "*All too often I have occasion to doubt whether the clients of a firm can have been fully advised of the relative merits and costs of the decision to instruct the solicitors to fulfill the role usually fulfilled by the Bar*". He believed there was substantial ground to question if clients were receiving full and detached advice from solicitors about whether their interests would be better served by instructing counsel rather than be represented by in house lawyers, who may be less experienced and more expensive. In short he doubted if clients always had freedom of choice. Where senior counsel was instructed, Mr. Justice Lightman spoke of, "*Firms increasingly foisting partners and staff as junior counsel on leaders they retain to obtain for their members' exposure and educational experience. If that were all and there was no need for a junior counsel who justified his presence on merit and value, and if no charge were made for the public relations or educational role of the solicitor, the situation would be defensible. But this is not in practice just to obtain exposure and experience: it is also to obtain fees. If the firm decides to provide exposure or education for its own members, it must be at its own expense: the client should not be expected to pay for it. Too often the client is paying and indeed at rates significantly exceeding the fees to be charged by counsel*".

To prevent exploitation of the special relationship with clients, and inflating the heavy cost of litigation even further, Mr. Justice Lightman said it was vital that solicitors should fully comply with their fiduciary duty to provide services to clients only where it is in their interests.

Advocacy and the Crown Prosecution Service

The Crown Prosecution Service ("CPS") describes itself as the "largest law firm" in the UK. Out of a total of about 8750 people, some 2700 of its employees are lawyers. The CPS is responsible for advising the police on cases for possible prosecution, reviewing cases submitted by the police, preparing cases for court and presenting cases in court. Every year it deals with many hundreds of thousands of cases in the magistrates' court and about 100,000 in the Crown Court.

Following its birth in 1986, lawyers employed by the CPS were introduced in the Magistrates' Court to conduct prosecutions, replacing police officers who had done so previously. At first complaints were made by magistrates, police and members of the public that the standard of advocacy shown by some advocates was not high. Also for a number of years, because of insufficient staff, contributed to by levels of low pay, the CPS found it necessary, particularly in London and some other areas, to brief solicitor agents and barristers in independent practice to appear before magistrates on its behalf.[23]

Prosecutions in the Crown Court were undertaken by barristers instructed by the CPS. Early suggestions that they too should be undertaken by CPS salaried lawyers were strongly opposed by the Bar. The Bar asserted that barristers in independent practice provided a vital safeguard against unjust or unfounded prosecutions. It was argued they brought with them a further review of the evidence, based on experience and a disinterested analysis, and, as ministers of justice, would not strive for convictions at all costs in court.[24] Questions were asked how independent barristers were in the face of CPS instructions and suggestions were made that the Bar's eloquent objections had much to do with preserving a great proportion of the work of the criminal bar.

Crown Court prosecution advocacy remained a sensitive issue. In 1999, representing a radical break with the past, the CPS started to undertake advocacy in the Crown Court. The principal reason for this was to reduce costs. Originally CPS Crown Court advocacy was confined to interlocutory matters, bail applications and putting the prosecution case before pleas in mitigation but expanded to some trials. In 2006 the CPS secured a guilty verdict after its first ever murder trial in which it was represented in court by its own lawyers.[25]

---

[23] See Gary Slapper and David Kelly, *The English Legal System*, 12th Edition, Routledge, 2011–2012, pp. 345–346. Also see *Happy Birthday CPS*, New Law Journal, 3rd May, 1996, page 617.

[24] Speaking at the Annual General Meeting of the Bar in 1998, Heather Hallet QC, chair of the Bar Council said "*I do oppose any extension of rights of audience to Crown Prosecution lawyers, which substantially undermines the role of the independent advocate in the prosecution process. As a matter of principle, total state control of the prosecution is not in the interests of justice. As a matter of practicality why increase the tasks of the CPS when they face extensive reorganization?*". *Counsel*, August, 1998, page 17.

[25] Law Society Gazette News: *CPS in –house murder win*, 17th August, 2006.

CPS Crown Court advocacy is performed by over one thousand higher court advocates[26] of whom nearly 70 percent are solicitors, the remainder being employed barristers who brought their rights of audience with them when they joined the service. Solicitors have to obtain the higher rights qualification via the exemption or accreditation route. They are also required to pass an internal higher court advocacy course, at the end of which they are assessed externally by advocacy trainers from Nottingham Law School. All CPS higher court advocates have very extensive experience of advocacy in the Magistrates court.

In a series of announcements between 2006 and 2010, then Director of Public Prosecutions (DPP), Kenneth MacDonald QC, made it clear in that the CPS would do much more higher court advocacy than it had traditionally done, partly to attract the strongest candidates, who want a career in all aspects of criminal law, to work for it and also to enable the DPP to hold prosecutors more accountable for their decisions. His aim was for the CPS to become an advocacy organization, rather than one in which advocacy had been secondary and often performed by the independent bar and solicitor agents.

Because of the nature of its work, the junior criminal bar was most affected by the CPS doing more Crown Court advocacy. Complaints arose in some parts of the country, that to achieve CPS area targets for the overall amount of advocacy undertaken, most, or all, interlocutory matters (Pleas and Case Management Hearings) were being conducted by CPS lawyers.[27] This was said to frequently lead to difficulties being experienced by independent barristers briefed later for trials because they lacked control of cases when vital earlier decisions were made. At a basic level dissatisfaction was expressed that barristers were receiving their briefs from CPS higher court advocates too shortly before trial.[28] Against this background, the Bar Council and the CPS agreed guidelines in late

---

[26] As of March 2010: *CPS Annual Report 2009–2010*, Director's letter to Attorney General. The number stood at 838 in March 2007: *CPS Annual Report 2006–2007*, page 7.

[27] See Mr. Geoffrey Vos QC, *Chairman's Column*, Counsel, July, 2007, page, 3.

[28] See *Memorandum submitted by the Criminal Bar Association to the House of Common's Justice Committee's Inquiry into the Crown Prosecution Service*, dated October, 2008, http://www.publications.parliament.uk, paras 14–24.

2006 designed to safeguard the junior bar.[29] Under them, external barristers were to be instructed at an earlier stage and follow the case through to trial, rather than most interlocutory matters being given to CPS advocates. Barristers would return plea and case management briefs only in exceptional circumstances. Further, under the guidelines, CPS in-house advocates were not to act as juniors to self-employed Queens' Counsels, unless they were sufficiently skilled and experienced to undertake the case themselves, and to handle it if the silk became unavailable for some unforeseen reason. The extent to which the guidelines were followed in the years immediately after they were issued was the subject of dispute between the Bar and the CPS.

In a highly contentious speech, delivered at the annual Bar Conference held in 2008, the chairman of the Criminal Bar Association, Peter Lodder QC, was disparaging of much CPS advocacy in serious trials. He said some CPS advocates had left the Bar because they had never risen above a modest practice. "*Now they have become the leading advocate in murder prosecutions, cases in which they would never have been instructed by the CPS while they remained in private practice*". He later added, in a newspaper interview: "*All this is done in the interests of economy. Watching the destruction of the system by the use of apparently cheap and inadequate labour is deeply upsetting and demoralizing to the professional Bar*".[30] In reply the Law Society President, Paul Marsh, said these comments were "*exactly what you would expect from a profession that is failing to deal with competition*" and there was no evidence of poor levels of advocacy by solicitors. Further, Mr. Marsh said "*advocates have to pass a demanding test in order to exercise higher rights of audience, whereas there is no quality assurance at the bar at all*". He added that the bar's decision to make such allegations in the press rather than by complaint to the regulator suggested they could not be substantiated.[31] A thematic Review carried out by Her Majesty's Crown Prosecution Service Inspectorate ('HMCPSI'), published in 2009 found tensions were easing between the CPS and the inde-

---

[29] *CPS/Bar Framework of Principles for Prosecuting Advocates in the Crown Court.* A copy appears as Appendix One of Memorandum, *supra.* Document also obtainable on Bar Council website, http://www.barcouncil.org.uk

[30] *The Times* 3rd November, 2008.

[31] *Law Society Gazette*, 6th November, 2008.

pendent bar and some members of the judiciary over the greater use of in-house advocates and a "*more collaborative and less combative*" approach was beginning to emerge.[32]

The HMCPSI Review, based on observations of numerous Crown Court, Magistrates and Youth Court trials, however, found a clear need to improve standards of CPS advocacy.[33] Too many cross-examinations were "*unstructured, lacking a theory of the case and frequently amounted to little more than "putting" the case*". At the Crown Court, "*the quality of cross-examination could be improved significantly if more consideration was given to exploring any inconsistencies given in evidence or interview and understanding how to make key points with the most dramatic effect that the jury will understand*". Greater planning of opening speeches to identify relevant issues and reasonably foreseeable defences was also necessary, as was more structuring of closing speeches. Weaknesses observed in case preparation and in presenting legal arguments were called to be remedied. Additionally, significant work was recommended to correct the *style* of some advocates who failed "*to present with an air of authority*", used inappropriate tone and pace and were insufficiently engaging. Other factors identified, although less significant, as negatively effecting the quality of advocacy included: inadequate clarity and voice projection; not making sufficient eye contact; "*failing to minimise distractions such as paper shuffling and specific mannerisms; and failing to use, where appropriate, simple and concise language*". To a far lesser extent, the Inspectorate observed examples of advocates dressing unsuitably for court, being discourteous to others there, and lacking awareness of the relevant practice and procedure, at its most basic resulting in not using correct forms of address for judges or magistrates.

In the wake of the HMCPSI Review, the Director of Public Prosecutions, Keir Starmer QC stated "*that high quality advocacy is a mark of a modern prosecution service*" and announced the introduction of the Advocacy Quality Management Strategy to monitor performance of in house advocates and to concentrate on their training.

---

[32] HMCPS Inspectorate *Thematic review of prosecution advocacy and case presentation*, Page 9.
[33] HMCPS Inspectorate *Thematic review of prosecution advocacy and case presentation*, Pages 12–14.

In a follow up report to the HMCPSI Review, written in 2012, the HMCPSI Chief Inspector warned that local management imposed cuts were damaging the effectiveness of in-house prosecutors in the Crown Court and the quality of their advocacy. He emphasized that good advocacy should be paramount and that CPS prosecutors should not be used just to save money.[34]

A barrister interviewed, who regularly prosecuted and defended in the Crown Court, thought that CPS higher rights advocates' style of advocacy was often briefer and more informal than that of independent barristers. She considered that their attachment to particular courts enabled them to know the ways and practices of judges who sat there better than advocates who are briefed in a number of courts.

"Lower Rights of Audience" for Lay Prosecutors in the Magistrates Court

Non-legally qualified support staff, Designated Caseworkers, ("DCWs"), from 1999 were allowed to assist qualified CPS lawyers in court and to handle straightforward guilty pleas, usually concerning minor motoring offences, before magistrates. In 2004 the Crown Prosecution Service permitted them to appear on its behalf in all non-contentious matters in the Magistrates Courts, including early administrative hearings and cases following a guilty plea where the court ordered a pre-sentence report. Their role was expanded further in 2005 to include uncontested bail applications and routine case management hearings at the Magistrates' court. The move was opposed by many legally qualified prosecutors. The First Division Association, the trade union which represents CPS lawyers, argued that the extension was solely driven by cost cutting and contrasted the minimal training received by DCWs with that of lawyers.[35]

The CPS in 2007 sought an amendment of the law to substantially expand what DCWs could undertake in the Magistrates to include prosecuting in all summary trials, involving both summary only and *either*

---

[34] In HMCPS Inspectorate *Follow up report to the thematic review of prosecution advocacy and case presentation*, March, 2012, page 3.
[35] *Fury over CPS caseworker plans*, Law Society Gazette, 6th October, 2005.

way offences (those that could be tried by a judge and jury if the defendant elects Crown Court trial), handling contested bail applications and applications for many court orders including anti –social behaviour orders, restraining orders, parenting orders and drinking and football banning orders.

The plan to widen the use of DCW's was very controversial. Worries were expressed about the quality of advocacy they might deliver given their comparative lack of legal knowledge and experience of contested matters. The chairman of the Magistrates Association said *"Magistrates deal with an enormous number of cases. We are most concerned that justice should always be fair and efficient. Our priority is that every matter should be presented to us by those with sufficient training and expertise"*.[36] In a briefing paper produced for Members of Parliament, before the second reading of the Bill containing the clause to enlarge the rights of audience of DCWs, the Law Society said it *"did not oppose deploying paralegals in appropriate cases as this will result in the time of legally qualified prosecutors being more productively used.* But added, *Allowing designated case workers to undertake summary trials or contested bail applications in relation to serious offences is inappropriate"*. The paper had concerns about the level of supervision DCWs received from Crown Prosecutors and their limited training, which it believed was confined to a two week residential course and continuing training. It considered this was wholly insufficient for the tasks of opposing bail and representing the Crown in a trial, which could lead to imprisonment for up to 12 months.[37] The very real possibility of a victim of crime seeing an accused prosecuted by a lay person but defended by a lawyer was broached. It was also pointed out that caseworkers, unlike lawyers, were not officers of the court or subject to any professional code of conduct. The short conclusions of the Law Society paper were that the government was trying to prosecute on the cheap. Witnesses and victims might be imperiled at trial. Victims might be deterred from allowing cases to go ahead if they fear they will not be handled properly.

---

[36] Cindy Barnett, The Times, July, 16th, 2007.
[37] Law Society Gazette, 13th March, 2008.

When the Bill was later before the House of Lords, the First Division Association, representing CPS prosecutors, expressed the view that the proposals to extend the powers of caseworkers were unworkable and would place an "impossible burden" on prosecutors to supervise caseworkers, who would need to be satisfied with the standard of presentation and prepared lines of cross-examination for each trial. The union predicted adjournments and delays would increase because caseworkers in court would frequently need to consult qualified prosecutors.[38]

The then Vice Chairman of the Bar, Mr. Timothy Dutton, QC, said the plan was against the public interest: *"Legally – qualified advocates are required because of the burden of responsibility, the advocacy skills needed for the cases, and the need to ensure independence of prosecutions in our criminal justice system........ Qualified lawyers are under a strict duty to be independent. Unqualified workers are not".*[39]

Mr. James Morton, a former criminal solicitor in the London courts, writer and legal historian, in an interview,[40] explained that when police officers acted as prosecutors in court, before the Crown Prosecution Service was introduced in 1986, many did not have a full understanding of the law of evidence in trials. They were not always corrected by court clerks. Miscarriages of justice did occur. In his opinion history could be repeated if DCWs were allowed to prosecute in summary trials.

The Director of Public Prosecutions robustly defended the move to devolve advocacy work.[41] He argued that the use of DCWs had been a success, freeing qualified lawyers to deal with serious and difficult cases and cutting trial delays. DCWs were adequately supervised and were of high quality, often entering the CPS on law scholarships and then moving on to take law degrees and become prosecutors. All had substantial experience and knowledge of the law and court procedure before being desig-

---

[38] Law Society Gazette, 13th March, 2008.

[39] *Wider role for CPS caseworkers 'not in public interest'* Law Society Gazette, 19th July, 2007. In response to concerns expressed by the Law Society, the Bar, the First Division Association of Civil Servants and by some DCWs, the Director of Public Prosecutions announced that he was negotiating with the Institute of Legal Executives to ensure caseworkers were adequately trained. The Times, 8th April, 2008.

[40] Conducted on 9th July, 2007.

[41] *Council hits out at CPS over casework extension*, Law Society Gazette, 26th July, 2007.

nated. He emphasised that they would be given full training and supervision for their additional duties.

The DPP insisted that he could not envisage any situation in which DCWs would be entrusted to handle cases where a defendant might go to gaol. Sir Kenneth MacDonald asserted that case workers performing advocacy in court was part of a wider trend across the professions in which more straightforward work is transferred to trained workers so as to allow professionals to focus their skills most productively.[42] Comparisons were drawn by him to nurse practitioners at doctors' surgeries, who, amongst other functions, can prescribe some medication, teaching assistants, based in classrooms to help teachers in their everyday work, and police community support officers, who usually patrol a beat and assist qualified police officers at crime scenes and major events. Whether these were apt comparisons for transferring courtroom advocacy to non-legally qualified personnel was questioned. What can, however, be said with certainty is that the use of lay persons as advocates before Magistrates runs against the move, over three decades ago, which was successful in 1986 with the creation of the CPS, to replace nonlegally qualified prosecutors with lawyers.

Despite objections made, the law was altered in 2008 to grant DCWs, of which there are several hundred, the expanded role sought by the CPS.[43] DCWs were renamed Associate Prosecutors in 2009. Although prosecuting in summary trials, they have not yet been deployed in those offences which carry imprisonment. All associate prosecutors are required to become members of the Institute of Legal Executives, and as such must comply with the Institute's code of conduct and guides to good practice.

For those who maintain a strong relationship exists between the quality of prosecution advocacy and how much the state is prepared to pay for it, the CPS strategies, largely driven by economy, of increasing the amount of higher court advocacy conducted by in-house barristers and solicitors

---

[42] The Times, July 16th, 2007. The National Audit Office and the Public Accounts Committee commented upon the use of DCWs, renamed *Crown Prosecution Service Associate Prosecutors* during 2009. Both recommended a greater use of them to increase the efficient running of the magistrates, court.

[43] Section 55 of the Criminal Justice and Immigration Act, 2008.

and expanding magistrates' court case presentation by nonadmitted law-yer Associate Prosecutors are highly doubtful.

Extended Rights of Audience for Fellows of the Institute of Legal Executives

Rights of audience spread some years ago beyond barristers and solicitors to Fellows of the Institute of Legal Executives who were allowed, in very limited circumstances, to represent clients in family and civil matters in the lower courts.[44] In 2006, the Lord Chancellor granted legal executives greatly extended rights in these areas and for the first time permitted them to appear in criminal courts. The Institute is now able to issue cer-tificates, following satisfactory completion of an advocacy training course lasting six days, in civil proceedings; family proceedings; and criminal proceedings. Holders of the Civil Proceedings Certificate are permitted to: appear in open court in the county court in all actions, except family proceedings; appear before Justices or a District Judge (Magistrates Court) in the Magistrates Courts in relation to all matters originating by complaint or application, including applications under the licensing, bet-ting and gaming legislation; appear before any tribunal under the super-vision of the Council on Tribunals where the tribunal rules provide for a non-discretionary right of audience being available to barristers and solic-itors; appear before Coroners Courts in respect of all matters determined by those courts and to exercise rights of audience similar to those exer-cised by solicitors and barristers.

Legal Executives who obtain a Family Proceedings Certificate, are allowed: to appear in court (including open court) in all County Court family proceedings; to appear before Justices or a District Judge (Magistrates' Court) in the Family Proceedings Courts; and to appear before Coroners' Courts in respect of all matters determined by those courts, and to exercise rights of audience similar to those exercised by solicitors and barristers.

---

[44] See Institute of Legal Executive Order 1998 which set out rights of audience available to legal executives.

Fellows to whom the Institute of Legal Executives awards a Criminal Proceedings Certificate are permitted: to appear before Justices or a District Judge (Magistrates' Court) in all adult magistrates courts in relation to all matters within that Court's criminal jurisdiction; to appear before Justices or a District Judge (Magistrates' Court) in all Youth Courts in relation to all matters within that court's criminal jurisdiction; to appear in the Crown Court or High Court before a judge in chambers to conduct bail applications; to appear in the Crown Court on appeal from the Magistrates' Court, the Youth Court or on committal of an adult for sentence; and to appear before Coroners' Courts in respect of all matters determined by those courts and to exercise rights of audience similar to those exercised by solicitors and barristers. In 2007, Fellows of the Institute of Legal Executives became eligible for judicial appointment, further advancing their position and status in court.[45]

Of the 7000 fellows of the Institute of Legal Executives, about 60 have become Legal Executive Advocates.

Quality Control of Advocacy

Satisfying formal controls of quality, additional and external to those imposed by lawyers' own individual professional bodies, seems to be a growing feature of advocacy which can now be undertaken by many more than previously.

The Bar in England and Wales responded to anecdotal accounts from magistrates and judges (which were often, it claimed, unsubstantiated) of poor quality court room advocacy, by setting up a Bar Quality Advisory Panel.[46]

The Panel, which began to operate on the 15th October, 2007[47] receives reports from judges solicitors and other barristers that barristers have provided below standard services. A barrister is able to refer him or herself to it as well. It does not have a disciplinary role and referral to it

---

[45] Under Part 2 of The Tribunals, Courts and Enforcement Act 2007.
[46] The Panel was first proposed in a consultation paper, *Bar Council Consultation Paper on Quality*, in April 2007. Bar News, June, 2007, page 1.
[47] *Counsel*, November, 2007, page, 4.

does not prevent any complaint being made to the Bar Standards Board, the Bar's regulatory body, established in 2006, as a result of the Bar Council (which now represents 15,000 barristers in England and Wales) separating its representative and regulatory functions. After seeking an explanation from the referred barrister, the Board, if it considers it necessary, offers him or her advice. This might include: to undergo a period of advocacy training or continuing education to deal with any shortcoming identified; to discuss the matter with his or her head of chambers, circuit leader, a bencher of his Inn of Court, or some other suitable person acting a mentor; to take specific action concerning his or her personal administration; and to take remedial action to improve his or her conduct or service in the future.

Following a request from the Bar Council, the Bar Standards Board amended the profession's training regulations to require barristers of four to six year's call to undertake three hours of advocacy training each year. Previously this was only compulsory for those of three year's call and under.

Possibly with an eye fixed on competition from solicitor advocates, the then Bar Council Chairman, Geoffrey Vos QC, said of these two measures:

> *The Bar Council wishes to ensure that barristers aspire to and achieve excellence, so that the future of the profession is assured.............. Quality control is not a threat to our independence. And it must not become burdensome or disruptive. It is, however, a necessary part of growing up. We are a big profession now, attracting entrants from all backgrounds. We must be able to produce evidence for our oft repeated assertion that we provide the highest quality advocacy and advice available anywhere.*[48]

The Bar Council supported a recommendation made in the Final Report of Lord Carter's Review of Legal Aid Procurement[49] that a Quality Assurance for Advocates scheme ("QAA"), based on principles of peer review and a rounded appraisal system, be established for all advocates

---

[48] Quoted in *The Times* by Frances Gibb, April, 10th, 2007.
[49] *Lord Carter's Review of Legal Aid Procurement: A market –based approach to reform.* House of Lords, published on 13th July, 2006.

working in the criminal, civil and family courts. According to the Review, the new quality monitoring system envisaged should be developed initially for publicly funded criminal advocates, then for publicly funded family and civil advocates and ultimately for all advocates, who should be graded according to skills and experience.[50]

Officials from the Ministry of Justice and the Legal Services Commission, which then ran legal aid, together with representatives from the judiciary, the Bar Council and Bar Standards Board, the Law Society, the Solicitors Regulatory Authority, the Institute of Bar Clerks, the Crown Prosecution Service and the Attorney General's Office formed a Working Group to develop a QAA. Because it was of the view that good quality of advocacy is particularly important in criminal defence, where an individual's liberty may be at stake, the Group decided to first develop a pilot scheme for assuring the quality of defence advocates in the Crown Court and above. Not just advocacy and legal knowledge, but the whole range of skills required of advocates was to be assessed including case management, client service and effective interaction with the wider justice system.

After considerable delay, agreement to establish a joint scheme, the Quality Assurance Scheme for Advocates ("QASA"), to assure the quality of criminal advocacy was finally reached in 2012 by the Solicitors Regulation Authority, Bar Standards Board and the Institute of Legal Executives. Although launched the following year, its implementation was repeatedly delayed, partly by a judicial review brought by the Criminal Bar Association.

Opponents saw the scheme as an unnecessary imposition based purely on anecdotal, rather than hard, evidence of poor quality advocacy. Colourful comparisons were drawn with a sledge hammer to smash a nut and building a tsunami defence around Alice Springs, the famed outback town in the middle of Australia.

Under QASA advocates, irrespective of their prior education and training and professional qualification, are assessed against a common set of standards. Judges evaluate the performance of advocates who perform Crown Court trials. Some judges welcomed the prospect of formally

---

[50] Recommendation 5.3, page 14.

assessing advocates. Others expressed reservations. They included Lord Justice Moses who considered evaluation of advocates by judges would damage the "*subtle relationship*" between them and "*pervert the purpose of the trial process.*" In particular, advocates seeking promotion to a higher grade (under the Quality Assurance Scheme there are four grades.) might refrain from pressing points not finding favour before judges, even though they may be correct. In this way an undesirable factor, risking injustice, could be introduced into advocacy.[51] The Law Society was similarly concerned about tensions between an advocate's duty to his or her client and the wish to ensure that the assessment goes well and also that the number of assessments would place a considerable burden on the judiciary.[52]

Notwithstanding lingering opposition of some advocates, it seems likely that QAA will be applied to all areas of publicly paid advocacy in the future and might possibly, as recommended by the Carter Review, be extended later to privately funded advocacy.

New Technology

In future technology will exert a stronger influence on advocacy. Almost all judges can now be seen taking a note of proceedings on a lap-top computer. The old adage that an advocate should "watch the judge's pen" to gauge the speed of his or her delivery has been adapted to "watch the Judge's fingers on the keyboard".

Advocates have been required to adapt to video conferencing ("VC") and video links. The Access to Justice Act 1999 allowed video-conferencing to be used in civil proceedings, including case management conferences, ancillary relief hearings, applications for permission to proceed with judicial review, where there are overseas or remote witnesses or in any civil cases in which the court directs the use of video and the parties involved consent to it.

Following the success of a pilot scheme involving the Royal Courts of Justice, Cardiff Civil Justice Centre and Leeds Combined Court in 2000,

---

[51] Interviewed by Joshua Rozenberg, *Law in Action*, BBC Radio 4, 19th June, 2012.
[52] Solicitor –advocates: raising the bar, Law Society Gazette, 22nd September, 2014.

the use of video conferencing substantially increased. Over sixty courts now have VC and it is possible for each to connect with each other and for multiple courts to be connected at once. For example, Bournemouth, Leeds and Manchester can be used to take evidence for a matter being heard at the Royal Courts of Justice. The lack of availability of expert witnesses constitutes a major source of delay in child care and supervision cases. To reduce this, all 53 Care Centres across England and Wales were provided with VC equipment to provide them with greater flexibility as to when and how expert witnesses will be heard by the court. Video conferencing is now available in nearly 160 Magistrates' Courts which are linked to prisons. In those courts prisoners are not usually required to be physically present for remands, bail applications and other matters. Video links have been installed in 85 Youth Courts so that child victims and witnesses no longer have to appear in person in the courtroom. The Prisons and Courts Bill 2017 contained provisions to permit greater use of live video or audio links in specified criminal proceedings. Matters currently conducted in a physical courtroom were to be dealt with in a "virtual – enabled" hearing – where some of the participants are elsewhere – or in a "fully virtual" hearing where there is no physical court room and all the participants take part using telephone or video conferencing facilities. In a fully virtual hearing, the court would be able to direct that proceedings be broadcast to screens in court buildings so the public and press may follow them. Wider broadcasting would not be permitted. Because of the 2017 May General Election the Bill was withdrawn. However it is anticipated these provisions will be revived in fresh legislation.

It is commonly agreed that successful advocacy requires keen sensitivity to the words and body language of witnesses and judges. Some barristers were interviewed after a case conducted by video link up as part of the pilot scheme conducted at the Royal Courts of Justice in 2000. Whilst they broadly approved of the use to which technology was being put, they said they were unable to pick up some of the judge's subtle nuances and body language on the monitors. One said, *"Advocates can usually tell when a judge is getting impatient, but something was lost in translation"*.[53]

---

[53] *Firm in court video link*, Law Society Gazette, October 26th, 2000, page 3.

It may be that as technology improves, and also as they gain more experience in video link cases, advocates will be able to detect subtle signs from judges and witnesses more acutely. There is certainly a strong case for advocacy training at colleges and elsewhere to include exercises involving V C.

Following pilot schemes using pre-recorded evidence in child abuse cases, the Lord Chancellor/Justice Secretary announced in 2017 that alleged adult victims of sexual offences will be able to choose to give evidence and be cross-examined on it before trials commence; their video recorded testimony being admitted during trial. Whilst welcomed as a means of avoiding alleged victims testifying unnecessarily long and preventing inadmissible evidence of sexual history being heard by juries, concern has been registered by some criminal advocates that they would be prevented from cross examining upon matters that arise at trial including the evidence of other witnesses.

Reception of Technology in the United States

In the United States, both at Federal and state court level, there has been considerable investment in technology.[54] Most courts can now display evidence by a document camera, a vertically mounted television camera that transmits an image of whatever item is placed on its base. Many courts have monitors, or a large screen and projector, allowing counsel, jurors, witnesses and judges to see evidence that has been put in digital form. In some high tech courts monitors are touch screen enabling witnesses to annotate displayed images, using related software. Key text or other parts may be emphasized or enlarged. Presentational software, such as Microsoft's *PowerPoint,* is increasingly employed by lawyers, especially in opening and closing speeches.

Technology expanded the ways in which evidence and arguments may be put to courts. It can transform what might otherwise be dry technical and difficult to understand reports into much more comprehensible

---

[54] For the extent of technology in Federal Courts see C. Wiggins, M. Dunn, and G Cort, *Federal Judicial Center Survey On Courtroom Technology.* Federal Judicial Center 2003. Further growth has occurred since this survey was published.

forms. Particularly in high value civil cases involving accidents, very expensive computer recreations are used more and more by lawyers in court.[55] Because they are such a powerful form of presentation, and may assume what is in dispute, their admissibility is sometimes challenged.

Advocates have to decide what will be the most persuasive means of presenting a case. This demands a knowledge of technology and how to operate it. Electronic methods of presenting documents and exhibits are marketed by companies to lawyers as a means of obtaining an advantage over opponents who might use no longer leading techniques such as models, charts graphs and photographs. Advocates generally make electronic presentations from a *litigation podium*. As the technology is comparatively new, technical problems still occasionally occur in court. The wise counsel will have a reserve traditional low –tech strategy in the event of technical difficulty to maintain the credibility of his or her case.[56]

Most who work with evidence presentation technology in America agree that it saves at least a quarter to a third of the time a traditional civil trial would take, although the amount of pretrial preparation required from advocates is often much more. Because of the increased speed of trials some attorneys report that they have little time to reflect on their case during trial and that this can contribute to stress.[57]

A feature of new court technology court is real – time transcription by which a court reporter, or stenographer, using a voice recognition computer system trained to his or her voice, can supply a rough transcript of the court's proceedings to counsel's computer notebook, where, if necessary, it can be later annotated. Real-time transcription, though expensive, has become more readily available. It can be transmitted through the Internet to the lawyer's office or elsewhere.

A lawyer can obtain almost instant assistance back, via his or her lap top computer, from an expert, who may be far away, on questions to ask

---

[55] In describing an aircraft crash simulation, made in America, that he had seen, Richard Susskind, former IT Adviser to the Lord Chief Justice and Gresham Professor of Law, observed, in an interview conducted on 21st February, 2001, that "*no amount of eloquent and descriptive advocacy could have rivalled it*".

[56] F. Lederer, *High tech trial lawyers and the court: Responsibilities, problems, and opportunities, an introduction.* 2003 William and Mary School of Law.

[57] F. Lederer, *Courtroom Technology: A Status Report.* (2006) William and Mary School of Law.

in cross-examination. Perhaps less helpfully, instructions from absent, but interventionist, clients located anywhere in the world could also be received on what to put to witnesses and points to make, lessening counsel's control of the case.

The expense of real time transcription precludes its use in most cases. Automatic voice recognition programmes, which do not need a stenographer are under development. In years hence it is likely that software systems sophisticated enough to recognize different voices in a courtroom will be available. Something that functions very like real time transcription, but much cheaper, may then be widely used in American courts and beyond. Reports of most cases could then be published virtually simultaneously on the Internet. Advocates in their submissions would need an even more immediate knowledge of relevant cases. This may not be too far off. Chinese courts are piloting speech recognition Artificial Intelligence ("AI") technology which produces real-time transcripts of hearings and which collates cases for judges to refer to when drafting judgments.[58] As courtroom technology is rapidly becoming an ordinary and necessary aspect of trial presentation in the United States, the ability of lawyers to use it effectively becomes ever more important. Many trial lawyers attend courses on what technology offers and how to work it. More law schools are following the example of William and Mary Law School – the home of the Courtroom 21 Project, an influential pioneer in the area of courtroom technology[59] – which for some years has required every second year law student to be instructed in basic use of courtroom technology and offers those interested in trial work a technology augmented trial advocacy course.[60]

---

[58] *Artificial Intelligence in the court room*, Law Society Gazette, 9th April, 2018.

[59] In 1993 the Project opened the Mc Gothlin Courtroom, still considered to be the most technologically advanced court in the world. With this courtroom, William and Mary Law School is exploring the place of information technology in litigation in the USA and the social consequences it may bring.

[60] F. Lederer, *High tech trial lawyers and the Court*, William and Mary School of Law, 2003.

As Yet, More Limited Use in England and Wales but Future Great Impact Predicted

Video conferencing apart, the use of technology in courts in England and Wales is much more limited than in America. A small number of Crown Courts do have monitors that display evidence. They are used in major trials involving fraud and terrorism. As a means of presentation, *Powerpoint* is not employed. In an interview the former Master of the Rolls and Lord Chief Justice, Lord Woolf, considered that it might be useful in closing speeches to juries in the Crown Court. A Lord Justice of Appeal saw little utility for it before the Court of Appeal. He did, however, strongly favour placing documents on DVD coupled with the technology that would allow them to be raised on monitors and which permitted participants in trials to make their own separate electronic notes on what they saw. Computer simulation was used in the Bloody – Sunday Inquiry in Northern Ireland,[61] conducted between 1998 and 2004 and published in 2010. Witnesses could "walk" around a virtual Londonderry in 1972 to help them recall events and where they were at the time.[62]

A government paper published in 2000,[63] which foresaw a much more rapid adoption of computer technology in the English and Welsh courts than has actually happened, predicted that advocates' verbal submissions would reduce in length: "*In the courtroom of the future it will not be necessary for a lawyer to state the agreed facts, history, relevant case law and statutes, when all of these materials are available in electronic form and are therefore more easily accessible in the courtroom*".

---

[61] Bloody Sunday was the name given to January 30th 1972 when 13 people were killed by soldiers on a banned civil rights march in Londonderry.

[62] Explained by Douglas McQuaid in the course of a lecture entitled *When two worlds collide: IT and Advocacy*. Gray's Inn, February, 2001. The Judicial Inquiry concluded in 2010. Lord Saville, who presided over it, was interviewed by Richard Susskind, President of the Society for Computers and Law, for a programme in the US television series, *The Digital Age*, broadcast in early 2011. He explained how digital technology had played a crucial role in its conduct, along with traditional forensic skills.

[63] *Civil Justice 2000, A Vision of the Civil Justice System in the Information Age*, Department of Constitutional Affairs, Section 3, paragraph 3.46.

Although at present behind the United States in its reception, court-room technology, which continues to develop briskly, will have a very important future bearing on advocacy in this country. Few advocates will escape its influence. Those who teach advocacy at professional law schools, and elsewhere, will have to become very familiar with IT and provide opportunities for students to use it. In *De Oratore*, Cicero advised those seeking to be advocates to speak the language of everyday life and to follow usages approved by the sense of the community. To this age old wisdom might now be added *"and use the technology of the time"*.

Impact on Jurors

Young people, especially, acquire much knowledge and information by looking at the internet and from other material on computers and smart-phones. Visual learning, rather than aural, is likely to increase as technology consolidates its position and advances. Proper functioning of a trial depends on jurors listening, often for prolonged periods. It is said some may lack sufficient ability to assimilate oral evidence of defendants and witnesses, especially if lengthy, submissions by advocates and what is said by judges.[64] Some have spoken of the oral tradition of advocacy in jury trials under imminent threat. Others think this is an exaggeration. Inevitably more demands will be made for information to be presented on screens in most cases, not just those that are protracted and complex.[65] How courts and advocates should respond to broad changes brought by IT requires detailed thought now, rather than later, when it may pose problems. A sensible response may be to commission research on how, if

---

[64] See Lord Judge, The Lord Chief Justice of England and Wales, *The Criminal Justice System in England and Wales Time For Change*, Speech To The University of Hertfordshire, 5th November, 2008, page 11. Also see report of a speech by Lord Judge in the *Times*, October, 2009. Interestingly, research by Professor Cheryl Thomas, *Are Juries Fair?*, Ministry of Justice, Research Series 1/10, did not show that younger jurors were less able to comprehend oral legal instructions than older jurors. In fact the contrary was found: understanding of directions fell as the age of the juror increased. In an interview, held on 11th May, 2010, Professor Thomas said further research, which differentiated in ages, was necessary, on jurors' capacity to follow complex evidence.

[65] The then Lord Chief Justice also suggested that in future, juries might be handed evidence on computers to take away and evaluate, *LCJ calls for court tradition rethink*. Law Society Gazette 22nd October, 2009, page 4. Such a course would have many ramifications.

at all, jurors' ability to follow live evidence and addresses by advocates and judges has been affected by new technology. Unless the law is changed, jurors in real cases could not be interviewed. Mock juries would have to be empanelled to hear simulated cases.

To reduce the amount of live oral evidence necessary for jurors to absorb, it has been proposed that criminal trials could follow civil trials by making witness statements, stand as examination in chief.[66] At first sight this may seem attractive. However, strong reservations exist. The way a person questions a witness when a statement is made may, unconsciously or consciously, distort recollections of events (this may be particularly relevant regarding suggestible persons) and fail to accurately convey his or her character in print. If a statement does not accurately capture the witness's version of events a clear risk arises that he or she will depart from it under cross-examination, thereby damaging credibility before a jury. It has also been said that an important function of examination in chief is to settle witnesses, many of whom have not given evidence in court before and may be nervous about doing so, and give them confidence before being cross-examined. Depriving them of this would be unfair and could reduce the quality of their evidence in cross-examination.[67] Further if jurors were given witnesses written statements, which stood as examination in chief, they would take them into the jury room when considering their verdict. The possibility would then exist

---

[66] To a limited extent, this is already possible under the "Section 9 procedure" (Criminal Law Act 1967) which allows a statement to be read by a prosecutor when it has been agreed with the defence that the maker is not required at court to be cross-examined. (Hearsay and other inadmissible evidence is edited out beforehand.) Section 10 Criminal Law Act, 1967 allows facts, which would otherwise be in issue, to be agreed between the prosecution and the defence. Also, under Section 27 Youth Justice and Criminal Evidence Act 1999 a video – recorded interview with a vulnerable witness before trial may be admitted by the court as the witness's evidence in chief.

[67] This view was put by a Lord Justice, interviewed on the 30th April, 2009. A similar opinion was expressed by a solicitor advocate who has represented clients in jury trials at the Crown Court and has also prosecuted there, when employed by the Crown Prosecution Service. In her view it was essential that jurors hear the witness's full story, not just cross-examination, in order to properly assess his or her credibility. She justified a distinction between practice in the criminal and civil courts on the grounds that in the former the liberty of the subject is at stake, whereas in the later, although very serious matters are decided, it is not. (Interview 30th April, 2009.)

that jurors would give greater importance to them than to their memories and notes of cross-examination.[68]

Rather than according witness statements the status of examination in chief, other measures may be adopted, to cope with jurors' perceived lesser ability to follow oral evidence. These include replacing jury trial in cases of serious fraud, which frequently demand listening to much evidence, with that by a judge and lay assessors, before whom advocacy would be markedly different, and by further removing the right to jury trial for lesser offences.[69]

Dangers of Internet Research by Jurors to Integrity of Trials

Danger to the integrity of jury trials posed by jurors using the internet and being influenced by what they find there, rather than by evidence admitted at trial, first came to public attention in 2008. A trial for manslaughter at Newcastle Crown Court had to be abandoned when it became known that a juror had conducted internet research into forensic science techniques relevant to the case and had discussed his findings with other jurors. Some of the questions the jury subsequently asked the judge revealed they had gained a knowledge of the case that had not been presented to the jury by the prosecution or the defence.[70] Also in 2008 a conviction for rape was quashed after evidence was presented that a juror consulted the internet on a Blackberry. Research published by Professor Cheryl Thomas in 2010[71] showed that some jurors in her study said they seen information about their case on the internet, whilst a smaller number admitted they had looked for it. Professor Thomas called for further research to study what type of judicial instruction would be most effective in preventing jurors from looking for information about their case on the internet. Later that year the Lord Chief Justice, Lord Judge, issued new guidance at the Court of Appeal requiring trial judges to give jurors

---

[68] This could perhaps be countered by a direction from the judge not to do so and by supplying them with by a written record of cross-examinations.

[69] This approach was thought more likely by Lord Justice interviewed on the 30th April, 2009.

[70] See *The Times*, 20th August, 2008.

[71] Cheryl Thomas, *Are Juries Fair?*, Ministry of Justice Research Series 1/10.

clear formal instructions they should not research cases on the internet or discuss them on social networking sites. Lord Judge said that internet research may consciously or unconsciously affect jury decisions, "*yet at the same time neither side at trial will know what consideration might be entering into their deliberations and will therefore not be able to address arguments about it. This would represent a departure from the basic principle which requires that the defendant be tried on the evidence admitted and heard by them in court.*"

Artificial Intelligence and Advocacy

Artificial Intelligence ("AI"), seen by some commentators as a fast incoming tide, and its effect on society is rightly much discussed. Some of the consequences foreseen for litigation and advocacy are mentioned briefly.

Machine learning allows a computer programme to analyse a set of data and then make predictions, or take decisions, based on what was learned. In 2016 University College London and the universities of Sheffield and Pennsylvania published research on application of an algorithm to data from each of 584 cases, concerning torture, degrading treatment and privacy, heard by the European Court of Human Rights.[72] In 79 percent of these cases the prediction was the same as the verdict given by the court. Using AI to predict the outcome of cases is very much in its infancy for domestic British civil cases. Although more in some areas of law than others, it may considerably inform advice given to clients whether to pursue litigation or alternatives including settlement. Numbers of cases going to court and the demand for advocates' services might be affected. If litigation is embarked upon insights from predictive AI could also influence tactics of advocates in court.

AI can identify trends, anomalies and inconsistencies in vast volumes of data. It will enable documents disclosed, which may be voluminous in complex litigation, to be analysed more speedily, thoroughly and possibly at less cost. Information may become available leading to evidence of lay and expert witnesses adduced by the opposing side being challenged

---

[72] Nikolaos Aletras, *Predicting judicial decisions of the European Court of Human Rights: A natural language processing perspective.* Peer J. Computer Science, 24th October, 2016.

more rigorously. Data upon which a party may wish to rely may also be examined more closely revealing both strengths and weaknesses, allowing adjustments to be made in litigation strategy and tactics.

AI that can function like the human brain, with independent consciousness, has not yet been developed and most likely never will be. It is only as good as those who train it to process information and the data it is fed. AI cannot be a substitute for the practical experience, common sense and emotional intelligence of advocates and judges, but may, however, act increasingly as a valuable support for litigators and advocates.

15

Some Conclusions

For the greater part of the period covered by this book much advocacy in England and Wales, especially for jurors, was directed to the passions, the emotions. It was often loud, long and declamatory, frequently diffuse and meandering, full of pathetic description, florid, extravagant in words and gestures to the point of theatricality. Advocacy was sometimes marked by intemperate exchanges amongst counsel and between counsel and judges, brow beating and bullying of witnesses. An important part of advocacy was to obscure and confuse, to cloak weaknesses in cases.

No longer prolix and longwinded, but highly focused and limited by considerations of time, advocacy is now vastly more subdued, undertaken in plain language, without the borrowed plumage of poetry and the classics, restrained by tight rules of procedure and evidence and, in a spirit of forensic enquiry, aimed at satisfying what is required by substantive law. Any appeal to the emotions of jurors is carefully disguised as reason or made subliminally. Advocacy now extends beyond the oral to that on paper and outside the court to various forms of arbitration and mediation.

Advocacy developed in the centuries surveyed not through logical overall planning but piecemeal, the result of many influences, most notably individual advocates, alterations in the law and broader social changes. Diverse identifiable key driving factors include:

© The Author(s) 2019   **327**
A. Watson, *Speaking in Court*, https://doi.org/10.1007/978-3-030-10395-8_15

Approaches, methods and styles of successful members of the bar. In a small profession, which, until very recently, lacked formal training in advocacy, junior advocates watched closely how leaders, "*big men*", performed in court and sought to emulate their triumphs. Those particularly observed, and who often took advocacy further along its path, include: Coke, Bacon, Cowper, Yorke, Murray, Burke, Sheridan, Garrow, Brougham, Scarlett, Erskine, Romilly, Copley, Curran, O'Connell, Phillips, Kenealy, Parry, Ballantine, James, Digby-Seymour, Hawkins, Clarke, Holker, Hardinge-Giffard, Russell, Isaacs, Muir, Wrottesley, Carson, Smith, Marshall-Hall, Hastings, Curtis-Benett, Birkett, DuCann, Carman, Gray, Arlidge and Beloff.

Judicial tastes. When sitting without jurors these have been strongly for practical and unadorned forms of advocacy. An orderly presentation of the facts, to which the law must be applied, being much appreciated by judges after which they generally prefer to be left alone, unexposed to rhetorical embellishment.

Consolidation of *stare decisis*, precedent, in the eighteenth and nineteenth centuries and its effect of focusing argumentation by lawyers on case law.

Changes in court trial procedure brought about by judges, for example in the eighteenth century allowing counsel to represent prisoners charged with felony (and in the civil context, over two centuries later, the High Court Practice Directions of the 1980s and 1990s), and under statute, notably the Prisoners' Counsel Act 1836, allowing defendants full representation by counsel.

Levels of respect and civility between advocates and between the bar and the Bench and the latter's ability to control proceedings in court and impose limits on counsel's forensic license.

Greater valuation of court time by judges and more willingness by them to impose time restraints on advocates.

Public and press opinion about what are acceptable advocates' tactics and oratory.

Rules of etiquette and conduct established by barristers and solicitors towards themselves, witnesses and parties and the extent of their enforcement by professional bodies – Bar Messes, the Bar Council and the Law Society.

Press reporting of court cases. A link existed, probably at its strongest in the nineteenth century, between the amount of publicity advocates received and their performance and conduct. The matter is again topical with televising certain court proceedings and calls by some to broadcast more.

Reforms in the law of evidence about who, and what, may be put before courts and informing the content of submissions made. Important examples are the rise of hearsay evidence and its demise in civil trials during the second half of the twentieth century, the ability of defendants to give evidence on their own behalf and expert evidence.

Laws of some complexity regulating the growth of industry, commerce, banking and international trade. The need to make submissions on detailed and exact statutory provisions restricted scope for rhetoric and promoted more precise, rather than unfocused and indiscriminate, examination of witnesses and strictly relevant closing speeches.

Major alterations in criminal and civil procedure during the nineteenth and twentieth centuries. Prominent statutory examples of the former include the Criminal Procedure Act 1851 and the Indictments Act 1915 and of the latter, the Judicature Acts 1873–1881 and Civil Procedure Rules, 1999.

Reduction from the mid-nineteenth century in the use of juries in both civil and criminal trial, lessening opportunities for passionate appeals to emotion, floral passages and histrionic gestures.

Widening horizons of jurors. Greater education amongst common jurors in the later Victorian era made them less susceptible to melodramatic appeals from advocates than before. Juries with broader perspectives, including some knowledge of science and Charles Darwin's theories, increasingly expected an appeal to reason presented in a matter of fact manner, rather than one pitched at their emotions and religious faith. Successful barristers recognised this and altered their approach accordingly.

Democratization of juries. The Juries Act 1974, which swept away the property qualification for jury service, led to a huge increase in the number of potential jurors, more women and a reduction in the minimum age for jury service to 18. Advocates became more aware than ever that in addressing juries they had to take into account a wider range of educational attainment and language in contemporary use and, when making allusions, the need to draw on popular culture, shaped by newspapers, novels, radio, films and television (and now increasingly the computer internet).

General styles of public speaking and discourse in society, for example the decline of declamation and grand oratory and the emergence of a more intimate conversational *fireside* approach.

Educational curriculum commonly received by judges and lawyers and its effect on selection of language and allusions made in court. The school syllabus altered substantially over the last half century with a much reduced place for the Classics, Latin and Greek, previously so prominent.

Formal teaching of advocacy to barristers and solicitors, only comparatively recently introduced and generally held to be beneficial.

Resources. A relationship, although not simplistic, exists between the quality of advocacy and the amount parties and the state are prepared to pay for it. This is particularly relevant to present policies of austerity resulting in cuts both to public funding of cases (legal aid) and to the Crown Prosecution Service.

New technology which has already started to exert an influence on advocacy and can be expected to do so powerfully in the future. Artificial Intelligence may in future play a role at least in the preparation of cases.

In the Preface to his book, *Advocacy and the Making of the Adversarial Criminal Trial 1800–1865*, Clarendon Press, 1998, David Cairns described the history of advocacy as neglected: *no more sophisticated or significant expression of the art of the lawyer has been studied less.* Inattention to the subject, in his view, exemplified the continuing gulf between the worlds of legal scholarship and legal practice. He expressed the wish that his book would stimulate further research and writing on advocacy. The subsequent two decades saw some impressive scholarly works on aspects of the subject. These include: Jan-Melissa Schramm's *Testimony in Victorian Law, Literature, and Theology*, Cambridge University Press, 2000, spanning the first half of the nineteenth century, John Langbein's *The Origins of the Criminal Trial*, Oxford University Press, 2003, covering the 1690s to the 1780s, Allyson May's *The Old Bailey and the Bar 1785–1834*, University of North Carolina, 2003 and Sadakat Kadri's *The Trial: A History from Socrates to O.J. Simpson*, Harper Collins, 2005. Notwithstanding these and other books, the history of advocacy, remains understudied, especially in the form of any comprehensive scholarly treatment spanning the centuries. Indeed, Geoffrey Robertson QC, in his

Preface to *Sir William Garrow, His Life Times and Fight for Justice*, by John Hostettler and Richard Braby, Waterside Press, 2009, criticises legal history's disdain of advocacy *in favour of teaching the tedious history of contract and land law, partly because of the inability of historians to comprehend the dynamics of forensic practice and how this impacts on the rules of the trial process.* The author of this book would be enormously delighted if it contributed to interest in the history of court advocacy and persuaded others to research it further especially the under examined late Nineteenth and opening decades of the twentieth century and the second half of the twentieth century, both periods in which great changes occurred. He would also be very pleased if it led to more scholarship and debate about the future of advocacy in the common law world.

Bibliography

Books, Pamphlets and Papers

Alverstone, Viscount Richard. *Recollections of Bar and Bench.* First published London, 1914 and re-published by Gaunt Inc, Florida, 1996.

Andenas, Mads and Fairgrieve, Duncan. *Tom Bingham and the Transformation of the Law: A Liber Amicorum.* Oxford University Press, 2009.

Andrews, William. *The Lawyer in History, Literature and Humour.* William Andrews and Co, London, 1896.

Ashton, A. J. *As I Went on My Way.* Nisbet and Co, London, 1924.

Aspinall, Arthur. *Lord Brougham And The Whig Party.* First published London, 1927 and republished by Nonsuch Publishing, 2005.

Atlay, J. B. *Famous Trials of the Century.* Grant Richards, London, 1899.

Baker, J. H. *The Order of Serjeants at Law.* Selden Society, London, 1984.

Baker, J. H. *A history of English Judges' Robes.* SN, 1978.

Baker, J. H. *An Introduction to English Legal History*, 4th Edition, Oxford University Press, 2002.

Ballantine, William. *A Barrister's Life.* Richard Bentley, London, 1880.

Bechhofer Roberts, C. E. *Lord Birkenhead*, Newnes, London, 1936.

© The Author(s) 2019
A. Watson, *Speaking in Court*, https://doi.org/10.1007/978-3-030-10395-8

Beer, Samuel B. *Britain Against Itself: The Political Contradictions of Collectivism.* Norton, New York, 1982.

Benson, Thomas, Edited, *Landmark Essays in Rhetoric,* Hermagoras Press, California, 1993.

Bentham, Jeremy. *The Works of Jeremy Bentham,* Russell and Russell, New York, 1962.

Bentley, David. *English Criminal Justice in the Nineteenth Century.* Hambledon Press, London, 1998.

Bergman, Paul. *Reel Justice.* Andrews and McMeel, Kansas City, 1996.

Birkett, Lord Norman. *Six Great Advocates.* Penguin, 1961.

Birkett, Sir Norman. *Presidential Address to the Holdsworth Club of the Faculty of Law. 7th May, 1954.* University of Birmingham.

Blair, Hugh. *Lectures on Rhetoric and Belles Lettres* (1783). South Illinois University, 2005.

Black, Jeremy. *Culture in Eighteenth-Century England. A Subject for Taste.* Hambledon and London, 2008.

Blom-Cooper, Louis. *The Birmingham Six and Other Cases.* Gerald Duckworth and Co Ltd, 1997.

Blom-Cooper, Louis. *The Law As Literature,* The Bodley Head, London, 1961.

Bowker, A. E. *Behind the Bar.* Staples Press, New York, 1949.

Bradley, Mark. *Classics and Imperialism in the British Empire.* Oxford University Press, 2010.

Bragg, Melvyn. *The Book of Books: A Biography of the King James Bible,* BBC Books, 2011.

Brougham, Lord Henry. *Speeches of Henry Lord Brougham.* Adam and Black, Edinburgh, 1838.

Bryce, J. C. *Rhetoric and Belles Lettres.* Clarendon Press, Oxford, 1983.

Bryman, A. *Social Research Method,* Oxford University Press, Oxford, 2008.

Cairns, David. *Advocacy and the Making of the Adversarial Criminal Trial, 1800–1865.* Clarendon Press, Oxford, 1998.

Campbell, George. *Philosophy of Rhetoric* (1776). Reprinted by Funk and Wignalls, London and New York, 1911.

Campbell, Lord John. *Lives of the Chancellors,* John Murray, London, 1856.

Campbell, Lord John. *Lives of the Chief Justices,* John Murray, London, 1858.

Carawan, Edwin. *Oxford readings on the Attic orators,* Oxford University Press, 2007.

Carman, Dominic. *No Ordinary Man: A Life Of George Carman Q.C.* Coronet Books, Hodder and Stoughton, 2002.

Carr, E. H. *What is History?,* Penguin, London, 1987.

Chitty, Joseph. *Practical Treatise on the Criminal Law*. London, 1816.

Cicero. *Brutus*. English Translation by G. L. Henrickson, W. Heinemann, London, 1939.

Clinton-Baddeley, V. C. *The Burlesque Tradition in English Theatre After 1660*, Methuen, London, 1952.

Cockburn, A. W. *In Limine: An Address on Advocacy to the Christ Church Law Club, May 15th, 1952*. Gestetnered and published by the Faculty of Law, University of Southampton.

Cohen, Herman. *A History of the English Bar and Attornatus to 1450*, Sweet and Maxwell, London, 1929.

Conley, J. and O'Barr, W. *Just Words: Law, Language and Power*. University of Chicago Press, 1998.

Cornish, William. *The Jury*. Penguin, 1971.

Cornish W. R. and G de N. Clark. *Law and Society in England 1750–1950*, Sweet and Maxwell, London, 1989.

Cox, Edward W. *The Advocate: His Training, Practice and Duties*. J. Crockford. London, 1852.

Crews, Clyde W. *Ten Thousand Commandments: An Annual Snapshot of the Federal Regulatory State*. Cato Institute, 2005.

Crook, J. A. *Legal Advocacy in the Roman World*. Duckworth, London, 1995.

Davis, Richard. *Intellectual Life in Jefferson's Virginia*. University of North Carolina Press, Chapel Hill, 1964.

De Romilly, Jacqueline. *The Great Sophists in Periclean Athens*. Clarendon Press, Oxford, 1992.

Dickens, Charles. *American notes for general circulation*. Chapman and Hall, London, 1848.

Disher, M. W. *Melodrama: Plots that thrilled*. Macmillan, New York, 1954.

Dixon, T. Thomas. *Weeping Britannia*, Oxford University Press, 2015

Donovan, J. W. *Tact in Court*. Sweet and Maxwell, London, 1915.

Downer, L. J. *Leges Henrici Primi: Edited With Translations and Commentary by L J Downer*. Oxford University Press, 1972.

Drake, Winifred. *The Trial of Harold Greenwood*, in the *Notable British Trials* series, W. Hodge and Co, Edinburgh and London, 1930.

DuCann, Richard. *The Art of the Advocate*. First Edition 1964 and Revised Edition 1993. Penguin Books.

Duman, Daniel. *The English and Colonial Bars in the Nineteenth Century*. Croom-Helm, London, 1983.

Duxbury, Neil. *The Nature and Authority of Precedent*, Cambridge University Press, 2008.

Erskine, Lord Thomas. *The Speeches of the Right Honourable Lord Erskine When at the Bar, with a Preparatory Memoir by the Right Honourable Lord Brougham.* James Ridgeway, London, 1910.

Evans, Keith. *Advocacy in Court.* Blackstone Press, 1995.

Fay, E. S. *The Life of Mr Justice Swift.* Methuen, 1939.

Fifoot, C. H. S. *Lord Mansfield,* Clarendon Press, Oxford, 1936.

Fisher, George. *Plea bargaining's triumph: A history of plea bargaining in America.* Stanford University Press, 2003.

FitzJames-Stephen, Sir James. *Digest of the Law of Evidence,* Macmillan and Co, London, 1877.

FitzJames-Stephen, Sir James. *A History of The Criminal Law of England.* Macmillan and Co, London, 1883.

Foote, John Alderson. *Pie powder from the Law Courts; being dust from the law courts, collected and recollected on the Western Circuit by a circuit tramp.* John Murray, London, 1911.

Ford, Douglas Morley. *Solicitors as Advocates.* Shaws and Sons, London, 1881.

Fordham, Edward. *Notable Cross-examinations.* Constable, 1951.

Forsyth, William. *Hortensius or the Advocate,* John Murray, London, 1849.

Friedman, Lawrence M. *A History of American Law,* Simon and Schuster, New York, 1973.

Friedman, Lawrence M. *American Law in the 20th Century.* Yale University Press, 2002.

Gabb, Sean. *Thomas Erskine: saviour of English Liberty,* Libertarian Alliance, 1990.

Galanter, Marc. *The Privatisation of Justice and the Vanishing Trial.* Paper presented at the Institute of Advanced Legal Studies, London, 27th June, 2006.

Garraghan, Gilbert. *A Guide to Historical Method.* Fordham University Press, New York, 1946.

Geoghegan, Patrick M. King Dan, *The Rise of Daniel O'Connell,* 1775–1829. Gill and Macmillan, 2006.

Genn, Hazel. *What is civil justice (and how much is enough) ?* Hamlyn Lecture, delivered at Faculty of laws University College London, 27th November, 2008.

Gibb, Andrew Dewar. *Judicial corruption in the United Kingdom.* W. Green, Edinburgh, 1957.

Gibbens, Brian. *Elements of Modern Advocacy,* Butterworths. London, 1979.

Gilbert, N. *From postgraduate to social scientist: a guide to key skills.* Sage, London, 2006.

Gilchrist, James P. *A Chronological Register of Principal Duels.* Bulmer and Nicol, London, 1821.

Gilmour, Ian. *The Making of the Poets. Byron and Shelley in their Time*. Pimlico, London, 2003.

Ginnell, Laurence. *The Brehon Law: A Legal Handbook*. T. Fisher Unwin, London, 1894.

Goldsmid, Louise. *Memoirs of Sir Francis Goldsmid*. C Kegan Paul and Co, London, 1882.

Goldstein, Laurence, *Precedent in Law*, Oxford, Clarendon Press, 1987.

Goodhart, Arthur. *Five Jewish Lawyers of the Common Law*. Oxford University Press, 1949.

Goodman, Andrew. *Influencing The Judicial Mind-Effective Advocacy in Practice*. XPL Publishing, 2006.

Grant, Kevin. *A Civilised Savagery: Britain and the New Slaveries in Africa*. Routledge, 2005.

Grant, Michael. *Cicero Selected Works*, Penguin, 1960.

Grasso, Christopher. *A Speaking Aristocracy*. University of North Carolina Press, 1999.

Graves, Robert. *Claudius the God*. Arthur Baker, 1934.

Graves, Robert. *The Greek Myths*. Combined Edition, Penguin, 1992,

Griffith, J. A. G. *The Politics of the Judiciary*. 5th Edition, Fontana Press, 1997.

Grimshaw, Roger and Mills, Helen. *Magistrates 'courts' and Crown Court expenditure, 1999–2009*. Centre For Crime and Justice Studies, 2010.

Gwyn, Aubrey S. J. *Roman Education from Cicero to Quintilian*. Teachers College Press, New York, 1926.

Haar, Charles M. *The Golden Age of American Law*. George Braziller, New York, 1965.

Hamilton, Richard. *All Jangle and Riot – a Barrister's History of the Bar*. Professional Books, 1986.

Handler, Philip. *Penal Reform and Trial Practice in England, 1808–1861*. Paper delivered to Institute of Advanced Legal Studies, London, 6th February, 2008.

Hans, Nicholas. *New Trends In Education In The Eighteenth Century*, Routledge and Kegan Paul, 1951.

Harding, Alan. *A Social History of English Law*. Penguin, 1966.

Hardwicke, Henry. *The Art of Winning Cases, or Modern Advocacy: A Treatise on Preparation for Trial and Conduct of Cases in Court*. Banks and Bros, Albany, New York, 1894.

Harris, Richard. *Illustrations in Advocacy*. Stevens and Haynes, London, 1915.

Harris, Robert. *Lustrum*, Hutchinson, London, 2009.

Hart, A. R. *A History of the King's Serjeants at Law in Ireland*. Four Courts Press, Dublin, 2000.

Hastings, Sir Patrick. *Cases in Court.* William Heinemann, London, 1949.

Hawkes, Terence. *Meaning by Shakespeare,* Routledge, London, 1992.

Hawkins, Henry. *Reminiscences of Henry Hawkins, Baron Brompton.* Edited by Richard Harris, K.C. Republished by Kessinger Publishing Co, USA, 2004.

Hawkins, William. *Treatise on the Pleas of the Crown.* London, 1721.

Hay, Douglas et al. *Albion's fatal tree: crime and society in eighteenth –century England.* Penguin, 1988.

Hazlitt, William. *Spirit of the age,* (1825) Republished by Kessinger Publishing Co, USA, 2004.

Heath, Jennifer. *The Veil: Women Writers on its History, Lore and Politics.* University of California Press, 2008.

Helmholz, R. H. et al. *The privilege against self-incrimination: its origins and development.* University of Chicago Press, 1997.

Heuston, R. F. *Lives of the Lord Chancellors 1885–1940.* Oxford, 1964.

Heward, Edward. *A Victorian Law Reformer. A Life of Lord Selborne.* Barry Rose, Chichester, 1998.

Hilberry, Sir Malcolm. *Duty and Art in Advocacy.* Sweet and Maxwell, London, 1946.

Holdsworth, Sir William. *Charles Dickens as a Legal Historian.* Yale University Press, New Haven, 1928.

Hood Phillips, O. *Shakespeare and the Lawyers,* Methuen and Co, 1972.

Hostettler, John. *Champions of the Rule of Law,* Waterside Press, 2011.

Hostettler, John and Braby, Richard. *Sir William Garrow, His Life, Times and Fight for Justice.* Waterside Press, 2009.

Hostettler, John. *The criminal jury old and new: jury power from early times to the present day.* Waterside Press, 2004.

Hostettler, John. *Lord Halsbury.* Barry Rose, Chichester, 1998.

Hostettler, John. *Thomas Erskine and trial by jury.* Barry Rose, Chichester, 1996.

House M. and Storey G. *Dickens's Letters,* Clarendon Press, Oxford, 1965.

Humphreys, Travers. *Criminal Days.* Hodder and Stoughton. London, 1946.

Hyndman, Michael. *Schools and Schooling in England and Wales,* a documentary history. Harper and Row Ltd, 1978.

Hynes, Steven and Robins, Jon. *The Justice Gap: whatever happened to legal aid?,* Legal Action Group, 2009.

Jardine, David. *Criminal Trials,* Charles Knight, London, 1832.

Jebb, John Claverhouse. *Attic Orators From Antiphon to Isaeos,* Cambridge Library Collection Classics, 2010.

Johnson, Cuthbert W. *The Life of Sir Edward Coke,* Henry Colborn, London, 1837.

Jonson, Ben. *On Lord Francis Bacon*, Harvard Classics, 1910.

Judd, Denis. *Lord Reading*. Weidenfeld and Nicolson, 1982.

Kee, Robert. *Trial and Error, the Guildford pub bombings and British Justice*. Hamish Hamilton Ltd, 1986.

Keeton, G. W. *Harris's Hints on Advocacy*. Stevens and Sons, London, 1943.

Kelly, Bernard. *Famous Advocates and their Speeches*. Sweet and Maxwell, London, 1921.

Kennedy, George. *Classical rhetoric and its Christian and secular tradition from ancient to modern times*. Croom – Helm, London, 1980.

Kennedy, George. *Quintilian*. Routledge, New York, 1996.

Kadri, Sadakat. *The Trial. A History from Socrates to O.J. Simpson*, Harper, London, 2006

King, P. *Crime, Justice and Discretion in England, 1740–1820*. Oxford, 2000.

Kirk, H. *Portrait of a Profession. A History of the Solicitor's Profession, 1100 to the Present Day*. Oyez Publishing, London, 1976.

Kleefeld, John C. *From Brehons to Brouhahas: Poetic Impulses in the Law*. Paper delivered on the 17th June, 2009 at the Institute of Advanced Legal Studies, London.

Korstal, R. W. *A Jurisprudence of Power; Victorian Empire and the Rule of Law*. Oxford University Press, 2005.

Langbein, John H. *The Origins of the Adversary Criminal Trial*. Oxford, 2003.

Lederer, F. *Courtroom Technology: A Status Report*. William and Mary School of Law, 2006.

Lederer, F. *High tech trial lawyers and the Court: Responsibilities, problems and opportunities, an introduction*. William and Mary School of Law, 2003.

Lee, Harper. *To Kill a Mockingbird*, J.B. Lippincot and Co, 1960.

Leich, Vincent B. *The Norton Anthology of Theory and Criticism*. W. W. Norton and Co, New York, 2001.

Lewis, J. R. *The Victorian Bar*, Robert Hale, London, 1982.

Lightman, Sir Gavin. *Advocacy –A Dying Art?* Lecture to Chancery Bar Association, January, 2004.

Lightman, Sir Gavin. *The Civil Justice System and the Legal Profession – The Challenges Ahead*. Edward Bramley Memorial Lecture, University of Sheffield, 2006.

Lustgarten, Edgar. *Rufus Isaacs, Advocate Impeccable*, BBC Radio 4, 1970.

Macauley Thomas H. *Critical and Historic Essays*. Longman, Green and Longman, London, 1877.

MacDonald, Kenneth. *Building a Modern Prosecuting Authority*. Paper delivered to the Centre for Crime and Justice Studies, Kings College, London, 23rd May, 2006.

MacPeake, Robert. *Advocacy Manual.* Oxford University Press, 2008.

MacKenzie, Ruth, Malleson, Kate, Martin, Penny and Sands, Philippe. *Selecting International Judges: Principle, Process, and Politics.* Oxford University Press, 2010.

Manchester, A. H. *A Modern Legal History of England and Wales 1750–1950.* Butterworths, London, 1980.

Manson, Edward. *Builders of Our Law During the Reign of Queen Victoria.* Horace Cox, London, 1895.

Marjoribanks, Edward. *For the defence: the life of Sir Edward Marshall Hall.* The Macmillan Company, New York, 1929.

Marshall, P. J. *The Impeachment of Warren Hastings.* Oxford University Press, 1965.

Martin, Sir Theodore. *A Life of Lord Lynhurst from letters and papers in possession of his family.* John Murray, London, 1883.

Mathew, Theo. *Forensic Fables.* Published in three books by Butterworths between 1926 and 1929. Complete Edition printed by Wildy and Sons, London, 1999.

May, Allyson. *Reluctant Advocates: The Old Bailey Bar and the Prisoners' Counsel Act 1836.* Paper given at the Institute of Advanced Legal Studies, London, 26th March, 2006.

May, Allyson. *The Bar and the Old Bailey, 1750–1850.* The University of North Carolina Press, Chapel Hill and London, 2003.

May, Allyson. *The Old Bailey Bar 1783–1834.* Thesis held at Lincoln's Inn Library. 1997.

May, James. Ed, *Brill's Companion to Cicero,* Brill, 2002.

McCall, G. and Simmons, J. *Issues in Participant Observation.* Addison and Wesley. 1969.

McConville, M. and Chui W. H. *Research Methods for Law,* Edinburgh University Press, Edinburgh, 2007.

McElhaney, J. W. *Trial Notebook.* 2nd Edition. ABA, 1987.

McRae, Donald. *The Old Devil Clarence Darrow: The World's Greatest Trial Lawyer,* Simon and Schuster, 2009.

Mellinkoff, David. *The Conscience of a Lawyer.* West Publishing Co, St Paul, 1973.

Millender, Michael. *The Transformation of the American Criminal Trial 1790–1875.* Doctoral Dissertation, Department of History, Princeton University, 1996.

Milsom, S. C. F. *Historical Foundations of the Common Law.* Butterworths. London.

Mitchell, John. *Jail Journal,* The Citizen, New York, 1854.

Mitchell, Paul. *The Making of the Modern Law of Defamation.* Hart Publishing, Oxford, 2005.

Montgomery Hyde, H. Norman Birkett. *The Life of Lord Birkett of Ulverston,* Hamish Hamilton, London, 1964.

Montgomery Hyde, H. *Carson; the life of Sir Edward Carson, Lord Carson of Duncairn,* Heineman, London, 1953.

Montgomery Hyde, H. *Sir Patrick Hastings, his life and cases.* Heinemann, London, 1960.

Montgomery Hyde, H. *The Trials of Oscar Wilde With an introduction by H. Montgomery Hyde.* Hodge. London, 1948.

Moorhead, R. and Sefton, M. *Litigants in person; Unrepresented litigants in first instance proceedings.* Department of Constitutional Affairs Research Series 2/05, 2005.

Mortimer, John. *Famous Trials,* Viking, 1984.

Mulcahy, Linda. *Architects of Justice: the Politics of Courtroom Design.* School of Law. Birkbeck College. Paper delivered at W G Hart Legal Workshop 2006 at Institute of Advanced Legal Studies, University of London.

Munkman, John. *Technique of Advocacy.* Stevens and Sons, London, 1951.

Murphy, Peter. *Murphy on Evidence.* Ninth Edition. Oxford University Press, 2005.

Murray, O. *The Oxford History of the Roman World.* Oxford University Press, New York, 1991.

Murray, Peter L. *Basic Trial Advocacy.* Maine Law Book Co, 2003.

O'Brien, R. Barry. *O'Brien's Life of Lord Russell.* Smith, Elder, 1901.

O'Flanagan, Roderick F. *The Munster Circuit.* Sampson, Low, Marston and Searle, London, 1880.

O'Tool, Fintan. *A Traitor's Kiss; The life of Richard Brinsley Sheridan 1751–1816.* Granta Books, 1998.

Oldham, James. *The Seventh Amendment and the Anglo-American Special Juries,* New York University Press, 2006.

Olsen, Kirsten. *Daily Life in 18th Century England,* The Greenwood Press, Westport Connecticut, 1999.

Page, Leo. *First Steps in Advocacy,* Faber and Faber, 1943.

Plamper, Jan. *The History of Emotions: An Introduction,* Oxford University Press, 2015.

Pannick, David. *Advocates.* Oxford University Press, 1992.

Pasley, Frederick D. *Not Guilty! The Story of Samuel Leibowitz,* G. P. Putnam, New York, 1933.

Phillips, Charles. *Curran and his contemporaries.* William Blackwood, London, 1850.

Phillipson, Nicholas. *The Scottish Whigs and the Reform of the Court of Session.* The Stair Society. Edinburgh, 1990.

Plotnikoff, Joyce and Woolfson, Richard. *Evaluating implementation of Government commitments to young witnesses in criminal proceedings.* National Society for the Prevention of Cruelty to Children, 2009.

Plowden, Alison. *Elizabethan England.* RDA Limited, 1982.

Pollock, Frederick and Maitland, William. *The History of English Law Before the Time of Edward 1st,* Cambridge University Press, 1898.

Powell, Jonathan and Paterson, Jeremy. *Cicero the advocate.* Oxford University Press, 2004.

Prest, Wilfred. *The Rise of the Barrister: A Social History of the English Bar 1590–1640.* Clarendon Press, Oxford, 1986.

Purcell, Edward. *Forty Years at the Criminal Bar; Experiences and Impressions.* Fisher Unwin, London, 1916.

Quintilian. *The Institutio Oratoria of Quintilian with an English Translation by H. E. Butler.* Heinemann, London, 1922.

Reinhold, Meyer. *The Classick Pages: Classical Reading of Eighteenth Century Americans.* Pennsylvania State University, 1975.

Rentoul, Sir Gervais. *The Art and Ethics of Advocacy.* Haldane Memorial Lecture, 1943.

Reynolds, Quintin. *Courtroom – The Story of Samuel S. Leiborwitz.* Victor Gollancz, London, 1950.

Robertson, Geoffrey. *The Justice Game.* Chatto and Windus, London, 1998.

Robson, Catherine. *Everyday Life and the Memorized Poem.* Princeton University Press, 2011.

Rodgers, Nigel. *The Rise and Fall of Ancient Rome.* Hermes House, 2004.

Rose, Jonathan. *The Intellectual Life of the British Working Classes.* Yale University Press, 2001.

Ross, David. *Advocacy.* Cambridge University Press, 2007.

Rovere, R. H. *Howe and Hummel.* Farrar Straus, New York, 1947.

Ruane, Janet. *Essentials of Research Methods: A Guide to Social Science Research,* Wiley – Blackwell, 2004.

Ryle, J. C. *Christian Leaders of the 18th Century: Estimation of Whitefield's Ministry.* Banner of Truth, 1869.

Sampson, AW. B. *Biographical Dictionary of the Common Law.* Butterworths, London, 1984.

Sarkar, S. C. *Hints on Modern Advocacy and Cross-Examination.* S. C. Sarkar and Sons (Private) Ltd, Calcutta, 1924.

Satre, Lowell J. *Chocolate on Trial; Slavery, Politics and the Ethics of Business,* Ohio University Press, Athens, 2005.

Scarlett, Peter Campbell. *A Memoir of the Right Honourable James, First Lord Abinger.* John Murray, London, 1877.

Schramm, Jan-Melissa. *Testimony and Advocacy in Victorian Law, Literature and Theology.* Cambridge University Press, 2000.

Scott, Sir Walter. *Guy Mannering,* 1815. P. D. Garside Edition, 1999.

Sedley, Sir Stephen. *The Future of Advocacy.* Lord Morris Memorial Lecture, Cardiff University, September, 1999.

Shetreet, Shimon. *Judges on Trial.* North Holland Publishing Company, 1976.

Skyrme, Sir Thomas. *The Changing Image of the Magistracy,* Macmillan Press, London, 1979.

Slapper, G. and Kelly, D. *The English Legal System,* Twelfth Edition, Routledge, London, 2011.

Smith, Adam. *Lectures on Rhetoric and Belles Lettres,* Indianapolis Liberty Classics, 1985.

Smith, F. E. First Earl of Birkenhead, *Famous Trials,* Hutchinson and Co, Ltd, 1930.

Smith, Roger. *Trial by Medicine,* Edinburgh University Press. 1981.

Smith, Sally. *Marshall Hall: A Law unto Himself,* Wildy, Simmonds and Hill Publishing, 2016.

Sprack, J. A. *Practical Approach to Criminal Procedure.* 11th Edition, Oxford University Press, 2006.

Stanhope, Philip, 4th Earl of Chesterfield. *Chesterfield's Letters.* J M. Dent and Sons, London, last reprint 1975.

Stebbings, Chantal. *Legal Foundations of Tribunals in the Nineteenth Century.* Cambridge University Press, 2007.

Stepniak, Daniel. *Overseas Themes and Lessons.* Paper produced for the Department for Constitutional Affairs Broadcasting Courts Seminar, 10th January, 2005.

Stevens, Robert. *The English Judges.* Hart Publishing, Oxford and New York, 2005.

Stray, Christopher. *Classics Transformed,* Clarendon Press, 1998.

Swift, Jonathan. *Gulliver's Travels.* 1726. Reprinted by Harmondsworth Press, Middlesex, 1985.

Thayer, James Bradley. *A Preliminary Treatise on Evidence at the Common Law*, Little Brown and Company, 1898.

Thomas, Cheryl. *Are Juries Fair?*, Ministry of Justice Research Series 1/10 (February 2010).

Thomas, John (Lord Justice Thomas). *The Maintenance of Local Justice.* The Sir Elwyn Jones Lecture, Bangor University, 8th October, 2004.

Tierney, Kevin. *Darrow: A Biography.* Thomas Y. Crowell, 1979.

Trollope, Anthony. *Orley Farm.* Folio, London, 1993.

Vidmar, Neil. *World Jury Systems.* Oxford University Press, 2000.

Vogel, Mary. *Coercion to compromise: plea bargaining, the courts and the making of political authority.* Oxford University Press, New York, 2000.

Von Arx, J. F. *Progress and Pessimism: Religion, Politics and History in Late 19th Century Britain.* Harvard University Press, 1985.

Von Mehren, Arthur T. and Murray, Peter L. *Law in the United States.* 2nd Edition. Cambridge University Press, 2007.

Walker, John. *Elements of Elocution.* 1799 Edition, Cooper and Wilson, London.

Walsh, Cecil Henry. *The Advocate.* Pioneer Press, Allahabad 1916.

Walton, Robert. *Random Recollections of the Midland Circuit.* Chiswick Press, 1869.

Watson, A. R. In Marutschke, Peter Ed, *Laienrichter in Japan, Deutschland und Europa. Should the Jury Return to Japan? And the question of mixed courts*, pp101–186. BWV, Berlin, 2006.

Watson, Eric. *The Trial of Thurtell and Hunt*, in the *Notable English Trial* series, William Hodge and Co, Edinburgh and London, 1920.

Wellman, Francis L. *The Art of Cross-examination.* Collier, New York, London, 1936.

Wellman, Francis L. *Luck and Opportunity*, Macmillan, New York, 1938.

Wiggins C., Dunn, M. and Cort G. *Federal Judicial Centre Survey On Courtroom Technology.* Federal Judicial Center, 2003.

Williams, Montagu. *Leaves of a Life being the Reminiscences of Montagu Williams QC*, Macmillan and Co., 1893.

Wilson, Ben. *The Making of Victorian Values*, Penguin, 2007.

Woodward, L. *The Age of Reform.* 2nd Edition, Oxford, 1962.

Wrottesley, F. W. *The Examination of Witnesses in Court*, Sweet and Maxwell, London, 1910.

Zander, Michael. *Cases and Materials on the English Legal System.* 10th Edition. Cambridge University Press, 2007.

Journal Articles

Aletras, Nikolaos et al. "Predicting judicial decisions of the European Court of Human Rights: A natural language processing perspective." *Peer J. Computer Science*, 24th October, 2016.

Alschuler, Albert. "Plea Bargaining and its history." *Law and Society Review*, Vol.91, No 4, 1979: 211–246.

Alschuler, Albert. "Comments on the Origins of the adversary Criminal Trial." *The Journal of Legal History*, Volume 26, No1, April, 2005: 79–85.

Baldwyn, J. and McConville, M. "Plea Bargaining and Plea Negotiation in England", *Law and Society Review*, Vol. 13, No 2 Winter, 1979: 287–387.

Beattie, J. M. "Garrow for the defence." *History Today*, Volume 41 Issue 2. Feb 1991a.

Beattie, J. M. "Scales of Justice: Defence Counsel and the English Criminal Trial in the Eighteenth and Nineteenth Centuries." *Law and History Review*, 1991b, Vol. 9, No 2: 221–267.

Beloff, Michael. "England's dying art." *New Statesman, Special Supplement: Are they off their trolleys? The Future of Legal Services.* 16th February, 2004: 16–17.

Berg, David. "Preparing Witnesses." *Litigation*, Vol. 13, No 2, 1987: 13.

Berlins, Marcel. "Why victim impact statements should be axed." *The Guardian*, December, 4th, 2006.

Berlins, Marcel. "Writ Large: George Carman." *The Guardian*, January, 8th, 2001.

Bingham, Lord Thomas. "The Role of an Advocate in a Common Law System." *Graya* – No 122, Hilary 2009 pp.17–24.

Birkett, Sir Norman. "The Advocate." *Graya*, No 46, Trinity, 1957: 89–96.

Blake, Leslie. "Famous cases: *R v Muller* – The nature of circumstantial evidence." *Estates Gazette*, October 14th, 1995.

Blake, Leslie. "Paper Hearings and Natural Justice." 2005, 12 *Journal of Social Security Law*, pp.26–35.

Botein, Stephen. "Cicero as a Role Model for Early American Lawyers: A Case Study in Early Classical Influence." *Classical Journal*. Vol. 73, 1978: 313–321.

Clark, Julian. "When witness training becomes tampering with the evidence." *Lloyds List*, March, 9th, 2005.

Cowper, Francis. "Holker and Kenealy." *Graya*, No 67, Easter, 1968: 17–18.

Davidson, Elizabeth. "Time to Dress Down?" *Counsel*, October, 2007:18–19.

DeStefano, John M. "On Literature As Legal Authority." *Arizona Law Review*, Vol. 49, 2007, pp. 521–552.

Domnarski, William. "Shakespeare In The Law." *Connecticut Bar Journal*, Vol. 67, 1993, pp. 317–350.

Ervo, Laura. "Scandinavian Trends in Civil Pre-trial Proceedings." *Civil Justice Quarterly*, Vol. 26, October, 2007: 466–483.

Fisher, G. "The Jury's Rise as Lie Detector." 1997, 107 Yale Law Journal.

Freedman, Monroe. "Counselling the Client: Refreshing Recollection or Prompting Perjury." *Litigation*, Spring, 1976.

Frenkel, John. "The New Advocacy." *The Law Society Gazette*. June, 16th, 1999: 41.

Friedman, Lawrence. "Plea bargaining in historic perspective." *Law and Society Review*, Vol. 91, No 4, 1979: 247–260.

Gibbons, Julian. "Those same old arguments" *New Law Journal*, October 23, 1998.

Girard, Philip. "Judging Lives: Judicial Biography From Hale to Holmes." *Australian Journal of Legal History*, 2003, Vol. 7.

Gleicher, Jules. "The Bard at the Bar: Some Citations of Shakespeare by the United States Supreme Court." *Oklahoma City University Law Review*, Volume 26, Number 1, 2001.

Golan, Tal. Tal "History of Expert Testimony in the English Court Room." *Science in Context* 12, 1 1999.

Gwynedd Parry, R. "Is legal biography really legal scholarship?" *Legal Studies*, Vol. 30 No. 2, June 2010.

Hanley, Connor. "The Decline of the Civil Jury in Nineteenth Century England." *Journal of Legal History*, Vol. 25, Number 1, April, 2005.

Harnett, Edward. "Questioning Certiorari: Some Reflections Seventy-Five Years After the Judges' Bill." 100 *Columbia Law Review*, 2000:1646–50.

Henley, Kate. "Higher Rights: Access all areas." *The Law Society Gazette*, January, 25th, 2007.

Hewson, Barbara. "Let us see your face." *Counsel*, June 2007:10–12.

Hilberry, Sir Malcolm. "Duty and Art in Advocacy." Graya, No 20, Easter, 1938:

Hilberry, Sir Malcolm. "The Kenealy Scandal." *Graya*, No 62, Michaelmas, 1965: 125–137.

Hoffman, Richard J. "Classics in the Courts of the United States. 1790–1880." *American Journal of Legal History*, Vol. 22, No1, 1978: 55–84.

Hungerford-Welch, Peter. "Advocacy." *New Law Journal*, 20th October, 2000:1532.

Ibbetson, D. "What is legal history?" *Current Legal Issues*, 6, 2003.

Jackson, R. M. "Incidence of Jury Trial During the Past Century." 1 *Modern Law Review*, 1937–38; 132–144.

Kahn, Ellison. "Literary Peregrination Through the Law Reports." *South African Law Journal*, Vol. 11, 229, (1997).

Kernan, Thomas J. "The jurisprudence of lawlessness." Green Bag 18, 1906; 588.

Kemplin, Frederick G. "Precedent and *Stare Decisis*: The Critical Years, 1800 to 1850." (1959) 3 *American Journal of Legal History*, 28–54.

Kurji, Fatim. "Justice for all." *Counsel*, June 2007: 14–16.

McCourt, John M. "Book Review of Courtroom – The Story of Samuel S. Lewiberwitz, by Quintin Reynolds." University of Pennsylvania Law Review, Vol. 99, 1950, pp. 434–437.

McGowan, Randall. "From pillory to gallows: The punishment of forgery in the age of the financial revolution." *Past and Present*, 1999, 165(1) pp. 107–140.

Langbein, John. "Understanding the short history of plea bargaining." *Law and Society Review*, Vol. 91, No 4. 1979: 261–272.

Levine, Linda and Saunders, Kurt. "Thinking like a Rhetor." *Journal of Legal Education* Vol. 43, 1993:108–122.

Lewis, Mark. "The Great Defender: Sir Edward Marshall Hall." The Law Society Gazette, July, 13th, 1988: 35–37.

Lemmings, David. "Criminal trial procedure in 18th Century England: The Impact of Lawyer." *Journal of Legal History*, Vol. 26, No1, April 2005, pp. 73–82

Lightman, Sir Gavin. "The case for judicial intervention." *New Law Journal*, December, 3rd, 1999, 1819–1836.

Litto, Frederic M. "Addison's Cato in the Colonies." *William and Mary Quarterly*, 3rd ser., Vol. 23, 1966: 431–449.

Lloyd, Sarah. "The Continuing Growth of the Collaborative Process." *Family Law*. Fam Law 37 (270), 1st March, 2007.

Lovell, Colin Rhys. "Trial of Peers of Great Britain." *The American Historical Review*, Vol. 55, No 1 (Oct 1949): 69–81.

Marshall-Andrews, Bob. "Court on Camera." *New Statesman, Special Supplement: Are they off their trolleys? The Future of Legal Services.* 16th February, 2004: 15.

May, Allyson. "Advocates and Truth-Seeking in the Old Bailey Courtroom." *The Journal of Legal History.* Volume 26, No1, April, 2005:71–77.

Montagu, Basil. "The Barrister". *The Jurist*, 1832: 94–100.

Morton, James. "Kings of the Court." *The Law Society Gazette*, February 22nd, 2007. Meyer, Phil, "Why a Jury Trial is More Like a Movie than a Novel." Journal of Law and Society, Volume 28, No 1, March, 2001:133–146.

Morton, James. "Uncovering the truth." Law Society Gazette, 18th October, 2007: 17.

Mullet, C. F. "Classical influences on the American Revolution." *Classical Journal*, Vol. 35, 1939–40: 92–104.

O'Barr, William and Lind, Allan. "The Power of Language: Presentational Style in the Courtroom." *Duke Law Journal*, 1978: 1375–1399.

Omerod, D. and Roberts A. "Expert Evidence: Where Now? What Next?" (2006) 5 *Archbold News* 5.

Ostrom, Brian J., Strickland, Shauna M. and Hannaford-Agor, Paula L. "Examining Trial Trends in the State Courts." Journal of Empirical Legal Studies, 2004: 755–782.

Pallis, Mark. "From the Bar to the small screen." *Counsel*, January 2010, pp. 27–29.

Phillips, J. H. "Practical Advocacy." (1988) 62 *Australian Law Journal*, 627–629.

Prest, Wilfred. "William Blackstone and the Historians." *History Today*, July, 2006: 44–49.

Pugsley, David. F. "Mr Justice Maule and the Western Circuit." *The Western Circuiteer*, Michaelmas Term 2000.

Punch, Mr. (Very possibly W.M. Thackeray). "Mr Punch to the Gentlemen of the Press." *Punch*, 1845:64–65.

Riddell, William Renwick. "Common Law and Common Sense". *Yale Law Journal*, Volume 27, No 8 (July, 1918), pp. 993–1007.

Riniker, Ursula. "Wigs, robes and other paraphernalia." *Justice of the Peace*, 9th September, 2000: 727.

Sheldon, John and Murray, Peter. Rethinking the rules of evidentiary admissibility in non-jury trials. 17 *Maine Bar Journal* 30 (2002).

Simon, Sir John. "Canadian Address." *Graya*, No 8, Easter, 1931: 32–35.

Soanes, Marcus. "Enhancing Education." *Counsel*, January, 2010, pp. 14–16.

Stirling, Sir James. "Advocacy and Acting." *Verdict*, Vol. 2. No1, 1966: 7–9.

Thornton, Brian. "The case of the disappearing court reporter". *Proof*, No 2., January, 2017.

Turner, Adrian. "Time For A New Look." *Justice of the Peace*, 30th September, 2006: 745.

Verkaik, R., Murray, N. and Ward, N. "Focus rights of audience." *Law Society Gazette*, 95/36 23 September, 1998, pp.20–23.

Vestey, Michael. "Murder most gripping." *The Spectator*, November, 23rd, 1996.

Vogler, Richard. "The International Development of the Jury: The Role Of The British Empire." *International Review of Penal Law*, Vol. 72, 2002.

Watson, Andrew. "Advocacy for the Unpopular." *Justice of the Peace*, Vol. 162, 1998: 478–80: 499–503 and 567–80.

Watson, Andrew. "Trial Advocacy Instruction from Harvard." *Justice of the Peace*, Vol.163, 1999a: 290–295.

Watson, Andrew. "Impeachments – Past, Present and Future?" *Justice of the Peace*, Vol. 163, 1999b: 468–472 and 491–494.

Watson, Andrew. "Witness Preparation in the United States and England and Wales." *Justice of the Peace*, Vol. 164, 2000: 816–822.

Watson, Andrew. "Changing Advocacy." *Justice of the Peace*. Volume 165, 2001: 743–749; 804–810 and 862–868.

Whittington-Egan, Richard. "God never gave her a chance – will you ?" *New Law* Journal, April 17th, 2000:522.

Wilson, A. "Expert Testimony in the Dock" (2005) 69 *Journal of Criminal Law* 330.

Newspapers and Journals

Bar News.
Counsel.
Daily Express.
Duke Law Journal.
Examiner.
Evening Standard.
Financial Times.
Era.
Guardian.
Irish Law Times.
Jurist.
New Law Journal.
Law Magazine and Review.
Law Review.
Law Society Gazette.
Law Times.
Legal Observer.

Morning Chronicle.
New Statesman.
New York Times.
Punch.
Solicitor's Journal.
Spectator.
Telegraph.
The Lawyer.
Times.
United States Democratic Review.

Index[1]

---

[1] Note: Page numbers followed by 'n' refer to notes.

© The Author(s) 2019
A. Watson, *Speaking in Court*, https://doi.org/10.1007/978-3-030-10395-8

Printed by Printforce, the Netherlands